THE HISTORY OF LANGUAGE LEARNING AND TEACHING
VOLUME II
19TH-20TH CENTURY EUROPE

LEGENDA

LEGENDA is the Modern Humanities Research Association's book imprint for new research in the Humanities. Founded in 1995 by Malcolm Bowie and others within the University of Oxford, Legenda has always been a collaborative publishing enterprise, directly governed by scholars. The Modern Humanities Research Association (MHRA) joined this collaboration in 1998, became half-owner in 2004, in partnership with Maney Publishing and then Routledge, and has since 2016 been sole owner. Titles range from medieval texts to contemporary cinema and form a widely comparative view of the modern humanities, including works on Arabic, Catalan, English, French, German, Greek, Italian, Portuguese, Russian, Spanish, and Yiddish literature. Editorial boards and committees of more than 60 leading academic specialists work in collaboration with bodies such as the Society for French Studies, the British Comparative Literature Association and the Association of Hispanists of Great Britain & Ireland.

The MHRA encourages and promotes advanced study and research in the field of the modern humanities, especially modern European languages and literature, including English, and also cinema. It aims to break down the barriers between scholars working in different disciplines and to maintain the unity of humanistic scholarship. The Association fulfils this purpose through the publication of journals, bibliographies, monographs, critical editions, and the MHRA Style Guide, and by making grants in support of research. Membership is open to all who work in the Humanities, whether independent or in a University post, and the participation of younger colleagues entering the field is especially welcomed.

ALSO PUBLISHED BY THE ASSOCIATION

Critical Texts
Tudor and Stuart Translations • *New Translations* • *European Translations*
MHRA Library of Medieval Welsh Literature

MHRA Bibliographies
Publications of the Modern Humanities Research Association

The Annual Bibliography of English Language & Literature
Austrian Studies
Modern Language Review
Portuguese Studies
The Slavonic and East European Review
Working Papers in the Humanities
The Yearbook of English Studies

www.mhra.org.uk
www.legendabooks.com

The History of Language Learning and Teaching

VOLUME II

19th–20th Century Europe

❖

EDITED BY
NICOLA McLELLAND AND RICHARD SMITH

l

LEGENDA

Modern Humanities Research Association
2018

Published by Legenda
an imprint of the Modern Humanities Research Association
Salisbury House, Station Road, Cambridge CB1 2LA

ISBN 978-1-78188-699-1 (HB)
ISBN 978-1-78188-372-3 (PB)

First published 2018

Copy-Editor: Richard Correll

CONTENTS

❖

ACKNOWLEDGMENTS

❖

Every chapter in this collection has been submitted to blind (i.e. anonymized) peer-review by at least two readers. We sincerely thank all those who read and commented on earlier drafts of chapters for their very helpful comments. We also acknowledge gratefully the generous support of the A. S. Hornby Educational Trust and, above all, the support of the Arts and Humanities Research Council network grant that led to the production of these three volumes [AH/J012475/1]. We owe a special debt of gratitude to Louis Cotgrove, our editorial assistant on this project. Finally, we thank the editors at Legenda, in particular Graham Nelson, and our contributors for their commitment and forbearance during the complex process of bringing this three-volume collection to publication.

CHAPTER 1

❖

From 'Glittering Gibberish' to the 'Mere Jabbering' of a Bonne

The Problem of the 'Oral' in the Learning and Teaching of French in Eighteenth- and Nineteenth-Century England

Michèle Cohen

This chapter argues that English attitudes to speaking French changed drastically between the early eighteenth century, when being able to speak French was necessary to a gentleman, and the early twentieth century, when the English gentleman was defined by his disdain for spoken fluency in French. To understand the reasons for the shift, the chapter investigates when and why the status of spoken French declined by analysing methods for teaching French pronunciation in a selection of textbooks which claim to teach how to speak the language; and attitudes to the teaching and learning of French in the testimony of witnesses to two Royal Commissions on secondary schools: the Clarendon Commission of 1864 and the Taunton Commission of 1868. This investigation reveals that attitudes of the English middle and upper classes to oral proficiency in French were complex and contradictory because this linguistic skill had always been freighted with cultural meaning relating variously to gender — masculinity, femininity and effeminacy; social class; the changing perceptions of the English and French tongues; as well as emerging notions of national character over the period. All this, the chapter concludes, explains why the condition which enabled French to become a subject in the secondary school curriculum in the early twentieth century was the *sacrifice* of oral proficiency.

Introduction

In late seventeenth-century England, writer Mary Astell commented that French had become so popular that almost as many 'Women of Quality' spoke French as men; and 'between 1694 and 1800, no less than 88 different grammars, dictionaries and methods, etc. of the French language were published in England' (Spink 1946: 155; see also Gallagher 2014). Although knowing French had long been central to the education of the English upper classes of both sexes, this suggests that the study of French was expanding at this time.

A number of factors contributed to this expansion. By the late seventeenth century, French was 'the language of the leading cultural and political power in Europe' (Howatt 2004: 56), spoken at all European Courts, and was the language of diplomacy. There were also domestic factors: following Louis XIV's revocation of the Edict of Nantes in 1685, many Huguenots moved to England and set up as tutors of French, either in the homes of the well-to-do or in private academies (Howatt 2004: 21). Another contributing factor was the establishment of the Hanover dynasty on the English throne in the early eighteenth century. The new king, George I, knew no English, but he knew French and official government reports had to be translated into French for him (Cowper 1864: ix). There were also cultural factors. The French tongue was highly valued at the time, unlike the English tongue. French was believed, by the English as well as the French, to possess unique clarity and precision and special elegance due to its softness and its nobility (Mah 1994). According to Voltaire, French had 'une délicatesse d'expression et une finesse pleine de naturel qui ne se trouve guère ailleurs' (Voltaire 1819: 275). English, by contrast, was full of harsh sounds and thus considered unpolished even by the English, and the early eighteenth century saw the development of a 'complaint literature' about the language (Milroy and Milroy 1991, p. 27). Jonathan Swift, for example, complained that English, 'already overstocked with Monosyllables', was further disfigured by 'the barbarous Custom of abbreviating Words' to form 'harsh unharmonious Sounds' like 'Drudg'd, Disturb'd, Rebuk't, Fledg'd' (Swift 1712: 22).[1] This was one reason why French was a necessary acquisition for young men of the elite and the gentry: it was believed to have a polishing and refining influence on the tongue of English speakers. This mattered because a gentleman was defined by his conversation (*The Tatler* 1709: No. 21).

In early eighteenth-century England, being able to speak French was 'by everyone acknowledged to be necessary' to a gentleman (Locke 1922 [1693]: 163.) By the early twentieth century, however, linguist and phonetician Harold Palmer (1968 [1917]: 166) described the typical English gentleman as one who:

> declares, with a tone savouring of pride and disdain, that the sounds of the language have no interest for him, who skips every chapter on pronunciation [...] [but who] will blush with shame if he so much as omits to dot an i when writing the language of which he claims to be master.

This chapter addresses two interlinked questions. First, when and why did the status of spoken French decline so drastically since Locke's comment as to produce Palmer's comment? Second, given this situation, how did French become a subject in the English secondary school curriculum in the early twentieth century?

The main explanation to date for these developments is that French became 'feminized' over the course of the nineteenth century, and to be included in the curriculum it had to be 'masculinized', that is, taught using the rigorous methods and discipline of Latin instruction (Bayley and Ronish 1992: 376). The problem with this explanation is that French instruction was always, to some extent, based on the methods of Latin instruction (see Gallagher 2014). I want to propose that something more radical took place. My argument is that French was accepted as a subject of the curriculum by *sacrificing* oral proficiency. While this has to do with gender — not only masculinity but effeminacy — it is not just about the relation of French to Latin. It is also intertwined with the shifting relations between the English and the French tongues, with ambiguities about *speaking* French throughout the eighteenth century, as well as with emerging notions of national character in late-eighteenth- and nineteenth- century England.

Teaching and Learning French in the Eighteenth Century[2]

One problem in researching the history of teaching and learning French is the lack of precision in the use of the terms 'speaking' and 'conversation' in eighteenth- and nineteenth-century textbooks. When authors claimed to be teaching *speaking*, this might refer to a variety of oral utterances, most of which would now be called *phonetic drill* rather than *speech*, while *conversation* might refer to reading out loud or repeating drilled sentences. Methodologically, my position is that the attempt to disambiguate what the past tangled together is anachronistic, for the very imprecision of the terms is one aspect of their complex cultural significance. Therefore I use the term 'oral'[3] to refer to these plural and multi-layered meanings, and the term 'speaking' only in a narrow sense, to convey a communicative function.

In the early eighteenth century, children of both sexes in families of rank and or wealth learned French, usually at home with a visiting tutor or a governess (Cohen 2003). Males would additionally spend time in France as part of their Continental tour to perfect their fluency and accent. French was also taught as a 'modern' subject in the many academies, private schools and boarding schools that flourished at the time (Hans 1966), but not at grammar schools — nor should it be, declared Lord Clarendon, Lord Chancellor under Charles II (Howatt 2004: 54).

Early eighteenth-century texts for teaching French were all constructed more or less on the same model. This consisted of a section on 'Grammar' and a larger section on 'Language'. The latter typically included vocabulary lists, arranged, first, hierarchically in the 'Great Chain of Being' — starting from God and the Archangels and leading to Man — and then topically: a section with 'Familiar Phrases',[4] which ranged from 'pour demander quelque chose' to 'expressions de tendresse', and a section with 'Familiar Dialogues' on a variety of topics from daily life, such as 'Entre une Dame et sa Femme de Chambre', 'Pour parler François' and 'Du Mariage: entre un père et sa fille' (Boyer 1729). Both 'Familiar Phrases' and 'Dialogues' were laid out in two columns with French on one side and English on the other, and were meant to be learned by heart. Early eighteenth-century authors all stressed constant oral practice as the best way to proficiency. The 'easiest Method to learn French is, to speak it often', says one character in a Familiar Dialogue (Boyer 1729: Dialogue X, 276). Most authors also recommended a foundation in grammar and joining rules to practice, for without grammar, wrote Guy Miège, learning a language is 'properly building in the Air' (Miège 1687, To the Reader).

The teaching of French was not gendered, but there was a gender difference in the *learners*: boys who studied Latin were familiar with its grammar and vocabulary, but their sisters were not. This mattered because French grammatical categories, as well as those of English, were at the time stretched onto the frame of Latin grammar. One consequence is that nouns were declined to show their supposed 'case', as in the following example:

Singular Masculine
Nom.	*Le Pain*: the Bread	
	Du Pain: some Bread	
Gen.	*Du Pain*: of or from the Bread	
	De Pain: of Bread	
Dat.	*Au Pain*: to the Bread	
	A du Pain: to Bread. (Boyer 1729: 53)	

However, lack of knowledge of grammar was not treated as a serious problem for girls, as Francis Cheneau (1723) and James Fauchon (1751) noted. This claim may also have been a way of advertising the efficacy of their method (see Fleming 1989).

From around mid-century, a shift is noticeable. Lewis Chambaud, a prolific author of French language-teaching texts, claimed that the best way to proficiency was understanding the rules of the language. In the introduction to his *Grammar of the French Tongue*, he defines *grammar* as 'the art of speaking a language' but, in addition, defines an *art* as 'a set of rules digested into a methodical order' (1758: 1). The key words here are 'rule' and 'methodical'. In the first part of the century, rules were a sort of *mode d'emploi*, a set of practical instructions to help composition, conversation and correctness. This is why Miège, who thought grammar necessary, allowed that learners could begin 'by learning texts by heart' first and 'come to rules later' (Howatt 2004: 63). For Chambaud, grounding in grammar first was necessary. There is no other way of attaining 'exactness and propriety in the writing and speaking of a language [...] than studying methodically the principles and rules of it' (1772: xx). He also criticized past methods for failing to teach pupils the 'grammatical dependence each word has upon another'. Attention to this dependence and to the 'right placing and using of words in speech require a constant and steady application of mind and [...] much meditating upon the language' (1772: xvii).[5] Chambaud's focus on grammar does not mean that he ignored the 'oral' dimension of the language: quite the contrary. 'The lesson must always begin with the pronunciation', he instructs the teacher in the preface to *The Art of Speaking French* (1772: viii). However, this practice used mostly nonsense syllables detached from meaning, as the excerpt from a table of syllables illustrates (Chambaud 1772: 11):

<u>ou</u>	<u>u</u>	<u>an</u>	<u>in</u>	<u>On</u>	<u>un</u>
hou	hu	han	hin	Hon	hun
mou	mu	man	min	Mon	Mun ...

This table is followed by tables of monosyllabic words, some meaningful, some non-sense; tables of words ending in 'consonants that ought not to be pronounced'; and a table of 'all the Monosyllables in the French Language', from '*a* to *zest*' (1772: 11-20).

Each table had to be fully mastered and memorized before the next was attempted. Although Chambaud mocked the Familiar Phrases and Familiar Dialogues , 'full', as he put it, of the 'oui Monsieur and non Madame' (1762: iii–iv) of earlier authors like Boyer and Cheneau, he does introduce them in one of his early texts, *The Elements of the French Language* (1762). On the other hand, *The Art of Speaking French* does not contain a single Dialogue, familiar phrase or 'communicative' vocabulary list. Yet Chambaud saw the method he had developed as providing the grounding indispensable for *speaking* French correctly. Lacking this grounding, he argued, children who are forced by their parents to speak French too soon, so that they can show them off, merely acquire 'the knack of talking a glittering gibberish, which no one can make anything of' (1772: xvi, xx). He even disapproved of the practice of sending boys to France to improve their French unless they had first been grounded in the principles of the language. His main tenet was that once the grammar of the language had been mastered through the application of mind to language, *speaking* would simply follow.

Another criticism that later eighteenth-century authors levelled at earlier methods was the amount of memorization involved in learning Familiar Phrases and Dialogues by heart. They presented grammar as an attractive way of avoiding memorizing such large chunks of language. Yet learners were now required to memorize '100, and, in some grammars, 160 pages of elementary rules' (Arleville 1798: Preface), interminable lists of verbal constructions, and nonsense syllables. Rote learning of grammar rules was justified by their systematic aspect and their appeal to the mind. Despite this enticement, by the close of the eighteenth century, authors noted that learning grammar was 'disagreeable', making the study of language 'dry, tedious and tiresome' or even 'disgustful' to young people (Picard 1790: Preface, [n. pag.]; Calbris 1797: Preface, [n. pag.]), and texts were published which claimed to make grammar less tedious, with 'new and original' plans (see Arleville 1798; Du Mitand 1784), or as 'abrégés' of the grammar (see Restaut 1798).

Although the debate about whether learning to *speak* French was best achieved by memorizing grammar rules or dialogues and French phrases was not resolved by the late-eighteenth century (see Chambaud 1772: xx), evidence strongly suggests that the early stress on the spoken language shifted to greater stress on grammar over the course of the century. This led modern linguists Richards and Rodgers to argue that from the early nineteenth century *speaking* had ceased to be the main goal of French study in many boys' schools. Instead, oral practice was limited to students reading aloud the sentences they had translated (Richards and Rodgers 2001: 4). However, contemporary comments suggest that the evidence is not as straightforward as Richards and Rodgers claim. Thus, on the one hand, Philip Le Breton, author of *Elemens de la Grammaire Françoise*, remarked: 'In the best schools, it is usually required that the pupils *converse* exclusively in French, at least during the [two or three] hours allotted to the study of that language' (Le Breton 1815: iv; Latin was usually allotted twelve hours a week). On the other hand, Newcastle Grammar School taught French 'precisely in the same way as the ancient languages, [...] grammar, not vocabulary, being the first consideration' (*Taunton Commission Report* [1867–68] 1970: VIII, 401). Another element complicates the claim by Richards and

Rogers: girls. At the same time as oral practice declined in boys' schools, 'French conversation' had become the obligatory accomplishment for young ladies. In Jane Austen's *Mansfield Park*, did Fanny Price's cousins not 'hold her cheap on finding out that she had but two sashes, and had never learnt French'? (Austen 1964 [1814]: 13).

The expansion in girls' learning of French was due to the influx of French émigrés during and after the Revolution. They were better teachers of French (Hegele 2011; Carpenter 1999), especially for the home education most middle- and upper-class girls were receiving (Cohen 2015). Aristocrats were sought because they could teach the French spoken at court, deemed the most elegant (Clapton and Stewart 1929; Carpenter 1999), but well-educated ladies of more modest birth also posted advertisements in the British press, such as the following:

> A FRENCH LADY about 30 years of age, good family, and who has received a very liberal education, but whose fortune has been injured by the Revolution of France, wishes to engage herself as companion to a Lady either in her own country, or in any other. She would willingly superintend Young Ladies as Governess to teach them her own language, geography, history, etc. (*Morning Chronicle* 1791)

Girls' schools also benefited from the Revolution. Abbey School for Girls in Reading, run by Mr and Mrs St. Quentin, hosted and employed many exiled aristocrats and 'the quality of French at the school soared'. One of the pupils, author Mary Sherwood, recalled that 'there was always some French gentleman present, and French only spoken' (Hegele 2011: 338). Even though moral educationist and author Hannah More was alarmed by 'the sacrifices which have been made, in order to furnish our young ladies with the means of acquiring the French language in the greatest possible purity', because the French were Catholics, she conceded that young ladies must be allowed to speak French, because the skill was so 'elegant and becoming' (More 1832 [1799]: 1, 328).

Approaches to the 'Oral' in the Nineteenth Century

While the teaching of French in boys' schools may have shifted away from the oral and especially from 'speaking', a number of textbooks published at the time claimed to teach how to speak the language. Who were the learners, and what methods were used? Since there has been no systematic investigation of the teaching of the 'oral' in the nineteenth century, my aim here is to examine what a variety of sources might tell us about attitudes to the teaching of *speaking* and about the methods for teaching it in the nineteenth century. To this end, I have selected three points of entry: textbooks, the Clarendon Commission of 1864, which investigated Public Schools, and the Taunton Commission of 1868, which investigated all other schools in England, including girls' schools.[6]

Textbooks

The textbooks selected all claim to teach how to *speak* French. Within the scope of this chapter I focus on examining how authors dealt with the pronunciation of the grammatical gender of nouns or the gender agreement of adjectives because speaking with grammatical correctness depends on these: for example, whether to voice or not to voice that final consonant, which still ambushes English speakers today.

Nicolas Gouin Dufief's *Nature Displayed in Her Mode of Teaching Language to Man* (1822 [1810]) announces that it is a 'new and infallible method' for learning to speak as well as write French. Dufief spends several pages on the pronunciation of the agreement of adjectives in the gender system. The thirteen-page list of adjectives 'which sound the same [in the masculine and the feminine] though written with an extra *e* for the feminine' includes words like *Eveillé/e, marié/e, salé/e, poli/e* but also, intriguingly, a large number of words such as *content/e, absent/e, léger/e, mauvais/e and commun/e* in which the final sound of the word actually changes in the feminine (1822: 1, 4-8, 13-26). Louis Philippe R. Fenwick de Porquet 's claim that an 'inability to converse in as nearly native a manner as possible is a mark of failure' (Beattie 1980: 82) suggests that he emphasized *speaking*, as promised by his *Truly Conversational Exercises for the French Language* (1846). De Porquet focuses on the gender of nouns. Having observed that French children seldom make mistakes in ascertaining whether a noun is masculine or feminine, he attributes this to the guidance of 'nature': words which end with a vowel 'the termination of which is soft, are conclusively of the weaker or softer gender, or feminine sex', whereas all nouns ending with a consonant are masculine 'because it sounds hard' (1846: 4-6). To illustrate this 'rule' he lists nouns such as *bonté, dent, maman, maison, faim, loi,* feminine because they end (orally) with a vowel sound. However, he also includes in this list feminine nouns such as *gloire, histoire, image, mémoire, cuillère* which end with an *e* when *written*, but *orally* with a notionally hard consonant sound. On the other hand, he lists nouns like *lit, canon, bâtiment* as masculine, presumably because of their final (written) consonant, even though they end *orally* with a notionally soft vowel sound. Ultimately, one is left to wonder what system De Porquet had in mind if the termination of *la mémoire* or *la dent* justifies their being placed in a feminine list, and that of *le bonheur* and *le bâtiment* justifies their being placed in a masculine list.

Other textbooks present different solutions to the problem. H. G. Ollendorf's *A New Method of Learning to Read, Write and Speak a Language in six months adapted to the French* initially explains the gender of nouns and adjectives by stating only that the feminine ends 'with the letter *e*'; and refers the learner to a later section within the text called 'A Complete Treatise on the Gender of French Substantives'. Here, twenty-seven pages list the gender of nouns on the basis of their written form alone, and there is no mention of pronunciation (Ollendorf 1882: 226, 414 -40). Achille Albitès's *How to Speak French* (1883) contains a section optimistically called 'French Gender Conquered: or the difficulty of French feminines and masculines solved by one single rule' (see Fig. 1). That single rule is: 'a noun is feminine having one of the following terminations: *ale, ole, ule; ure, ère, eur*' and so on for twenty-four terminations. The rule for the masculine is simpler: 'A noun is masculine having none of [these] terminations'. Nonetheless, the many exceptions for the masculine spread over the next five pages. The single reference to pronunciation in the whole section is provided by a phonetic rendition of the feminine sounds listed: *ahl-ol-ül; ür-air-urr* etc. (Albitès 1883: 27-30, 65-68).

THE RULE.

A NOUN IS
FEMININE,

having
one of the following Terminations:

ale, ole, ule; ure, ère, eur;

rre, lle, ie; ée, ue, ion;

be, ce, de; fe, ne, pe;

se, te, té; ve, he, aison.

(OR, *tié.*)

*(As: Cathédrale, Ecole, Nature, Faveur, Terre, Conversation,
Clémence, Beauté, Amitié, Marche, Maison.)*

☞ *Pronounce the lines nearly thus:*

*Ahl-ol-ül; ür-air-urr ;— rruh-lluh-ee ; eh-ü-eong ;
buh-suh-duh ; fuh-nuh-puh ;—suh-tuh-tey ; vuh-uh-aizong.*

A NOUN IS MASCULINE

having none
of the Terminations above.

(Examples: port, canal, canon, ordre, café, crime, village.)

FIG. 1.1. Albitès 1883: 67.

The striking thing the textbooks tell us is that while aiming to give primacy to pronunciation, authors themselves remained tied to the written form, even though this produced errors and incoherence. Nevertheless, while the popularity of such texts suggests that learning to speak French remained fashionable,[7] evidence from the two Royal Commissions on Education from the 1860s also suggests that the status of spoken French was declining.

French in the *Clarendon Commission Report on Education in Public Schools* (1864)

Testimonies from witnesses about the teaching of French in the *Clarendon Commission Report on Education in Public Schools* (2004 [1864]) provide evidence about headmasters' attitudes to modern languages (at the time French and German), about masters' teaching, and also, uniquely, about former pupils' learning experience. Intriguingly, while most textbook authors advertised their methods with the alluring promise that learners would attain spoken fluency in minimal time, public-school educators considered speaking French an aim *not* attainable in a school,[8] claiming that it was not 'practicable'. Reverend H. M. Butler, Headmaster of Harrow School (1859–85), was unequivocal:

> What we have to consider is how far we can introduce the study of a subject like modern languages without fatally, or, at least, without seriously or dangerously, infringing upon the time [usually 12 hours a week] given to what is our main study, *i.e.* classics.

When, in response to Butler, Lord Clarendon suggested a 'middle term between a thorough training and two hours a week, which is no training at all', Butler replied that to give French (or German) more hours would 'damage the intellectual tone of the place' and impair 'the genuine education of the mind' that Classics alone provide because it was easier for boys to expend less 'intellectual labour' on a 'collateral' subject like French.[9] As a former Harrow pupil recalled: '[I]dleness in learning a modern language passed more easily than idleness in reference to any other branch of study' (*Clarendon Commission Report* 1864: IV, 169, 170, 394, 226).

Monsieur Ruault, French teacher at Harrow, explains how the language was taught in Public Schools: 'French is taught grammatically, and boys attain a very fair knowledge [...] sufficient to enable them to acquire afterwards, in a short time, what cannot be taught in a public school; that is, the power of speaking [...] fluently' (Clarendon 1864: IV, 218). This statement also encapsulates Butler's view that it was 'comparatively less important that a boy should be able to express himself fluently and gracefully in French [...] than that he should have something to say which is worth expressing' (Clarendon 1864: IV, 169, 170). The sole aim of public schools was to discipline and strengthen the mind by teaching subjects which required continuous mental exertion, such as Latin and Greek. French was ill-suited to this end because it was so easy that it could be learned 'empirically', that is, orally, as a vernacular or 'half-native tongue' at home (Clarendon 1864: III, 241).

French in the *Taunton Commission Report* (1868) on Education in All Non-Public Schools

The sections about French instruction in the Assistant Commissioners' reports to the Taunton Commission, which investigated non-public schools in England, including girls' schools, provide an overall picture of the state of modern-language teaching in mid-nineteenth-century secondary schools.

French in Boys' Schools

Assistant Commissioner Bryce's survey of the teaching and learning of French in Lancashire offers the most extensive and detailed assessment of the state of French instruction in boys' schools at the time.[10] He concluded that both the teaching and the learning of French were 'loose and inexact' and the teaching 'usually unintelligent', with too much stress on 'idioms and pronunciation, and too little on the main outlines of etymology and syntax' (*Taunton Commission Report* 1868: IX, 645). Bryce's analysis of the 'causes' of poor French instruction provides a unique insight into perspectives on language teaching at the time:

> One cause of these defects seems to be that French is a living language, and in teaching living languages men are apt to hesitate between two modes of treatment, the strictly grammatical and the colloquial.[11] Each has its merits. The colloquial is pleasanter [...] but [...] it is apt to become superficial. The grammatical is surer in the end, but it must be handled thoroughly, and it must consist in making the leading principles of etymology and syntax clear. [...] French teachers, as a matter of habit, choose to teach the grammar, but they seldom succeed in making the learner exact, and they endeavour to supplement his want of accuracy by running over a great deal of ground in hasty translations, by giving a number of petty phrases to be learnt, and by encouraging the boy in a notion that French is a thing which may be in a measure 'picked up' without systematic study. If truly colloquial teaching can be given, it will have its value, and that a high one; the misfortune is that the possibility of colloquial practice, if the pupil should go to France, becomes an excuse for the slovenly treatment of the grammar. (IX, 644-46)

Bryce exposes tensions in language-teaching pedagogy and practice which indicate that in boys' schools, at least, the separation of 'grammar' from 'speaking' was intensifying. This may have been due to the growing importance assigned to grammar, whose 'principles and rules' were deemed, by intellectual giants such as J. S. Mill, as 'the means by which the forms of language are made to correspond with the universal forms of thought' (Mill 1931 [1867]: 150), while speaking was increasingly devalued, as revealed by the Assistant Commissioners' comments about French in girls' schools.

French in Girls' Schools

Girls' schools were investigated by the Taunton Inquiry only because pioneers of female education, especially Emily Davies, requested that the scope of the Inquiry be extended to include them (Cohen 2005: 77; Stephens 1927: 131-32). The Assistant Commissioners raised several points of criticism. The teaching of French in girls' schools had the wrong priorities and methods: 'a pure Parisian accent was regarded as of more consequence than grammatical knowledge'; gaining fluency was 'more important than the evil of incorrectness'; the practice of enforcing the constant use of French for a fixed number of hours outside class, common in the best girls' schools, was 'mischievous' and fostered 'slovenliness'. Moreover, girls were taught 'conversationally'; and because French lessons were conducted entirely in French, opportunities for explaining grammar (in English) were lost (*Taunton Commission Report* 1868: VII, 524; VIII, 250; IX, 297). It is worth noting here that the exact opposite had been said seventy years earlier, when Gratte and Lévizac had insisted on the constant use of French in classrooms *especially* when teaching grammar, so as not to waste any opportunities of using the language (Gratte 1791; Lecoutz de Lévizac 1797). Nevertheless, one Assistant Commissioner also remarked that girls 'knew French better than the boys' (*Taunton Commission Report* 1868: VIII, 49). This might seem startling in view of the other comments, except that it was no praise. The purpose of learning a language was to 'form the mind' not to give 'a knowledge of the language' (V, 190). Thus girls' superior oral performance had no educational value or status and was, instead, evidence of educational failure: their minds had not been trained by learning French (VIII, 250; IX, 809).

The comments about French in both Royal Commission reports expose the strength of opposition to teaching spoken or 'colloquial' French on the part of the education authorities. Why had *speaking* French become a site of such contention?

The Problematization of the 'Oral'

To understand this problematization, it is necessary to examine the ambiguities and contradictions concerning the oral in England since the early eighteenth century. In the late seventeenth century, French was 'almost naturalized through Europe' (Howatt 2004: 53) and was the medium of communication of the European cosmopolitan elite. It was thus essential for the English ruling class to speak it fluently, with a perfect accent. This was a crucial reason why young men of rank and wealth spent time in France on their Grand Tour, when they were expected to master the language. Many did, like young George Lyttelton, who went on the Tour aged nineteen in 1728 and whose letters to his father show both his written fluency and desire to converse in French (Boulton and McLoughlin 2012: 38). The emphasis on acquiring the spoken tongue suggests that the proficiency of returned Grand Tourists would be valued once they were back in England. Surprisingly, the contrary was the case. They were criticized for showing off their French by sprinkling French 'smatterings' in their English. This 'code-switching' was viewed by eighteenth-century critics not as evidence of imperfect knowledge of the foreign tongue, but as 'breaking' the native tongue. Far from promoting fluency in foreign languages, critics complained, travel just produced broken tongues and conversational nonsense (Cohen 1996, 2001). Samuel Foote's two plays, *The Englishman in Paris* and *The Englishman Return'd*, produced in early 1750s, are not the first but they are the best satire of the linguistic transformation expected — yet not welcomed — of the Grand Tourist. In *The Englishman returned*, young Buck now 'Maister of the Accent', utters what sounds like a jumble of broken English and French:

> *Buck.* Not a word, mi Lor; *jernie*, it is not to be supported! — after being *rompu tout vif*, disjointed by that execrable *pavé*, to be tumbled into a kennel by a filthy *charbonnier*, a dirty retailed of sea coal, *morbleu* [...] and then the murderous hootings of that detestable *canaille*, that murtherous mob. (Foote 1794 [1756]: I: 13, 18)

Despite his satire, Foote did not consider that travel on the Grand Tour or learning French should cease. This, however, is precisely what Richard Hurd (later Bishop of Worcester) recommended ten years later. Hurd (1764) not only criticized travel abroad but was one of the first to argue that learning French was a waste of time (Cohen 2005).

In 1771 the grammarian V. J. Peyton articulated a patriotic critique of the English ruling class for preferring foreign languages to English:

> What emolument would it be to Britain if the great men in power [...] would pay the same veneration to their native language, or at least would please to promote a learned English education [...] instead of being enthusiastically in love with other tongues, especially the French, as if to make Britons learned, to learn Greek, Latin or French was the *conditio sine qua non*. (Peyton 1771: 13)

Those men in power were aristocrats such as Lord Pembroke, whose letters to his son show that he too practised code-switching, for example: 'I should be vastly sorry to arrive in England & *d'y avoir du tout à faire avec ce Seigneur là* [...]'. Elsewhere he writes: 'there is certainly no eternal obligation on my part to bring in Hamilton, *bon gré, malgré* all possible circumstances' (Herbert 1950: II, 349, 431). Aristocratic ladies sojourning in France also interspersed French phrases in their English texts: 'I have got a Box at the French Play *qui me fait grand plaisir*, and I must go and write about it', Lady Sutherland wrote from Paris to Lady Stafford (Granville 1916 [1790]: 31).

In *A Comparative View of the French and English Nations* (1785) John Andrews went further in his objections. Learning to *speak* a foreign language was 'an insipid occupation to a solid thinking mind' because it was just a matter of learning 'combinations of sounds and letters' (Andrews 1785: 318). He specifically disparaged even the desire to acquire a correct French accent by introducing a new dimension into the debate, namely, 'national' masculinity: the attention to diction necessary for speaking French, he opined, 'frequently destroys manliness of thinking' (1785: 318). For a man to be concerned with his pronunciation now resonated with connotations of effeminacy and un-Englishness.

At the turn of the century, the educationist Reverend William Barrow scorned the study of French, both on the Grand Tour, which he opposed, and in English schools. He maintained that it took too much time, time which was robbed from the study of the classics, so that 'the sterling metal of Greek and Roman literature is exchanged for an adulterate currency, and ornaments of French plate'. He also denounced the 'inflated efflorescence of Gallick oratory' used by some English writers, which 'tends to corrupt the purity and destroy the character of our English diction, and [...] reduce us to babble a dialect of France' (1802: II, 112-13).

The English turn against French took place at the same time as a number of other cultural developments. One was the revival of interest in Anglo-Saxon, construed as a 'pure' form of English when it had been 'undefiled', before it had deviated 'towards a Gallick structure and phraseology', namely, Norman French (Johnson 1755, Preface: 9). The idea of a 'pure' English implied a rejection of the French invader in both body and tongue,[12] a rejection of heteroglossia and of bilingualism.[13] Two other shifts took place which are significant for the change in attitude towards *speaking* French because they were closely intertwined with the waning of politeness as a dominant social practice and of conversation as the supreme definition of the English gentleman (Cohen 2001; 2005).

The first was a radical reversal in the power relations between the French and English tongues (Cohen 1996 and 1999; Crowley 1996). The harsh monosyllabic sounds of English, deplored early in the century, now defined it as masculine and sincere, like its speakers; conversely, the very qualities which had made French the most refined language in Europe earlier in the century now served to define it as an effeminate tongue (Andrews 1785; Jardine 1788).

The second was a radical reversal towards 'taciturnity', long held to be a national trait (Cohen 1999). Deemed in the early eighteenth century to result from the 'Clog upon [the] tongue' of the Englishman (Wilson 1729: 32; Cohen 1996), taciturnity became, at the end of the century, the emblem of his self-discipline and of the depth and strength of his mind, both associated with the masculine national character. This was in explicit contrast to Frenchmen, whose volubility denoted their shallow superficiality, in their case also a national character trait. As Mary Wollstonecraft put it:

> The French [...] if they have not the depth of thought which is obtained only by contemplation, they have all the shrewdness of sharpened wit; their acquirements are so near their tongue's end that they never miss an opportunity of saying a pertinent thing, or tripping up, by a smart retort, the argument with which they have not strength fairly to wrestle. (1794: v, 504-05)

The strength of the relation of taciturnity to depth of mind intensified over the course of the nineteenth century, notably in Carlyle's celebration of the 'talent of Silence', a silence that characterized his strong and manly heroes (1940 [1840]: 411; see also Vance 1985 and Langford 2000) and may account for the late-nineteenth-century belief that modern languages, learned to be spoken, have the 'inherent' effect of 'weakening the mind' and making it more superficial (Sweet 1964 [1899]: 230).

While the late eighteenth-century English turn against French was related to changes in attitude to the Grand Tour, and thus mainly to men, ambivalence about speaking French also appears from the mid-eighteenth century in diaries as well as in prescriptive conduct, educational and moral literature, in which knowing French but never speaking it is a signifier of virtue for both sexes. Eighteen-year-old Fanny Burney wrote in her diary that she had 'taught myself that charming language (French) for the sake of its bewitching authors. [...] I shall never want to speak it' (1913 [1768-78]: 1, 102). In David Fordyce's *Dialogues Concerning Education*

(1745-48) two young ladies are praised because they know French but make no display of that acquirement: 'No one could have guessed from Cleora's behaviour that she spoke both French and Italian'; and 'the well brought up daughter of a gentleman [...] reads and talks the French prettily, but neither values herself for it, nor is forward to shew it' (1745: I, 146). The difference between virtuous young ladies and others is also illustrated in the contrast between two female characters in Thomas Day's highly popular moral novel *The History of Sandford and Merton*. Matilda, brought up by a 'fashionable' mother, 'talks French even better than she does English', signifying her frivolity. Miss Simmons, an orphan brought up by an uncle who gave her an education which disqualifies her for fashionable life, has read the best French as well as English authors but does not speak French — a symbol of her seriousness (Day 1890 [1783-89]: 225-26.) Although moral paragon Count Altenberg is said to speak fluent French, he does not utter a single French word throughout Maria Edgeworth's 631-page novel *Patronage* (1986 [1814]). Miss Porson, the virtuous English governess in Catherine Sinclair's novel *Modern Accomplishments*, has contempt for mere training in tongues because it tells of an education meant just to display in the drawing room (Sinclair 1838).

In view of the different and contradictory attitudes to the 'oral' I have reviewed so far, what were the conditions that made it possible for French to be accepted as a subject in the curriculum of secondary schools in the early twentieth century? This question concerned mainly boys since, as Sara Burstall, first Headmistress of Manchester High School, would point out years later, 'French has always been a subject in girls' secondary education' (Burstall 1907: 109).

What French in the Curriculum?

Both Max Müller, Taylorian Professor of Modern Languages at Oxford and witness to the Clarendon Commission, and Charles Cassal, Professor of French at University College London and witness to the Taunton Commission, agreed that French could be taught in secondary schools. However, their perspectives on how this should be done differed significantly. Müller argued that French could be taught at public schools as long as it was 'grafted on to the knowledge of Latin'. He explained that 'if a competent Latin master were to teach French [...] the mass of conjugations and declensions' that is French would be 'properly traced back to Latin'. Not only might 'a great deal of time and tedious work [...] be saved' but it would actually be of interest to boys' minds:

> Many of the rather puzzling rules of French grammar become at once intelligible to a boy if, by a reference to Latin, he is made to see the reason why. [...] A boy might be puzzled to know why *leur* in French should not take the feminine termination; but if it is explained to him that it came from the Latin *illorum*, he would never dream of putting the feminine termination (*Clarendon Commission Report* 1864: IV, 396-97).

Cassal's argument for teaching French in schools was based on three claims. The first was that French was a *difficult* language, which should be taught 'not only practically' but 'in a philosophical or scientific way'.

The French language, if it has no flexional declensions, has at least a verb which is as complicated almost as the Latin verb. As to the French syntax, it is at least as difficult as the Latin. [...] French is more difficult to study in its derivation, in its syntax, in its structure, than the Latin language. Now why could we not treat it philosophically? (*Taunton Commission Report* 1867-68: v, 188)

Cassal knew that he was courting contention. As he was to put it a few years later, 'I know I shall horrify some learned classicists if I say that French is more difficult than Latin or Greek' (Cassal 1885: 8). His second, equally bold claim was that French grammar could be used to train the mind. He explained to Lord Taunton: '[W]hat I mean to state is not that French could or should be substituted for Latin; but that French might be the medium of developing the mind, exactly as Latin and as Greek'. His third and most provocative claim was that studying French could help the study of Latin, making Latin 'infinitely more interesting, if French was placed on the same level with it, and if each was used to explain the other' (*Taunton Commission Report* 1867-68: v, 188). Cassal's arguments were not just diametrically opposed to Müller's, but subversive in his daring to challenge the inviolable superiority of Latin.

Where Müller and Cassal agreed was in excluding oral French from the curriculum. Müller argued scornfully that '[s]ervants and couriers speak French very well, simply because their sphere of thought is very narrow, very limited indeed' (*Clarendon Commission Report* 1864: IV, 394). He was not alone in this view. R. W. Hiley, in an article entitled 'The study of modern languages in England' in the *Journal of Education* in 1887, argued that grammar should be 'rigidly learned', for it was 'the pith and marrow of a language, and not the mere jabbering taught by a "bonne"' (Radford 1985: 212). Cassal opposed teaching pupils to speak French at school because it was 'merely empirical' and 'superficial learning' (*Taunton Commission Report* 1867-68: v, 188). For French to become part of the curriculum, the oral had to be sacrificed. In effect, this meant that the 'Frenchness' of French was removed from the tongue. Why was this acceptable?

Two factors could plausibly have contributed to this perspective. The first, noted in both the Clarendon and the Taunton Reports, was that male French teachers were not respected: they had a reputation for being unable to keep discipline in the class, and their French accent in English made them figures of ridicule to schoolboys. This, combined with pupils' low esteem of French (*Taunton Commission Report* 1867-68: VII, 392; IX, 646; *Clarendon Commission Report* 1864: IV, 170, 272), led to the recommendation that only a well-educated Englishman, one who would also be a gentleman, should be a French master, with the help of a Frenchman as assistant (1867-68: VII, 298-99; 1864: IV, 396).Twenty years later, this had become so commonplace that Cassal (1885: 7) lamented that it was 'no longer necessary to know French in order to teach it'. In fact, he added, the teaching of French has deteriorated so much that 'the men who speak and understand French are relatively few; those who can make an after dinner speech even fewer'. Yet, he noted, 'educated ladies generally speak French at least, simply because in every respectable girls' school there is at least one French sous-maitresse' (1885: 7). By the early twentieth century the men in power, far from being 'in love with other tongues', as Peyton had complained in 1770, were unable to 'show a minimal working knowledge of the key languages of European diplomacy' (Radford 1985: 210).

It could be argued that the Reform Movement of the 1880s and 1890s would change all that (Bayley 1998). Walter Rippman, 'a leading figure' in the Reform Movement and a professor of French in top girls' schools, was critical of methods in which 'grammar was made the centre of instruction' and of the 'translation' method. He advocated that 'attention be paid to the spoken language in the first place', that the pupil 'be led to express his own ideas' and made 'conversation in the classroom as the starting point' (McLelland 2012: 123, 127, 128, 133). Had the 'oral' gained a foothold in secondary classrooms? Richard Smith argues, however, that the Reform movement made 'slow progress' in Britain. He identifies several reasons for this, including the 'continuing low status of living languages in schools', the lack of training in the spoken language for language teachers, and the entrenchment of the grammar-translation method in grammar schools as a result of the 'continuing dominance of the University-led system of examinations' (Howatt & Smith 2002: iv, x).

The second concerns the examination system, which continued to constrain the teaching of the oral in schools in the twentieth century. The Board of Education Regulations of 1902 and the Regulations for Secondary Schools of 1904 established French as a subject in the curriculum, along with Latin and German (Gordon and Lawton 1978: 20-23; Dalglish 1996: 217, 224). However, as the *Acland Report on Examinations in Secondary Schools* (1911) noted, 'the subjects which flourish most in schools are those which are most easily tested by the simplest form of examination, namely, by a paper examination'. Subjects requiring other more practical methods, such as the oral method of teaching modern languages, are neglected (1911: 74).

Conclusion

This chapter has explored why the ability to speak French, highly valued in early eighteenth-century England, came to be derided by the early twentieth century, and whether this negative perception affected how French was taught as a subject in the curriculum of secondary schools in the early twentieth century. I have argued that the 'oral' had always been problematic but that this was not simply an educational issue. Rather, the historical perspective adopted to explore the trajectory of the 'oral' since the eighteenth century shows the extent to which the linguistic skill of 'speaking' French in England has been freighted with the social and cultural burdens of gender, social class and national character. While the effects of these factors on how the oral was conceived and taught have not been explored here, the evidence adduced in this chapter has shown that the history of the 'oral' and its meanings can be a means of identifying ideas and shifts in language education since the eighteenth century.

I thank Marjorie Lorch, Nicola McLelland and the anonymous reviewer for their judicious and challenging comments on earlier versions of this chapter.

Bibliography

ALBITÈS, ACHILLE. 1883. *How to Speak French, or French and France: Facts, Inductions, Practice* (London: Longmans)

ARLEVILLE, BRIDEL.1798. *Practical Accidence of the French Tongue upon a more Extensive and Easy Plan than any Extant* (London: The Author)

ANDREWS, JOHN. 1785. *A Comparative View of the French and English Nations* (London: T. Longman; G. G. J. & J. Robinson)

AUSTEN, JANE. 1964 [1814]. *Mansfield Park* (New York: Bantam)

BARROW, WILLIAM (Reverend). 1802. *An Essay on Education*, 2 vols (London: Rivington)

BAYLEY, SUSAN N. 1998. 'The Direct Method and Modern Language Teaching in England, 1880-1918', *History of Education*, 27: 39-57

——, and DONNA Y. RONISH. 1992. 'Gender, Modern Languages and the Curriculum in Victorian England', *History of Education*, 21: 363-82

BEATTIE, NICHOLAS. 1980. 'Nineteenth-Century Foreign Language Textbooks: Observations and Speculations', *Modern Languages*, 61: 81-88

BOARD OF EDUCATION. 1911. *Report of the Consultative Committee on Examinations in Secondary Schools (Acland Report)*, 2 vols (London: HM Stationery Office)

BOULTON, JAMES T., and T. O. McLOUGHLIN (eds). 2012. *News from Abroad: Letters Written by British Travellers on the Grand Tour, 1728–71* (Liverpool: Liverpool University Press)

BOYER, ABEL. 1729 [1694]. *The Compleat French Master for Ladies and* Gentlemen, 10th edn (London: Longman) <https://books.google.co.uk/books?id=MXU0AAAAYAAJ> [accessed 19 August 2015]

BURNEY, FANNY. 1913. *The Early Diary of Fanny Burney, 1768–1778*, ed. by Annie Raine Ellis (London: Bell)

BURSTALL, SARA A. 1907. *English High Schools for Girls: Their Aims, Organisation, and Management* (London: Longmans)

CALBRIS, B. 1797. *The Rational Guide to the French tongue containing rules for learning the language without disgust, and for speaking it with facility*, Part II, *A French plaidoyer between five young ladies* (London: Debrett)

CARLYLE, THOMAS. 1940 [1840]. *On Heroes, Hero Worship, and the Heroic in History* (London: Chapman and Hall)

CARPENTER, KIRSTY. 1999. *Refugees of the French Revolution: Émigrés in London, 1789–1802* (Basingstoke: Macmillan)

CASSAL, H. CHARLES S. 1885. *The State and Prospects of the Study of French in England* (London: Brown)

CHAMBAUD, LEWIS. 1772. *The Art of Speaking French or the French language methodised* (Dublin: Walker)

——. 1758. *A Grammar of the French Tongue* (London: Millar)

——. 1762. *The Elements of the French Language* (London: Beckett & de Hondt)

CHENEAU, FRANCIS. 1752 [1723]. *The True French Master* (Eton: Pote)

CLAPTON, GEORGE. T., and WILLIAM STEWART. 1929. *Les Etudes Françaises dans l'Enseignement en Grande Bretagne* (Paris)

The Clarendon Report: English Public Schools in the Nineteenth Century. 2004. Intro. by Christopher Stray, 4 vols (London: Thoemmes)

COHEN, MICHÈLE. 1996. *Fashioning Masculinity: National Identity and Language in the Eighteenth Century* (London: Routledge)

——. 1999. 'Manliness, Effeminacy and the French: Gender and the Construction of National Character in Eighteenth-Century England', in *English Masculinities, 1660 –1800*, ed. by Tim Hitchcock and Michèle Cohen (London: Longman)

——. 2001. 'The Grand Tour: Language, National Identity and Masculinity', *Changing English: Studies in Reading and Culture*, 8: 129-41

——. 2003. 'French Conversation or "Glittering Gibberish"? Learning French in Eighteenth-Century England', in *Expertise Constructed: Didactic Literature in the British Atlantic World, 1500–1800*, ed. by Natasha Glaisyer and Sara Pennell (Farnham: Ashgate), pp. 99–117

——. 2005A. 'Language and Meaning in a Documentary Source: Girls' Curriculum from the Late Eighteenth Century to the Schools Inquiry Commission, 1868', *History of Education*, 34: 77-93

——. 2005B. '"Manners" Make the Man: Politeness, Chivalry and the Construction of Masculinity, 1750-1830', *Journal of British Studies*, 44: 312–29

——. 2015. 'The Pedagogy of Conversation in the Home: Familiar Conversation as a Pedagogical Tool in Eighteenth- and Nineteenth-Century England', *Oxford Review of Education*, 41: 447-63

COWPER, MARY (Lady).1864. *Diary of Mary, Countess Cowper, Lady of the Bedchamber to the Princess of Wales, 1714–1720* (London: Murray)

CROWLEY, TONY. 1996. *Language in History: Theories and Texts* (London: Routledge)

DALGLISH, NEIL. 1996. *Education Policy Making in England and Wales: The Crucible Years, 1895–1911* (London: Woburn Press)

DAY, THOMAS. 1890 [1783-89]. *The History of Sandford and Merton* (London: Routledge)

DUFIEF, NICOLAS G. 1822 [1810]. *Nature Displayed in her Mode of Teaching Language to Man; being a new and infallible method of acquiring languages with utmost rapidity*, 2 vols (London: Dufief)

DU MITAND, HUGUENIN. 1784. *A New French Spelling Book* (London: S. Crowder)

EDGEWORTH, MARIA. 1986 [1814]. *Patronage* (London: Pandora)

FAUCHON, JAMES. 1751. *The French Tongue* (Cambridge: Bentham)

FENWICK DE PORQUET, LOUIS. P. R. 1846. *Truly Conversational Exercises for the French Language* (London)

FLEMING, JULIET. 1989. 'The French Garden: An Introduction to Women's French', *English Literary History*, 56: 19-51

FOOTE, SAMUEL. 1794 [1756]. *The Englishman Return'd from Paris*, The Minor Theatre Series, 5 (London: Jarvis)

FORDYCE, DAVID.1745-48. *Dialogues Concerning Education*, 2 vols (London)

GALLAGHER, JOHN J. 2014.'Vernacular Language Learning in Early Modern England' (unpublished doctoral thesis, University of Cambridge)

GORDON, PETER, and DENIS LAWTON. 1978. *Curriculum Change in the Nineteenth and Twentieth Centuries* (London: Hodder and Stoughton)

GRATTE, HENRI. 1791. *Nouvelle Grammaire Françoise à l'Usage de la Jeunesse Angloise* (London)

HANS, NICHOLAS. 1966. *New Trends in Education in the Eighteenth Century* (London: Routledge and Kegan Paul)

HEGELE, ARDEN. 2011. '"So she has been educated by a vulgar, silly, conceited French governess!" Social Anxieties, Satirical Portraits, and the Eighteenth-Century French Instructor', *Gender and Education*, 23: 331-43

HERBERT, LORD (ed.). 1950. *Pembroke Papers: Letters and Diaries of Henry, Tenth Earl of Pembroke and his Circle*, 2 vols (London: Jonathan Cape), II: *1780–1794*

HOWATT, ANTHONY P. R., with H. G. WIDDOWSON. 2004. *A History of English Language Teaching*, 2nd edn (Oxford: Oxford University Press)

——, and RICHARD C. SMITH (eds). 2002. *Foundations of Foreign Language Teaching: Nineteenth-Century Innovators*, 5 vols (London: Routledge)

HURD, RICHARD. 1764. *Dialogues on the Uses of Foreign Travel Considered as a Part of an English Gentleman's Education: Between Lord Shaftesbury and Mr Locke* (London: Millar)

JARDINE, ALEXANDER (Captain).1788. *Letters from Barbary, France, Portugal, etc.*, 2 vols (London: Cadell)

JOHNSON, SAMUEL. 1755. *A Dictionary of the English Language* (London: W. Strahan)

LANCASTER, THOMAS.1797. *A Plan of Education* (London: Robinson)

LANGFORD, PAUL. 2000. *Englishness Identified: Manners and Character, 1650–1850* (Oxford: Oxford University Press)

LE BRETON, PHILIPPE. 1815. *Elemens de la Grammaire Françoise* (London)

LECOUTZ DE LÉVIZAC, ABBÉ J. P. V. 1797. *L'Art de Parler et d'Ecrire Correctement la Langue Françoise* (London)

LEVESON-GOWER GRANVILLE (Earl).1916. *Private Correspondence 1781 to 1821*, ed. by Castalia, Countess Granville, 2 vols (London: Murray)

LOCKE, JOHN. 1922 [1693]. *Some Thoughts Concerning Education* (Cambridge: Cambridge University Press)

MACLURE, J. STUART. 1968. *Educational Documents England and Wales: 1816 to the Present Day* (London: Methuen)

MAH, HAROLD. 1994. 'The Epistemology of the Sentence: Language, Civility, and Identity in France and Germany, Diderot to Nietzsche', *Representations*, 7: 64-84

MCLELLAND, NICOLA. 2012. 'Walter Rippman and Otto Siepmann as Reform Movement Textbook Authors: A Contribution to the History of Teaching and Learning German in the United Kingdom', *Language and History*, 55: 123-43

———. 2015. *German through English Eyes: A History of Language Teaching and Learning in Britain, 1500–2000* (Wiesbaden: Harrassowitz)

MIÈGE, GUY. 1687. *The Grounds of the French Tongue* (London: Bassett)

MILL, JAMES. S. 1931 [1867]. 'Inaugural Address at St Andrews', in F. A. Cavanagh, *James and John Stuart Mill on Education* (Cambridge: Cambridge University Press), pp. 150-51

MILROY, JAMES, and LESLIE MILROY. 1991. *Authority in Language: Investigating Language Prescription and Standardisation* (London: Routledge)

MORE, HANNAH. 1832 [1799]. *Strictures on the Modern System of Female Education*, 2 vols (Philadelphia: Woodward)

OLLENDORF, HEINRICH G. 1882. *A New Method of learning to read, write and speak a language in six months. Adapted to the French*, 9th edn (London: Whittaker)

PALMER, HAROLD. E. 1968 [1917]. *The Scientific Study and Teaching of Languages* (Oxford: Oxford University Press)

PEYTON, V. J. 1771. *The History of the English Language* (London: Hilton)

PICARD, GEORGE. 1790. *A Grammatical Dictionary* (London)

RADFORD, HARRY. 1985. 'Modern Languages and the Curriculum in English Secondary Schools', in *Social Histories of the Secondary Curriculum*, ed. by Ivor Goodson (London: Falmer Press), pp. 203–37

RESTAUT, PIERRE. 1798. *Abrégé des principes de la grammaire françoise* (London : De la Grange)

RICHARDS, JACK, and THEODORE RODGERS. 2001. *Approaches and Methods in Language Teaching* (Cambridge: Cambridge University Press)

SINCLAIR, CATHERINE. 1838. *Modern Accomplishments or the March of Intellect* (Edinburgh: Whyte)

SPINK, J. S. 1946. 'The Teaching of French Pronunciation in England in the Eighteenth Century, with Particular Reference to the Diphthong *oi*', *The Modern Language Review*, 16.2: 155-63

STEPHEN, BARBARA. 1927. *Emily Davies and Girton College* (London: Constable)

STUBBS, MICHAEL. 1990. *Knowledge about Language: Grammar, Ignorance and Society* (London: Institute of Education, University of London)

SWEET, HENRY. 1964 [1899]. *The Practical Study of Languages* (London: Oxford University Press)

SWIFT. JONATHAN. 1712. *A Proposal for Correcting, Improving and Ascertaining the English Tongue* (London: Tooke)

The Tatler. 1709. No. 21, 26 May to 28 May

TAUNTON COMMISSION. 1970 [1867–68]. *Reports from Commissioners.* (Schools Inquiry). 24 vols (Shannon: Irish University Press)

VANCE, NORMAN. 1985. *The Sinews of the Spirit: The Ideal of Christian Manliness in Victorian Literature and Religious Thought* (Cambridge: Cambridge University Press)

VICE, SUE. 1997. *Introducing Bakhtin* (Manchester: Manchester University Press)

VOLTAIRE. 1819. 'Franc ou Franq; France, François, Français', in *Œuvres Complètes De Voltaire*, XXXI, *Dictionnaire Philosophique* (Paris: Dupont)

WILSON, THOMAS. 1729. *The Many Advantages of a Good Language to Any Nation* (London)

WOLLSTONECRAFT, MARY. 1794. *A Historical and Moral View of the Origin and Progress of the French Revolution and the effect it has produced in Europe* (London: Johnson)

Notes to Chapter 1

1. See McLelland (2015) for a discussion of German attitudes to monosyllables.
2. This section is loosely based on my chapter 'French Conversation or "Glittering Gibberish"? Learning French in Eighteenth-Century England' (2003).
3. This term was never used in nineteenth-century texts.
4. 'Familiar Phrases' were brief exchanges intended to provide pupils with phrases or sentences which would now be called 'functional'.
5. See John Stuart Mill for an articulation of the relation of 'grammar' to mind in his 'Inaugural Address at St Andrews' (1931 [1867]: 150–51).
6. For a succinct description of the terms of reference of these two Royal Commissions on Education, see Maclure 1968: 83–84; 89–91.
7. Ollendorf's and de Porquet's texts were highly popular in their time (Beattie 1980), while Albitès' edition of 1883 is the fourteenth.
8. Rugby School was an exception (*Clarendon Commission Report* 1864, IV: 284–86).
9. 'Collateral' was the name given to subjects other than Classics.
10. James Bryce was one of the eight Assistant Commissioners appointed to inspect English secondary schools. He was appointed to Lancashire.
11. That is, 'spoken' French.
12. England feared French military invasion, especially in the second half of the eighteenth century.
13. I use Bakhtin's definitions of 'heteroglossia' (Vice 1997: 19, 49).

CHAPTER 2

❖

Grammar-Translation: Tradition or Innovation?

Sonya Kirk

There is a prevalent view that the Grammar-Translation method was the dominant means of foreign language instruction from antiquity until the Reform Movement of the late nineteenth century and that, when modern-language learning was introduced into schools, the Grammar-Translation method was followed, as that method had been used in teaching Latin and Greek. Yet, as Howatt (2009: 467) and others have observed, the Grammar-Translation method originated in the late eighteenth century as a 'methodological compromise' which *began* in modern-foreign-language teaching, rather than in the application of classical language methodology to modern-foreign-language teaching. This chapter re-examines the definition and development of the Grammar-Translation method. Beginning with an overview of the fundamental features of the approach, it then explores the two key questions suggested by its treatment in much secondary literature to date: 1. the evidence for its use in the teaching of the classical languages in the nineteenth century; and 2. to what extent the method was innovative in its time, rather than merely conservative and backward-looking, as it is so often portrayed.

There has been a broad consensus that, until the emergence of the Reform Movement in the late-nineteenth century, the Grammar-Translation method was the most popular method for teaching modern foreign languages because it had been the preferred method for teaching classical languages since antiquity. As recently as 2013, Yu contended in the *Routledge Encyclopedia of Language Teaching and Learning* that 'Latin and Greek were taught through the Grammar-Translation method only [...] and it became very natural that, when students began learning a modern foreign language [...] the same language teaching method was imitated' (2013: 288). This opinion is echoed in several authoritative treatments (e.g. Stern 2003 [1983]: 455; Grenfell and Harris 1999: 11; Richards and Rodgers 2001: 4; Anderman and Rogers 2005: 18; Harden 2006: 35; Farman 2007:8; Musumeci 2011: 45-46; Yule 2014: 190), which all contend that the Grammar-Translation method was the 'traditional' method of language teaching. Some sources go so far as to claim that the terms 'Grammar-Translation method' and 'Classical Method' are synonymous, due to the widespread use of the Grammar-Translation method in teaching Latin and Greek (e.g. Zimmerman 1997: 6; Grenfell and Harris 1999: 11; Larsen-Freeman 2000: 11; Yu 2013: 287; Wheeler 2013: 153). This tendency to view the Grammar-Translation method as 'old' or 'traditional' has led to some circular reasoning in typical assessments of it: Grammar-Translation was the only method for teaching languages, so it was used to teach the only languages being taught (the classical languages). Many believe that when modern-language learning was introduced, the Grammar-Translation method was therefore used almost by default, since that was the method which had been used for teaching classical languages (cf. Council of Europe and European Commission 2000: 11; Anderman and Rogers 2005: 18; Yu 2013: 288). This chapter will question these assumptions. As discussed below, the belief that the Grammar-Translation method is a traditional method from antiquity appears to have little basis. Similarly, there is little evidence for the contention that the Grammar-Translation method was originally used to teach the classical languages, which calls into question the often-mentioned idea that modern-foreign-language teaching inherited the Grammar-Translation method from classical language teaching.

In order to explore these points, it is important to first understand what the Grammar-Translation method *is*, or was. Despite wide use of the term (usually disparagingly), there is no standard definition of the Grammar-Translation method; there is, therefore, a tendency to regard any means of language teaching that includes learning grammar and undertaking translation as an example of the Grammar-Translation method by default. Yet, regardless of the purported widespread use of Grammar-Translation, there are no definitions or manifestos written by nineteenth-century advocates of Grammar-Translation. Modern definitions of Grammar-Translation, meanwhile, vary in their specific wording, but there are aspects which are generally agreed upon and which are assumed to form the core, fundamental principles of the method. I have adopted the following working definition, based on eight commonly cited factors:

1. Instruction is conducted in the mother tongue of the pupil (Prator and Celce-Murcia 1979; Stern 2003 [1983]; Richards and Rodgers 2001; Howatt and Smith 2002a);
2. Rules of grammar are explicit (Chastain 1976; Prator and Celce-Murcia 1979; Stern 2003 [1983]; Richards and Rodgers 2001; Howatt and Smith 2002a);
3. Grammar is taught using specific technical terminology (Chastain 1976; Prator and Celce-Murcia 1979; Stern 2003 [1983]; Richards and Rodgers 2001; Howatt and Smith 2002a);
4. Examples of grammar rules in use are provided (Chastain 1976; Stern 2003 [1983]; Richards and Rodgers 2001; Howatt & Smith 2002a);
5. The learner is presented with ample opportunities to translate from the mother tongue into the foreign language and vice versa (Prator and Celce-Murcia 1979; Stern 2003 [1983]; Richards and Rodgers 2001; Howatt and Smith 2002a);
6. Instruction and translation are graded in a step-by-step manner of increasing complexity (Stern 2003 [1983]; Richards and Rodgers 2001; Howatt and Smith 2002a);

7. Vocabulary is taught through bilingual vocabulary lists (Chastain 1976; Prator and Celce-Murcia 1979; Stern 2003 [1983]; Richards and Rodgers 2001);
8. Reading and translation are the goal of instruction (Chastain 1976; Prator and Celce-Murcia 1979; Stern 2003 [1983]; Richards and Rodgers 2001).

These criteria come from modern treatments of language teaching rather than from those who used the method in previous centuries. This is unfortunate but necessary — perhaps surprisingly so — since the term 'Grammar-Translation' is relatively new. As we shall see below, the label 'Grammar-Translation' originated at the end of the nineteenth century and was used pejoratively by those who advocated increased speaking and listening in foreign-language classrooms. Thus 'Grammar-Translation' was identified largely by the features which stood in opposition to newer, more spoken-language-based, methods. So, to understand the Grammar-Translation method, we need to consider not its definition but its history as a label.

Unfortunately, the Grammar-Translation method is often given only a brief and broad treatment in modern commentary, where it is usually regarded as a regrettable traditional legacy that flourished in the nineteenth century. This is coupled with a tendency to over-simplify the state of language teaching and learning in the nineteenth century. In fact, Decoo observes: 'The history of language teaching in the nineteenth century is an intricate one. It is not the often mentioned, simplistic opposition between the dreary, antique "Grammar-Translation" method and the "reform method" that tried to overturn it' (Decoo 2011: 54). As to the origins of the Grammar-Translation method, modern sources which treat its history generally give inconsistent information: estimates of how long the Grammar-Translation method has been in use range from more than two thousand years to one hundred years, but these estimates are rarely supported with further evidence. For example, Benson (2000: 36) contends that the Grammar-Translation method was created as early as the second century BCE, while Yu (2013: 287) states that Grammar-Translation was 'the method of studying Latin and Greek adopted by Europeans in the Middle Ages'. Kelly (1976: 51) offers the proposal that Grammar-Translation 'had existed during the Renaissance'. Other sources are still less precise, referring to the Grammar-Translation method as 'a classical inheritance' (Joseph 2002: 29), contending that it was 'clearly rooted in the formal teaching of Latin and Greek which prevailed in Europe for many centuries' (Rivers 1968: 14) or simply stating that the origins of the Grammar-Translation method 'can be traced back to the annals of history' (Grenfell and Harris 1999: 11). Such general pronouncements as these are not supported by evidence, however.

A small number of contentions about the history and origin of the Grammar-Translation method do have better support. Stern (2003 [1983]: 453-54) shows that it was developed by German scholars while Howatt (1984: 132) and Vermes (2010: 85) each specify that the method originated in Prussia at the end of the eighteenth century. Unlike the general statements that the Grammar-Translation method is vaguely 'old', the contention that it developed around the late eighteenth or early nineteenth century has more support. In Howatt's assessment, the Grammar-Translation method was not a wholesale importation of a classical-language-teaching methodology imposed on modern-foreign-language teaching, but rather a 'methodological compromise' which 'retained most of the negative features of traditional language teaching while at the same time refusing to give modern languages what they most needed — a central role for the spoken language' (Howatt 2009: 467). Howatt (1984: 132) finds that the first textbook to utilize what became known as the Grammar-Translation method was Johann Valentin Meidinger's 1783 *Praktische Französische Grammatik*. Meidinger (1756-1822), a Prussian language teacher of French and Italian, wrote in his preface that he intended to clarify grammar and make the learning process easier for pupils. Meidinger's text meets the eight criteria established above for Grammar-Translation. It was written in the learners' mother tongue (in this case German) for German learners, and consisted of a series of lessons centred on explicit grammatical rules with examples of usage. Meidinger does not claim that reading or translating is the goal of instruction, but this is a logical conclusion given the text's emphasis on reading rather than speaking or listening. Crucially, the text also includes an innovation compared to earlier textbooks: translation exercises from French into German and from German into French, which become increasingly complex as new grammatical concepts are mastered. Lists of vocabulary to be learned at each stage are also given. The addition of these new features by Meidinger contributed to the success of his textbook (see Macht 1994: 7); and other language learning textbooks by Prussian authors for various languages written on the same model (with some modifications) soon appeared. For example, Meidinger's work was followed by texts for learning French or English written by Johann Heinrich Philipp Seidenstücker (1765-1817), Johann Franz Ahn (1796-1865), and Karl Ploetz (or Plötz) (1819-1881), all of whom utilized the basic principles found in Meidinger's textbook (Wheeler 2013: 113).

Another name commonly associated today with the fledgling Grammar-Translation method is that of Heinrich Gottfried Ollendorff (1803-1865) (see Howatt 1984: 141–45; Richards and Rodgers 2001: 6; Decoo 2011: 56; Wheeler 2013: 115-19, 128, 132 ff.). Ollendorff's method, which adopted many of Meidinger's principles, was applied to textbooks published for teaching several foreign languages. Regardless of the target language, the format and arrangement of each textbook were virtually identical. Wheeler (2013: 115) writes that 'Ollendorff approached language teaching as a business' and Howatt (1984: 141) observes that 'the Ollendorff industry must have been a large-scale international publishing operation'. Ollendorff's textbooks were 'essentially translations of each other' (Wheeler 2013: 115); they were all published in the format of combined grammar and vocabulary, followed by translation exercises. It was this format that caused the name of Ollendorff to be associated by later commentators with the Grammar-Translation method (e.g. Kelly 1976: 53; Linn 2006: 78; Decoo 2011: 56; Wheeler 2013: 115), though some contemporary American sources (e.g. Porter 1846: 103; A. N. G. 1849: 250; Pinney and Arnoult 1867: 3) considered that Ollendorff's method was based on that of Jean Manesca (1778?-1838), a French teacher in New York who developed an *oral* system of language teaching. Howatt (1984: 145) also notes that Ollendorff's texts were considered conversational; indeed, although teaching

Latin orally was not a popular idea in general in the nineteenth century,[1] Ollendorff published an unusual textbook in 1844 intended to teach Latin to French speakers through oral methods (Ollendorff 1844).

Of course, neither Ollendorff nor any of the other authors mentioned above used the term 'Grammar-Translation'. Instead, we find references to the Ollendorff Method, 'Meidinger's Methode',[2] 'Seidenstücker's Methode'[3] and the 'Ahn'sche Methode';[4] and, although there does not appear to be a method associated with the name of Plötz, the author himself termed his method the 'stufenweise fortschreitende Methode' [the step-by-step progressive method], which emphasized what he considered its distinguishing feature (Ploetz 1853).[5] The innovations introduced by Meidinger, and adopted or adapted by Seidenstücker, Ahn, Plötz, Ollendorff and others, were broadly based on the 'practical' approach mentioned in the title of the Meidinger's textbook, though the term 'practical' as Meidinger employed it did not convey the same meaning that it does today. Howatt (1984: 132) explains that in the nineteenth century a 'practical' language course was 'one which required *practice*'. This 'practical' approach to foreign language was a departure from the neo-Humanist approach to foreign-language education at the end of the eighteenth century, which valued the study of foreign languages less as a way to gain tools for communication and more as a contribution to the 'mental training of pupils' (Macht 1994: 1; McLelland 2015: 69).

So, while the innovative aspects of Grammar-Translation within Meidinger's textbook of 1783 may not appear particularly ground-breaking to modern eyes, they are strikingly different from other textbooks of the time. Consider the elements Loonen (1991: 106) attributes to a 'typical textbook' published between 1500 and 1800:

— a short preface
— dialogues
— a grammar section
— personal and commercial letters
— idiomatic phases

and sometimes also:

— a word list (or vocabulary)
— a list of proverbs
— a table of English money
— some texts
— a list of abbreviations
— other practice material.

Loonen (ibid.) notes that none of the textbooks he surveyed included 'verses, songs, plays, pictures, simplified reading material (except the spelling books), graded phrases', etc.; and he does not mention any presence of the type of translation exercises associated with the Grammar-Translation method, which indicates that they were not normally found in 'typical textbooks'. For example, Johann König's *A Royal Compleat Grammar, English and High-German*, which was published in twelve editions between 1715 and 1802, has been called 'the most successful text-book for

English as a foreign language in the eighteenth century' (Hüllen 1995: 45). This book contained a grammar, followed by dialogues which were presented as 'routine formulae' rather than authentic conversation practice (Hüllen 1995: 51), and finally a section regarding rules for writing letters, but practice exercises such as we find in Meidinger's text are conspicuously absent.

In order to explore further the argument that the Grammar-Translation method was co-opted from Latin textbooks, it is also worthwhile to compare the innovations found in Meidinger's textbook with contemporary Latin textbooks. For instance, the 1779 edition of Thomas Ruddiman's (1674-1757) popular and enduring textbook *Rudiments of the Latin Tongue* lacks several elements of the Grammar-Translation method. Ruddiman's *Rudiments* follows a Catechetical method (see below) throughout, presenting grammar in a series of questions and answers in both Latin and the native language. Unlike Meidinger's textbook, Ruddiman's *Rudiments* offers no opportunities to practise; there are no exercises or translations to undertake, nor are there lists of vocabulary to be learned. To cite another example, the *Compendium Latinae Grammaticae* (1781) by Joannes Rhenius, a Latin textbook for German-speakers, also heavily utilized the Catechetical method and was written in the Latin language rather than the native German of the intended readers. Again, the *Compendium* offered no exercises, opportunities to practice or vocabulary lists as one would expect to find in a textbook based on the Grammar-Translation method.

It is worth reiterating here that the first textbook credited with using the Grammar-Translation method was not a Latin textbook from antiquity, but an eighteenth-century textbook for French; and that the authors who initiated, imitated and refined this method were Prussian authors of modern language textbooks (Howatt 1984: 132; Decoo 2011: 56; Titone 2013: 387). Yet the Grammar-Translation method and the classical languages have come to be closely identified with one another. The reason for this association, and the possible genesis of the name 'Grammar-Translation', can be found in the work of Wilhelm Viëtor (1850-1918), a language teacher in Germany. In 1882 he published the pamphlet *Der Sprachunterricht muß umkehren! [The Teaching of Languages Must Start Afresh!]*,[6] which is credited with sparking the so-called Reform Movement in language teaching towards the end of the nineteenth century. Viëtor disdained language teaching by focusing on grammar and setting students to conducting translations rather than speaking and listening and learning to be effective communicators (Jaworska 2009: 15; Byram 2000: 957), which led to a tendency of both Viëtor and those who adhered to his thinking to paint with a very broad brush. As a consequence of this generalized thinking, the label of 'Grammar-Translation' was subsequently applied to many language instructional approaches which taught grammar directly and practised translation as a means of teaching, regardless of how grammar was taught or how translation was used as a teaching tool.

Viëtor's choice of title indicated his call for a change from an 'old' way of teaching language and he began by establishing just what the 'old' method entailed. As Cook observes, this was a necessary step in order to reject that method:

> All new movements need an old regime to replace — one they can caricature and ridicule, whose weaknesses will nicely show off their own virtues in contrast. In Grammar Translation, the orthodoxy of their time, both the Reform Movement and the new Direct Method language schools found an easy target. (Cook 2010: 9)

Viëtor associated grammar and translation with the 'old' way in which Latin and Greek were taught. He then identified those supposedly old, ineffective methods used to teach classical languages with the equally ineffective way in which modern foreign languages were taught in his day: 'Widerspreche mir, wer kann: Läßt ihn die Schule endlich frei, so ist dem abgehetzten Schüler die Sprache der alten Römer und Hellenen, ja das lebendige Englisch und Französisch der Gegenwart im wahren Sinne des Wortes fremd wie zuvor' [Contradict me, whoever can: when the school finally releases him, to the harried pupil the language of the ancient Romans and Greeks, indeed the living English and French of the present, are to him in the true sense as foreign as before] (Viëtor 1882/1905: 26).[7] Viëtor did not regard the 'old' as 'tried-and-true', but as something that no longer functioned well and that needed to be replaced or repaired. In Viëtor's view, presenting grammar rules in a progressive manner and translating phrases or sentences to practise those rules had become so odious that it inspired a war-cry: 'Mehr Stimmen schon, und nicht wenige altklassische, erheben sich zu dem Ruf: Tod den Regeln und Sätzen!' [More and more voices already, and not a few classicists' voices, are raised to the call: death to rules and sentences!] (Viëtor 1882/1905: 30). Viëtor cited V. H. Günther, author of *Der Lateinunterricht am Seminar*, published in 1881, who had observed the effect of 'rules and sentences' in classrooms:

> Nur wenn ein neuer Abschnitt beginnt, der nach einer neuen Regel und nach neuen Formen schematisiert ist, gibt solcher Unterricht dem Geiste der Schüler einen kleinen Ruck, ein anderes Register wird aufgezogen, der Schüler achtet wieder auf die ersten paar Sätze, und nach der kurzen Mühe ihrer Übersetzung kann die alte Schnurre von neuem beginnen. (Günther 1881, in Viëtor 1882/1905: 23)

> [Only when a new section begins, which is schematized by a new rule and new forms, does such teaching give to the spirit of the pupils a little jerk, another register is opened up, the pupil pays attention again to the first few sentences, and after a short effort of its translation, the old farce can start anew.]

Viëtor further quoted Günther's views that pupils were taught foreign languages 'mindlessly': 'Er lese nur gedankenlos seine Regel, gedankenlos lerne er sie auswendig, und gedankenlos übersetze er dann die nach ihrer Schablone verfaßten Übungssätze' [He [the pupil] is expected to read his rule mindlessly, to learn it mindlessly by heart, and mindlessly to translate the exercise sentences which have been fashioned according to its template] (Günther 1881, quoted in Viëtor 1882/1905: 23). Viëtor agreed with Günther, writing that pupils learned to translate foreign language texts 'mechanisch' [mechanically] (Viëtor 1882/1905: 23).

Finally, after much discussion of grammar rules and how and why they were taught, Viëtor presents the reader, in the pamphlet's third edition, with the term 'grammatisierend-übersetzende' [grammatical-translating] (Viëtor 1882/1905: 47), not as a method but disparagingly referred to as a 'Betrieb' (Viëtor 1882/1905: 47), suggesting a 'business' or 'process'. However, two pages later Viëtor also uses the phrase the '"grammatisierend–übersetzende" Methode' ['grammatical-translating' method] (Viëtor 1882/1905: 49, quoted in original). It is a very short step from the 'grammatisierend–übersetzende Methode' [grammatical-translating method] to the *Grammatik-Übersetzungsmethode* [Grammar-Translation method], as the method came to be known. It should be stressed, however, that neither the original 1882 edition of *Der Sprachunterricht muß umkehren*, nor the second edition from in 1886, included any mention of 'grammatisierend–übersetzende' either as a *Betrieb* or a *Methode*. However, as Howatt and Smith (2002b: xii) note, the term 'Grammatik- und-Übersetzungsmethode' did appear in Viëtor's (1902) *Die Methodik des neusprachlichen Unterrichts* (p. 24). Citing this 1902 reference, they note that it 'is possible that Viëtor himself invented the [Grammar-Translation] label', though they caution that 'this is not clear'.

Whether or not he invented this label, Viëtor's work certainly bears some responsibility for the close association made between the Grammar-Translation method and the perception of classical-language teaching as dreary and ineffective. Viëtor makes no reference to the idea that the Grammar-Translation method was introduced by innovative modern-foreign-language teachers like Meidinger, who were genuinely trying to make learning easier.

While Viëtor did not regard the Grammar-Translation method as contributing to the ease of learning, he did believe it was easier to teach, going so far as to claim that in classrooms where grammar and translation were the focus, the teacher was 'as good as dead' (Der lebendige Lehrer ist so gut wie tot (Viëtor 1902: 24, cited by Howatt and Smith 2002b: xii)). Wheeler (2013: 120) concurs that part of the appeal of the Grammar-Translation method was how easy it was to implement. Despite the negative reputation of the Grammar-Translation method, Howatt (personal communication cited in Weir 2013: 16) notes that textbooks using the Grammar-Translation method 'replaced existing grammar manuals, which had offered no pedagogical guidance at all, with an organised sequence of lessons in which a selection of specific grammar rules were taught and exemplified in a step-by-step manner'. Texts structured on the basis of Grammar-Translation offered an organized sequence of lessons that taught specific grammar rules, exemplified them and then gave opportunities to practise those rules in a step-by-step manner. This was easy to abuse; those who lacked teaching skills or who had a weak grasp of Latin must surely have greeted this step-by-step method with enthusiasm. Although the Grammar-Translation method was originally intended to make things easier for *pupils* by teaching language in a graded manner and giving them the opportunity to practise and master a concept before moving on to learn another (instead of simply committing grammar rules to memory), part of the reason it was easy to attack was the mechanical, mindless way that unskilled *teachers* implemented it (Kelly 1976: 278).

The question still remains as to whether or to what extent nineteenth-century textbooks followed the Grammar-Translation method for the classical languages. To answer this question, at least with regard to Latin textbooks, I examined a corpus of fifty nineteenth-century German-Latin textbooks and fifty nineteenth-century English-Latin textbooks used for instruction in the Latin language at secondary level and published between 1801 and 1900,[8] against the eight characteristics of the Grammar-Translation method given above. The findings are perhaps surprising. The Grammar-Translation method did *not* appear in the majority of texts; only nine English-Latin textbooks and ten German-Latin textbooks met all eight of the criteria for Grammar-Translation. The majority of the Latin textbooks in the corpus met some of the criteria; eighty-six of the one hundred texts conduct instruction in the students' mother tongue, but just seventeen textbooks present opportunities to translate both into and out of Latin; fewer than half present information in a graded manner, and only eighteen provide bilingual vocabulary lists. Thus, only a small proportion of the texts in the corpus satisfy all eight of the criteria, with only nineteen Latin textbooks following the Grammar-Translation method, as defined here, in its entirety.

The majority of the nineteenth-century Latin textbooks within the corpus followed other teaching methodologies. For instance, it was considered perfectly reasonable in the nineteenth century that pupils could not be expected to translate any Latin at all until they understood all the rules of grammar and had developed a good vocabulary, a 'grammar-first' method that entailed learning lists of vocabulary words and all the rules of grammar by heart before applying those words and rules to the translation of a Latin text. This method is found in thirty-six German-Latin textbooks and thirty-seven English-Latin textbooks. According to my corpus of nineteenth-century textbooks, this, rather than the Grammar-Translation method, was the dominant method.

Nor is it accurate to say that the Grammar-Translation method was the 'traditional' language-teaching method handed down from antiquity. That honour more properly belongs to the Catechetical method, which originated in the philosophical dialogues of Greek and Latin and is attested for Latin teaching as far back as the fourth century BCE. The Catechetical method (from κατηχέω [to instruct orally]) developed from the use of scripted conversations or dialogues as a method of teaching spoken language. Over time, these dialogues evolved into scripts which simply posed a series of questions, asked by the master, and answers which pupils would give verbatim. Kelly (1976: 49–50) notes that sometime between the third and sixth centuries AD 'grammarians rid themselves of the fiction that their treatises represented a conversation, but often kept a question-and-answer form'. It was this form of the Catechetical method as a series of memorized questions-and-answers that 'remained normal [in language teaching] until the early nineteenth century' (Kelly 1976: 50) and is found in a limited number of textbooks in the corpus: the Catechetical method appears in seven textbooks, with only one textbook, Pinnock's *Catechism of Latin Grammar* (1831), adhering to the Catechetical method throughout.

The one common factor amongst the nineteenth-century Latin textbooks in the corpus was a focus on reading and writing rather than speaking and listening. However, this focus on reading and writing does not mean that the text or the teacher were following the Grammar-Translation method, but only that grammar and translation were aspects of language teaching and learning. The tendency to apply the label 'Grammar-Translation' to any means of instruction that includes learning grammar and translating text is as imprecise as stating that every language-teaching method that involves speaking and listening is the audio–lingual method. Yet such negative associations persist: I have heard many language teachers lament that their students lack sufficient knowledge of grammar to undertake serious study of foreign languages, but any suggestion of increasing the role of teaching grammar evokes unconsidered reactions based on scorn for the Grammar-Translation method. For instance, a statement in 2013 to the UK Parliament by Secretary of State for Education Michael Gove which highlighted, among other changes to the Literacy and Foreign Language curriculum, 'a new stress on learning proper grammatical structures and practising translation' (Gove 2013: Sec. 2, para. 11), was met with outcries of fear about 'a return to grammar-translation methodology' (Hawkes 2013: Sec. 6, para. 1), which one commentator claimed (without supporting documentation) is 'a widely discredited approach to language learning' (Smith 2013: para. 3). Such responses are best tempered with the words of Wheeler:

> If it's possible to feel sorry for a language-teaching method, the poor Grammar-Translation Method deserves our sympathy. It started out with the best of intentions. (Wheeler 2013: 119)

Bibliography

ANDERMAN, GUNILLA, and MARGARET ROGERS. 2005. *English in Europe: For Better or Worse.* Edited by Gunilla Anderman and Margaret Rogers (Clevedon: Multilingual Matters)

A. N. G. 1849. 'Ollendorff's New Method', *The Literary World*, III: 249–50

BENSON, MALCOLM J. 2000. 'THE SECRET LIFE OF GRAMMAR-TRANSLATION', IN *Change and Continuity in Applied Linguistics* (Clevedon: British Association for Applied Linguistics), pp. 35–50

BUTTERFIELD, DAVID. 2011. 'Neo-Latin', in *A Companion to the Latin Language*, ed. by James Clackson (Chichester: Wiley-Blackwell), 303–18

BYRAM, MICHAEL (ed.). 2000. *Routledge Encyclopedia of Language Teaching and Learning* (London: Routledge)

CHASTAIN, KENNETH. 1976. *Developing Second Language Skills: Theory to Practice* (Boston, MA: Houghton Mifflin)

COOK, GUY. 2010. *Translation in Language Teaching: An Argument for Reassessment* (Oxford: Oxford University Press)

COUNCIL OF EUROPE and EUROPEAN COMMISSION. 2000. *Methodology in Language Learning* (Council of Europe)

DECOO, WILFRIED. 2011. *Systemization in Foreign Language Teaching: Monitoring Content Progression* (New York: Routledge)

FARMAN, SARAH. 2007. *Der Beitrag Der Linguistik Zur Grammatikvermittlung: Theoretische und Unterrichtspraktische Ansätze* (Norderstecht: GRIN)

FICK, JOHANN CHRISTIAN. 1793. *Praktische Englische Sprachlehre für Deutsche beyderley Geschlechts: Nach Der in Meidingers Französischen Grammatik Befolgten Methode* (Erlangen: Walther)

———. 1800. *Praktische Englische Sprachlehre für Deutsche beyderley Geschlechts: Nach Der in Meidingers Französischen Grammatik Befolgten Methode* (Erlangen: Walther)

——. 1808. *Praktische Englische Sprachlehre für Deutsche beyderley Geschlechts: Nach Der in Meidingers Französischen Grammatik Befolgten Methode* (Erlangen: Walther)

——. 1852. *Praktische Englische Sprachlehre für Deutsche beyderley Geschlechts: Nach Der in Meidingers Französischen Grammatik Befolgten Methode* (Erlangen: Walther)

GOVE, MICHAEL. 2013. 'Oral Statement to Parliament: Curriculum, Exam and Accountability Reform', *Hansard Debates*, 7 February <https://www.gov.uk/government/speeches/curriculum-exam-and-accountability-reform>

FILIPPI, P. A. DE. 1866. *Praktischer Lehrgang Zur Schnellen, Leichten Und Doch Gründlichen Erlernung Der Italienischen Sprache*, I (Vienna: Manz)

GREENE, GEORGE. 1854. 'Ollendorff's German Method', *The New York Quarterly*, 4: 537–60

GRENFELL, MICHAEL, and VEE HARRIS. 1999. *Modern Languages and Learning Strategies: In Theory and Practice* (London: Routledge)

G. S. 1864. 'Our Continental Correspondence', *American Literary Gazette*, 5: 70–72

HARDEN, THEO. 2006. *Angewandte Linguistik und Fremdsprachendidaktik* (Tübingen: Narr Francke Attempto)

HAWKES, RACHEL. 2013. 'National Curriculum Reform: Languages', *Tes Connect* <https://www.tes.co.uk/article.aspx?storyCode=6318981>

HOWATT, A. P. R. 1984. *A History of English Language Teaching* (Oxford: Oxford University Press)

——. 2009. 'Principles of Approach', in *Handbook of Foreign Language Communication and Learning*, ed. by Karlfried Knapp and Barbara Seidlhofer (Berlin: de Gruyter), 467–90

——, and RICHARD SMITH. 2002A. 'General Introduction', in *Modern Language Teaching: The Reform Movement*, I: *Linguistic Foundations* (London: Routledge)

——, and RICHARD SMITH. 2002B. 'Introduction', in *Modern Language Teaching: The Reform Movement*, V: *Bibliographies and Overviews* (London: Routledge)

HÜLLEN, WERNER. 1995. 'The Path through an Undergrowth: A Royal Compleat Grammar, English and High-German (1715) by John King Alias Hans König', *Paradigm*, 17 [n. pag.] <http://faculty.education.illinois.edu/westbury/paradigm/hullen.html>

JAWORSKA, SYLVIA. 2009. *The German Language in British Higher Education* (Wiesbaden: Harrassowitz)

JOSEPH, JOHN E. 2002. 'Is Language a Verb?', in *Language in Language Teacher Education*, ed. by H. R. Trappes-Lomax and Gibson Ferguson (Philadelphia, PA: Benjamins), pp. 29–47

KELLY, L. G. 1976 [1969]. *25 Centuries of Language Teaching*, 2nd edn (Rowley, MA: Newbury House)

KIRK, SONYA. 2016. *'Whatever you do, do not let a boy grow up without Latin': A Comparative Study of Nineteenth-century Latin Textbooks in English and Prussian Education* (unpublished doctorial dissertation, University of Nottingham)

LANGSTEDT, FRIEDRICH LUDWIG. 1797. *Uebungen Zum Englisch-Schreiben für junge Leute beiderlei Geschlechts in abgekürzter Verbindung mit gemeinnützigen und wissenswerthen Kenntnissen nach Den Haupttheilen der Sprachlehre in Meidingers und Meinekes Methode* (Nuremberg: Raspe)

LARSEN-FREEMEN, DIANE. 2000. *Techniques and Principles in Language Teaching*, 2nd edn (Oxford: Oxford University Press)

LICHTENTHAL, PIETRO. 1812. *Kurzgefaßte Practische Englische Sprachlehre nach Meidinger's Methode* (Vienna: Doll)

LINN, ANDREW. 2006. 'English Grammar Writing', in *The Handbook of English Linguistics*, ed. by Bas Aarts and April McMahon (Oxford: Blackwell), 72–92

LONGINO, JOHANN BAPTIST. 1803. *Französische Sprachlehre nach Meidingers Beliebter Methode* (Cologne: Hass)

LOONEN, P. L. M. *'For to learne to buye and sell': Learning English in the Low Dutch Area between 1500 and 1800: A Critical Survey* (Amsterdam: APA-Holland University Press)

MACHT, KONRAD. 1994. 'Practical Skills or Mental Training? The Historical Dilemma of Foreign Language Methodology in Nineteenth and Twentieth Century Germany', *Paradigm*, 14 [n. pag.] <http://faculty.education.illinois.edu/westbury/paradigm/macht.html>

MAGER, KARL. 1846. *Die Modernen Humanitätsstudien*, III: *Die genetische Methode des schulmäßigen Unterrichts in fremden Sprachen und Litteraturen* (Zurich: Mener and Zeller)

MANESCA, LOUIS. 1870. *The Serial and Oral Method of Teaching Languages* (Philadelphia, PA: DeSilvers)

MCLELLAND, NICOLA. 2015. *German through English Eyes* (Wiesbaden: Harrassowitz)

MÜHLMANN, GUSTAV. 1843. *Elementarbuch der Lateinischen Sprache nach Seidenstücker's Methode* (Leipzig: Schumann)

MUSUMECI, DIANE. 2011. 'The Context of Second-Language Teaching', in *The Handbook of Language Teaching*, ed. by Michael H. Long and Catherine J. Doughty (Oxford: Wiley-Blackwell), pp. 42–62

OLLENDORFF, H. G. 1844. *Nouvelle Méthode pour Apprendre à Lire* (Frankfurt: Jugel)

PINNEY, NORMAN, and ÉMILE ARNOULT. 1867. *Pinney and Arnoult's French Grammar* (New York: Mason)

PINNOCK, WILLIAM. 1831. *A Catechism of Latin Grammar, containing principally the Eton Accidence* (London: [n. pub.])

PLOETZ, CARL. 1853. *Elementarbuch Der Französischen Sprache* (Berlin: Herbig)

——. 1865. *Elementarbuch der Französischen Sprache: Nach Seidenstücker's Methode* (New York: Steiger)

PORTER, NOAH. 1846. 'The Youth of the Scholar', *Bibliotheca Sacra*, 3: 95–121

PRATOR, CLIFFORD H., and MARIANNE CELCE-MURCIA. 1979. 'An Outline of Language Teaching Approaches', in *Teaching English as a Second or Foreign Language*, ed. by Marianne Celce-Murcia and L. McIntosh (Rowley, MA: Newbury House), 3–5

RICHARDS, JACK C., and THEODORE S. RODGERS. 2001 [1986]. *Approaches and Methods in Language Teaching*, 7th edn (Cambridge: Cambridge University Press)

RIVERS, WILGA. 1968. *Teaching Foreign Language Skills* (Chicago, IL: University of Chicago Press)

Routledge Encyclopedia of Language Teaching and Learning. 2000. Ed. by Michael Byram (London: Routledge)

SCHNITZER, K. F. 1848. *Zeitschrift für das Gelehrte- und Realschulwesen* (Stuttgart: Ebner and Seubert)

SMITH, STEVE. 2013. 'Why Michael Gove Is Wrong to Advocate Translation', <http://frenchteachernet.blogspot.co.uk/2013/02/why-michael-gove-is-wrong-to-advocate.html>

STERN, H. H. 2003 [1983]. *Fundamental Concepts of Language Teaching*, 12th edn (Oxford: Oxford University Press)

TITONE, RENZO. 2013 [2004]. 'History: The Nineteenth Century', in *The Routledge Encyclopedia of Language Teaching and Learning*, ed. by Michael Byram and Adelheid Hu, 2nd edn (Abingdon: Routledge), 386–94

VERMES, ALBERT. 2010. 'Translation in Foreign Language Teaching: A Brief Overview of Pros and Cons', *Eger Journal of English Studies*, 10: 83–93

VIËTOR, WILHELM. 1902. *Die Methodik des neusprachlichen Unterrichts: Ein geschichtlicher Überblick in vier Vorträgen* (Leipzig: Teubner)

——. 1905. *Der Sprachunterricht Muß Umkehren! Ein Beitrag zur Überbürdungsfrage* (Leipzig: Reisland)

WEIR, CYRIL J. 2013. 'An Overview of the Influences on English Language Testing in the United Kingdom, 1913–2012', in *Measured Constructs*, ed. by Cyril J. Weir, Ivana Vidakovie and Evelina D. Galaczi, Studies in Language Testing, 37 (Cambridge: Cambridge University Press), pp. 1–102

WHEELER, GARON. 2013. *Language Teaching through the Ages*, Routledge Research in Education, 93 (New York: Routledge)

YU, WEIHUA. 2013 [2004]. 'Grammar-Translation Method', in *The Routledge Encyclopedia of Language Teaching and Learning*, ed. by Michael Byram and Adelheid Hu, 2nd edn (Abingdon: Routledge), 287–89

YULE, GEORGE. 2014 [1985]. *The Study of Language*, 5th edn (Cambridge: Cambridge University Press)

ZIMMERMAN, CHERYL BOYD. 1997. 'Historical Trends in Second Language Vocabulary Instruction', in *Second Language Vocabulary Acquisition: A Rationale for Pedagogy*, ed. by James Coady and Thomas Huckin. Cambridge: Cambridge University Press , pp. 5–20

Notes to Chapter 2

1. In the first decade of the twentieth century, Dr W. H. D. Rouse, Headmaster of The Perse School in Cambridge, received a grant from the Board of Education to conduct an experiment in teaching Latin orally. However, even in the twentieth century, the use of oral or direct methods for the teaching of Latin 'never won widespread acclaim' (Butterfield 2011: 316).

2. See, for instance, Volume 3 of Karl Mager's *Die modernen Humanitätstudien* (Mager 1846: 58), as well as language textbooks by Fick (1793, 1800, 1852, 1808), Langstedt (1797), Longino (1803) and Lichenthal (1812).

3. Plötz wrote a French text in 1865 (Ploetz 1865) and Gustav Mühlmann a Latin textbook in 1843 (Mühlmann 1843), both of which were 'nach Seidenstücker's Methode'. Unfortunately, I was unable to locate a copy of Mühlmann's text in time to include it in the corpus for this research.

4. De Filippi makes reference to the 'Ahn'sche Methode' (Filippi 1866: iii), as does an advertisement in the Munich *Allgemeine Zeitung* from July 1860. It also appears in academic journals (e.g. Schnitzer 1848: 133).

5. See, for example, the *Praktische Englische Sprachlehre für Deutsche beyderley Geschlechts* (Graz, 1793); George Crabb, *Neue practische englische Grammatik* (Frankfurt, 1803); D. P. Lichtenthal, *Kurzgefasste englische Sprachlehre* (Wien, 1812); H. E. Lloyd, *Theoretisch-praktische englische Sprachlehre* (Hamburg, 1816); T. S. Williams, *Theoretisch-practische englische Schul-Grammatik* (Hamburg/London, 1836) and so forth.

6. Alternatively: *Language Teaching Must Transform!* or *Language Teaching Must Change Direction!*. There have been many translations over the years.

7. Though originally published in 1882 and re-printed in 1886, I cite here the 1905 edition of the pamphlet, which included changes and edits.

8. Full details of this corpus can be found in Kirk 2016.

CHAPTER 3

❖

Ioannis Carassoutsas (1824-1873): médiateur culturel, professeur et auteur de manuels pour l'enseignement du français

Despina Provata

Ioannis Carassoutsas (1824-1873), a representative of the First Athenian School of literary production, one of the first Greek francophone poets and well known as a translator of works including Victor Hugo's *Notre Dame de Paris*, was also one of the most important nineteenth-century textbook authors for the teaching of French in Greece. Following a brief description of the overall affinity that Carassoutsas established with the French language — which reached its peak with his poetic work in French — this study focuses on his contribution to the teaching of French in Greece in the nineteenth century and considers the three textbooks that he published: his *Γραμματική της γαλλικής γλώσσης* [*Grammar of the French Language*] (1852); his *Χρηστομάθεια Γαλλική* [*French Chrestomathy*] (1855); and his *Λεξικόν των συνωνύμων της γαλλικής γλώσσης* [*Dictionary of Synonyms in the French Language*] (1865). By studying the context and content of the textbooks, this chapter outlines the author's pedagogical choices and sheds light on the methods that he adopted in the teaching of French. A common thread through the three textbooks is the comparative approach he adopted to language teaching. In his *Grammar*, Carassoutsas presents the language through a set of rules and exceptions but at the same time refers to the Greek language in a contrastive attempt to indicate the particularities of French. The consolidation of language teaching was achieved with the help of his *Chrestomathy*, which presented excerpts from literary works selected by the author and which served at the same time as an initiation for Greek students into French literature and civilization. Finally, Carassoutsas's dictionary of synonyms was the first of its kind in Greece and also followed the same method of comparative identification of the peculiarities of the French language.

Introduction

Dans le contexte de l'institution du nouvel État grec issu de la guerre d'Indépendance (1821-29), le monde de l'enseignement s'efforce de constituer une production nationale de publications destinées à l'enseignement scolaire conforme aux nouvelles options politiques et valeurs idéologiques. Avec l'institutionnalisation de l'enseignement du français en Grèce à partir de 1836, date à laquelle est promulgué le premier programme scolaire, l'objectif premier des pédagogues est de mettre à disposition des hellénophones des manuels adaptés à leurs besoins spécifiques, tout en ayant recours à des modèles étrangers. Ainsi, de nombreux érudits et professeurs de français se lancent dans la rédaction de manuels scolaires destinés à l'enseignement du français.[1]

Parmi ceux-ci, nous proposons d'étudier la contribution de Ioannis Carassoutsas. Cette figure notable des lettres grecques, longtemps méconnue, a laissé une œuvre multiple et polyvalente située au carrefour de plusieurs disciplines, dont le dénominateur commun est toujours la langue française. Ce n'est qu'au XXe siècle que la critique littéraire se penche sur l'œuvre poétique de ce représentant de l'École Athénienne[2] pour tenter de comprendre pourquoi il a été méprisé de ses contemporains en tant que poète. Cléon Paraschos relève alors ses accents poétiques subtils, sa sensibilité particulière, son expression sobre et tendre à la fois (Paraschos 1962: 22-40). Carassoutsas est aussi l'un des premiers auteurs francophones grecs, ainsi que le traducteur réputé de *Notre-Dame de Paris* de Victor Hugo et de *La Cabane de l'oncle Tom* de Harriet Beecher-Stowe. Il est enfin, au regard du sujet qui nous occupe dans la présente étude, l'auteur de trois manuels utilisés durant toute la deuxième moitié du XIXe siècle dans les établissements scolaires en Grèce: une *Grammaire de la langue française* publiée en 1852, qui a connu par la suite quinze éditions et réimpressions différentes, une *Chrestomathie française* en date de 1855 qui a connu trois rééditions et un *Dictionnaire des synonymes de la langue française* publié en 1865, puis de nouveau en 1868.

Nous tenterons de mettre ici en évidence le rôle éducatif dévolu à ces ouvrages tel qu'il apparaît à travers le paratexte et les contenus. Nous examinerons en outre le rôle qu'ils ont pu jouer dans la diffusion de la langue et de la culture françaises en Grèce car, longtemps en usage, ces manuels y ont initié plusieurs générations. Mais avant de porter notre attention sur ces ouvrages éducatifs, il nous semble nécessaire de rappeler le parcours personnel de Carassoutsas, sa formation et ses rapports avec la langue française, qui ont fait de lui une figure de médiateur culturel entre la France et la Grèce.

Ioannis Carassoutsas et la langue française

Pour ce qui est de la biographie de Carassoutsas, nous disposons de très peu de renseignements. L'érudit Anghélos Vlachos, qui fut son ami intime, nous trace le portrait d'un homme éprouvé à la santé frêle, qui a traversé de nombreuses épreuves, des maladies, des amertumes et qui s'est rapidement retiré de la vie mondaine avant de donner une fin tragique à sa vie en mars 1873 (Vlachos 1901: 56-82).

Né en 1824 dans la ville cosmopolite de Smyrne, Carassoutsas émigre avec sa famille à Hermoupolis, la capitale de Syra, qui jouit de la protection qu'offre la France à cette île à forte population catholique, et qui connaîtra une prospérité éclatante au cours du XIXe siècle (Kolodny 1969: 189-220). C'est là que Carassoutsas fait ses études secondaires, y apprend le français, et sans doute aussi l'anglais.[3]

Jeune élève encore, il y publie en 1839 son premier recueil intitulé *Λύρα* [*Lyre*] qui laisse déjà apparaître ses orientations poétiques: sensibilité et lyrisme romantiques associés à l'amour de la patrie, vénération de la culture antique, sentiment religieux, réflexion philosophique, tout cela associé à des convictions démocratiques (Protopapa-Bouboulidou 1976: 29). Néanmoins, Carassoutsas, qui est reconnu par Linos Politis (1979: 177) comme 'la voix la plus sympathique de la poésie en katharevousa'[4] — cette langue savante qui s'impose comme langue écrite au XIXe siècle —, est animé de la volonté de ne pas succomber à l'imitation facile des accents romantiques français, comme l'ont fait nombre de ses confrères de l'École Athénienne, même s'il suit avec intérêt les événements littéraires et politiques européens, souvent à la source de son inspiration. En effet, la poésie devient pour Carassoutsas — qui souhaite participer, au même titre que ses confrères européens au dialogue établi au sein l'intelligentsia de son époque — une passerelle lui permettant d'établir des contacts entre son pays et l'Europe.

Ainsi, il prend la plume tantôt pour s'adresser aux poètes qu'il admire, tels Béranger ('Εις τον θάνατον του φιλέλληνος ποιητού Βερανζέρου' [À la mort du poète philhellène Béranger]) ou à Byron ('Στροφαί εις Βύρωνα' [Strophes à Byron]), tantôt pour se prononcer sur des questions de politique européenne. Citons à titre d'exemple ses poèmes inspirés des luttes pour l'unité italienne: 'Επωδοί. Οι Γάλλοι εις Ιταλίαν' [Refrains. Les Français en Italie]; 'Ωδή εις Κάρολον Αλβέρτον' [Ode à Charles-Albert]; 'Αι σφαγαί της Νεαπόλεως' [Les Massacres de Naples] (Carassoutsas 1849: 39-41, 67-70, 71-73). Avec ces vers, il diffuse dans son pays les idéaux démocratiques et humanitaires qui, au lendemain du printemps des peuples de 1848, se sont emparés des sociétés européennes qui désiraient un gouvernement libéral. Cette veine initie de la sorte un transfert culturel qui se concrétisera davantage avec son œuvre poétique francophone.

En effet, souhaitant entretenir des canaux de communication avec l'Europe, Carassoutsas écrit ou se traduit en langue française, témoignage supplémentaire de l'importance qu'acquiert la langue française dans son expression poétique. Dans ces poèmes, qu'il s'exprime 'Sur la mort de Chateaubriand' afin de révéler à l'Europe l'émotion suscitée par la mort du philhellène chez les Grecs (Carassoutsas 1849: 77-82), ou qu'il satirise la vie politique et culturelle de son pays dans 'Le Distributeur d'un journal français à ses abonnés' (Carassoutsas 1849: 83-84), son objectif est d'atteindre le public non-hellénophone, résidant en Grèce ou au-delà des frontières de son pays. C'est aussi de la langue française qu'il se servira pour défendre les intérêts de sa patrie. Ainsi, lorsque Lamartine, le poète qu'il admire tant,[5] publie en 1858 une *Histoire de la Turquie* qui présente une image embellie de l'Empire ottoman, il exprime son indignation dans son *Épître à M. de Lamartine au sujet de son histoire de la Turquie*, texte rédigé initialement en grec mais qu'il a traduit lui-même en français pour le publier à Paris en 1858. Dans d'autres circonstances, il aura encore recours au français et composera quelques poèmes, sans grandes prétentions littéraires, mais révélateurs de l'importance qu'acquiert cette langue dans sa propre production littéraire. Par cette œuvre poétique francophone, bien que maigre, Carassoutsas prend place parmi les premiers écrivains grecs d'expression française. Il cultive désormais un terrain dans lequel se réalise l'osmose entre les deux cultures, grecque et française (Provata 1990: 19-21). Parallèlement, il s'initie à la traduction avec des extraits de la tragédie *Esther* de Racine et des *Fables* de La Fontaine[6] avant de publier en 1867 la traduction de *Notre-Dame de Paris* de Victor Hugo.

La langue française devient ainsi le fil conducteur de l'œuvre de Carassoutsas. Elle lui permet d'exprimer sa sensibilité poétique, ses attentes, voire une certaine idéologie. Après s'être en quelque sorte approprié la langue de l'Autre, après s'être ainsi affirmé en partie différent de l'environnement culturel grec dominant, et bien qu'il fût jusqu'alors un poète prolixe, Carassoutsas se voit contraint pour des raisons de subsistance de s'orienter vers l'enseignement et la rédaction de manuels de la langue française.

Ioannis Carassoutsas et l'enseignement du français

Nous ignorons tout de la formation qu'a pu avoir Carassoutsas avant d'entamer sa carrière de professeur de français. Comme de nombreux autres professeurs de son époque, il n'a reçu aucune formation spécifique — si ce n'est les cours du Gymnase de Syra — et n'a jamais voyagé en France. Il est d'abord nommé à Nauplie en 1850,[7] puis à Athènes en 1852 où il enseigne jusqu'en 1861, date à laquelle il est muté en province, au Gymnase de Chalkis fondé la même année. Mais en 1864, alors qu'il est en poste au Gymnase du Pirée, il soumet sa démission à cause des nombreux problèmes de santé qu'il affronte, dus, selon l'acte de sa mise à la retraite, à des problèmes causés lors du service. Il sera désormais réduit à vivre sur une maigre pension, égale au quart de ses revenus, ce qui aggrave encore davantage autant ses problèmes de subsistance que sa santé déjà fragile et le conduit finalement au suicide.

Carassoutsas consacra sa vie à la promotion de la langue et de la culture françaises en Grèce. Dans ses ouvrages, il encouragea systématiquement la jeunesse grecque à se lancer dans l'étude de cette langue qui constituait à ses yeux la clé avec laquelle 'le jeune Grec pourra ouvrir les coffres où gisent les trésors de l'humanité' (Carassoutsas 1856: iv). Image qui montre à quel point le français représentait pour lui l'ouverture au monde nécessaire à la jeunesse grecque, une langue de civilisation, véritable passerelle culturelle pour conquérir les trésors de l'humanité. Pour ce Grec cultivé, la langue française est perçue comme un moyen qui d'une part permettra la marche en avant vers le progrès tant recherché par la société néohellénique, et qui d'autre part, pourra garantir sa participation et sa reconnaissance par les nations européennes que l'on considérait comme 'civilisées'.

Sa *Grammaire de la langue française*, parue en 1852, deux ans après sa nomination à Nauplie, est le fruit de son expérience d'enseignant. Il y expose à l'intention des élèves des écoles grecques, les raisons pour lesquelles le français, expression d'une culture d'exception, est, selon lui, le complément nécessaire de la bonne éducation de tout jeune Hellène. Car pour lui, cette langue est 'nécessaire à l'érudit, au savant, au commerçant, et de manière générale à toute personne aspirant à une éducation libre' (Carassoutsas 1865: iv). Cette idée n'est pas neuve: Adamance

Coray, le représentant grec le plus illustre de l'esprit des Lumières et promoteur de l'enseignement en Grèce, avait l'intime conviction que l'apprentissage du français, langue porteuse des valeurs de la Révolution, était susceptible d'éveiller chez ses compatriotes assujettis le désir pour la liberté (Coray 1829: 90).

Carassoutsas réaffirme l'idéologie si souvent répétée depuis le XVIIe siècle, d'après laquelle le français était considéré comme une langue quasi parfaite et complète. Il reconnaît l'universalité de la langue française — à laquelle il accorde d'ailleurs l'importance qu'avaient le grec et le latin pour l'antiquité — et estime que la seule connaissance du français suffit pour accéder aux sources du savoir. Car, il n'existe pas d'ouvrage 'quelque peu renommé de n'importe quelle langue du monde' (Carassoutsas 1856: iv), insiste-t-il, qui n'ait pas été traduit en français. Nul besoin, donc, conclut Carassoutsas, d'investir dans le multilinguisme et dans l'apprentissage de l'anglais ou de l'allemand, qu'il reconnaît toutefois comme des langues 'utiles'. Le public auquel il s'adresse, outre les classes nombreuses des élèves, comprend aussi cette nouvelle bourgeoisie, porteuse d'une culture européenne, qui adopte le français comme langue de communication signalant par ce choix son appartenance à l'élite. La majorité des lecteurs de Carassoutsas, écrit à juste titre le journal *Athina* (Αθηνά) 'appartiennent à des familles de bonne condition qui connaissent bien la langue [française], sont des locuteurs naturels, et dont les enfants apprennent tout naturellement de leurs parents la langue comme il se doit' (*Athina* 1857: 3).

Cependant, c'est précisément ce contact direct avec la langue française tel qu'il s'opère au sein de la famille hellénique, qui peut receler, selon Carassoutsas, des dangers pour la langue maternelle. Le rôle de l'enseignant est de protéger cette dernière face aux 'imitations de mauvais aloi'. Car la langue grecque, insiste Carassoutsas, 'non encore construite et formée, ressemble aux métaux qui fondent dans le creuset de l'ouvrier, dans lequel peuvent facilement s'introduire des substances étrangères' (Carassoutsas 1856: vi). Le professeur de français, endosse donc une double et lourde responsabilité: enseigner la langue française tout en veillant à empêcher la 'dégénération' de la langue grecque.[8] Son premier souci doit être de sauvegarder la langue maternelle face aux 'barbarisants', dit Carassoutsas, ceux qui transgressent les règles grammaticales de leur langue et qui sans jugement transposent dans la langue grecque des particularités syntaxiques du français. Ce sont, poursuit-il, 'ces gallicismes, étrangers à la nature de la langue grecque, que l'on doit éviter comme un fléau' (Carassoutsas 1856: vii). Le rôle des professeurs de français est d'attirer l'attention de leurs élèves sur les structures grammaticales, comme par exemple la construction des divers verbes, en leur faisant remarquer, dans une approche contrastive, les ressemblances et différences du français d'avec la langue grecque (Carassoutsas 1856: 120). Un procédé qui à ses yeux devrait permettre le meilleur apprentissage de la langue mais aussi le renforcement de la langue maternelle.

Une grammaire adaptée aux besoins des élèves grecs

Cette optique particulière, ce double souci linguistique, est à la source du fondement théorique des manuels de Carassoutsas. Ceux-ci, qui sont exclusivement destinés à des apprenants hellénophones, ont toutes les explications grammaticales ou lexicales données en grec et doivent être adaptés à leurs besoins spécifiques. Carassoutsas adopte donc systématiquement dans sa grammaire l'approche contrastive des deux langues et ne manque pas de critiquer ses prédécesseurs d'avoir simplement reproduit, plus ou moins fidèlement, les grammaires françaises. Il est en effet à bon droit persuadé que dans l'apprentissage de la langue étrangère, on doit pouvoir tirer profit des connaissances linguistiques et syntaxiques préalablement acquises par les élèves et propres à leur langue maternelle. D'où l'examen comparé des deux systèmes linguistiques.[9]

Cela ne veut pas dire qu'il ne suit pas des modèles grammaticaux français éprouvés de la méthode traditionnelle, à savoir la présentation, en introduction, des sons du français et de leur prononciation et, ensuite, des parties du discours au nombre de dix. Il aura pour modèle des grammaires françaises, surtout celle de Noël et Chapsal[10] et se servira en outre de celle de Ch. P. Girault-Duvivier.[11] On le sait, l'une des particularités de la langue française, langue non flexionnelle, à laquelle l'élève grec devra se familiariser est l'absence des déclinaisons. Animé d'un grand souci pédagogique, Carassoutsas n'hésitera pas à recourir au besoin à des grammairiens plus anciens; comme il l'avoue dans la préface de la 3e édition de sa grammaire, il s'est aussi servi des ouvrages de N.-F. de Wailly,[12] P. Restaut[13] et E. Condillac[14] qui maintiennent dans leurs grammaires l'appellation de *cas* pour désigner ce qui correspond aux cas des Grecs (Carassoutsas 1859: 17).

Si Carassoutsas accorde une grande importance à la théorisation grammaticale, il est en même temps désireux d'apprendre aux élèves à parler correctement le français. Aussi insiste-t-il sur l'acquisition d'une bonne prononciation. Il reconnaît qu'il est 'difficile d'interpréter des sons étrangers à partir de leur transcription écrite, lesquels ne peuvent être enseignés que de vive voix' (Carassoutsas 1856: 2). Il va donc tenter une phonologie comparée, et confronte régulièrement les sons français à ceux du grec. Or, comme on sait, certains phonèmes de la langue française, notamment les nasales sont complètement étrangères au système phonétique du grec. Il est remarquable que l'auteur tente alors de décrire, aussi minutieusement que possible, la position des organes vocaux lors de la production des sons en question. Il aura même parfois recours à la comparaison avec la prononciation du grec ancien:

> [L]a prononciation du *u* ne peut pas être expliquée par une lettre grecque. Lorsqu'il est prononcé, la bouche se forme comme lorsqu'on prononce la diphtongue *ou* mais avec plus de crispation autour des lèvres; c'est-à-dire qu'il est un peu plus fin du *ou* et sa prononciation se rapprocherait à celle de l'upsilon des anciens. (Carassoutsas 1856: 3)

Mais force lui est de reconnaître, en définitive, que 'l'écoute directe' et la 'vive voix' sont quelquefois irremplaçables.

La théorisation grammaticale est complétée par des exercices de cacographie qui consistaient à fournir aux élèves des textes dans lesquels des fautes grammaticales et syntaxiques avaient été délibérément introduites afin de les entraîner à les corriger.[15] Ceci leur permettait d'approfondir les règles avant d'aborder des textes qu'ils étaient censés traduire dans leur langue maternelle. Enfin, un chapitre consacré à la versification française permettait de découvrir l'alexandrin, l'art poétique français ainsi qu'un choix de poésies, une pratique qui sera d'ailleurs institutionnalisée plus tard, en 1882, par la loi sur les manuels scolaires.[16]

La *Chrestomathie française*

Si la grammaire disséquait la langue et la présentait comme un ensemble de règles et d'exceptions, l'apprentissage se couronnait, dans les classes supérieures, par des activités didactiques d'application qui se faisaient à l'aide de chrestomathies. Ces recueils de textes littéraires, qui servaient de support à l'apprentissage et à l'approfondissement de la langue, transmettaient en même temps une certaine image de la culture française.

Il convient ici de noter que durant presque tout le XIXe siècle, la littérature française sera en Grèce le complément de l'enseignement de la langue. Or, ces florilèges de textes français devaient eux aussi se conformer aux consignes de l'État et obtenir une autorisation officielle du ministère de l'Instruction publique avant d'être introduits dans les classes. Car, au même titre que les manuels utilisés dans les classes de grec ou d'histoire, et conformément aux buts éducatifs de l'époque, ces manuels de français devaient souscrire aux valeurs morales convenues tout en desservant les objectifs que le jeune État s'était fixés, à savoir l'éducation morale et intellectuelle des élèves. De la perspective qui était la leur, ces florilèges contribuèrent eux aussi à la construction de l'identité nationale (Provata 2011: 281-92).

Le choix des textes comme la méthode adoptée revenaient aux auteurs, et ceci jusqu'en 1884, date à partir de laquelle les contenus des manuels sont définis par le ministère. Lorsque Carassoutsas expose dans son 'Avis aux lecteurs' sa démarche théorique, il distingue les chrestomathies en deux types. La première catégorie, qui recueille des extraits courts et variés de différents auteurs, serait plutôt destinée à des débutants; la seconde opte pour la présentation des œuvres entières, permettant ainsi aux élèves des classes plus avancées, non seulement d'approfondir l'étude de la langue mais aussi de se faire une idée beaucoup plus complète de la littérature française et de pouvoir mesurer la valeur de chaque auteur à l'aune de l'histoire de la littérature. Dans son manuel, Carassoutsas s'efforce justement de combiner ces deux tendances. Ceci explique que l'on y trouve un peu de tout: des maximes, des anecdotes, des dialogues moralisateurs, des fables, des poésies, des portraits, des descriptions, des discours, des morceaux d'histoire.

Les pièces choisies proposent des échantillons de la littérature française des XVIIe, XVIIIe, et XIXe siècles suivant un double objectif pédagogique. Objectif pratique d'abord, car ces passages, longs ou courts, se mettaient au service de l'objectif linguistique qui était l'apprentissage de la langue; ainsi chaque texte est accompagné de commentaires explicatifs et grammaticaux, rédigés dans la langue maternelle des élèves et qui renvoient à la *Grammaire de la langue française* de Carassoutsas. Objectif culturel ensuite, car ils initiaient les élèves à la littérature française et aux œuvres des prosateurs et poètes que l'auteur considérait comme les meilleurs ou les plus représentatifs. Aussi Carassoutsas propose-t-il des extraits d'œuvres littéraires de Bossuet, Fénelon, Molière, Marmontel, Florian, Mably, André Chénier, Chateaubriand, Mme de Staël, Sismonde de Sismondi, Pierre Daru, Villemain, François Guizot, Xavier de Maistre, Lamartine, Victor Hugo, Casimir Delavigne, Auguste Marseille Barthélemy. De plus, il met à disposition des apprenants deux tragédies intégrales — *L'Iphigénie* de Racine et *Mérope* de Voltaire — mais encore un chant de l'*Henriade* de Voltaire, plusieurs fables de La Fontaine et des satires de Boileau. Bien que Carassoutsas ait eu sous la main des florilèges ou autres chrestomathies publiés en France, comme notamment *Les Leçons de littérature et de morale* de Noël et de la Place et la *Chrestomathie française* de Vinet (Choïda 2003: 300), son ouvrage porte néanmoins son empreinte personnelle, visible dans le choix des textes qui laissent entrevoir ses propres choix idéologiques et politiques: critique de la tyrannie à travers l'extrait de *Angelo, tyran de Padoue* de Hugo, critique véhémente de l'Empereur dans 'Bonaparte' de Lamartine, éloge de la tyrannicide libératrice, dans le poème 'Charlotte Corday' d'André Chénier.

Car Carassoutsas souhaite que son ouvrage soit un instrument d'introduction des valeurs et principes culturels nouveaux. Il a en effet la conviction profonde que les deux piliers de l'éducation du jeune Hellène doivent être la langue et culture de la Grèce ancienne, d'une part, et, d'autre part, la langue et culture françaises. En comparant la littérature française aux littératures d'autres pays, il estime que la supériorité de la première réside dans le fait que ses représentants visent non à affirmer leur gloire personnelle mais à joindre l'utile à l'agréable à l'intention des lecteurs. Il conseille même aux jeunes prosateurs grecs d'étudier la littérature française pour profiter non seulement de sa qualité majeure qui est le 'bon sens pratique', mais aussi de son caractère 'méthodique, clair, intègre et toujours séduisant' (Carassoutsas 1855: 16). Il appuie ses propos par un argument d'autorité, en prenant pour exemple le patriarche des lumières néohelléniques: 'Adamance Coray qui seul parmi nous ou avec quelques-uns encore connaissait l'art d'écrire doit les vertus de sa langue, d'une part à l'étude attentive de nos illustres ancêtres et deuxièmement à la fréquentation continue des auteurs français' (*ibid.*). Outre l'appropriation efficace de la langue, les textes littéraires français ont aussi une valeur esthétique et peuvent donc servir un objectif stylistique.

Pour faciliter l'approche des textes, Carassoutsas fait précéder sa chrestomathie d'une présentation sommaire de la littérature française, intitulée 'Abrégé de la littérature française' (Ἔκθεσις Συνοπτικὴ τῆς Γαλλικῆς Φιλολογίας). Si son point de départ est le XVIe siècle, il insiste surtout sur la présentation des auteurs des XVIIe et XVIIIe siècles, ceux qui forment, comme l'a montré André Chervel, le canon littéraire scolaire suivi en France (Chervel 2008: 434). Quant à la littérature contemporaine, Carassoutsas lui réserve dans son ouvrage une place réduite. Il ne semble du reste pas beaucoup l'apprécier, notamment pour ce qui est du roman, en raison d'une part des difficultés que ce genre littéraire a rencontrées en Grèce, surtout dans la première moitié du XIXe siècle, et d'autre part à cause de la volonté fermement réitérée par les auteurs des manuels de fournir aux élèves des textes à caractère moral. Les romans français sont en effet taxés d'immoralité à cette époque en Grèce, et Carassoutsas s'indigne de l'accroissement de leur nombre aux dépens de la poésie lyrique, genre considéré plus noble.

On ne s'étonnera donc pas de constater que dans la chrestomathie de Carassoutsas la poésie occupe la part du lion et que le roman en est pour ainsi dire absent, représenté seulement par un extrait de la *Corinne* de Mme de Staël. La prose est représentée par des morceaux qui exaltent l'antiquité grecque,[17] par des leçons morales ou des épisodes historiques.[18] Ainsi, au moment où se construit l'identité nationale par l'enseignement, la reconquête du patrimoine antique est en partie assurée par la médiation des textes français, puisque les chrestomathies puisent copieusement dans les sources offertes par la France. La culture de la France participe à la formation de celle de la Grèce et les chrestomathies françaises deviennent des instruments précieux pour l'élaboration d'une idéologie et pour la formation des individus-citoyens dont avait besoin l'État grec à ce stade de sa constitution.

Dans ce processus, il est intéressant de noter que l'objectif premier, à savoir l'apprentissage du français, n'a paradoxalement pas été toujours atteint au niveau souhaité. En effet, les chrestomathies privilégiaient surtout la langue soutenue des auteurs classiques. Or Carassoutsas, quoique suivant fidèlement le canon littéraire et tenant le roman pour délétère, estime que mis à part les trésors de la littérature classique auxquels l'élève doit s'initier, l'apprentissage de la langue doit se faire à partir de textes modernes. Déplorant le fait que la plupart des manuels enseignent un français désuet qui n'est plus celui parlé en France, il inclut dans son manuel des extraits de prosateurs contemporains, comme Villemain, Guizot et Chateaubriand: 'ce sont justement les modernes, dit-il, qui peuvent servir d'exemple à l'élève pour apprendre la langue comme elle est écrite et parlée de nos jours' (Carassoutsas 1855: iii).

Le *Dictionnaire des synonymes*

Ce souci de communiquer aux élèves la réalité de la langue vivante, se trouve à l'origine de la dernière initiative pédagogique de Carassoutsas, le *Dictionnaire des synonymes de la langue française* (Λεξικόν των Συνωνύμων της Γαλλικής γλώσσης) publié en 1865. Complément obligé des grammaires et des chrestomathies, le dictionnaire pédagogique proposé à cette époque est le plus souvent bilingue. Mais ce dictionnaire particulier, d'un genre nouveau pour la Grèce, était à ses yeux destiné à contribuer au perfectionnement de l'oral et du travail réalisé dans le cadre de la traduction. Dans son prologue, l'auteur présente successivement les lexicologues français qui ont fait des dictionnaires des synonymes et qui constituent ses sources: Gabriel Girard, Nicolas Beauzée, Roubaud, D'Alembert, Diderot, Condillac, Pierre-Benjamin Lafaye et François Guizot, sans toutefois préciser de quel ouvrage il s'est servi. Nous avons cependant pu constater après collationnement, que ses entrées comme les exemples fournis suivent en grande partie de près les entrées du *Dictionnaire universel des synonymes de la langue française* (1839). Ce dernier contenait les synonymes proposés par les auteurs cités — à l'exception de Lafaye dont les travaux sont postérieurs — et a constitué aussi la base pour le dictionnaire des synonymes de Guizot.

Dans son dictionnaire, Carassoutsas suit la voie de la simplification qui s'imposait pour un ouvrage à usage scolaire pour non-francophones. Il reste en outre fidèle à l'objectif constant qui était le sien, à savoir l'approche comparée des deux langues, qui constitue à la fois la difficulté mais aussi le défi de sa démarche: 'il fallait donner une forme et un type grecs, écrit-il, à des notions françaises, et de plus conserver, là où il était possible, la correspondance du grec aux synonymes français' (Carassoutsas 1865: iii). Et comme dans ses autres ouvrages, ici encore toutes les explications et les commentaires sont fournis en grec.

Carassoutsas va jusqu'à proposer dans sa préface la méthode qu'il estime la plus adéquate pour l'enseignement des synonymes en classe de langue. L'élève, écrit l'auteur, 'après avoir traduit deux pages d'un texte français, devrait chercher les synonymes des mots dans le dictionnaire et les apprendre. Le professeur lui poserait par la suite des questions pour vérifier ses connaissances'. Une deuxième approche, poursuit Carassoutsas, consisterait à donner aux élèves une liste de mots à mémoriser, et les inciter à les utiliser par la suite dans le texte (Carassoutsas 1865: iii-iv).

Conclusion

Les trois ouvrages pédagogiques de Carassoutsas nous permettent, à travers leur paratexte et leurs contenus, de reconstituer les fondements intellectuels, voire idéologiques de l'auteur, tout en nous renseignant, à un plus large plan, sur les démarches méthodologiques mises en œuvre dans la deuxième moitié du XIXe siècle pour l'enseignement du français en Grèce, qu'en règle générale on méconnaît. Ils nous permettent, en outre, de compléter l'itinéraire individuel de Carassoutsas et la place importante qu'il occupe dans les lettres grecques du XIXe siècle. Par son œuvre poétique, traductologique et pédagogique, Carassoutsas devient en effet un médiateur culturel entre la France et la Grèce.

Ces documents nous permettent de compléter nos connaissances de l'histoire quelquefois mouvementée des manuels de français en Grèce. La *Grammaire de la langue française* est l'un des manuels les plus importants de la deuxième moitié du XIXe siècle, fait qui est attesté par les nombreuses éditions et réimpressions qu'elle connut jusqu'à la fin du siècle, la dernière datant de 1891.[19] Approuvée par le ministère de l'Instruction publique pour être utilisée dans les Écoles helléniques et les Gymnases, la grammaire de Carassoutsas se trouve en plus en 1857 au centre d'une querelle d'érudits qui se déploie dans les pages des journaux athéniens. Face à lui, Georges Doukas, professeur de français et également auteur d'une grammaire publiée en 1855, l'accuse de plagiat, d'omissions, d'absence de méthode et de cohérence dans la présentation des phénomènes grammaticaux, d'ignorance de la prononciation correcte des mots. Les arguments de Doukas, exposés dans une brochure intitulée *Collation de la première édition de la Grammaire française de G. Doukas publiée en 1853 et de la deuxième édition de celle de M. Carassoutsas publiée en 1856* ne sont pas toujours justes car il ignore volontairement — ou même passe sous silence — les nouveautés qu'a essayé d'introduire Carassoutsas dans sa grammaire (Papadaki and Provata 2011). Mais malgré le bruit provoqué (à moins que cela ne le fit connaître encore davantage), le manuel de Carassoutsas connaît un bel essor et initie plusieurs générations à la langue française, avec pour compléments sa chrestomathie — qui connut elle quatre éditions — et son dictionnaire des synonymes.

Comme on a pu le voir, Carassoutsas, qui doit aujourd'hui sa renommée dans les lettres grecques d'abord à son œuvre poétique puis à son œuvre de traducteur, a laissé une œuvre de pédagogue qui est loin d'être négligeable. Ses manuels ont contribué à l'acculturation française de plusieurs générations de jeunes Hellènes par l'étude de la langue et de la littérature françaises. Tout en ayant scrupuleusement suivi les prescriptions morales de l'enseignement grec, en proposant des lectures destinées à édifier la conscience nationale, politique et religieuse du nouvel État grec, ses ouvrages portent néanmoins l'empreinte personnelle de l'érudit qu'il a été. Carassoutsas a enfin l'insigne mérite d'avoir contribué à un enseignement littérairement contextualisé de la langue étrangère tout en étant animé du souci de ne pas nuire à la culture nationale.

Bibliography

Primary sources

Αθηνά – Athina, n° 2607, 23 octobre 1857: 3–4
CARASSOUTSAS, IOANNIS. 1839. *Λύρα* [*Lyre*] (Ermoupoli: Polyméri)
——. 1849. *Απάνθισμα ποιητικόν* [*Florilège poétique*] (Athens: Aggelidou)
——. 1855. *Χρηστομάθεια Γαλλική* [*Chrestomathie française*] (Athens: Vlastou) (Rééditions: 1859, 1865, 1876)
——. 1856 [1852]. *Γραμματική τής Γαλλικής Γλώσσης* [*Grammaire de la langue française*] (Athens: Philadelphéos)
——. 1859. *Γραμματική τής Γαλλικής Γλώσσης* [*Grammaire de la langue française*], 3ᵉ édition, revue et complétée (Athens: Vlastou)
——. 1865 [1868]. *Λεξικόν τών συνωνύμων τής Γαλλικής Γλώσσης* [*Dictionnaire des synonymes de la langue française*] (Athens: Grypari and Kanariotou)
CARASSUZA, JEAN [CARASSOUTSAS, IOANNIS]. 1858. *Épître à M. de Lamartine au sujet de son 'Histoire de la Turquie' avec une notice sur l'état actuel de la Grèce et de l'empire Ottoman* (Paris: Garnier)
Dictionnaire universel des synonymes de la langue. 1839. Nouvelle Édition (Paris: Loquin)
DOUKAS, GEORGE. 1855. *Γραμματική της Γαλλικής Γλώσσης* [*Grammaire de la langue française*] (Athens: Anghélidou)
[P], 1857. *Παραβολή της πρώτης εκδόσεως της του Γ. Δούκα Γαλλικής Γραμματικής εκδοθείσης κατά το 1853 προς την δευτέραν έκδοσιν της του κ. Καρασούτσα εκδοθείσαν το 1856* [*Collation de la première édition de la Grammaire française de G. Doukas publiée en 1853 et de la deuxième édition de celle de M. Carassoutsas publiée en 1856*] (Athens: Kotsambasopoulou)

Secondary sources

ANTONIOU, DAVID. 2012. *Διδάσκαλοι-Καθηγητές της Γαλλικής γλώσσας στα ελληνικά σχολεία του 19ᵒᵘ αιώνα* [*Maîtres-Professeurs de langue française dans les écoles grecques du XIXᵉ siècle*] (Athens: CIREL)

CHERVEL, ANDRÉ. 2008. *Histoire de l'enseignement du français du XVIIe au XXe siècle* (Paris: Retz)

CHOÏDA, KONDYLIA. 2003. 'Το μάθημα των γαλλικών στα Ελληνικά σχολεία της Μέσης εκπαίδευσης του ελεύθερου κράτους και του έξω ελληνισμού κατά τον 19° αιώνα' [Le Cours de français dans les écoles grecques du secondaire, de l'état libre et des territoires assujettis durant le XIXe siècle] (unpublished doctoral dissertation, Université Aristote de Thessalonique)

CORAY, ADAMANCE. 1829. *Άτακτα* [Mélanges], II (Paris: Eberhard)

KOLODNY, EMILE. 1969. 'Hermoupolis-Syra: naissance et évolution d'une ville insulaire grecque', *Méditerranée*, 10: 189-220

MATTHAIOU, ANNA, and PATSIOU, VIKY. 1989. *Η βιβλιοθήκη του Γυμνασίου Σύρου. Κατάλογος εντύπων (1526–1920)* [*La Bibliothèque du Gymnase de Syra. Catalogue des imprimés (1526–1920)*] (Ermoupoli: Morfotiko Idryma Kykladon)

PANAYOTOPOULOS, I. M. 1973. 'Καρασούτσας τις' [Un certain Carassoutsas], *Νέα Εστία*, 92: 184-89

PAPADAKI, MARIA, and PROVATA, DESPINA. 2011. 'Η *Γραμματική της Γαλλικής Γλώσσης* του Ιωάννη Καρασούτσα. Συμβολή στη μελέτη της διάδοσης της γαλλικής γλώσσας στην Ελλάδα κατά τον 19° αιώνα' [*La Grammaire de la langue française* de Ioannis Carassoutsas. Contribution à l'étude de la diffusion de la langue française en Grèce au XIXe siècle], in *Διασταυρώσεις — Croisements*, ed. by Rhéa Delvéroudi et al. (Athènes: Kardamitsa), 245-59

PARASCHOS, CLÉON. 1962. 'Ιωάννης Καρασούτσας' [Ioannis Carassoutsas], in *Δέκα Έλληνες Λυρικοί* [*Dix poètes lyriques grecs*] (Athens: Féxis), pp. 22–40

PARISSIS, S. 1884. *Ανωτέρα και Μέση Εκπαίδευσις (1833–1884)* [*Enseignement secondaire et supérieur (1833–1884)*], 2 vols (Athens: 'O Palamidis'), II

POLITIS, LINOS. 1979. *Ιστορία της Νεοελληνικής λογοτεχνίας* [*Histoire de la littérature néo-hellénique*] (Athens: Morfotiko Idryma Ethnikis Trapezis)

PROTOPAPA-BOUBOULIDOU, GLYKERIA. 1976. *Η Αθηναϊκή Σχολή* [*L'École Athénienne*] (Ioannina : n. pub.)

PROVATA, DESPINA. 1990. 'Écrire en français en Grèce au XIXe siècle', in *Écrivains grecs de langue française* (= special number of *Nouvelles du Sud*, 13), pp. 13-25

——. 2011. 'Construction identitaire et enseignement du français en Grèce au XIXe siècle', in *Identities in the Greek world (from 1204 to the present day)*, ed. by Konstantinos Dimadis, 5 vols (Athens: European Society of Modern Greek Studies), V, 281-92

VLACHOS, ANGELOS. 1901. 'Ιωάννης Καρασούτσας' [Ioannis Carassoutsas], *Ανάλεκτα* [Mélanges], II (Athens: Sakellariou), pp. 56-82

Notes to Chapter 3

1. Selon Antoniou (2012: 82), le pourcentage des professeurs de français qui ont rédigé des manuels s'élève à 31.90%.
2. Groupe de poètes qui ont donné voix au romantisme en Grèce.
3. La langue française était enseignée au Gymnase de Syra depuis sa fondation en 1833. Parmi les titres de la collection de la Bibliothèque du Gymnase de Syra, se trouve un ouvrage de Carassoutsas portant une dédicace de la main de l'auteur au Gymnase de Syra, ce qui renforce l'hypothèse qu'il a été scolarisé dans cet établissement (Matthaiou and Patsiou 1989: 10-11).
4. Toutes les citations provenant du grec sont traduites par l'auteur de l'article.
5. Il est d'ailleurs l'un des poètes qui traduiront en grec le 'Lac' de Lamartine.
6. Ces traductions seront incluses plus tard dans son recueil poétique intitulé *Βάρβιτος* [*Violoncelle*] (1860).
7. On ne doit pas exclure, cependant, le fait qu'il ait pu aussi enseigner à Hermoupolis mais aucune indication n'existe dans ce sens.

8. Il ne faut pas oublier que la Grèce se trouve alors en situation de diglossie: la 'katharevousa', langue purifiée qui ne contient pas de mots 'barbares' — car, en théorie, les mots étrangers en sont bannis — est la langue de l'écrit. Face à elle, la langue populaire, le démotique, est la langue parlée, réservée à l'usage quotidien. Cette diglossie reflète aussi une opposition d'ordre socioculturel car elle souligne les différences entre le peuple et l'élite.

9. Pour une approche détaillée de la grammaire française de Carassoutsas, on peut consulter Papadaki et Provata (2011).

10. La *Nouvelle grammaire française* (1823) de François Noël (1756-1841) et Charles-Pierre Chapsal (1787-1858) utilisée comme manuel dans les écoles, connut un succès phénoménal et devint un ouvrage de référence pour la grammaire scolaire en France.

11. Charles-Pierre Girault-Duvivier (1765-1832) publia sa célèbre *Grammaire des grammaires, ou analyse raisonnée des meilleurs traités sur la grammaire française* en 1811.

12. Noël-François de Wailly (1724-1801) publia, en 1754, les *Principes généraux et particuliers de la langue française.*

13. Pierre Restaut (1696-1764) est l'auteur des *Principes généraux et raisonnés de la Grammaire française* (1730), premier manuel élémentaire composé pour l'étude du français.

14. Étienne Bonnot de Condillac (1714-1780) est l'auteur des *Principes généraux de grammaire pour toutes les langues: avec leur application particulière à la langue française,* publié en 1775 comme premier tome du *Cours d'étude pour l'instruction du Prince de Parme.*

15. Les exercices de cacographie, inventés au XVIIIᵉ siècle, sont largement utilisés au XIXᵉ siècle dans les écoles en France. Voici, à titre d'exemple, des phrases tirées de la grammaire de Carassoutsas, dans lesquelles sont délibérément introduits des fautes de langage que les élèves doivent corriger: 'L'exemple d'une bonne vie est la meilleure leçon qu'on peut donner au genre humain'; 'Les hommes passent comme les fleurs, qui, épanoui le matin, le soir sont flétri et foulé aux pieds' (Carassoutsas 1856: 147, 148).

16. La loi de 1882 concernant la rédaction des manuels scolaires, exigeait que les grammaires scolaires destinées aux classes des gymnases comportent un chapitre sur la versification française (Parissis 1884: 445).

17. Les élèves grecs pouvaient lire, par exemple, un passage intitulé 'Les Grecs et les Romains', extrait de l'œuvre *Observations sur l'histoire de France* de l'Abbé Mably.

18. On pouvait aussi lire, par exemple, des extraits des *Martyrs* de Chateaubriand ou de *l'Histoire de Charles XII* de Voltaire.

19. Depuis sa première édition, en 1852, elle a connu neuf éditions, dont certaines ont été réimprimées plus d'une fois, dans des villes différentes et/ou chez des imprimeurs différents. Au total, on l'a dit, la bibliographie dénombre quinze éditions et réimpressions différentes.

CHAPTER 4

❖

Manuels scolaires de français écrits par des grecs pour des grecs au 19ᵉ siècle

Étude de cas: un manuel de Georges Theocharopoulos

Constantin (Konstantinos) Mytaloulis

The purpose of this chapter is to examine various historical aspects of Greek textbooks for teaching French as a foreign language in Greece, used by the Greek educational system, before and after the birth of the New Hellenic State, which was officially recognized in 1830. The willingness of the Greek State to integrate French language teaching into school curricula was accompanied by a growing number of school textbooks (grammars, dictionaries) in Greece and an increase in the number of publications of textbooks for French, written by Greeks for Greeks. We shall outline the model followed during the nineteenth century for the production and publication of French-language school textbooks. To do so, we present a short historical overview of the textbooks for teaching French as a foreign language in Greece. Additionally, we present and examine, as an illustration, the textbook of G. Theocharopoulos (1839) for teaching French. Our presentation of Greek textbooks for French dating from the nineteenth century will focus not only on how they were written, but also on their structure, contents, methodological approaches and the underlying culture conveyed.

À travers cet article nous allons présenter des éléments historiques de la publication de manuels de français langue étrangère en Grèce au cours du 19ᵉ siècle avant de continuer avec l'étude et l'analyse (au sens de dissoudre) du manuel de français de Georges Theocharopoulos, *Dialogues familiers précédés de quelques phrases faciles de plusieurs dialogues de Fénelon en français et en grec* (1839).[1] Les données auxquelles nous allons faire référence ont toujours un rapport avec le contexte de l'enseignement du français langue étrangère en Grèce.

Bref aperçu historique du français langue étrangère en Grèce au 19ᵉ siècle[2]

Depuis 1790, date qui correspond selon Jean Caravolas à la publication par Georges Vendotis du premier manuel de français langue étrangère pour des Grecs, nous constatons une hausse du nombre de publications s'agissant de ce type de manuels, comme la *Grammaire* de Nicolas Caradja (Vienne, 1806), ou la réédition de la *Grammaire de la Langue française* de Vendotis (Venise, 1810). De nouvelles grammaires paraissent, comme la *Grammaire française théorique et pratique*, de Stéphanos Partzoulas (Vienne, 1814) ou plus tard, en 1832, des adaptations de la *Grammaire* de Ch.-F. Lhomond (Odessa, Imprimerie de l'École des commerçants grecs), ou de la *Grammaire de la Langue Française* du Français Hippolyte Teisonnière (Athènes, 1837). Vers 1838, Noël et Chapsal voient publier deux de leurs ouvrages, la *Nouvelle Grammaire française* (Athènes, 1838), ainsi que l'*Abrégé de la Grammaire Française ou Extrait de la Nouvelle Grammaire* (Athènes, 1839), tous deux traduits par Georges Theocharopoulos. Ces traductions portent souvent l'intitulé d'"adaptation au public grec" ou "adapté et enrichi pour les élèves grecs", mais elles ne présentent que peu de changements par rapport au texte d'origine, comme par exemple la *Méthode d'Ollendorff révisée et amendée, traduite et enrichie de lettres et dialogues* d'Oikonomidis (Athènes, 1865).

Le manuel *Chrestomathie Française* (1859) de Ioannis (Jean) Karasoutsas (ou Karasousas), professeur des collèges, écrivain et poète, comporte une collection d'extraits d'œuvres d'écrivains français, comme Racine (*Iphigénie*), Voltaire (*L'Histoire de Charles XII, Mérope*), Chateaubriand (*Le Génie du Christianisme*, Lamartine (*Voyage en Orient*) ou Fénelon (*Les Aventures d'Aristonoüs*). Les manuels de Karasoutsas, que ce soit *La Chréstomathie Française* ou *La Grammaire de la Langue Française* de (1852), doivent leur importance au fait qu'ils ont été approuvés par le comité du ministère de l'Éducation grec et grâce à leurs multiples rééditions.[3] Par exemple, *La Grammaire de la Langue Française*, selon Antoniou (2012), connait neuf éditions jusqu'en 1884.

La *Nouvelle méthode pratique et facile pour apprendre la langue française* (1860) de D. F. Ahn (1796-1865) (dont le premier cours est paru en 1860 et le deuxième cours paru en 1861, selon *Le Catalogue annuel de la librairie française* de Charles Reinwad (1861)), ainsi que la *Méthode d'Ollendorff* (Athènes, 1886) marquent une volonté de renouveler les manuels choisis pour l'enseignement du français en Grèce.

Schinas et Levadeus publient leur dictionnaire français-grec en 1861 en deux tomes (1032 et 1464 pages), basé sur les tout nouveaux et très complets dictionnaires de Bescherelle et Poitevin, tous les deux publiés en 1856. Dans le prologue, les auteurs consacrent neuf pages à survoler l'histoire de la langue française. Nous y trouvons mention des influences qu'elle a subies et de l'existence de mots d'origine latine (*lupus-loup, palatium-palais*), allemande (*marche, halte, maréchal, bivouac*) ou grecque, surtout parmi les termes scientifiques (*cardiaque, apoplectique*) (Schinas et Levadeus 1889). Les auteurs introduisent ensuite un extrait des *Serments de Strasbourg*, des extraits de l'*Histoire de la conquête de Constantinople* ou *Chronique des empereurs Baudouin et Henri de Constantinople* (1207-13) de Geoffroy de Villehardouin et des écrits de Jean de Joinville, le biographe de saint Louis. Des références à des œuvres d'autres époques enrichissent cet aperçu de l'itinéraire de la langue française (Montaigne, l'Académie française, les érudits et savants du siècle des Lumières). Le *Dictionnaire du dialecte grec* de Dimitris Scarlatos (Athènes/Constantinople, 1874) signale l'introduction des dictionnaires bilingues dans le monde de l'éducation francophone pour les Grecs.

En 1878, la *Grammaire de la langue française* d'Ioannis Karasoutsas (deux cent pages), amendée et révisée par Georges Karasoutsas pour sa huitième édition de 1878, est enseignée dans les écoles grecques. En première page, nous est présenté l'avis du comité qui approuve cette grammaire (signé par le ministre de l'époque) et qui la recommande aux enseignants des écoles. Il est à noter que l'auteur, dans sa préface, reproche aux auteurs de grammaires contemporains de n'avoir produit que de mauvaises traductions des grammaires françaises, alors que lui-même a complété celle qu'il a traduite en utilisant *La Grammaire des Grammaires* de Girault Duvivier (1811), et celle de Noël et Chapsal, et le *Dictionnaire de l'Académie*.

En 1880, c'est *La Grammaire de la langue française théorique et pratique à l'usage des collèges* (sixième édition, deux cent pages) qui domine. Elle est rédigée par le professeur de français Georgios Zades, à Patra (première édition: 1872). Dans sa préface, celui-ci renseigne les lecteurs sur les œuvres qu'il a utilisées pour la rédiger: *La Grammaire des grammaires* de Girault-Duvivier, *La Grammaire Générale* de Napoléon Landais, et la cinquantième édition de la *Grammaire* de Noël et Chapsal. Il incrimine lui aussi les autres auteurs pour les erreurs et les lacunes de leurs manuels, et souligne que le sien débarrasse les élèves de la méthode lourde d'Ollendorff .[4]

En 1894, *La Grammaire de la Langue Française* de D. Panopoulos est le seul manuel approuvé par le ministère de l'Éducation publique et des Affaires religieuses. En première page, l'éditeur insère la décision qui porte la signature du ministre et de l'époque, Dimitris Kallifronas. Il n'y figure pas de préface ou d'avant-propos de l'auteur comparant son manuel à d'autres, ni de texte mis en exergue pour vanter les qualités de l'ouvrage, comme c'était le cas pour les auteurs des manuels antérieurs. Peut-être cela est-il dû au fait que ce manuel avait été approuvé sur concours.[5] Les manuels approuvés pouvaient être utilisés dans les écoles pour une période de quatre ans et l'introduction d'autres manuels dans l'enseignement était strictement interdite.[6]

Les auteurs de divers manuels ou méthodes que nous présentons n'hésitent pas à utiliser les ouvrages qui existent sur le marché international à cette époque. Ces maîtres-auteurs ont sans doute contribué à ce que nous appelons la *disciplinarisation du français* en Grèce. Les maîtres deviennent auteurs, et les titres des manuels sont très souvent identifiés à leurs patronymes.[7] Il se produit donc un glissement sémantique, une synecdoque comme disent Carla Pellandra et Javier Suso López (2012: 96): 'on parle d'un Goudar, d'un Marin ou d'un Chantreau' pour définir le manuel produit par ces auteurs. Il est presque certain que de la même façon les élèves et les professeurs de français en Grèce parlaient d'un Panopoulos, d'un Scarlatos, d'un Théocharopulos, etc.

En effet, parmi les 163 professeurs de français grecs recensés par Antoniou (2012) depuis 1833 jusqu'en 1900, cinquante-deux parmi eux ont publié un manuel de français comme G. Zades, I. Karasoutsas, N. Kontopoulos, D. Kontogeorgis, G. N. Oikonomidis, A. Syrigos et Th. Kyprios, tandis que parmi les 107 professeurs de français étrangers, quinze se sont occupés de la rédaction, traduction et publication d'un manuel de français comme C. Cambiol ou Kambiolis, H. Téisonnière, C. Nonnote, Eugène Brissaud et Xavier de Bouge (Antoniou 2012). Ces professeurs-auteurs publient des manuels dont le titre diffère selon le contenu: *Grammaire*, *Abrégé de la grammaire française*, *Chrestomathie française*, *Syllabaire français*, *Dictionnaire grec-français, ou Méthode d'apprentissage de la langue française, Manuel de l'étudiant grec* etc. Ces manuels, retrouvés dans des bibliothèques grecques comme la bibliothèque de l'Institut pédagogique grec, la Bibliothèque nationale de Grèce, ainsi que des bibliothèques en ligne comme les archives du laboratoire de bibliologie du musée Benaki ou la bibliothèque numérique Anemi de l'université de Crète, peuvent présenter aux chercheurs un panorama de ces productions ambitieuses. Ce grand nombre de publications de manuels comprend les livres appelés 'grammaires', qui n'étaient autres que des manuels et des dictionnaires. Notons cependant que les dictionnaires et les grammaires étaient utilisés dans les écoles grecques en tant que manuels au début du XIXe siècle, comme *L'enseignement exact de la Grammaire française* de Nicolas Caradja (1806), ou la *Grammaire de la langue française* de Georgios Vendotis (1810).

Par ailleurs, les soixante-dix-huit premières pages du *Dictionnaire du François-Grec* de Grigorios Zalikoglou de Thessalonique (Paris, 1809; 576 pages) sont consacrées à une série d'explications des phénomènes grammaticaux et syntaxiques de la langue française, de la conjugaison des verbes réguliers et irréguliers, etc. Il en résulte qu'à l'époque, faute de manuels de français, ces dictionnaires bilingues comprenaient l'équivalent d'un manuel entier, à côté de la traduction des mots.

Après la mise en place du nouveau système éducatif en Grèce (1834), et même avant, des auteurs grecs rédigent des manuels de français à l'intention d'un public hellénophone. Déjà, en 1831, *Ο εισηγητής της Γαλλικής Γλώσσης* (*Introduction à la langue française*) d'Anastasios Herkoulides, le premier manuel qui ne porte ni le titre de *Grammaire* ni celui de *Dictionnaire,* est publié en Grèce. Ce livre est inspiré de la *Méthode Universelle* de Jacotot (Caravolas 2015) qui contient des textes littéraires qui ne sont pas tirés uniquement des *Aventures de Télémaque* (1699) comme le fait Jacotot (Jacotot 1829). Ce roman pédagogique de Fénelon permet aux enseignants de réveiller dans l'esprit des élèves, à travers les aventures de Télémaque et du sage Mentor, des sujets de la mythologie et des images qui évoquent l'ambiance antique comme les batailles, les amours et la descente aux enfers.

Avec son manuel *Dialogues Familiers*, Georges Theocharopoulos (Athènes, 1839) est l'un des premiers à considérer les petits dialogues comme des éléments constitutifs dominants de l'enseignement ou comme outils fondamentaux de l'enseignement du français langue étrangère en Grèce. Cet ouvrage ne comporte que des dialogues familiers, assortis des *Dialogues de Morts* (1712) de Fénelon.

Theocharopoulos, né à Patras en 1770 hellénophone, a enseigné aux gymnases du Péloponnèse et de Constantinople et a été instituteur des Ypsilanti et d'autres hospodars (titre attribué aux seigneurs et aux gouverneurs de Valachie, de Moldavie ou autre région balkanique). Il a vécu à Paris (Moulias 1993: 63) et donnait des cours à des hellénistes et des philhellènes comme Wladimir Brunet de Presle, qui a pris des cours de grec moderne avant de suivre les cours du philhellène Charles Benoît Hase à l'École des langues orientales. Sandrine Maufroy (2005b: 221), afin de nous renseigner sur la vie de Theocharopoulos, nous donne une lettre de Theocharopoulos adressée à Hase: il lui présente sa situation déplorable et demande une aide financière afin qu'il puisse quitter la France et se rendre en Grèce via Munich:

sexagénaire, éloigné des siens, frappé dans ce qu'il avait de plus cher, il a tout fait jusqu'ici pour n'être point à charge à cette France hospitalière où tout Hellène trouve un si touchant accueil, et pour se procurer par son travail les moyens de retourner dans le pays de ses pères; mais il n'a pu recueillir le prix de ses efforts. Il avait déjà repris le chemin de la Grèce en passant par Bruxelles où il donnait ses soins à l'édition d'un dictionnaire grec-français, pour laquelle il avait traité avec un imprimeur-libraire de cette ville, lorsque la révolution Belge, cause ou prétexte de la rupture de ce traité, le réduisit à vendre ses vêtements pour revenir à pied vers ce Paris où il avait laissé des hommes généreux et de nobles caractères. Dans cette capitale même, la stagnation du commerce l'empêchant de tirer parti de ses connaissances littéraires, il a été obligé, il y a quatre mois, de se défaire, au vil prix de six sols par volume, de 500 grammaires qu'il y avait en dépôt. Le faible produit de cette vente, qui soulagea quelque peu sa détresse pendant la saison rigoureuse, est enfin épuisé, et maintenant il ne lui reste absolument rien. Il a donc résolu de retourner dans sa patrie; mais, privé de toutes ressources, il lui est impossible de subvenir aux frais que nécessitera son voyage d'ici à Munich où il trouvera des amis et les moyens de continuer sa route.

Nous avons sélectionné à présenter le manuel bilingue (français-grec) de Georges Theocharopoulos *Dialogues familiers précédés de quelques phrases faciles de plusieurs dialogues de Fénelon en français et en grec* (Athènes, 1839) qui peut refléter à la fois la diversité et les ressemblances du contenu (éléments langagiers et culturels) avec d'autres manuels de français des XIXe et XVIIIe siècles, utilisés au sein du système éducatif grec. Ce manuel a été publié aussi en 1827 (français-anglais-grec) et en 1828 (français-anglais-grec) à Paris, et à Athènes en 1842 (français-grec) et 1845 (français-grec) (Tsigris 2002: 94).[8] Notre choix de présenter le manuel de 1839 s'explique par le fait que la traduction de G. Theocharopoulos est publiée quatre à cinq ans après le premier effort sérieux d'organisation du système éducatif grec, en 1834. Il est évident que l'auteur a reproduit une grande partie de l'édition de 1828 en ôtant les phrases et dialogues en anglais. D'ailleurs, l'édition de 1839 a plus de pages (270) par rapport à celles de 1827 et 1828 (175 pages).

Quant à l'importance accordée par Theocharopoulos aux œuvres de l'excellent helléniste que fut Fénelon, rappelons que celles-ci ont pénétré dans la péninsule balkanique au début du XVIIIe siècle. La première traduction de l'œuvre *Les Aventures de Télémaque* (1699) en grec moderne qui ouvre la voie à sa diffusion dans les Balkans date de 1742. Elle est due à Athanassios Skiadas; la deuxième, celle de Dimitrios Govdelas, paraît en 1801; et la troisième, celle de Konstantinos Ikonomos, vers 1808.

Cette œuvre de Fénelon est largement utilisée dans les écoles grecques, bien avant et après la Révolution des Grecs contre le joug ottoman. Nous apprenons par la monographie de Caravolas sur la vie de Jules David que cet helléniste français et professeur de français se servait de l'œuvre de Fénelon dans son cours du collège de Chios (Chevalier 2010).[9] L'étendue des œuvres de Fénelon en tant que romans pédagogiques justifie alors le choix de Theocharopoulos à ce que son manuel contienne les *Dialogues des morts* de Fénelon.

Présentation du manuel de Theocharopoulos (1839)

Le manuel de Theocharopoulos est divisé en quatre parties principales: la première partie présente des phrases familières ou courantes (1839: 5-11): pour demander quelque chose: ('je vous prie'; 'donnez-moi'; 's'il vous plaît'; 'prêtez-moi!'); pour remercier et faire compliment ou amitié ('je vous remercie!'; 'je vous rends mille grâces!'; 'honorez-moi de vos commandements!'; 'faites mes baisemains à M.'); pour consulter ou considérer ('que faut-il faire?'; 'que ferons-nous?'). Il est aussi question du parler, du faire, d'entendre ('parlez haut!'; 'taisez-vous!'; 'je vous entends fort bien!'); connaître, oublier, se ressouvenir ('nous nous connaissons'; 'vous souvenez-vous de cela?'); ou bien de l'âge, de la vie, de la mort ('je me porte bien!'; 'avez-vous encore père et mère?'; 'ma mère est remariée'; 'combien de frères avez-vous?'; 'ils sont tous morts!').

La deuxième partie offre des échantillons de dialogues familiers sur un grand nombre de thématiques (1839: 13-144). Voici quelques exemples: compliments ('Bon jour!'; 'Je vous souhaite le bon jour!'; 'Comment se porte madame votre épouse?'); pour rendre visite et s'informer de la santé ('Je n'ai pas fermé l'œil de toute la nuit'; 'Elle a mal à la tête'); pour prier, demander ou offrir ('Faites-moi ce plaisir'; 'Accordez-moi cette grâce, cette faveur'; 'Daignez accepter cette légère marque de ma reconnaissance'); pour consentir ou accorder, refuser ou s'excuser et remercier ('volontiers'; 'de tout mon cœur'; 'J'y consens'; 'Ordonnez et vous serez obéi'; 'Je vous suis infiniment obligé'); pour interroger et pour répondre ('Est-il bien vrai?'; 'Je l'ai entendu dire'); pour douter, consulter, affirmer, nier ('J'en crois rien'; 'J'en doute').

L'objectif de la troisième partie (1839: 153-98) est de permettre l'accès à des textes littéraires par le biais des *Dialogues des morts* de Fénelon. L'étendue de l'enseignement de la langue à travers ces œuvres est vaste. À titre d'exemple, il suffit de donner les résultats de la consultation du catalogue électronique de la Bibliothèque nationale de France sur les *Aventures de Télémaque*, fournis par Nadia Minerva (2003): 'quelque 630 exemplaires (sans compter les œuvres complètes et les "choix" innombrables où figure *Télémaque*), échelonnés de façon très irrégulière entre 1699 et 2003: plus de 3/5 jusqu'à 1850, un autre cinquième entre 1851 et 1900'.

Enfin, la quatrième partie (1839: 204-61) donne des modèles de 'Lettres et billets d'affaires' pour remercier, inviter, recommander quelqu'un, demander de l'argent qui est dû, écrire une lettre de change à vue, une lettre de quittance, etc. Bref, des références qui appartiendraient aujourd'hui à ce qu'on appellerait visée actionnelle (la fameuse tâche du CECRL). En effet, depuis les XVIIe et XVIIIe siècles, il est très habituel de comporter dans les manuels utilisés en Europe pour l'enseignement d'une langue étrangère des éléments qui regardent les échanges financiers ou des détails sur l'achat et la vente des produits (voir Loonen 1991: 18-23 et McLelland 2015: 53-54).

À la suite de ces quatre parties principales, un guide de deux pages intitulé 'Des titres' donne au lecteur l'occasion d'apprendre la façon dont on s'adresse aux personnes importantes (le pape: 'Saint Père'; les rois: 'Votre Majesté'; et particulière-ment le roi de France: 'Votre Majesté Très Chrétienne'; le roi d'Espagne: 'Votre

Majesté Catholique', etc.). L'auteur choisit de présenter un essai en grec sur la signification du choix du nombre douze (la douzaine, les Apôtres, les dieux grecs etc.). Cette petite sous-partie de douze pages n'a aucun rapport avec l'enseignement du français, mais elle pourrait être prise comme un effort de création d'un manuel interdisciplinaire. Enfin, le manuel se clôt avec un tableau des principaux homonymes français et la mise à jour d'une nouvelle loi royale d'Othon (du 22 juin 1838) sur la division territoriale du nouvel État grec (183: 261).

Remarques générales

Ce manuel présente un grand nombre de situations à travers des dialogues qui sont susceptibles de susciter l'intérêt des apprenants. Ce sont ces dialogues qu'on appelle en didactique moderne les dialogues de situation.[10] H. Besse souligne qu'ils sont produits en opposition aux dialogues qui peuvent se tenir dans n'importe quel lieu, à n'importe quelle heure: 'appeler le garçon à la terrasse d'un café, lui commander quelque chose, le remercier, relève d'un dialogue de situation' (Besse 1992: 65).

Nous voyons que les phrases choisies dans cet ouvrage de G. Theocharopoulos, bien que différentes dans leur lexique en fonction des situations, appartiennent toutes aux mêmes registres de langue, que nous considérons comme standard ou soutenu. Il n'y aucune nuance de langage familier comme c'est le cas dans les manuels de FLE surtout ceux du début du XXIe siècle; on vouvoie même les enfants (La gouvernante des enfants: 'Où est votre poupée?' (1839: 135)). L'auteur combine des phrases et des dialogues de la vie ordinaire avec des dialogues tirés de l'œuvre de Fénelon, rédigés dans un langage soutenu. De cette façon, il pense pouvoir concilier deux registres de langue, le standard et le soutenu dans le même manuel didactique. Voici un exemple de registre standard et soutenu des dialogues quotidiens:

> — Quel tintamarre faites-vous là? (1839: 10).
> — Accordez-moi cette grâce, cette faveur. Vous ne sauriez me faire un plus grand plaisir (1839: 17).

Et un exemple de texte soutenu/littéraire des dialogues entre Socrate et Alcibiade (1839: 187):

> Socrate: Ce qu'on appelle conquête devient le comble de la tyrannie et l'exécration du genre humain, à moins que le conquérant n'ait fait sa conquête par une guerre juste, et n'ait rendu heureux le peuple conquis en lui donnant de bonnes lois.
>
> L'auteur, au début du livre, en guise d'introduction, s'explique sur les raisons pour lesquelles il publie ce manuel: 'La langue écrite d'un peuple diffère de la langue parlée. La première est étudiée dans les textes des historiens, dans les poètes, dans les orateurs; la seconde ne peut être bien apprise qu'au milieu des cités étrangères'. Et il continue: 'Pour ceux qui ne peuvent pas voyager, la seule ressource, le meilleur guide, c'est la conversation avec quelques nationaux et la lecture de dialogues (1839: β).

Concernant le contenu de manuels, celui-ci est progressivement enrichi par un grand choix de thèmes. Tous les sujets sont adaptés à la vie d'un adulte. On est loin de la publication des manuels de FLE du XXe siècle, manuels attrayants, conçus spécialement pour attirer l'intérêt, attiser la curiosité et susciter la motivation chez des jeunes apprenants de différentes tranches d'âge. Cependant, ce manuel s'inscrit dans le cadre de productions pédagogiques qui introduisent, souvent inconsciemment, des notions qui n'appartiennent pas tout à fait au domaine linguistique du français (c'est-à dire l'enseignement de tel ou tel phénomène grammatical ou syntaxique), afin que les élèves prennent conscience du monde, et non pas seulement du sujet de telle ou telle discipline, en l'occurrence la langue française (par exemple des termes qui touchent à l'histoire, la littérature ou la philosophie).

Quant aux thématiques culturelles, nous avons procédé à une catégorisation (Mytaloulis 2014) de celles[11] de ce manuel selon les grilles d'évaluation existant aujourd'hui (Cordier-Gauthier, 2000): la France, les relations internationales, la vie quotidienne, la famille, les voyages, l'éducation, le cadre de vie, les finances, les sciences.

Pour ce qui est de la France géographique, des villes et lieux de France, de Paris et de ses monuments l'auteur ne donne presque aucun renseignement, à deux exceptions près: sur 'un voyage au Midi de la France':

— C'est un des meilleurs climats de l'Europe. Il y a peu d'Anglais qui voyagent, qui manquent de passer par la Provence et le Languedoc.
— Voilà du Bourgogne et du Bordeaux. Le vin de Bourgogne est préférable au commencement du repas. (1839: 42, 43)

L'auteur ne fait pas non plus référence à des personnages politiques ou à des célébrités. Les conditions historico-politiques ne permettaient pas alors de citer le moindre nom, d'autant plus qu'un tel manuel, publié en 1839, était destiné à une période longue. Une fois un manuel était approuvé, son utilisation durait plusieurs années après sa première publication. La moindre prise de position politique pouvait avoir des effets négatifs sur la décision des comités qui approuvaient les manuels.

En ce qui concerne les relations internationales et les systèmes politiques, nous pouvons signaler une référence précise à la monarchie, régime cité dans les dialogues: 'Après le dîner: allons faire une promenade au parc. Nous y verrons le roi. Pour le voir de plus près il faut aller un dimanche à la chapelle royale'. Toutefois, le dialogue 'Des nouvelles' fait allusion à l'instabilité politique des sociétés:

— De quoi parle-t-on en ville? N'avez-vous pas entendu dire que nous allions avoir la guerre? Il n'y a que huit jours que la paix a été signée et vous pouvez croire que la guerre recommence? Le commerce a un grand besoin de la paix pour se relever. (1839: 86)

Concernant le système administratif et les institutions de l'époque, le dialogue 'Avec les commis de douanes' (1839: 104) constitue un indice: 'N'avez-vous rien contre les ordres du gouvernement? Non, je n'ai pas [sic] aucun objet prohibé. Cela ne suffit pas; nous avons des ordres d'être très sévères [...] la contrebande est très active'.

En revanche, les dialogues concernant la vie quotidienne, l'alimentation et la gastronomie contiennent une pléthore de références aux habitudes de la classe aisée ('Chez le restaurateur' (1839: 45); 'Pour déjeuner' (1839: 36); 'Pour acheter des meubles' (1839: 130); 'Dans un café' (1839: 48)). Notons qu'il existait à l'époque des cafés pour des non-fumeurs, le tabagisme s'étant répandu surtout pendant la deuxième moitié du XXe siècle ('Entrons dans un café où l'on ne fume pas'). Pour les loisirs, nous retrouvons des phrases sur le jardinage, les promenades, les jeux, les échecs et les dames, la chasse et la pêche (1839: 113): 'Pour nager: Allons nous baigner [...] dans la rivière ou dans la mer?'; ou sur le dessin: 'Votre sœur dessine très bien'.

Concernant la famille et les relations homme-femme, nous donnons une phrase dont le contenu paraît moderne pour les mœurs de la société chrétienne orthodoxe grecque de l'époque: 'Ma mère est remariée'. En effet, la question du veuvage est un élément culturel qui reflète les mœurs de l'époque. Les orthodoxes suivent les catholiques pour lesquels la question du veuvage n'est qu'une apparence; la mort n'a pas rompu l'union 'puisque le mari, vivant au ciel, continue de protéger mystérieusement son foyer' (Beauvalet et Walch 1995: 615), en Grèce aussi bien qu'en Occident.[12]

Le dialogue fabriqué 'Parlant avec une personne qui va se marier' témoigne bien de la conception du mariage et de la tradition de la dot dans:

— Quelle est la demoiselle que vous épousez?
— C'est la fille d'un banquier et une enfant unique.
— Elle a sans doute une grande dot.
— Oui, mais c'est le moindre de ses avantages. Les qualités de son cœur et de son esprit sont supérieures à tout le reste. (1839: 118)

Le dialogue 'La toilette d'une femme' nous transmet les habitudes vestimentaires et le rituel de l'habillement féminin au XIXe siècle, mais on prête attention aussi à la mode masculine. Voyons le dialogue 'Avec un tailleur':

— Il me faut un habit; montrez-moi vos échantillons. J'aimerais bien ce bleu céleste.
— Elle est très à la mode, et vous ira très bien. (1839: 102)

Les voyages occupent une grande partie des dialogues. Les difficultés, les dangers et les soucis des voyageurs sont présentés de façon claire. Voici quelques exemples: 'Pour voyager: je pars demain pour Athènes; si vous voulez être de la partie, il ne tient qu'à vous. Nous voyagerons à frais communs. Il n'y a donc rien à craindre des voleurs' (1839: 87). Des accidents arrivent souvent: 'Des accidents qui peuvent arriver en route: postillon arrêtez, une soupente est cassée. Un cheval vient de s'abattre, le postillon est tombé' (1839: 90).

Pour ce qui est des voyages marins, la menace des pirates préoccupe les capitaines des vaisseaux et les voyageurs (1839: 98):

Il n'y a rien à craindre sur mon bord [...]. Nous ne pensons pas tant aux naufrages qu'aux corsaires. Il y a peu de temps de l'avoir échappé belle [...]. Nous étions à la hauteur de l'île de Ténédos quand un Algérien tomba sur nous à l'improviste.

Les thématiques sur l'école et l'éducation sont présentes dans le dialogue: 'La leçon: Savez-vous votre leçon? Vous êtes un peu paresseux. Vous causez au lieu d'étudier' (1839: 23).

Références à l'Angleterre

Il est intéressant d'ouvrir ici une parenthèse afin de présenter quelques points qui regardent les Anglais et l'Angleterre[13] d'autant plus que cette édition bilingue de 1839 est basée sur le manuel trilingue de 1827 et 1828 dont le titre en anglais est: *Familiar dialogues preceded by some easy phrases and followed by several dialogues from Fenelon in French, English and Greek* (Paris: Bobée et Hingray, 1828).[14]

La visite aux jardins de Vauxhall (1839: 55) est une référence à un spectacle musical à Londres. Présentons un extrait du texte anglais plein de points culturels (1828: 43):

> Since we have resolved to go to Vauxhall, we must determine how we shall go [...]. I don't like crossing the Thames [...]. Let's rather take a hackney coach. Well, what do you think of Vauxhall? It is a terrestrial paradise. The great number of lights produce a very fine effect [...]. What do you think of Mrs B? She has a sweet, natural, harmonious voice. One may say with justice that she is one of the best singers in England.

La traduction de cet extrait d'abord en français, puis en grec comporte comme il est évident des erreurs. L'auteur traduit souvent mot-à-mot. Cette pratique ne correspond pas à une traduction du sens exact de la phrase. Des expressions comme 'with justice, avec justice, δικαίως' ou la phrase qui regarde Mme B — 'je ne m'ennuierais jamais de l'entendre; Δέν πλήττω ποτέ νά τήν ἀκούω' — dont la traduction en anglais est 'I should never be tired of hearing her' montrent l'*injustice* de sa traduction. Mais quelle est cette chanteuse mystérieuse Mrs B (Mme B)? Si on juge par l'année de publication du livre (1827 et 1828) elle pourrait bien être soit Bellchambers qui a chanté en 1818, soit, ce qui est le plus possible, Maria Theresa Bland réputée de sa voix mélodieuse.[15]

Un point qui montre que ce manuel est basé sur le manuel trilingue français-anglais-grec du même auteur est l'importance qu'il donne aux langues française et anglaise, soulignée à travers les dialogues 64, 65 et 66, intitulés 'Sur la langue anglaise' et 'Sur la langue française' (1839: 121).

Toutefois, les phrases qui montrent la difficulté des Français à prononcer le *th* anglais font la preuve que Theocharopoulos s'intéressait au marché français qui était plus large par rapport à celui d'une Grèce qui sortait à peine de quatre cents ans de joug ottoman:

> — Que pensez-vous de l'anglais? What do you think of the English language? Πῶς σάς φαίνεται ἡ ἀγγλική γλῶσσα;
> — Very difficult. Très difficile! Πολλά δύσκολος!
> — Prononcez-vous bien le *th*? Do you pronounce the *th* well? Προφέρετε καλά τό *th*?

Il est bien connu que ce sont les Français qui ont du mal à prononcer le morphème anglais *th* puisque ce son n'existe pas en français, mais il existe en grec!

L'auteur met l'accent sur les bonnes recommandations nécessaires pour trouver un domestique dans le dialogue 'Pour louer un domestique':

> — Qui vous a adressé à moi? De quel pays êtes-vous?

— Je suis Grec.

— Savez-vous écrire?

— Oui, monsieur; je puis aussi me faire entendre dans plusieurs langues.

— Combien demandez-vous de gages?

— J'ai toujours gagné cinq cents francs et la nourriture. (1839: 121)

Nous pouvons noter la présence d'éléments de la vie à Londres, ainsi que certaines des caractéristiques des Anglais:

> Quand êtes-vous revenu de l'Angleterre? Et que pensez-vous des Anglais? Quoique les Anglais n'aiment pas beaucoup les étrangers, ceux-ci sont toujours bien accueillis des personnes auxquelles ils sont recommandés [...]. On soupe fort tard en Angleterre [...]. Je n'ai pas traversé la Tamise. Louons plutôt un fiacre. (1839: 55)

Ces références qui regardent le mode de vie à l'anglaise et sa comparaison avec celui en France montrent bien que ce manuel était d'abord destiné aux Français qui désiraient apprendre l'anglais.

Pour les thèmes relatifs à des domaines tels que *urbanisation*, *architecture*, *maisons*, *environnement*, nous trouvons intéressante la présentation des rues londoniennes, ainsi qu'une petite comparaison entre Paris et Londres:

> 'Pour aller voir la ville' (1839: 68)

> Londres est-il aussi beau que Paris? Les rues de Londres sont beaucoup plus belles et larges. Mais, il n'y a pas tant de beaux bâtiments et de monuments publics qu'à Paris. [...] Les rues sont bien alignées et bien pavées. La ville est bâtie sur le rivage de la mer.

Concernant l'argent, le dialogue 'Avec un banquier' (1839: 81) nous donne le contexte des échanges bancaires. On retient que le problème majeur de l'époque est celui de la fiabilité des titres. On peut payer avec des lettres de change ou des pièces d'or:

> — Monsieur, je suis porteur d'une lettre de change. Est-elle payable de vue?

> — J'ai quelques doutes sur la bonté de ces deux pièces d'or; l'empreinte de l'une est presque effacée et l'autre me paraît rognée. N'avez-vous un trébuchet? Nous allons la peser. Il y manque cinq grammes. Je serai obligé de faire le protêt.

> — J'en recevrai avec plaisir en une traite sur Constantinople, à trente jours au cours de la place.

On utilise aussi des monnaies françaises et anglaises: 'Chez un marchand de bas: Je vous en donnerai quinze francs, douze schillings et six pence. Je vous ai dit mon dernier mot' (1839: 66).

Les thèmes de la santé, des sciences et de la technologie trouvent leur place dans le dialogue 'Avec le médecin, le chirurgien, le dentiste' (1839: 77): 'Voyons votre langue. Elle est bien chargée. Vous avez besoin d'être purgé. Il serait bon de vous mettre un vésicatoire'; et dans 'Voyage sur un bateau à vapeur': 'Avez-vous déjà voyagé sur un bateau à vapeur? La première invention vient d'un Anglais, nommé H. Bull en 1736' (1839: 140).[16] Les sciences et les nouvelles inventions technologiques occuperont une place importante dans les manuels de français langue étrangère, surtout à partir de la dernière décennie du XXe siècle.

Certains thèmes sont absents ou rares: rien sur la presse et les sports, qui à l'époque sont presque inexistants tels que nous les connaissons aujourd'hui. N'oublions pas que les compétitions sportives sont récréées surtout grâce à la réhabilitation des Jeux olympiques par le baron Pierre de Coubertin, en 1896.

Des références aux fêtes religieuses ou folkloriques ne font pas partie des choix de Theocharopoulos. Le rapport des sociétés occidentales avec la religion et l'église apparaît à travers des phrases du type: 'Qui est-ce qui prêche aujourd'hui?', 'Ses sermons ne m'ennuient pas'. Par contre, dans les manuels actuels, rares sont les éléments ayant une connotation religieuse. Ils comportent des photos de cathédrales, d'églises ou de mosquées présentées sous un aspect plutôt culturel ou touristique.[17]

Dans les manuels publiés au XIXe siècle par des Grecs, les comparaisons entre la France et la Grèce sont rares. La Grèce, en tant que nouvel État à peine reconnu par la communauté internationale, n'a alors rien à 'exporter'. Sa seule consolation consiste à présenter les années glorieuses de Byzance et de l'Antiquité grecque, les œuvres et la gloire des philosophes et savants. L'auteur, dans sa préface, justifie le choix de présenter des dialogues de Fénelon par le fait qu'ils comportent des éléments de Lucien et de Platon.

Enfin, un détail significatif rend évident le fait que ce manuel de Theocharopoulos que nous venons d'examiner n'est pas un plagiat d'un autre livre. Dans toutes les deux éditions (celle de 1828 et celle de 1839), il fait la publicité de sa propre grammaire à travers le dialogue intitulé 'Sur la langue française':

> — Je vous trouve bien occupé. Quel livre lisez-vous donc avec tant d'attention?
> — J'étudie la grammaire française cette grammaire qu'un Grec de Patras G. Theocharopoulos a traduit à l'usage des Hellènes. Il a rendu un véritable service à son pays en facilitant à ses concitoyens l'étude d'une langue si utile et si universelle.
> — I find you very much occupied. What book are you reading with such attention?
> — I am studying the french grammar wich [sic] a Greek from Patras George Theocharopoulos has translated for the use of the Greeks; he rendered a real service to his country by facilitating the task of learning a language so useful and so universal as this. (1828: 75; 1839: 124)[18]

Le type d'organisation du contenu d'un manuel comme celui du manuel que nous venons de présenter fait une longue tradition en Europe. Loonen (1991: 108) parlant de la période entre 1500 et 1800 dit qu'un manuel typique de langue comporte une préface courte, une section de grammaire, des phrases et expressions idiomatiques, des dialogues et des lettres personnelles ou commerciales.[19]

En général, les thématiques de chacun de ces dialogues pourraient bien être des éléments constitutifs des manuels modernes, dont les unités sont organisées de la même manière depuis plus de cinquante ans, c'est-à-dire autour d'un dialogue central, suivi par l'analyse des phénomènes syntaxiques et grammaticaux. Contrairement aux manuels des XXe et XXIe siècles, celui-ci n'offre que des dialogues. Cependant, l'association des dialogues et de la grammaire dans un même manuel tarde encore à venir.

Conclusion

Nous avons voulu à travers cet article donner quelques renseignements sur l'histoire des manuels de français langue étrangère en Grèce du 19ᵉ siècle. Les manuels auxquels nous avons fait référence ici nous permettent de montrer comment les Grecs ont pu les rédiger et les publier contribuant ainsi à tracer les premières lignes de la disciplinarisation du français langue étrangère en Grèce par rapport aux manuels scolaires. Cet effort pédagogique de la rédaction et publication de manuels de français langue étrangère a mis l'accent sur son enseignement systématique et a abouti à la stabilisation du français en tant que matière enseignée dans les écoles grecques. La présentation du manuel de Theocharopoulos nous a fourni des renseignements sur la façon d'organiser un manuel destiné aux apprenants grecs en insistant sur ses thématiques culturelles. Nous avons aussi touché à un nombre de points concernant les références faites par l'auteur à l'Angleterre et le mode de vie des Anglais du fait que les premières éditions de ce manuel ont été trilingues (français-anglais-grec). Ce manuel basé sur ses éditions plus anciennes (1827 et 1828) sera réédité à Athènes en 1842 et 1845. Cette vie longue démontre son importance.

De manière générale, l'étude de n'importe quel manuel de français de cette période, après l'organisation du nouvel État grec, nous permet de repérer d'une part ses éléments structurels, et de l'autre, la conception de l'enseignement de la culture par le choix de certains éléments culturels ou au contraire leur absence. Ce choix nous donne une idée de la vision du monde des auteurs, souvent obligés de maintenir des équilibres entre le contenu, l'ordre établi et les mœurs de leur époque. La recherche sur le manuel peut ainsi contribuer à ce que le manuel scolaire devienne ou continue à l'être un objet d'étude.

Bibliography

ANTONIOU, DAVID. 2012. *Professeurs- Enseignants de français dans les écoles grecques du XIXe siècle: Éléments biographiques et bibliographiques, contribution à l'enseignement et à la diffusion de la langue et de la civilisation françaises* (en grec: Δάσκαλοι και καθηγητές της Γαλλικής Γλώσσας στα Ελληνικά Σχολεία του 19ου αιώνα) (Athens: CIREL)

BEAUVALET, SCARLETT, and AGNÈS WALCH. 1995. 'Le Veuvage: une expérience de spiritualité conjugale. Trois témoignages de veuves catholiques (1832-1936)', *Histoire, économie et société*, 14: 609-25 <http://www.persee.fr/web/revues/home/prescript/article/hes_0752−5702_1995_num_14_4_1793> [accessed 4 October 2015]

BERTHET, ANNIE ET AL. 2006. *Alter Ego 1* (Paris: Hachette)

BESSE, HENRI. 1992. *Méthodes et pratiques des manuels de langue* (Paris: Didier)

CARAVOLAS, JEAN. 2015. 'Le Premier Manuel de français publié en Grèce', in *Documents pour l'histoire du français langue étrangère ou seconde*, 54: 63-78

CHARAUDEAU, PATRICK. 1987. 'L'Interculturel: nouvelle mode ou pratique nouvelle' (propos recueillis par Bouacha, Abdelmadjid Ali), in *Le Français dans le monde* (special number), 253: 46−52

CHEVALIER, JEAN-CLAUDE. 2010. 'Jean Antoine Caravolas: Jules David et les études grecques (1783−1854)', in *Documents pour l'histoire du français langue étrangère ou seconde*, 45, online at <journals.openedition.org/dhfles/2486> [accessed 6 February 2018]

COKE, DAVID, and ALAN BORG. 2011. *Vauxhall Gardens: A History*, The Paul Mellon Centre for Studies in British Art (Yale: Yale University Press) <http://www.vauxhallgardens.com>

CORDIER-GAUTHIER, CORINNE. 2000. 'Essai de caractérisation du discours du manuel de Français Langue Etrangère: parcours à travers les manuels utilisés au Canada (1970–1995), repérage et description de leurs éléments constitutifs' (doctoral thesis, Université Paul Valéry - Montpellier III) [published 2004 (Lille: ANRT)]

GELADAKI, SONIA. 2002. 'La Législation sur les manuels scolaires pendant la période de Kapodistria' (en grec), in L'Education à l'aube du XXIe siècle. Actes du 2e colloque du Laboratoire de l'archive historique de l'éducation néo-hellénique et internationale, Université de Patras, oct. 2002 <http://www.eriande.elemedu.upatras.gr/eriande/synedria/synedrio2/praktika/geladaki.htm> [accessed 7 February 2018]

GERMAIN, CLAUDE. 1993. Évolution de l'enseignement des langues: 500 ans d'histoire (Paris: Clé International

GIOGIA, MARIA, and IRINI PAPOUTSAKI. 2009. Action. Fr-gr 1 (Athens: OEDB)

JACOTOT, JOSEPH. 1829. Enseignement Universel: cours complet d'Écriture Théorique et Pratique (Paris : D'Arbé Ainé), online at <https://babel.hathitrust.org/cgi/pt?id=umn.31951000928593h;view=1up;seq=9> [accessed 7 February 2018]

KLIPPEL, FRIEDERIKE. 1994. Englischlernen im 18. und 19. Jahrhundert: Die Geschichte der Lehrbücher und Unterrichtsmethoden (Münster: Nodus)

LE TELLIER, CHARLES-CONSTANT. 1827. Grammaire Françoise à l'usage des pensionnats, 39th edn (Brussels: De Mat) online at <https://books.google.gr/books?id=hZY8AAAAcAAJ&printsec=frontcover&hl=el&source=gbs_ge_summary_r&cad=0#v=onepage&q&f=false> [accessed 7 February 2018]

LOONEN, PETRUS LEONARDUS MARIA. 1991. For to learne to buye and sell: Learning English in the Low Dutch Area between 1500 and 1800: A Critical Survey, Studies of the Pierre Bayle Institute (Amsterdam: APA-Holland University Press)

McLELLAND, NICOLA. 2015. German through English Eyes: A History of Language Teaching and Learning in Britain, 1500–2000 (Wiesbaden: Harrassowitz)

MARTINEZ, PIERRE. 1996. La Didactique des langues étrangères, Que sais-je? (Paris: puf)

MAUFROY, SANDRINE. 2005A. 'Hellénisme, Philhellénisme et transferts culturels triangulaires: le cas de Charles Benoît Hase', in Revue Germanique Internationale, 1-2: 109-23

——. 2005B. 'Lettre de Georges Theocharopoulos à Charles Benoît Hase, Paris, 27 mai, 1838', Revue Germanique Internationale, 1-2: 219-34

MINERVA, NADIA. 2003. 'Les Aventures de Télémaque. Trois siècles d'enseignement du français. I', Documents pour l'histoire du français langue étrangère ou seconde <http://dhfles.revues.org/1287> [accessed 20 July 2016]

MOULIAS, CHRISTOS. 1993. Γεώργιος Β. Θεοχαρόπουλος Πατρεύς [1770–1852?]. Ένας άγνωστος πατρινός λόγιος [Georgios B. Theocharopoulos of Patras (1770–1852?): An Unknown Scholar of Patras] (Patras : n. pub.)

MYTALOULIS, KONSTANTINOS (Constantin). 2014. 'L'Enseignement du français et son histoire dans les manuels scolaires en Grèce: aspects culturels' (doctoral thesis, University of Paris 3, published 2016 (Lille: AWRT))

PELLANDRA, CARLA, and JAVIER SUSO LÓPEZ. 2012. 'Vers une disciplinarisation du FLE: enseignants, apprenants et institutions', in Histoire internationale du français langue étrangère ou seconde: problèmes, bilans et perspectives, ed. by Marie-Christine Kok-Escalle, Nadia Minerva and Marcus Reinfried, Le français dans le monde. Recherches et applications, 52 (Paris: Clé internationale), pp. 94-108

PORCHER, LOUIS. 1995. Le Français langue étrangère: émergence et enseignement d'une discipline, Ressources Formation (Paris: CNDP Hachette)

PROVATA, DESPINA. 2015. 'Se former pour enseigner ou enseigner pour se former: formations et parcours d'enseignants en Grèce au XIXe siècle', in *Documents pour l'histoire du français langue étrangère ou seconde*, 55: 101-19

——, and MARIA PAPADAKI. 2011. Ή Γραμματική της Γαλλικής Γλώσσης του Ιωάννη Καρασούτσα. Συμβολή στη μελέτη της διάδοσης της γαλλικής γλώσσας στην Ελλάδα κατά τον 19ο αιώνα', σε συνεργασία με τη Μαρία Παπαδάκη στον τόμο Διασταυρώσεις, επιμ. Ρ. Δελβερούδη et alii, Α. Καρδαμίτσα, 2011, σ. 245-59 ['La Grammaire de la langue française de Ioannis Karassoutsas. Contribution à l'étude de la diffusion de la langue française en Grèce au XIXe siècle', in *Croisements*, ed. by R. Delvéroudi et al. (Athens: Kardamitsa), pp. 245-59]

REINWALD, CHARLES. 1862. *Le Catalogue annuel de la librairie française, quatrième année, 1861* (Paris: Reinwald)

SCHINAS, MICHAEL, and JOANNIS NIKOLAIDIS LEVADEUS, 1889. *Dictionnaire français-grec* (Athens) [Σχινάς, Μιχαήλ, και Ιωάννης Νικολαΐδης Λεβαδεύς, Λεξικόν Γαλλοελληνικόν]

THEOCHAROPOULOS, GEORGES. 1839. *Dialogues Familiers précédés de quelques phrases faciles de plusieurs dialogues de Fénelon en français et en grec* (Paris: Bobée et Hingray)

TSIGRIS, CHRYSSOULA. 2002. 'La Diffusion et l'Enseignement du français en Grèce au XIXe siècle à travers les programmes institutionnels et l'analyse du discours des manuels' (unpublished doctoral thesis, University of Paris 3)

Websites

Digital Library of Modern Greek Studies <http://anemi.lib.uoc.gr>
Research workshop of the Benaki Museum <www.benaki.gr/bibliology/index.htm>
SWIGGURN, S., and M. KOHLI. 1997-2011. *The Ships List* <http://www.theshipslist.com/ships/lines/bull.shtml>

Other sources

Archives générales de l'État grec GAK/A.YEDE (1833-1848)

Notes to Chapter 4

1. Dans la British Library et dans la Bibliothèque Nationale de France, il existe une édition trilingue (grec-français-anglais) de 1827 (Paris). Nous remercions Michèle Cohen et Nicola McLelland de nous avoir aidé à trouver la forme numérique du manuel trilingue de l'édition de 1828.
2. Les manuels (grammaires, dictionnaires) présentés ci-dessous ne font pas partie de la bibliographie de la fin de cet article.
3. Sur l'œuvre de I. Karasoutsas voir la contribution de Provata (2015) et Provata (2011).
4. Sur la méthode d'Ollendorf, voir: Wheeler (2013: 112-21) et McLelland (2015: 86-88).
5. Un concours de rédaction de manuels se lance par un comité du ministère de l'Éducation qui approuve les manuels et fixe leur prix d'achat. En 1882, la loi de Charilaos Trikoupis AMB du 4 septembre, stipule que le concours de rédaction de manuels (appelés aussi livres didactiques) aura lieu tous les quatre ans. Le temps jusqu'à la décision finale atteindra les quatorze mois. Un seul livre est approuvé pour chaque discipline. Voir: Geladaki Sonia, 'La Législation sur les manuels scolaires pendant la période de Kapodistria' (en grec), in *L'Éducation à l'aube du XXIe siècle. Actes du 2e colloque du Laboratoire de l'archive historique de l'éducation néo-hellénique et internationale, Université de Patras, oct. 2002* <http://www.eriande.elemedu.upatras.gr/eriande/synedria/synedrio2/praktika/geladaki.htm>.
6. Article 7, loi AMB, du 22 juin 1882, Archives générales de l'État grec GAK/A.YEDE (1833-1848).

7. Sur la formation et le recrutement des maîtres et des professeurs de français voir Provata (2015).

8. Selon Tsigris ce manuel est publié en 1827 à Athènes tandis que selon notre recherche, le lieu de cette première publication est Paris. Le manuel de 1827 est édité par l'Imprimerie et Fonderie de G. Doyen alors que le manuel de 1828 est publié chez l'Imprimerie Bobée et Hingray.

9. <journals.openedition.org/dhfles/2486>.

10. La grande importance des dialogues en tant qu'outils d'apprentissage d'une langue étrangère dans les manuels de langue, est avérée depuis l'Antiquité. Chez les Romains, ils sont employés dans l'enseignement du grec. Au Moyen Âge, le latin est enseigné par le biais de manuels de conversations appelés 'colloques', synonymes de dialogues. Comenius suggère de rédiger des dialogues théâtraux en guise d'activités pédagogiques dans les manuels de langue, ce qu'il met en pratique dans l'*École du jeu* (1656), une pièce de théâtre en cinq actes (Germain, 1993: 44, 55, 115-17).

11. Pour le terme culture nous retenons les définitions données par: a) Pierre Martinez (culture cultivée, culture quotidienne); b) Patrick Charaudeau (l'ensemble de pratiques sociales et ensemble de discours construits sur des pratiques); et c) Louis Porcher (les sous-parties de la culture), dans la mesure où elles sont applicables à l'analyse des éléments culturels présents dans les manuels de FLE.

12. La femme peut ou doit rester veuve, comme le dit saint Paul, Épître aux Corinthiens, 7. 39-40.

13. Georges Théocharopoulos avait de bons rapports avec la langue anglaise. Il a traduit le dictionnaire anglais-français de Poppleton: *Vocabulaire français-anglais, grec moderne et grec ancien, contenant à la tête une exposition abrégée de la prononciation et de l'orthographe grecques et à la fin cinq tableaux alphabétiques avec le décret sur la division et le mode de gouvernement du royaume de la Grèce. Traduit du vocabulaire anglais-français de Mr. le Professeur Poppleton, augmenté et enrichi de notes philologiques, critiques et grammaticales épuisées dans les écrits du Savant Koray et dans d'autres différentes sources. À l'usage des compatriotes jeunes Hellènes et à celui des étrangers amis des Muses* (Munich: Wolf, 1834).

14. Voir réf. 9.

15. <http://www.vauxhallgardens.com/vauxhall_gardens_singers_page.html> [consulté le 25 juillet 2016]. Nous retrouvons sur ce site une liste de chanteurs solo [solo singers] qui ont chanté aux Vauxhall Gardens de 1745 à 1859. Cette page fait partie d'un site sur l'histoire de Vauxhall Gardens 1661-1859, créé par David Coke et complété par Coke et Borg (2011): David Coke et Alan Berg, *Vauxhall Gardens: A History* (Yale: Yale University Press).

16. H. Bull n'a pas inventé le bateau à vapeur. En 1885 il a fondé la société britannique *New York and Porto Rico Steamship Co.* <http://www.theshipslist.com/ships/lines/bull.shtml>.

17. Par exemple la photo de la mosquée de Paris, du manuel: *Alter Ego 1* (Berthet et al. 2006: 47), ou les photos de la tour Hassan, ainsi que la statue du Christ Rédempteur dans le manuel *Action-fr. gr 1*, Athènes (Giogia et Papoutsaki 2009: 162).

18. Il s'agit sans doute de la *Grammaire françoise de M. Charles-Constant Le Tellier, Professeur de Belles-Lettres, traduite en grec moderne sur la 39° édition, et augmentée d' une introduction et de remarques essentielles, à l 'usage des jeunes Hellènes, par Georges Theocharopoulos de Patras* (Paris: Didot, 1827), <https://books.google.gr/books?id=hZY8AAAAcAAJ&printsec=frontcover&hl=el&source=gbs_ge_summary_r&cad=0#v=onepage&q&f=false>. Le Tellier est connu pour la rédaction de fameuses *Cacographies* ou *Cacologies*.

19. Il note, parlant des manuels anglais-flamands/néerlandais: 'A typical textbook would contain: a short preface; a grammar section; idiomatic phrases; dialogues; and personal and commercial letters'.

CHAPTER 5

La langue française en Moldavie: entre héritage et tradition

Olga Turcan

This chapter focuses on two important arguments justifying the place occupied by the French language in Moldova: the historical legacy and the tradition of teaching. It provides an overview of the evolving role of French in the Moldovan context. It covers the period from the eighteenth century, when French spread widely in Europe, including in the Romanian Principalities, until 2011, when this language retained its leading position in Moldovan teaching. This chapter outlines the principal channels through which French spread in Moldova, mainly in the educational field, by retracing the various cultural and political influences due to the geographical position and complex history of the country. It also highlights the reasons for the tradition of teaching French in the Soviet period that has strongly marked its place in Moldova after independence (1991). The chapter is based on the author's doctoral research results, in particular on a *corpus* made up of archive documents, a sociolinguistic survey, recent regulations, interviews with people working in the education system and the French-speaking world (*Francophonie*) in Moldova, media articles and statistical publications.

Introduction

Nos recherches ont été effectuées dans le cadre d'un doctorat à l'Université de Strasbourg. La thèse intitulée 'Le Français en Moldavie: entre héritage, tradition et mondialisation' et soutenue en mars 2014 interroge la place du français en Moldavie dans des contextes d'héritage historique, de tradition d'enseignement et de mondialisation. Dans ce travail, le nom de 'Moldavie' renvoie au territoire de l'actuelle République de Moldavie (ou Moldova), pays frontalier de la Roumanie et de l'Ukraine. Pour effectuer cette étude[1] sur la langue française en Moldavie, nous avons élaboré un corpus constitué de documents d'archives, d'une enquête sociolinguistique, de textes réglementaires, d'entretiens avec des acteurs du système éducatif et de la francophonie en Moldavie, d'articles de médias et de publications statistiques. Cette contribution[2] s'articulera autour de deux arguments justifiant la place importante occupée par le français en Moldavie — l'héritage historique et la tradition d'enseignement — et permettra d'avoir un aperçu de la place évolutive du français en contexte moldave.[3]

En 2007, au début de nos recherches doctorales, un de nos questionnements portait sur les raisons de la place dominante du français dans l'enseignement des langues étrangères en Moldavie, situation quantitative unique et supérieure par rapport à tout autre pays d'Europe — en dehors de ceux qui l'ont en tant que langue officielle — pays où l'anglais occupait depuis longtemps une position dominante.[4] De nombreux discours des acteurs éducatifs ou décisionnels moldaves faisaient référence à l'héritage historique et à la tradition d'enseignement. Ainsi, nous nous sommes intéressée à la 'présence' historique du français en Moldavie, ainsi qu'aux origines de la tradition de son enseignement.

Comme la frontière entre les termes d'''héritage' et de 'tradition' est en permanente mouvance en fonction du moment où l'on se situe, nous avons opté pour un jalonnement temporel pour essayer d'éviter l'ambiguïté. L'héritage historique se rapporte ainsi à la période d'avant 1940 (année où la Moldavie est rattachée à l'U.R.S.S.) et la tradition se réfère à la période qui lui succède jusqu'à aujourd'hui, car plusieurs dates importantes peu après 1940 posent le fondement de cette tradition d'enseigner le français. Dans les années 1940, notamment, sont créées les premières facultés de langues étrangères à enjeux importants dans la formation de professeurs de français et la diffusion du français en Moldavie.

Autour de l'héritage du français

L'interrogation sur l'héritage du français nous fait remonter au XVIIIe siècle, lorsque la langue française a connu une diffusion dans toute l'Europe, y compris dans le territoire de la Moldavie. Dans cette démarche de contextualisation historique et diachronique, nous avons étudié les voies de diffusion du français en Moldavie et les acteurs de sa médiation, vu sa position géographique et son histoire complexe. L'étude de nombreuses sources historiques permet de voir que les changements politiques traversées par la Moldavie influencent la situation du français, son statut et ses fonctions.

Voici d'abord un abrégé chronologique de l'histoire de Moldavie (cf. Figure 5.1): partie de la principauté de Moldavie, apparue sur la carte politique de l'Europe en 1359, le territoire de l'actuelle république est dominé par l'Empire ottoman à l'aube du XVIIIe siècle. Après la défaite des troupes moldaves en 1711, le gouvernement de l'Empire ottoman installe Nicolae Mavrocordato sur le trône de Moldavie et inaugure, symboliquement, le règne des Phanariotes. Dans la période 1812-1918, la Moldavie est rattachée à l'Empire russe; de 1918 à 1940, elle fait partie de la Grande Roumanie; de 1940 à 1991, la Moldavie est rattachée à l'U.R.S.S. (désormais URSS) jusqu'à l'obtention de son indépendance le 27 août 1991.

La langue française a connu plusieurs voies et acteurs pour sa diffusion sur ce territoire qui a subi de multiples dominations et influences culturelles et politiques: les Phanariotes, les Français — de passage ou émigrés — , les enseignants de français de différentes origines, les Roumains eux-mêmes, les 'Russes francisés' (Brunot 1967: 7). Nombreux sont les secteurs qui adoptent et font circuler cette langue:

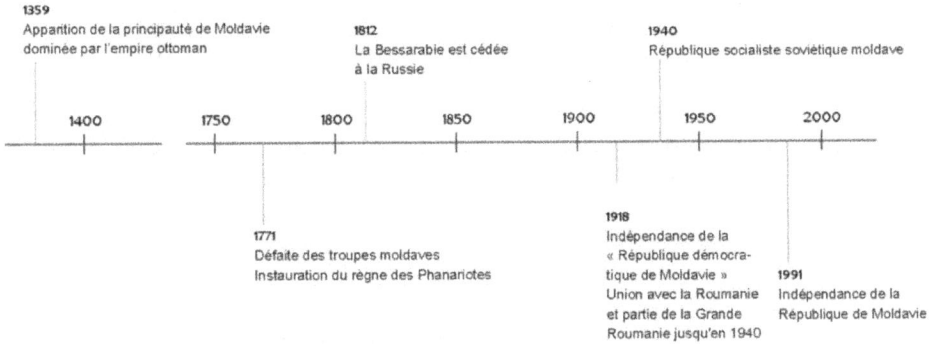

FIG 5.1. Repères chronologiques de l'histoire de Moldavie

l'éducation, le théâtre, la presse, le commerce, l'armée, la diplomatie, la littérature, etc. Nous évoquerons plus en détails ici les voies par lesquelles le français s'est répandu en Moldavie et insisterons sur l'éducation et l'enseignement en français.

La diffusion de la langue française en Moldavie (et en Valachie) emprunte différentes voies au XVIIIe siècle:

a) *La voie du pouvoir politique et de la diplomatie*
Pour le gouvernement de l'Empire ottoman et les princes phanariotes nommés à la tête des principautés de Moldavie et de Valachie, le français représente l'outil indispensable à maîtriser dans le domaine de la politique (étrangère) et des relations diplomatiques au début du XVIIIe siècle. L'administration de haut niveau constituant la couche sociale dominante qui entoure le prince s'empare de cette langue à usage diplomatique, succombe à son prestige et en même temps le renforce, par les attributs de la domination. Le français a été progressivement choisi dans les correspondances diplomatiques, en faisant son chemin en tant que 'langue des traités', à partir de 1714 — le traité de Rastatt[5] (Seguin 1999: 251).

b) *La voie de l'éducation*
Le français fait partie d'abord d'une éducation en famille avec des précepteurs,[6] personnalités françaises, grecques ou d'autres nationalités, renommées auprès du prince ou moins connues auprès des familles des boïars. La diffusion du français relève d'un processus qui commence par le 'haut' de la société et qui touche, par un système d'imitation, ceux qui aspirent à une ascension sociale. Ensuite, l'enseignement du français devient accessible à un nombre plus grand d'apprenants inscrits dans les écoles privées. Il est souvent dispensé par des Grecs, rarement par les Français, car ils sont encore en nombre réduit sur le territoire des principautés roumaines.

c) *La voie de la culture*
Les princes phanariotes éclairés et les familles de nobles roumains se focalisent autour du 'français considéré [...] comme symbole, icône de la culture' (Rey, Duval et Siouffi 2011: 45). Pour eux, cette culture renvoie à la politesse, aux mœurs, au raffinement qui sont retrouvés dans la mode, la cuisine, le théâtre français, etc. Le monde des salons se distingue par leur marque dominante — les échanges en langue française; les officiers, avec leur appartenance à la noblesse,

y prennent part. Ceux qui veulent faire partie des couches dominantes, de près ou de loin, vont adopter le français de la même manière, autant qu'ils le peuvent.

Les livres en français circulent, la presse en français est lue, le français des Lumières ne s'arrête pas à la frontière des Principautés danubiennes. D'un côté, les princes phanariotes, les boïars moldaves et valaques et tous ceux qui souhaitaient les imiter, augmentaient la demande de ressources pour l'éducation en langue française. De l'autre côté, les éléments suivants concouraient à satisfaire cette demande: les précepteurs, les enseignants grecs et français, les commerçants de livres, les pensions françaises se multipliaient, car les démarches administratives étaient simples et le manque d'écoles publiques assez important en Moldavie, selon Dumas (2012: 6).

A cette multiplicité des voies, énumérées *supra*, s'oppose l'unicité des couches sociales qui transportent la langue française — la classe sociale dominante. La diffusion du français ne concerne pas tant le critère territorial ou un espace géopolitique (principautés roumaines ou pays européens), mais plutôt le statut social des locuteurs qui l'adoptent non seulement en tant qu'outil de communication, mais aussi et surtout comme instrument de pouvoir, signe de distinction et marque de prestige. La France favorise l'engouement envers la langue française et envers tout ce qui est français. En effet, la volonté du roi de France est de consolider le statut et l'usage du français et, par conséquent, son pouvoir royal: il encourage l'utilisation du français dans tous les domaines de la science; il fait même introduire subrepticement le français dans le traité de paix de Rastatt (déjà mentionné), fait qui marque ses débuts de langue diplomatique en Europe.

Une continuité peut être observée dans la diffusion du français au XIXe siècle où il garde encore son statut de langue élitaire, tout en devenant l'apanage de la couche sociale émergeante de l'*intelligentsia* qui la parle ou l'emploie pour ses produits ou créations (littéraires, scientifiques ou culturelles). Cette intelligentsia, assez hétérogène, est composée d'autochtones d'origine moldave, roumaine, grecque ou autre, de Russes ou de Français installés en Moldavie suite aux nombreux changements politiques, en commençant par l'année 1812 lorsque sa partie méridionale, appelée aussi *Bessarabie*,[7] devient région et ensuite *goubernie* russe.

Le champ de l'éducation reste primordial pour la diffusion du français. Dans les écoles paroissiales de Bessarabie déjà existantes, ainsi qu'au Séminaire théologique de Chisinau,[8] créé en 1813, le français constituait une matière optionnelle. Au 'pensionnat pour les nobles' ou Séminaire pour Fils de Nobles (des garçons de 8 à 12 ans), ouvert en 1816 auprès du Séminaire précité suite à l'insistance des boïars moldaves et avec l'accord du tsar Alexandre Ier, la langue française était parmi les matières obligatoires (avec le russe, le roumain, le grec, le latin et l'allemand). Dans les premiers lycées et écoles secondaires fondés dans les différentes villes principales des districts de Bessarabie dans la seconde moitié du XIXe siècle, la langue française figure parmi les matières obligatoires, ainsi que parmi celles facultatives (l'allemand et le russe étaient également étudiés, le plus grand nombre d'heures étant accordé au russe).[9]

Pourtant, la présence du français reste encore limitée dans l'enseignement. Ceux qui souhaitent continuer à l'apprendre ou à le parfaire partent à Odessa, à Iassi — deux villes à proximité de Chisinau avec une présence française croissante au XIXe siècle, mais aussi à Bucarest ou à Paris, car les voyages et les études en France se pratiquent de plus en plus fréquemment. La ville portuaire d'Odessa — 'capitale' de la 'Nouvelle Russie', d'après le souhait de Catherine II — est gouvernée de 1803 à 1814 par le duc de Richelieu, futur ministre de Louis XVIII. Le duc lui-même a été à l'origine de plusieurs projets culturels: la fondation d'un théâtre, d'un lycée, d'une grande imprimerie, d'un journal. En 1815, on y trouve une puissante colonie française et occidentale. La langue française était enseignée au lycée fondé à la demande de Richelieu et ouvert en 1818, sous la direction de l'abbé Nicole qui a élaboré son plan d'études et a recruté des enseignants qualifiés en France. A part ce lycée prisé par les familles moldaves, le français était enseigné dans les écoles paroissiales organisées par les Jésuites, ainsi que dans les pensions privées tenues par les Français (Polevchtchikova 2013: 187-204).

A la même époque, la ville d'Iassi (Moldavie occidentale) garde sa proximité physique et culturelle à l'égard de Chisinau. A moins de 130 km de la ville de Chisinau, elle constitue une fenêtre 'francophone' pour la Bessarabie et surtout pour la partie méridionale dans la seconde moitié du XIXe siècle (trois départements — Cahul, Izmaïl et Bolgrad — sont revenus à la Moldavie roumaine en 1856 jusqu'en 1878). A cette époque, Iassi connait une nouvelle vague d'immigration française dans un contexte qui lui est favorable: le prestige de la langue française s'y maintient depuis le siècle précédent et l'enseignement du français, proposé dans les pensions françaises, y est toujours assez prisé.

A l'Académie princière de Iassi (comme à celle de Bucarest) fondée au début du XVIIIe siècle, la langue française était enseignée et certaines matières comme les mathématiques, la philosophie, la géographie ou l'histoire étaient enseignées en français. En 1813, le cours théorique et pratique de géométrie (avec des applications à l'aide d'instruments apportés de Paris et de Vienne) est tenu en français, faute de manuels roumains (Camariano-Cioran 1974: 108). Ce cours a été suivi par des fils de boïars, de citadins, ainsi que par le fils du prince. Ces études débouchaient, en partie, sur des postes importants à la Cour des princes phanariotes qui exigeaient la connaissance du français.

Ces deux foyers de la langue française, Odessa et Iassi, à proximité de Chisinau, favorisent la formation des intellectuels de Bessarabie qui adoptent cette langue dans leur parcours politique ou littéraire. Un exemple dans ce sens est C. Stamati-Ciurea qui est envoyé à Paris pour faire ses études et y devient diplomate par la suite; il écrit en français, russe, allemand et roumain (Calendar National 2008: 460-62).

Au XXe siècle, trois grandes périodes ont marqué, chacune à leur façon, l'histoire de la Moldavie, avec des incidences sur la place du français. La situation du français, héritée des siècles précédents, est préservée dans la première moitié du XXe siècle (1918-40) lorsque la Bessarabie fait partie de la Grande-Roumanie. Le roumain retrouve son statut de langue de l'administration et de l'enseignement.

La nouvelle orientation de la politique générale roumaine qui visait la création de nouvelles écoles publiques et l'accroissement de la dotation des bibliothèques de

Chisinau en livres (en français également) constituent un avantage pour la diffusion de la langue française en Bessarabie. Il est important de mentionner ici l'action de la France qui, à travers son Service des œuvres françaises à l'étranger, notamment la mission universitaire et la section du livre français, intervient en Bessarabie pour une 'rapide diffusion du français dans les régions nouvellement acquises à la Roumanie' (Godin 1998: 10).

Plusieurs documents attestent la présence et la diffusion de la langue française, notamment dans le domaine éducatif. Nous évoquerons brièvement quelques exemples. Le Général Le Rond (MAE 2007: 210) et Ciobanu (1941: 93-94) mentionnent l'existence de deux lycées français à Chisinau. D'après ces deux sources qui se réfèrent à deux années différentes, ces établissements sont fréquentés par un public différent selon la nationalité et/ou le genre: 'deux lycées français, l'un pour les garçons, l'autre pour les filles, tous deux presque exclusivement fréquentés par les israélites [...] des minorités juives et russes' (1922) *versus* 'deux lycées français pour sujets roumains' (1938).

De l'étude des documents sur quelques établissements de la capitale,[10] nous retenons quelques éléments sur le français. D'abord, le fait qu'il était la seule langue, à part le roumain, enseignée à toutes les classes, dont celles de la section qui formait les futures enseignantes (dans le premier lycée cité). Ensuite, l'existence d'une tradition d'enseigner cette langue et la présence d'enseignants francophones natifs (dans le deuxième lycée). Enfin, la création d'une institution comme l'Université populaire en 1918, à l'initiative d'un groupe d'intellectuels afin de promouvoir les connaissances de différents domaines de la science ainsi que les valeurs culturelles roumaines au sein de la population, mettait à la disposition d'un public adulte des livres en français, grâce à la contribution importante de l'Université de Iassi et de l'Académie Roumaine. A l'issue de leurs études aux lycées de Chisinau, les jeunes avaient la possibilité de suivre des études en langue française à Iassi, à Bucarest, qui ouvraient également la voie pour des études à Paris. Déjà avant 1918, la France était 'la principale pépinière des universitaires roumains' (Boia 2006: 8).

Cette première partie ne présente qu'un aperçu de la présence du français dans l'enseignement en Moldavie, situation complexe qui constitue ce qu'on appelle 'héritage' du français ou héritage francophone. Plusieurs aspects sont développés dans notre travail de thèse, certains d'entre eux méritent un approfondissement dans le cadre des recherches ultérieures.

Autour de la tradition du français

Le jalonnement pour lequel nous avons opté afin de délimiter sur l'axe du temps les périodes de l'''héritage' et de la 'tradition' (l'année 1940) ne comporte pas uniquement des raisons pratiques (éviter l'ambiguïté). Nos recherches ont montré que la place qu'occupe le français dans la République de Moldavie, après l'indépendance, surtout dans le domaine de l'enseignement, a son point d'ancrage dans les mesures de politique linguistique éducative mises en place dans la période soviétique. Appuyée sur l'héritage des siècles passés, la tradition de l'enseignement du français s'est instituée dans les premières décennies après 1940, comme nous le verrons. Suite au pacte germano-soviétique 'de non-agression' d'août 1939 et au traité de Vienne de 1940, la Bessarabie est rattachée à l'URSS et en fait partie pendant environ un demi-siècle en tant que *République socialiste soviétique moldave*.[11] Dans ce contexte politique, les relations de l'URSS avec la France auront une influence sur la diffusion du français dans l'URSS, avec des spécificités pour la Moldavie.

Dans le contexte où la situation du français sur le plan international après 1945 est 'ambiguë' et défavorable (Coste 1998: 76), la création des postes d'action culturelle dès 1945 a eu 'd'importantes et durables conséquences' (*idem*) pour la mise en œuvre d'une politique culturelle et linguistique de la France. Elle contribuera par la suite à son rapprochement culturel avec l'URSS: dès octobre 1957, la première commission mixte se réunit à Paris. Dans tous les domaines, l'équilibre des échanges franco-soviétiques était respecté, sauf pour celui de la langue française:

> Le dessein proclamé des Soviétiques était alors d'affecter 35% des élèves de leurs écoles secondaires à l'apprentissage du français (contre 40 % à l'anglais et 25% à l'allemand). En France, [...] le russe n'a jamais atteint 1%. (Girard 1984: 74)

Les données statistiques publiées par les sources soviétiques indiquent pour l'année scolaire 1958-59 l'allemand en tant que langue étrangère la plus répandue dans les écoles de l'URSS, la deuxième place revient à l'anglais et la troisième au français (De Witt 1961: 114-15).

Contrairement à la situation générale du français en URSS, les documents d'archives[12] sur la création des premières facultés de langues étrangères en Moldavie dans les années 1940 permettent de constater que le français occupe une place importante et devance les autres langues étrangères enseignées (l'allemand, l'anglais, l'espagnol et l'italien). Des documents d'archives, il en ressort que l'Institut pédagogique[13] (I.P.) de Balti, créé en 1945, était l'institution qui avait des enjeux importants dans la formation de professeurs de français en Moldavie et en URSS et, par conséquent, dans la diffusion ultérieure du français dans les écoles moldaves. En 1954, sa Section des Langues étrangères est réorganisée: la Faculté des langues étrangères de l'Institut pédagogique de Chisinau est transférée à celui de Balti. Sa chaire de français compte désormais onze enseignants, formés à Moscou, Saint-Pétersbourg, Kiev, Kharkov et Odessa, alors que celles d'anglais et d'allemand ne disposent que de trois enseignants chacune.

En 1959 est créée la Faculté de Langues étrangères à l'I.P. de Balti. En effet, les trois sections de langues étrangères (français, anglais, allemand) de la Faculté de Philologie forment la Faculté de Langues étrangères. Pendant environ vingt ans, la section de langue française aurait ainsi été le plus grand centre de l'URSS où l'on formait les professeurs de français, avec plus de 250 étudiants. Les premières promotions de diplômés de l'Institut pédagogique de Balti (et de Chisinau) ont fait émerger par la suite des professeurs de renom, auteurs de manuels, dictionnaires, grammaires et pionniers dans l'enseignement de plusieurs domaines disciplinaires de la linguistique française au sein des départements de français du milieu universitaire et de la recherche de Moldavie (Gutu 2006: 37-40). De même, des dizaines de diplômés ont travaillé en tant qu'interprètes dans plusieurs pays: Algérie, Congo, Egypte, Inde, Indonésie, etc. Les documents attestent qu'une place nettement plus importante qu'aux autres langues est accordée au français à l'admission à la Faculté des Langues étrangères de Balti. En 1977 ou 1979, par exemple, il y a soixante-quinze places pour le français, vingt-cinq pour l'anglais et vingt-cinq pour l'allemand.[14]

A l'époque soviétique, on formait donc beaucoup plus de professeurs de français par rapport à l'anglais, allemand ou à d'autres langues. Ils étaient des acteurs-clés dans la diffusion du français, souvent la seule langue étrangère proposée dans les écoles. Les données statistiques indiquent pour l'année 1981 que 72% des élèves moldaves apprennent le français, pourcentage qui reste inchangé jusqu'en 1991. Trois éléments de différents ordres (historique, politique, linguistique) pourraient expliquer la place importante accordée à la formation des professeurs de français et, de cette manière, à la langue française en Moldavie:

1) la présence historique du français dans la Principauté moldave, dont la Bessarabie faisait partie avant 1812, mais aussi la continuité de sa diffusion au XIXe siècle et dans la première moitié du XXe siècle (cf. sujet traité *supra*);

2) la 'réelle volonté politique' (Girard 1984: 74) de la part de Moscou de soutenir l'enseignement du français dans les écoles soviétiques pour donner suite à la politique de diffusion du français engagée par la France après 1945. A cela se rajoute la volonté politique des autorités locales moldaves de soutenir l'enseignement du français;

3) la proximité ou la parenté des langues roumaine et française à travers leur origine latine, mais également par le biais de l'emprunt français en roumain qui remonte au XVIIIe siècle. Selon Boia (2006: 3), 'dans le langage courant, un mot sur cinq en moyenne est d'origine française'.

Nous nous attarderons sur le deuxième et troisième éléments d'explication. Concernant la volonté politique, nous nous interrogions sur les raisons de la continuité de la diffusion prédominante du français en Moldavie à l'époque où Moscou favorisait plutôt l'enseignement de l'allemand et de l'anglais. Dans ce cadre, deux autres questions se posent:

> 1. S'agit-il d'une politique conjoncturelle: Moscou profite-t-il d'un état de fait — d'une présence du français dans l'enseignement moldave due à des raisons historiques — pour créer et développer à l'Institut de Balti, en Moldavie, un grand centre de formation de professeurs de français, mais aussi de traducteurs, interprètes, etc. en URSS?
> 2. S'agit-il de la réforme de la décentralisation de 1957 mise en place par Moscou qui aurait favorisé le choix des politiques moldaves à l'égard de l'enseignement des langues et, par conséquent, la préservation de la situation historiquement privilégiée du français sur son territoire? Difficile de trouver une réponse, vu que le sujet des rapports entre Moscou et les républiques soviétiques est très vaste et constituerait en soi l'objet d'une autre recherche.

Ces deux questions sur le poids de la politique moldave et de celle de Moscou à l'égard du français privilégié en Moldavie, pourraient constituer en même temps des éléments de réponse. Elles se résument au fait que les deux — la politique conjoncturelle et la réforme de la décentralisation — y contribuent dans une certaine mesure. Cela pourrait se jouer également à d'autres niveaux: non seulement en Moldavie, en URSS ou Chisinau — Moscou, mais également URSS — France et URSS — Etats-Unis.[15]

Par rapport au troisième élément d'explication — la proximité linguistique, auquel plusieurs sources font référence — il faut rappeler que la parenté linguistique entre le roumain et le français à l'époque soviétique pouvait être perçue uniquement à l'oral ou phonétiquement, car il s'agissait de deux alphabets totalement différents pour l'écriture de ces deux langues (cyrillique et respectivement latin). En effet, suite à l'orientation de la politique linguistique stalinienne, le roumain de RSSM, appelé 'moldave', passe à l'alphabet cyrillique russe. Cette situation a duré environ cinq décennies, lorsqu'une réforme de l'orthographe a été mise en place pour le retour à l'alphabet latin en août 1989. Le passage à l'écriture latine a été facilité par le français qui était appris majoritairement dans les écoles moldaves et qui a servi à la réappropriation de la langue nationale. 'Ecrivez comme en français!' était la consigne que les professeurs de roumain donnaient à leurs élèves du secondaire en référence à la graphie latine, à quelques différences près. C'était également une référence pour les adultes qui devaient acquérir l'écriture latine du roumain et qui, pour la plupart d'entre eux, avaient appris le français pendant leur scolarité (Bondarenco 2006: 20). Le français a, donc, joué un rôle important dans la préservation des racines latines des Moldaves dans cette période de rattachement à l'URSS.

Ces trois éléments énumérés *supra* ont contribué fortement à instituer la tradition de l'enseignement du français en Moldavie, celle dont on parla après 1991 et encore aujourd'hui, mais il ne faut pas oublier une autre dimension de ce contexte, celle qui relève de la perception de la langue française par les acteurs sociaux[16] et nous nous référons ici au prestige de la langue, à la littérature et culture françaises appréciées en Moldavie.

La tradition en (dé)faveur du français: 1991–2011

L'année 1991, lorsque la Moldavie obtient son indépendance,[17] amène un tournant dans l'enseignement des langues dites étrangères dans la mesure où les relations de l'Etat moldave avec les pays où l'on ne parle pas roumain ou russe s'intensifient. Le Ministère de l'Education met en place de nouvelles mesures qui offrent plus de place à la matière 'langue étrangère' par l'introduction d'une deuxième langue (LV2) au collège ou lycée, à côté du roumain (langue officielle) et du russe (langue de 'communication inter-ethnique'). De l'état des lieux sur l'enseignement des langues étrangères dans l'enseignement pré-universitaire[18] de 1993, il ressort que 71,3% des élèves étudient le français et 23,5% l'anglais. En 2001, dix ans après l'Indépendance, on observe une baisse du nombre d'élèves pour le français et une augmentation de celui pour l'anglais. Cette évolution, à petits pas, amènera ces deux langues à un certain équilibre quantitatif, mais aussi à un renversement des statistiques générales en faveur de l'anglais en 2011:[19] 48,2% des élèves étudient le français et 49,9% l'anglais. Ces données quantitatives ne peuvent pas en elles seules expliquer la situation complexe de la langue française en Moldavie depuis 1991, mais elles constituent un indicateur de changement auquel plusieurs acteurs et facteurs sociaux, éducatifs, politiques et économiques ont contribué.[20]

Quel a été le rôle de la 'tradition' dans cette période de vingt ans après 1991? Dans le discours des différents acteurs sur le français en Moldavie que nous avons pu recueillir dans le cadre de nos recherches doctorales (entretiens, enquête sociolinguistique, articles de presse, rapports d'activité, procès-verbaux de réunion etc.), l'emploi du terme de 'tradition' est récurrent. Il sert d'argument pour les actions mises en place en lien avec le français.

En effet, l'Etat moldave s'appuie sur la tradition de l'enseignement du français dans ces démarches pour intégrer l'Organisation internationale de la Francophonie (OIF) en 1996. L'Alliance française et l'Agence universitaire de la Francophonie (AUF) trouvent un terrain propice en Moldavie pour mener leur action. Dans l'enseignement public moldave à partir de 1997, deux projets majeurs pour le français ont vu le jour: les filières universitaires francophones dans le supérieur et les classes bilingues dans le primaire et secondaire (projet démarré en 1998). Les deux sont liés à l'activité de l'AUF avec laquelle le gouvernement moldave a signé un accord le 13 novembre 1997 à Hanoi.

Les actions de militantisme et de défense du français de la part de certains enseignants ou responsables des établissements scolaires ou universitaires font également référence à la 'tradition' du français à perpétuer. De même, les représentations sociolinguistiques des élèves ou des parents d'élèves en faveur de l'apprentissage du français s'appuient en partie sur la 'tradition' et déterminent le choix du français lorsqu'il est possible.

Si l'argument de la 'tradition du français' ou de la 'tradition francophone' en Moldavie a joué souvent en faveur de cette langue, elle l'a aussi été implicitement en sa défaveur. En effet, la tradition du français dans l'enseignement (la place importante qu'il occupait dans les programmes scolaires, le nombre d'écoles où il était enseigné, le nombre d'apprenants du français, etc.) a été considérée par certains acteurs décisionnels moldaves comme un état de fait acquis après 1991, ce qui a déterminé en partie leur inaction à son égard et, dans une certaine mesure, le déclin constant de la place du français. Devant le recul progressif du nombre d'élèves qui étudient le français et le renversement des statistiques générales en faveur de l'anglais en 2011, aucune mesure de soutien du français ne figurait dans les textes de politique éducative produits par le Ministère de l'Education, ni par le Gouvernement moldave. Au contraire, les autorités politiques moldaves annonçaient clairement des objectifs pour le renforcement de l'enseignement de l'anglais. La Moldavie n'échappe pas aux effets linguistiques de la mondialisation à tendance homogénéisante, induite par un marché libéral: 'Il serait donc économique d'apprendre l'anglais puisque tout le monde l'apprend et qu'ainsi tout le monde pourra se comprendre' (Calvet 2002: 210). Cela dit, dans quelle mesure la tradition pourra encore contribuer à la promotion du français en Moldavie, sans une volonté politique derrière?

Conclusion

Partagé entre l'héritage, la tradition et la modernité, on pourrait se poser les questions suivantes: Pourquoi l'Etat moldave a-t-il besoin aujourd'hui du français? Pourquoi les citoyens moldaves ont-ils besoin du français? La réponse peut sembler évidente: pour le rôle que peut avoir le français dans le développement de l'Etat et de ses citoyens, un rôle revisité qui permettrait dans le contexte actuel de répondre à cette finalité d'évolution. Nous avons recensé six fonctions importantes du français dans ce sens: langue d'accès au savoir, langue de la recherche, de la mobilité (académique et professionnelle), langue du développement économique et du rapprochement avec l'UE, ainsi que vecteur de la diversité linguistique et culturelle. Certains de ses fonctions ou enjeux sont mis en exergue plus que d'autres par les acteurs exogènes de la francophonie (l'Alliance française, l'OIF, l'AUF), comme le montrent leurs actions, discours et documents de politique pour la promotion du français (Turcan 2014: 246-333). Depuis une dizaine d'années, la dimension économique et la dimension politique de l'accompagnement de la Moldavie dans la voie de l'intégration européenne sont des arguments incontournables dans le discours en faveur du français.

Si les acteurs exogènes suivent les lignes prioritaires de la politique à l'égard du français de la francophonie institutionnelle, le contexte moldave impose une adaptation et une concrétisation de celle-ci. D'où la nécessité de se réunir entre acteurs exogènes et endogènes pour une réflexion de fond qui permettrait de revisiter le rôle du français et de fixer des objectifs qualitatifs et quantitatifs pour les années à venir, dans un cadre de concertation et de synergie.

Bibliography

BOIA, LUCIAN. 2006. 'Sur la diffusion de la culture européenne en Roumanie (XIXe siècle et début du XXe siècle)', in *Modèle français et expériences de la modernisation. Roumanie, 19e-20e siècles*, ed. by Turcanu Florin (Bucharest: l'Institut Culturel Roumain), pp. 1-29

BONDARENCO, ANA. 2006. 'La francophonie et l'uniformisation dans le contexte de la République de Moldova', in *Actes du colloque international. La Francopolyphonie comme vecteur de la communication* (Chisinau: ULIM), pp. 17-24

BRUNOT, FERDINAND. 1967 [1934; 1935]. *Histoire de la langue française, des origines à 1900* ou à *nos jours*, VIII: *Le français hors de France au XVIIIe siècle*, 2nd edn, 2 vols (Paris: Colin)

Calendar National. 2008. Publication de la Bibliothèque nationale de la République de Moldavie <www.bnrm.md/index.php?lang=ro&pid=calendar-national> [accessed 2 February 2015]

CALVET, LOUIS-JEAN. 2002. *Le marché aux langues: les effets linguistiques de la mondialisation* (Paris: Plon)

CAMARIANO-CIORAN, ARIADNA. 1974. *Les Académies princières de Bucarest et de Jassy et leurs professeurs* (Thessaloniki: Institut d'Etudes Balkaniques de Thessalonique)

CIOBANU, STEFAN. 1941. *La Bessarabie: sa population, son passé, sa culture* (Bucharest: Imprimerie nationale)

COSTE, DANIEL. 1998. 'De 1940 à nos jours: consolidations et ajustements', in *Le Français dans le monde: recherches et applications*, ed. by Willem Frijhoff and André Reboullet (= *Histoire de la diffusion et de l'enseignement du français dans le monde*, special number) (Paris: Clé International), pp. 75-95

DE WITT, NICHOLAS. 1961. *Education and Professional Employment in the U.S.S.R.* (Washington: National Science Foundation)

DUMAS, FELICIA. 2012. 'La Langue française et son enseignement en Roumanie: tradition, histoire et actualité', *Éducation et sociétés plurilingues*, 33: 3-14

GIRARD, MARCEL. 1984. 'Moscou et Pékin: deux postes d'action culturelle, deux moments de l'histoire', in *Aspects d'une politique de diffusion du français langue étrangère depuis 1945: matériaux pour une histoire*, ed. by Daniel Coste (Paris: Hatier), pp. 73-76

GODIN, ANDRÉ. 1998. *Une passion roumaine: histoire de l'Institut français de Hautes Etudes en Roumanie (1924-1948)* (Paris: L'Harmattan)

GUTU, ION. 2006. 'Aspects historiques de la francophonie moldave', in *Actes du colloque international 'La Francopolyphonie comme vecteur de la communication'*, ed. by Ana Guțu (Chisinau: Institut de Recherches Philologiques et interculturelles — ULIM), pp. 36-40

LEBEL, GERMAINE. 1955. *La France et les Principautés danubiennes (du XVIe siècle à la chute de Napoléon Ier)* (Paris: Presses Universitaires de France)

MINISTÈRE DES AFFAIRES ÉTRANGÈRES (éd). 2007. *Documents diplomatiques français, 1922, Commission des Archives diplomatiques — Direction des Archives*, 1 (1er janvier-30 juin), VII (Paris: Lang)

POLEVCHTCHIKOVA, ELENA. 2013. 'Les Français et les Russes dans les établissements éducatifs d'Odessa (1803-1822)', in *Le précepteur francophone en Europe (XVIIe-XIXe siècles)*, ed. by Vladislav Rjéoutski and Alexandre Tchoudinov (Paris: L'Harmattan), pp. 187-204

REY, ALAIN, FRÉDÉRIC DUVAL and GILLES SIOUFFI. 2011. *Mille ans de langue française, histoire d'une passion*, II: *Nouveaux destins* (Paris: Perrin)

SEGUIN, JEAN-PIERRE. 1999. 'La langue française aux XVIIe et XVIIIe siècles', in *Nouvelle histoire de la langue française*, ed. by Jacques Chaurand (Paris: Seuil), pp. 225-304

TURCAN, OLGA. 2014. 'Le français en Moldavie: entre héritage, tradition et mondialisation' (unpublished doctoral thesis, University of Strasbourg)

———. 2015. 'Le français en Moldavie: entre héritage, tradition et mondialisation', in *Usages du français et pratiques de l'enseignement en Europe balkanique, centrale et orientale [...] XVIII-XXe siècles*, ed. by Despina Provata and Marie-Christine Kok-Escalle (= *Documents pour l'histoire du français langue étrangère ou seconde*, 54), pp. 195-208

Notes to Chapter 5

1. Thèse en deux volumes: un volume de texte, 362 pages (avec un CD 'Enquête sur la langue française en Moldavie' (2009)) et un volume d'annexes.

2. L'article fait suite à la communication présentée au Congrès international sur l'histoire de l'enseignement et de l'apprentissage des langues étrangères et secondes, 1500-2000, *Connecting cultures?*, à l'Université de Nottingham, 2 - 5 July 2014.

3. Le compte-rendu de la thèse paru en 2015 présente également cette trame historique de la diffusion du français en Moldavie, ainsi que d'autres aspects traités dans la thèse qui ne font pas l'objet de cet article (cf. Turcan 2015).

4. l'Organisation Internationale de la Francophonie. 2007. *La Francophonie dans le monde 2006-2007* (Paris: Nathan), p. 18 <http://www.francophonie.org/IMG/pdf/La_francophonie_dans_le_monde_2006-2007.pdf>.

5. 'accidentellement en 1714 — le traité de Rastatt' (Seguin 1999: 251), 'avec la réserve de la primauté du latin' en 1736, dans la convention de Vienne, ainsi qu'en 1748 — le traité d'Aix-la-Chapelle et 'sans condition ni réserve' à partir du traité de Hubertsbourg, en 1763, jusqu'à celui de Versailles (*ibid.*, Seguin cite Brunot) (Turcan 2014: 32).

6. Germaine Lebel consacre un chapitre (1955: 188-98) aux précepteurs et secrétaires français.

7. *Bessarabie* est une autre dénomination du territoire de la République de Moldavie, à l'exception de quelques régions frontalières du sud et du nord qui font à présent partie de la Roumanie et de l'Ukraine.

8. Chisinau est le centre administratif de la Bessarabie à partir de 1812 et la capitale de l'actuelle République de Moldavie.

9. Concernant l'emploi des langues, il est à préciser que vers 1870, l'emploi de la langue roumaine est absolument défendu dans les écoles béssarabiennes, malgré le fait que les Moldaves roumains

formaient une majorité de plus de 70 % de la population (Zasciuc cité par Ciobanu 1941: 39-40).

10. Lycée de filles de l'Eparchie, section 'Ecole normale'; Lycée de garçons 'B. P. Hasdeu', l'Université Populaire.

11. Créée le 2 août 1940 par la loi du Soviet suprême de l'URSS, son territoire correspond aux deux tiers de la Bessarabie, qui faisait partie de la Roumanie avant la Seconde Guerre mondiale, et à un petit morceau (longeant la rive gauche du Dniestr) de la Podolie ukrainienne, appelée Transnistrie.

12. Documents des archives de la période 1975-2010, en roumain et en russe, émis par le Ministère de l'Education de la République de Moldavie, consultés dans le cadre du travail documentaire à Chisinau, en 2010: décisions/ arrêtés ou procès-verbaux de réunion relatifs aux programmes scolaires, à la formation des professeurs de français, à l'accueil des délégations françaises en Moldavie, aux professeurs invités de France, aux bourses d'études pour le perfectionnement du français, à l'édition de manuels de français et d'autres langues étrangères enseignées.

13. En Moldavie, l'institut pédagogique était un établissement public d'enseignement supérieur qui formait des enseignants, en général, des instituteurs pour le primaire et des éducateurs pour le niveau préscolaire.

14. D'après l'Annexe à l'Arrêté ministériel n° 650 du 15 décembre 1978 sur l'admission dans l'enseignement supérieur en 1979.

15. Ce sujet serait à approfondir par un autre travail de recherche ultérieur.

16. Nous consacrons une partie de notre thèse aux représentations de la langue française (Turcan, 2014: 178–95).

17. Le 27 août 1991, le Parlement moldave adopte la Déclaration de l'Indépendance de la République de Moldavie (Moldova). Les régions de Transnistrie (le territoire entre le fleuve Dniestr et la frontière internationalement reconnue entre la République de Moldavie et l'Ukraine) et de Gagaouzie, située près de la frontière sud avec l'Ukraine, autoproclament leur souveraineté en septembre 1990. Le Parlement moldave a officiellement reconnu l'autonomie de la Gagaouzie en décembre 1994, mais n'a jamais reconnu, comme d'ailleurs la communauté internationale, la 'République moldave du Dniestr' avec sa capitale à Tiraspol, ni eu le contrôle de ce territoire.

18. Source: *Le Bulletin de l'Enseignement*, n° 13 (1993), édition informative du Ministère de la Science et de l'Enseignement de la République de Moldavie (Chisinau: Edition Didactica): 12-13.

19. D'après la Publication statistique 'L'Education en République de Moldova 2010-2011' élaborée par le Bureau National de la Statistique de Moldavie en 2011.

20. Nous consacrons un chapitre de notre thèse (Turcan 2014: 74-195) à la question sur l'existence d'une politique linguistique (éducative) à l'égard du français, sujet que nous n'aborderons pas dans cette contribution.

CHAPTER 6

❖

To Kill Two Birds with One Stone: Combining Language and Content since the Nineteenth Century

Tim Giesler

The German *Realanstalten* (literally, 'real institutions', including both *Realschulen* and *Bürgerschulen*) of the second half of the nineteenth century were secondary schools founded to prepare pupils for non-academic technical and mercantile careers. For that purpose they focused — as the name *Realschule* suggests — on 'realia' (subject knowledge in science and technology) as well as on modern foreign languages. The success of these schools can be attributed mainly to the Industrial Revolution, which reached Germany in the second half of the nineteenth century and strongly demanded a trained workforce of both technicians and merchants. Towards the end of the century the *Realgymnasien* and *Oberrealschulen*, which had arisen from the *Realschulen*, became entitled to grant access to all subjects at universities. Most of today's secondary schools in Germany which emphasize sciences and modern foreign languages were originally *Realgymnasien*. The combination or integration of subject knowledge and language teaching in such schools — in the form of realia, *Landeskunde* or cultural content within the foreign language course or as a separate CLIL (Content and Language Integrated Learning) subject — has a long tradition. However, this tradition is often overlooked in favour of teleological historiography which constructs and advertises paradigm changes. This chapter provides evidence that, contrary to the claims made in mainstream didactic and applied linguistic research, elements of content and language integration have been common and central to foreign language education in Germany for many years.

A 'Mythology' of Language Teaching?

Authorities in the field of English-language education are not, in general, particularly eager to include a historical perspective in their work, except in order to explain and justify the present. The 'preface history' (Depaepe 2010: 33) which results usually serves as a foundation for teleological argumentation which presents modern teaching methods as superior to their predecessors. There is a common tendency, then, to highlight the impact of reforms like the late nineteenth-century *Neusprachliche Reformbewegung* (Reform Movement) (cf. Howatt with Widdowson 2004: 187-98) or the Communicative Turn (ibid.: 326-40) almost a century later. However, this tendency is misleading, masking the alternative view that central elements of language teaching persist and can be found throughout the centuries, albeit adapted to changing contexts. Howatt and Smith (2014: 76; referring to Hunter and Smith 2012) express this vividly as follows:[1]

> 'Potted histories' have tended to prevail which reproduce a kind of mythology intended to set off the past from the present, itself viewed as superior [...], they tend to over-emphasize the prevalence of breaks or 'paradigm shifts' rather than continuity and tradition.

In the tradition of the preface or 'potted history', the vast majority of German researchers today claim that teaching content knowledge in another language (labelled 'CLIL' — Content and Language Integrated Learning — or *Bilingualer Sachfachunterricht* [bilingual subject-teaching]) was 'invented' in Germany in the 1960s in the spirit of German–French reconciliation after the war (Breidbach 2007: 51). However, this chapter adopts an alternative view to mainstream research and deconstructs the 'myth' (Depaepe: 2010: 32) that content instruction and language teaching have only recently begun to be integrated.

In this chapter, then, I shed light on the type of subject knowledge that found its way into English-language teaching in nineteenth-century Germany and examine mechanisms behind this which predated even the Reform Movement. Although the late nineteenth-century reformers collaborated internationally and managed to provide both a theoretical and a practical foundation for their teaching methods / methodologies, their immediate influence on teaching practice on a broader level was probably a lot less prominent (Schleich 2015: 112). In other words, their *influence* on theoretical debates was much stronger than their *impact* on teaching (cf. Smith 2011 for this distinction). As we shall see, there is little doubt that it was not the reformers but many of their forerunners who introduced subject knowledge or *realia*[2] into classroom practice.

The Context: German *Realanstalten*

The institutional context focused upon in this chapter is that of the (often neglected) German *Realanstalten*. When looking at Germany's (in fact, typically Prussia's) nineteenth-century school system, historians of education tend to concentrate mainly on two school types only, located at extreme ends of the stratified school system: the *Volksschule* and the *Gymnasium*. The former enabled at least a basic education for almost everybody, while the latter served as a model for secondary education around the world. Without question, both school types had their merits; yet for those interested in the history of modern language teaching these two school types present more of a dead end than a potential topic for more detailed investigation: the traditional *Gymnasium* (grammar school) saw itself as a palladium for the classics, and modern languages played a subordinate role there, if any. At *Volksschulen*, apart from experiments in Hamburg (cf. Lehberger 1990) and Bremerhaven (cf. Körtge 1999) in the 1860s to 1870s, modern languages were not taught at all. The school type where modern languages were an integral part of the curriculum was the *Real-*, or *Bürgerschule*. In the early twentieth century, a proportion of these schools received a status similar to the classical *Gymnasien*, becoming entitled to grant full university access. Different types of *Realgymnasien* specialized in teaching modern languages or sciences and increasingly became an alternative to the grammar schools, which came to be seen, more and more, as relatively 'old-fashioned'. A large number of modern *Gymnasien* originated as such schools and the classics are no longer taught as main subjects there.

Shifting the research focus onto *Real-* and *Bürgerschulen*, therefore, seems to be a crucial step in the investigation of the history of modern languages and the way culture and content found their way into modern language teaching methodologies, especially given that their curricula encompassed content other than literary texts and their translation. As we shall see, geography and history teaching, for instance, were combined with language teaching in *Realschulen* long before the late twentieth century and its alleged novelties like CLIL.

Content in Foreign Language Teaching

Thornbury (2011: 192, referring to Richards and Schmidt 2002) identifies different general 'options' of language teaching. A closer look at the development of modern language teaching in institutional settings indeed uncovers a remarkable stability of many of the central features or options mentioned. Although denominations and concepts do change, the leeway in decision making in teaching designs seems to be quite limited. One such evergreen is the methodological continuum between grammar-based approaches to language learning on the one hand and more 'natural' acquisition on the other; and the struggle between them: 'the formal and functional' or 'accuracy *versus* fluency' dimensions (Thornbury 2011: 192). No matter how fierce the theoretical discussion may be, in the end classroom teaching usually combines both approaches in an 'eclectic' way. Hence, one might argue that real-life teaching generally settles down somewhere in the middle between the ends of the continuum. Interestingly, though, this does not seem to be the case for the 'segregated *versus* integrated' dimension (ibid.) in question here. At least in higher grades in Germany — when the language competence level of the pupils has reached a relatively high level after several years of tuition — English language and subject knowledge are usually taught in an integrated or combined way: in other words, the pendulum swings to one side only.

Most researchers seem to agree that CLIL approaches in Germany started in the 1960s under the rather inelegant name of *Bilingualer Sachfachunterricht* (Breidbach 2007: 27; Bonnet, Breidbach and Hallet 2009: 172). The usual common feature is that subject knowledge is taught in a foreign language — typically in one of the dominant school languages, French or English (thus, in fact the so-called 'bilingual' courses are usually taught monolingually in the target language). The two subjects most commonly integrated are geography and history (Mentz 2010: 34).

Describing this as a novelty of the second half of the twentieth century is clearly short-sighted as the integral elements of what is described as CLIL today have long been a part of language teaching in general. Beyond the German context, Mehisto, Marsh and Frigols (2008: 9) identify a much longer tradition:

> The term CLIL [...] was coined in 1994 in Europe. However, CLIL practice has a much longer history. The first known CLIL-type programme dates back some 5000 years to what is now modern-day Iraq. The Akkadians, who conquered the Sumerians, wanted to learn the local language. To this end, Sumerian was used as a medium of instruction to teach several subjects to the Akkadians, including theology, botany and zoology. If Sumerian instructors were true to the basic principles of CLIL, they supported the learning of Sumerian, as well as the learning of the content in theology, botany and zoology.

The same authors continue by placing Latin instruction at medieval universities and the hiring of foreign governesses or tutors in the same category. Still, this tradition is mainly ignored in the literature (e.g. Doff 2010: 10; Biederstädt 2013: 6). In addition to the examples stated in Mehisto et al., we can find more predecessors of combining language and subject teaching in the German institutional context as well:

★ Subject knowledge — especially in geography and history — has long played an integral part in foreign language teaching in Germany

★ Academic subjects in which subject knowledge was taught in a foreign language can also be found in nineteenth-century curricula.

Traces of integrating content and language teaching can, for example, already be found in 1791 in Schulze's commercial school [*Handelsschule*] in Berlin:

> In den mittleren und obern Klassen (es waren vier Klassen vorgesehen) traten an seine Stelle [gemeint sind die Sprechübungen, TG] außer Korrespondenz mit Lektüre verbundener <u>Realsprachunterricht</u>. Diese obern Klassen hießen deshalb 'Realklassen'. Ihr Zweck war — wie Dr. Schulze schrieb — mit 'einem Stein zwei Würfe zu tun', indem hier 'die französische Sprache als Vehikel des wissenschaftlichen Unterrichts in der Kommerzgeographie, Warenkunde, Technologie und Geschichte usw. gebraucht wurde'. Selbstverständlich wurden dabei die auf der Unterstufe begonnenen <u>Sprechübungen</u> fortgesetzt, aber hier an die Stoffe des 'wissenschaftlichen Unterrichts' angeschlossen; denn es war der Grundsatz an der Schulzeschen Schule, daß die fremde Sprache 'nicht bloß als Büchersprache, sondern auch, und vornehmlich, als Konversationssprache kultiviert' wurde [...]. Zugrunde gelegt wurde dem Realsprachunterricht die '<u>Lektüre</u>'. Dr. Schulze hatte selbst eine Anzahl Lesebücher veröffentlicht, die aus fremdsprachlichen Aufsätzen fremdnationaler Autoren zusammengesetzt waren, hie und da jedoch auch kurze von ihm selbst verfaßte Darstellungen gaben. (Dietze 1927: 22)

> [Besides correspondence, the middle and higher grades were exposed to <u>real language teaching</u> [*Realsprachunterricht*] in combination with readings. These higher grades were thus called 'real grades'. Their object was — according to Dr. Schulze [the school's headmaster] — to 'kill two birds with one stone' by 'using the French language as the medium of the scientific teaching in

commercial geography, the study of goods, technology, history etc.'. Of course the speaking practice of the lower grades was continued and merged with the scientific course; it was the principle of Schulze's school that the foreign language was 'cultivated not only as a bookish language but also, and in particular, as a conversational language'. [...] The basis for the real language teaching [*Realsprachunterricht*] was the 'reading'. Dr. Schulze himself had published a number of textbooks that were compiled from foreign language essays by foreign authors, here and there also giving some short account written by the author himself.][3]

This description quite closely fits generally accepted definitions of modern CLIL, for example that provided by Mehisto et al. (2008: 11; see also Breidbach 2007: 26): 'The CLIL strategy, above all, involves using a language that is not a student's native tongue and/or vocational level subjects such as maths, science, art or business. However, CLIL also calls on content teachers to teach some language.'

What is especially striking is the immediate relevance of the content knowledge for the future merchants attending the school — they learn how to correspond with others and are provided with knowledge which is of immediate professional (or vocational) use.

More generally, Klippel (1994: 357) argues for the second half of the nineteenth century that:

> Die thematische Ausrichtung ihrer Texte lag den Lese- und Lehrbuchverfassern am Herzen und wurde häufig in den Vorworten erörtert und begründet. Fünf große Themenkomplexe bildeten den gemeinsamen Nenner für eine ganze Anzahl von Englischlehrbüchern: Alltagswelt, Allgemeinwissen, Landeskunde, Geschichte und Literatur.

> [The topical focus of the texts was close to the textbook authors' hearts and was often discussed and justified in the prefaces. Five big topical fields were common to a number of English textbooks: everyday life, general knowledge, applied geography [*Landeskunde*], history and literature.]

She also states (ibid: 360) that:

> Für viele [Lehrbuchautoren] war die Verknüpfung zwischen englischem Sprachunterricht mit gleichzeitiger Information selbstverständlich, einige von ihnen sahen sogar eine enge Zusammenarbeit zwischen den dem englischen Sprachunterricht und Sachfächern vor. Gerade um eine Überbürdung der Schüler wegen des umfangreichen Lehrstoffs abzubauen, sollten geeignete Themenbereiche aus diesen Fächern, z.B. Geographie oder Geschichte, im Englischunterricht behandelt und wiederholt werden.

> [Many [textbook authors] found the combination of English language teaching and information self-evident, and some of them even saw a close collaboration between English language teaching and content subjects. Especially to counter overloading the pupils with extensive subject matter, suitable topic areas from these subjects, for example geography or history, should be dealt with or repeated in the English lessons.]

To sum up, subject knowledge was indeed an integral part of language teaching at German schools, especially at commercial and middle schools in which modern languages played an important role. These, in turn, were of major importance to future merchants, who had the chance to study them in traditional merchant cities like Bremen in preparation for careers in trade with England and the United States. In fact, the Bremen *Bürgerschule* was the first public school in Germany to teach English as the first foreign language, with as many as eight lessons a week from 1855 onwards (Giesler 2013: 114). In addition, geography and history were taught in English as separate subjects in the two highest grades, although the focus there was at least partly still on language teaching, as we learn from one of the Bremen teachers Friedrich Werner (1866: 37), who explains the rationale for the subject being taught in English to his pupils' parents:

> Die englische Geographie in der II. Klasse der Bürgerschule, die zum Gegenstande England und die Vereinigten Staaten hat, steht als Unterrichtsgegenstand nicht isolirt da, sondern bildet einen untergeordneten Theil des Unterrichts im Englischen. Außer der Mittheilung geographischer Kenntnisse, soll nämlich der mündliche und schriftliche Gedankenaustausch im Englischen geübt werden. Es ist darum wohl selbstverständlich, daß dieser Unterricht ganz in englischer Sprache ertheilt wird, und das die Schüler angehalten werden, nicht nur einzelne Fragen in dem fremden Idiom zu beantworten, sondern sich auch gelegentlich zusammenhängend über das Dagewesene auszusprechen.

> [The English geography in the second [i.e. second highest] grade of the *Bürgerschule*, which deals with England and the United States, is not an isolated subject but a subordinate part of English language teaching. Apart from teaching geographical knowledge, the oral and written exchange of ideas in the English language should be practised. This is why it is self-evident that this course should be fully held in the English language and that the pupils are expected not only to answer questions in the foreign idiom but also occasionally to talk coherently about the content.]

Werner even published *Geographische Charakterbilder über das Britische Reich und die Vereinigten Staaten* [*Geographical Character Sketches about the British Empire and the United States*], a selection of English texts to teach geography. Klippel (1994: 342) refers to this coursebook as an early example of non-fiction being used in the late nineteenth-century classroom for teaching English as a foreign language, but it was in fact a collection of texts compiled specifically for the geography courses at his school. Similar self-published text selections with 'subject' content, e.g. from geography or history, had already been used at some late eighteenth-century commercial schools (Dietze 1927: 22-23).

Indeed, at first glance, these examples might appear to suggest that the main aim was language teaching. However, cultural aspects and developing an understanding of foreign nations were considered important in their own right as well, belying the image we might have of the 'nationalist' nineteenth century:[4]

> Es sollte uns freuen, wenn mancher unserer Schüler, der jetzt in weiter Ferne weilt, ein richtiges Verständniß für fremde Nationalitäten auch durch den Unterricht in der englischen Geographie gewonnen hat. Ohne den eigenen Patriotismus zu behelligen, ist es nämlich gewiß eine sehr dankbare Seite des Unterrichts in der Geographie, die Vorurtheile, die so Mancher gegen

fremde Länder und fremde Völker zu seinem eigenen Nachtheile zur Schau trägt, verschwinden zu sehen. In England und Amerika hat sich überdies ein so gesundes, kräftiges Leben entwickelt, und die Charakterstärke, diese edle Zierde des Mannes, ist in jenen Ländern so sprüchwörtlich geworden, daß diese Einem wohl Achtung einflößen kann, selbst wenn man den Schwächen und Mängeln, die ja jedes Volk hat, Rechnung trägt. (Werner 1866: 39)

[It should please us when some of our pupils who are now far away have won an understanding of foreign nations partly through the English geography [that we teach]. Without damaging one's own patriotism it is surely a thankful side of our geography course to see the prejudices against foreign peoples, which some of us display to their own disadvantage, disappear. In England and America, such a healthy and strong life has developed and the moral fibre, this noble quality of mankind, has become proverbial in an awe-aspiring way even when considering the weaknesses and faults of every people.]

England and the USA are assigned the quality of role models for Bremen merchants here, with the close mercantile connection having obvious repercussions on the school curriculum in this respect. So, in addition to providing material for practising spoken and written English, geography lessons were used to counteract stereotypical images of the target cultures. This feature of the Bremen 'English geography' lessons strongly resembles the demands placed on modern CLIL classes.

Understandably, teaching subject knowledge in English can only be found at schools with an extended English language course and where English was usually the first foreign language. Although the Bremen *Bürgerschule* may serve as an early example not only for integrating subject knowledge into foreign language teaching but also for teaching other subjects in the foreign language, it was not the only example. At the *Realschule* in Bremerhaven (Bremen's extraterritorial port located at the mouth of the river Weser), which was founded in 1867, the geography course could be held in English or French — depending on the individual teacher. The curriculum for the last year of schooling (*Prima*) reads:

Der Unterricht wird in englischer Sprache ertheilt. Außerdem wird, so lange der geographische Unterricht in der Hand des Lehrers des Englischen liegt, die Geographie Englands, der britischen Besitzungen und der vereinigten Staaten englisch vorgetragen und repetiert.

[The lessons are held in the English language. In addition, as long as the geography lessons lie in the hand of the teacher of English, the geography of England, of the British colonies and the United States is presented and repeated in English.] (Hildebrand 1883: 26)

At the Bremen *Bürgerschule*, the teaching of history and geography in English (and later in French as well) was discontinued after 1885 (Reiche 1905: 86), mainly because of a standardization of the different German school systems after the unification of the Reich in 1871. Still, subject knowledge has never left English-language teaching completely: *Realienkunde* and early twentieth-century *Kulturkunde* were cases in point (these being the dominant approaches to knowledge about the target culture as recognized at the time), both of which only partly served as a basis for understanding literary texts (Hüllen 2005: 114-18). During the heyday of *Kulturkunde*, Hugo Dietze (1927: 24) analysed the similarities and continuities of both approaches when he termed the *Realsprachunterricht* at Schulze's late eighteenth-century Berlin commercial school 'wirtschaftliche Kulturkunde' [economic cultural studies]:

> Alles, was das Wirtschaftsleben betraf, stellte Schulze mehr oder weniger in den Vordergrund, so daß seine Kulturkunde nicht allgemeine, sondern vorzugsweise wirtschaftliche Kulturkunde war. Das Ästhetische, Schöngeistige spielte nur die Rolle von Begleiterscheinungen. Es wurde nicht vermieden, aber in der Regel doch nur hinzugezogen, wenn es zu den vorgeführten wirtschaftlichen Kulturerscheinungen irgendwie in Beziehung stand. Die Schulzeschen Schüler sollten vor allen Dingen von dem fremden Kulturleben das kennenlernen, was sie als zukünftige Kaufleute brauchen konnten.

> [Schulze foregrounded everything concerning the economic life so that his *Kulturkunde* was not a general, but rather an economic one. The aesthetic aspects only played the role of concomitants. They were not avoided but generally only consulted when somehow related to economic cultural phenomena. Schulze's pupils should primarily get to know those elements of the foreign cultural life that they could use as future merchants.]

Whereas nineteenth-century Prussian *Realschulen* at least partly had to fulfil neo-Humanist demands of providing general knowledge and thus had a focus on the 'aesthetic', the early Bremen *Bürgerschule* — although not explicitly mentioned by Dietze — can be seen as a missing link. Later on, following the Prussian example, literature studies became more important there as well; hence language education had to become more a part of general education, leaving a utilitarian or economic focus aside.

The 1960s and 1970s saw a renaissance of a more practical approach towards knowledge about target countries in Germany (Dietze 1927: 140-45), often described as *Landeskunde*. The latter still serves as the knowledge base of intercultural approaches. In all these contexts — and especially in CLIL or 'bilingual' teaching scenarios since the 1960s — subject knowledge has played an integral part in institutional language teaching in Germany.

Conclusion

Looking at the German institutional context of schooling, there is strong evidence, visible even in this small selection of sources, that language teaching usually combined elements of subject and language — especially in long courses when English or French rather than Latin was the first foreign language taught. The decisions that teachers and curriculum-designers have needed to make are thus not whether to integrate content at all, but rather what content to integrate. This may be different in more specialized language teaching set-ups (e.g. Business English courses) or in other national traditions; but for state schools in Germany it has definitely been a central, traditional feature. Hence, the combination of subject and language teaching should be seen as a common and central element of language teaching, not as the extraordinary approach it is usually treated as.

Long English courses which aimed at a high language competence demanded challenging content that could be discussed, read and written about. The aspired-for qualification profile for the pupils dictated what subject knowledge to teach: thus, non-literary subject knowledge could be interpreted as a sign of a prominent economic influence on schools. It can be seen that pronounced combinations of subject and language teaching mainly seem to develop when schools are understood as institutions qualifying pupils for an international market.

The examples above illustrate the role of non-literary content in language teaching at *Realanstalten* and commercial schools that mainly taught future merchants. Its importance and relevance were especially visible in a merchant city like Bremen with a direct economic relationship between politics and schools. The role of non-literary content became less pronounced in the dominant Prussian school system adopted after the German unification in 1871, when history and geography taught in English (and later French) disappeared as the economic influence on the school system diminished (Giesler 2013: 119-22). Following a stronger 'cultural' focus and a more prominent role of literary content in the early twentieth century, in a modern 'globalized' world and with the growing economic influence on teaching (e.g. through 'standardization' (Tröhler 2013)), we nowadays find a renaissance of vocational subject knowledge in language teaching.

Taking these deliberations into consideration, it seems that interpreting the history of language teaching as composed of sudden revolutions which then again serve as preface-histories for today's ('superior') ways of teaching is a misconception. Rather than that, ideas, concepts or methodologies should be productively understood in their continuity: developments in the context of schooling have a *longue durée*. The options or dimensions within these methods and methodologies (Thornbury 2011) neither reflect innovative ideas, nor are they mainly (and all of a sudden) influenced by paradigm shifts. When it comes to practice, they are customized to the specific teaching context in which language teachers and curriculum designers work. So, when modern languages like English took on a more prominent role in the German schools, the teaching of them demanded meaningful and challenging content which was integrated into the language course.

The continuity of schooling — or even its strong persistence against change and reform — has been shown for the twentieth-century United States by Tyack and Tobin (1994), who devised the notion of the 'grammar' of schooling, in which it seems not that 'innovations [...] change schools, but [...] schools change reforms' (ibid.: 478). Within the context of institutional schooling, the same might be true for individual subjects like foreign language teaching (cf. Giesler 2015). In the German context, 'to kill two birds with one stone' via integration of language and subject teaching within the English (or French) course, or in the form of a separate subject, is not an innovation but a persistent feature.

Bibliography

Primary sources

HILDEBRAND, L. 1883. *Die Realschule in Bremerhaven: Geschildert in Anlaß der Feier ihres 25jährigen Bestehens am 2. April 1883* (Bremerhaven: the Author)

W[ERNER, FRIEDRICH]. 1866. 'Die englische Geographie in der II. Klasse der Bürgerschule', in *An das Elternhaus: Mittheilungen aus der Bürgerschule und Töchterbürgerschule*, published by authority of the principal of the *Bürgerschule*, 6(5): 37-39. Staatsarchiv Bremen, Za-231

WERNER, FRIEDRICH. 1867. *Geographische Charakterbilder über das Britische Reich und die Vereinigten Staaten als stoffliche Grundlage für den mündlichen und schriftlichen Gedankenaustausch in den obern Klassen höherer Unterrichtsanstalten* (Bremen: the Author)

Secondary sources

BIEDERSTÄDT, WOLFGANG. 2013. 'Ein innovatives Unterrichtskonzept', in *Bilingual unterrichten: Englisch für alle Fächer*, ed. by Wolfgang Biederstädt (Berlin: Cornelsen Scriptor), pp. 5-14

BONNET, ANDREAS, STEPHAN BREIDBACH and WOLFGANG HALLET. 2009. 'Fremdsprachlich handeln im Sachfach: Bilinguale Lernkontexte', in *Englischunterricht: Grundlagen und Methoden einer handlungsorientierten Unterrichtspraxis*, ed. by Gerhard Bach and Johannes Timm, 4th edn (Tübingen: Francke), pp. 172-98

BREIDBACH, STEPHAN. 2007. *Bildung, Kultur, Wissenschaft: Reflexive Didaktik für den bilingualen Sachfachunterricht* (Münster: Waxmann)

DEPAEPE, MARC. 2010. 'The Ten Commandments of Good Practices in History of Education Research', *Zeitschrift für pädagogische Historiographie*, 16: 31-34

DIETZE, HUGO. 1927. *Methodik des fremdsprachlichen Unterrichts an Handelsschulen* (Leipzig: Gloeckner)

DOFF, SABINE. 2010. 'Theorie und Praxis des bilingualen Sachfachunterrichts', in *Bilingualer Sachfachunterricht in der Sekundarstufe: Eine Einführung*, ed. by Sabine Doff (Tübingen: Narr), pp. 11-25

GIESLER, TIM. 2013. 'Die bremische Bürgerschule: Kommunikativer Englischunterricht für Kaufleute', in *Schulsprachenpolitik und fremdsprachliche Unterrichtspraxis: Historische Schlaglichter zwischen 1800 und 1989*, ed. by Friederike Klippel, Elisabeth Kolb, and Felicitas Sharp, Münchener Arbeiten zur Fremdsprache-Forschung, 26 (Münster: Waxmann), pp. 113-24

——. 2015. 'Here be dragons — Von einer "Mythologie" zu einer "Morphologie" des Fremdsprachenunterrichts', *IJHE Bildungsgeschichte*, 5: 146-61

HOWATT, A. P. R., with H. G. WIDDOWSON. 2004. *A History of English Language Teaching*, 2nd edn (Oxford: Oxford University Press)

——, and RICHARD SMITH. 2014. 'The History of Teaching English as a Foreign Language, from a British and European Perspective', *Language and History*, 57: 75-95

HÜLLEN, WERNER. 2005. *Kleine Geschichte des Fremdsprachenlernens* (Berlin: Erich Schmidt)

HUNTER, DUNCAN, and RICHARD SMITH. 2012. 'Unpackaging the Past: "CLT" through *ELTJ* Keywords', *ELT Journal*, 66: 430-39

KLIPPEL, FRIEDERIKE. 1994. *Englischlernen im 18. und 19. Jahrhundert. Die Geschichte der Lehrbücher und Unterrichtsmethoden* (Münster: Nodus)

KÖRTGE, HERBERT. 1999. *Das Schulwesen in Alt-Bremerhaven von der Gründung der ersten Schule 1831 bis zur Eingliederung der Stadt in Wesermünde 1939* (Bremerhaven: Körtge)

LEHBERGER, REINER. 1990. *'Collect All the English Inscriptions You Can Find in Our City': Englischunterricht an Hamburger Volksschule 1870 –1945* (Hamburg: Curio)

MEHISTO, PEETER, DAVID MARSH and MARÍA JESÚS FRIGOLS. 2008. *Uncovering CLIL: Content and Language Integrated Learning in Bilingual and Multilingual Education* (Oxford: Macmillan)

MENTZ, OLIVIER. 2010. 'Alle Fächer eignen sich — oder doch nicht? Überlegungen zu einem bilingualen Fächerkanon', in *Bilingualer Sachfachunterricht in der Sekundarstufe: Eine Einführung*, ed. by Sabine Doff (Tübingen: Narr), pp. 29-43

REICHE, ARMIN. 1905. *Die Entwicklung des Realschulwesens in Bremen insbesondere der Realschule in der Altstadt: Ein geschichtlicher Rückblick* (Bremen: Guthe)

RICHARDS, JACK C., and RICHARD W. SCHMIDT (eds). 2002 [1985]. *Dictionary of Language Teaching and Applied Linguistics*, 3rd edn (Harlow: Longman)

SCHLEICH, MARLIS. 2015. *Geschichte des internationalen Schülerbriefwechsels: Entstehung und Entwicklung im historischen Kontext von den Anfängen bis zum Ersten Weltkrieg* (Münster: Waxmann)

SMITH, RICHARD. 2011. 'Applied Linguistic Impact and Influence: Historical Perspectives', paper given at 44th Annual Meeting of the British Association for Applied Linguistics, University of West of England, Bristol

——, and MOTOMICHI IMURA. 2004. 'Lessons from the Past: Traditions and Reforms', in *English Language Teaching: The Case of Japan*, ed. by V. Makarova and T. Rodgers (Munich: Lincom-Europa), pp. 29-48

THORNBURY, SCOTT. 2011. 'Language Teaching Methodology', in *The Routledge Handbook of Applied Linguistics*, ed. by James Simpson (London: Routledge), pp. 185-99

TRÖHLER, DANIEL. 2013. 'Standardisierung nationaler Bildungspolitiken: Die Erschaffung internationaler Experten, Planern [sic] und Statistiken in der Frühphase der OECD', *IJHE Bildungsgeschichte*, 3: 60-77

TYACK, DAVID, and WILLIAM TOBIN. 1994. 'The "Grammar" of Schooling: Why Has It Been So Hard to Change?', *American Educational Research Journal*, 31: 453-79

TYACK, DAVID, and LARRY CUBAN. 1995. *Tinkering toward Utopia: A Century of Public School Reform* (Cambridge, MA: Harvard University Press)

Notes to Chapter 6

1. In a similar spirit, Smith and Imura (2004: 40) illustrate a specific Japanese tradition in English-language teaching which again shows substantial persistence and resistance to change, thus highlighting the mistaken nature of 'reformers' overriding belief in the superiority of their own favoured methods'.

2. Within the German context, the term 'realia' (*Realien*) refers to content connected to 'real' life — not just to objects brought into the classroom as the term is often understood in English-speaking countries. The place of *Realien* in schools was established in opposition to the intellectual sphere, which had been idealized by the Neo-Humanists since the late-eighteenth century.

3. The emphasis in the original; English translations are by the author.

4. Although there were, of course, nationalist tendencies in the Hanseatic cities as well, they had traditionally built their wealth on international trade relations and were thus strongly influenced by their overseas partners.

CHAPTER 7

❖

'Let Girls Chat about the Weather and Walks': English Language Education at Girls' Secondary Schools in Nineteenth-Century Germany

Sabine Doff

In nineteenth-century Germany, learning to make conversation in French and English was typically considered to be an integral part of a 'proper' education for girls from upper middle-class families (so-called *höhere Töchter*, i.e. 'higher daughters', who needed to be provided with a secondary education befitting their families' status), on a par with playing an instrument or doing needlework. Thus modern languages had an important status at *höheren Mädchenschulen* (girls' secondary schools), a school type which was nationalized and thus became very prominent in Germany during the last third of the nineteenth century. In this context, choosing contents and matching methodology, as well as defining objectives with regard to learning (about) language and culture, involved a difficult balancing act between formalistic and utilitarian traditions — as was true of conceptualizations of teaching at girls' secondary schools in general. This chapter argues that within this context modern languages played a significant role as school subjects, contributing to the establishment of a state system of secondary education for girls and young women in Germany especially towards the end of the nineteenth century. A distinctive 'female' approach to modern-language learning and teaching developed that can readily be associated with the so-called 'marketplace tradition' of language learning and teaching. This approach (or at least distinct traces of it) prevailed in secondary education in Germany for boys as well as girls well into the twentieth century.

Introduction

This chapter investigates the 'female' approach to English-language learning in late nineteenth-century Germany in the framework of the state school system that was becoming institutionalized and clearly differentiated according to learners' gender. Following a brief overview of modern language education in eighteenth- and nineteenth-century Germany, the chapter examines contents, methods and aims of teaching and learning English at secondary schools for boys and girls in turn. I show that as secondary education for girls was institutionalized in Germany (1872 onwards) there was inclusion of both formalistic aspects referring to the educational standards typical of grammar schools for boys and of elements of a clearly utilitarian approach. This utilitarian approach was in line with a long 'female' tradition of modern language learning which was given added momentum by the Reform Movement at the end of the nineteenth century; distinctive elements of this approach persisted in modern language curricula for both sexes well into the twentieth century.

Between Marketplace and Monastery: English-Language Education in Germany in the Eighteenth and Nineteenth Centuries

A central motivation for many learners in the long history of language teaching has been the need to communicate in everyday and professional life, for example, with merchants, traders and travellers. The type of language teaching influenced by this kind of motivation and thus geared towards language use has often been referred to as the 'marketplace tradition' (for example, McArthur 1998). Some of its distinct characteristics are a focus on oral competence and methods following the principle of 'learning by doing'. The complementary type of language teaching, labelled the 'monastery tradition', was originally influenced by the medieval training of religious novices in Latin as an international language (ibid.). Language teaching methods in this tradition favour rote learning combined with repetition, the study of canonical texts, and grammatical analysis. The primary motivation for language learning is anchored in the academic field, that is, learning to read and write a language in order to be able to understand writings in the original version. Languages provide access to certain fields of knowledge; and educational institutions and forms of language teaching in this tradition do not therefore have a primarily utilitarian benefit but are education-oriented. The history of language teaching has always been characterized by this tension between use and education, with one or the other tending to be favoured at different times or in different contexts. This certainly applies to the two hundred years of teaching English in Germany between 1800 and 2000, during which — as this chapter argues — market and monastery traditions were clearly linked to the learners' gender.

The eighteenth century marks the beginning of the meteoric career of English-language education in Germany (see, for example, Hüllen 2005, Klippel 1994). In the first half of the century, English was only sporadically present in schools and universities. However, an interest in the language was continuously being fed at this stage in Germany by a growing desire to read: formative works on politics, science, philosophy, theology and art and works of English literature attracted a large number of educated adult readers. These works could only be read in the original in many cases due to a lack of translations, therefore reading in English became a central skill, whether in home-, school- or self-study. This was reflected in a number of textbooks from this period which served as models for many decades to come (for example, *A Complete English Guide for High Germans* by Hans König / John King, which was first published in 1706 and revised and re-edited in many versions subsequently, the latest one being dated 1802 (see Hüllen 1991)). These textbooks typically included a grammar part and, in addition, discussions/ dialogues, a dictionary, lists of key words or short reading texts. The grammar parts of most textbooks for English from this period were based on Latin grammar, but with rules written in German, and there were illustrations with example sentences which often came from well-known literary works.

The number of self-taught adult learners of English in the nineteenth century continued to rise. The new phenomenon was that in this century English teaching was established in both boys' and girls' schools as a school subject, yet with different *foci* that demanded adaptation and differentiation of content, material and method to address the specific target group adequately. Although the overall goal of teaching English was language proficiency, sub-objectives were weighted differently depending on the type of school and gender of the learners, and these sub-objectives were hotly debated throughout the century. In the context of secondary education for boys (see below), the argument was mirrored in the competition between the so-called 'real institutions' (*Realanstalten*) that were emerging in the last third of the nineteenth century and the traditional grammar schools. Whereas the former put a focus on natural sciences and modern foreign languages in the context of useful training for present needs (in the 'marketplace tradition'), the latter focused on classical languages in association with a Humanist and formal education (in the 'monastery tradition'). This chapter argues, however, that at this stage the most progressive foreign language teaching (in a rather radical version of the 'marketplace tradition') was probably that at girls' schools, where principles that today are related to designations such as 'English as a language of communication' were realized. This led to heated expressions of views about goals and methods for the teaching of English, as exemplified in the following quotation (which gives this chapter its title):

> Ich schätze es gering, einen Menschen perfect Englisch sprechen zu hören, das kann jeder brauchbare Kellner, er muß es können; das französische Institutsgeplapper der Mädchen ist nicht viel werth, denn sie wissen schließlich doch nicht, warum nach dieser und jener Conjunction der Conjunctiv steht, ob sie auch die Regel wissen, daß er steht. [...] Lassen wir Mädchen parliren vom Wetter und von Spaziergängen, dem Gebildeten ist es um etwas anderes zu thun. Er will, er soll eindringen in den Genius der Sprachen, er soll die Gedanken der Nationen, die Ideen der Fremden, nicht ihre Wörter beherrschen, er solle stehen auf sprachhistorischem Boden und die Art Sprachen zu studiren, diese Methode soll und muß vom Gymnasium ausgehen. Der Gebildete, das Gymnasium, die einzige und wirkliche Pflanzschule der Gebildeten, muß Opposition machen gegenüber diesem rohen Sprachstudium. (Reinhardstöttner 1868: 13-14)

> [I do not greatly value hearing a man speak perfect English, any skilled waiter can do that; girls babbling in institution French is not worth much because they do not actually know why after this or that conjunction a subjunctive comes,

even if they know the rule. [...] Let girls chat about the weather and walks, the educated [man] has something else to do. He wants to — he should — penetrate the genius of languages, he should study the ideas of nations, the ideas of foreigners, not master their words, he should have to study the historical background of languages and the type of languages, this method should and must come from the grammar school. The educated person from the grammar school, the only and real nursery of the educated, must be opposed to this crude language study.][1]

Towards the end of the nineteenth century a group of foreign-language teachers (together referred to nowadays as the 'Neusprachliche Reformbewegung' [Modern Language Reform Movement] turned against this position. The reformers demanded that living languages should be taught as such (unlike classical languages): that is, there should be increased importance placed on the spoken language, with grammar given a subservient role; teaching should be done in the foreign language; and translation reduced. Yet the reformers were not the first to practise and conceptualize a marketplace-tradition approach to language learning and teaching in the institutionalized school system of nineteenth-century Germany: as we shall see, secondary education for girls and young women was way ahead of them. First, though, we consider language education for boys and the Reform Movement in more detail.

Language Education in Boys' Secondary Schools

In nineteenth- and early twentieth-century Germany the institutionalization of secondary education for boys seems to have been ahead of that relating to girls' secondary education for about a hundred years.[2] This 'delay' influenced the didactic decisions (about what, how and why to teach) taken for secondary education for both boys and girls. The development of boys' secondary education in nineteenth-century Germany is often described as having the following three phases (cf. Jeismann 1987):

* Up to 1840 the *Gymnasium* (the German grammar school based mainly on Humboldt's ideas) developed as *the* leading type of school providing secondary education for boys from the upper classes;

* Within the next phase of system formation, competing types of secondary schools for boys evolved alongside the *Gymnasium*: the so-called *Realanstalten* (see Giesler in this volume);

* The final third of the nineteenth century is a phase of system consolidation, the eventual outcome of which was that different kinds of secondary school for boys gained equal status. This applies, for example, to the so-called *Realgymnasien* and *Oberrealschulen*, which in the early twentieth century gained a somewhat similar status to the classical *Gymnasium* once they, too, were entitled to grant full university access. There were different types of *Realgymnasien* that specialized, for example, in teaching sciences or modern languages. Given the focus on modern languages rather than sciences in girls' schools, only the second type of *Realgymnasium* can serve as a reference point for comparisons with girls' secondary schools.

On the one hand, the *Gymnasium* pursued traditions of the older Latin schools (see, for example, Hüllen 2005: 41-46); on the other, it integrated nineteenth-century Humanist approaches (including the teaching of modern languages) according to the financial and political resources available. However, in most of the secondary boys' schools — irrespective of school type — the idea prevailed that modern languages must be taught according to the grammar-translation methods common for Latin and Greek. The role played by the classical languages at a traditional *Gymnasium* was often assigned to French (and later also to English) at boys' secondary schools where Latin was not taught. This is stated explicitly, for example, in the 1892 curriculum for English and French at *Realanstalten* for boys in Prussia: 'Die Aufgabe der sprachlich-logischen Schulung, welche an lateinlehrenden Anstalten vorzugsweise der lateinischen Grammatik und den angeschlossenen Uebungen zufaellt, ist an lateinlosen durch die französische Grammatik und die entsprechenden Uebungen zu loesen' [The function of language- and logic-training which at schools with Latin is assigned to Latin grammar and related exercises is taken over at schools without Latin by French grammar and related exercises] (*Centralblatt* 1892: 69; cf. Panning 1898). This quotation illustrates that, apart from the introduction of English and French, there was nothing new at a typical secondary school for boys towards the end of the nineteenth century: since the aims of foreign language teaching remained more or less the same (irrespective of the language taught), the method of teaching the classical languages (with a focus on grammar and translation, i.e. the 'grammar-translation method' (see, for example, Hüllen 2005: 92-97)) was simply transferred to teaching modern languages, until something new — in this case the Reform Movement — began to have an effect.

The initial impetus for this movement is commonly seen as Wilhelm Viëtor's work with the title *Der Sprachunterricht muss umkehren!* (*Language Teaching Must Start Afresh!* (1882)). The Reformers (that is, the leaders of the reform movement that spread across Europe and later became known as the *Neusprachliche Reformbewegung* (cf. Howatt with Widdowson 2004: 187-209)) were a small number of modern-language teachers (among them Hermann Klinghardt, Felix Franke and Gustav Wendt) who argued that modern languages, that is, English and French, needed a distinct teaching methodology, different from that for Latin, which had to take into account that both were spoken languages. The three main principles underlying the reformers' writings and classroom experiments were: the primacy of speech; the centrality of the connected text as the kernel of the teaching-learning process; and the absolute priority of an oral classroom methodology (ibid.: 189). These principles were specified, for example, in Gustav Wendt's manifesto entitled 'Die Wiener Reformthesen' [The Vienna Reform Theses] (see Wendt 1898/99, 1900/01). Grammar was seen as a means to an end (i.e., being competent in using the language) rather than as an end in itself. Translation (in particular into German) was reduced to a minimum, as was the use of German in general in the foreign-language classroom.

The reformers' ideas can be seen as a reaction to the deficient state of teaching modern languages to boys. While their immediate impact on the theoretical discourse about language education is undisputed (see, for example, Howatt with Widdowson 2004: 187–209; Howatt and Smith 2002), their influence upon language classrooms in the context of boys' secondary education seems to have been clearly limited (Klippel 2013). Thus, for actual widespread practice of a marketplace tradition-oriented approach to modern-language teaching in schools, on which the reformers must have drawn, we need to look elsewhere.

Language Education in Private and State Girls' Secondary Schools

The 'Female' Tradition of Language Education

When we take a closer look at what, how and with what aims modern languages were taught at private and state schools for girls, it becomes clear that many elements of the approach promoted by the reformers were rooted in a long tradition of language teaching in Europe carried out by female native speakers working as governesses (see, for example, Hardach-Pinke 1993; Lehmann 1904). The governesses (and, in particular, governesses in private secondary institutions for girls) strengthened their female learners' oral competence and combined it with appropriate behaviour in and knowledge of French and English culture. This twofold aim was in line with the idea that a so-called 'higher daughter' should be able to make conversation in a foreign language and learn useful skills like, for example, needlework. This criterion of usefulness was prominent across the subjects taught to girls in many European countries for most of the nineteenth century (see Jacobi 2013: 220ff.). It was realized, for example, at the *Société des jeunes dames* run by 'Mamsell' Ackermann in Danzig in the late eighteenth century, where young ladies were trained in French conversation and appropriate socio-cultural behaviour by means of role plays imitating afternoon teatime in a French upper-class household. Ackermann's exclusively female learners took turns at playing the role of the hostess and her guests. Using French was only one of the tea-time rules which the girls quickly became used to, as one of them, Johanna Schopenhauer (later to become the mother of Arthur Schopenhauer), reports in her autobiographical notes (Schopenhauer 1996 [1839]; see also Schreiner 1992: 202-03, 207).

Many ideas which the reformers presented, for example in their Vienna manifesto, can be found as elements in this governess teaching tradition. Looking more closely at nineteenth-century modern language teaching at higher secondary girls' schools, it becomes obvious that the principles the reformers formulated at the end of the nineteenth century had been realized within the context of teaching modern languages to girls for at least a century. These principles were probably known to, and appreciated by, at least some of the reformers precisely *within* the context of secondary education for girls. This hypothesis is supported by the fact that a number of prominent reformers including, for example, Wilhelm Viëtor, had done a considerable part of their teaching at girls' secondary schools.

By contrast with the women who had practised a marketplace-oriented approach for modern language teaching for some time, reform-minded male teachers found efficient ways of making their voices heard, for example as speakers at the Weimar conference that officially marked the institutionalization of a secondary state-school system for girls in Germany (1872); or in newly founded associations (for example, the *Allgemeiner Deutscher Neuphilologenverband* (*ADNV*), founded in 1880). As Christ (1987: 828) has described, the first generation of male modern-language-teacher reformers understood themselves to be, and acted as, a group:

> Die Generationsgenossen stehen in engem, persönlichem und beruflichem Kontakt; sie empfinden das Bedürfnis, sich zusammenzuschließen; denn sie arbeiten unter relativ homogenen Bedingungen — an Realgymnasien, Realschulen und höheren Mädchenschulen. [...] Die hier zu besprechende Generation ist noch eine reine Männerversammlung. Von Frauen als Fremdsprachenlehrerinnen in Höheren Mädchenschulen ist noch nicht oder nur am Rande die Rede. Dies wird sich mit der Jahrhundertwende ändern (Christ 1987: 828).

> [These fellows are close in their private and professional lives; they feel they need to stand side by side since they work in similar conditions — at *Realgymnasien*, *Realschulen* and girls' secondary schools [...]. This generation is a purely male assembly. Women do not play a (significant) role yet as modern language teachers at girls' secondary schools. This is about to change with the turn of the century.]

To sum up: what the reformers advocated was not new — it was an approach which had been practised in the context of secondary education for girls for nearly a century by female governesses. Yet their male colleagues at the end of the nineteenth century found more efficient ways of implementing these ideas and thus succeeded in integrating them, as the last part of this chapter will show, into curricula of the state school system for girls as well as for boys.

Institutionalization of Girls' Secondary Schools

The final third of the nineteenth century brought something fundamentally new into the field of secondary education for girls. After the so-called Weimar Conference of 1872, the government of a newly unified Germany stepped up efforts to institutionalize and nationalize a system of state secondary education for girls (Doff 2002: 112–246). At this conference in Weimar, a large number of influential (male) teachers from the field (the so-called *Mädchenschulpädagogen*) had met with politicians and a very small number of female colleagues to lay out the general conditions for two new secondary school types: the *höhere Mädchenschule* and the *Mittelschule* for girls. The distinct characteristic which separated one from the other was that a second foreign language was required in the former, but not in the latter (which usually offered either French or English). This meant that both English and French became mandatory school subjects at every *höhere Mädchenschule* that was run or acknowledged by the state.

This development was indeed new and thus presented the state with a huge challenge: the need for teachers of modern languages, particularly for girls (but also for boys), skyrocketed. Only male teachers had previously been admitted to official employment in the context of state secondary education for girls as well as boys.

Latin and Greek had formed a substantial part of their own education at school and university, but hardly any of them were proficient in modern languages, let alone in teaching them. This is why female teachers eventually surfaced on the agenda of state secondary education in Germany (Doff 2007), but since they were not officially admitted to the state system of teacher education for secondary schools until the late nineteenth century, the prospective female teachers had often qualified abroad and thus spent a considerable amount of time in France and Britain. There, they had been trained as teachers or worked as governesses or teachers (often in the context of private education) and thus had become experienced pedagogues, but also proficient speakers of French and English. Briefly, this advantage over their male counterparts is one of the main reasons why around the turn of the twentieth century female teachers were admitted into German state girls' secondary schools, and later also into secondary schools for boys.

A look at the curricula for modern languages at girls' secondary schools reveals that there was indeed a modern-language-teaching approach that differed significantly from that for boys described in the curriculum from 1892 cited above. This approach was supported by the reformers' theses. This hypothesis is supported by the 1894 Prussian curriculum equivalent for higher girls' schools, which states:

> Der Unterricht in den fremden Sprachen hat die unmittelbare Aufgabe, die Schülerin zu befähigen, einen leichteren französischen oder englischen Schrift-steller zu verstehen, gesprochenes Englisch und Französisch richtig aufzufassen, und die fremde Sprache in den einfachen Formen des täglichen Verkehrs mündlich wie schriftlich mit einiger Gewandtheit zu gebrauchen. (*Centralblatt* 1894: 466)

> [The direct aim of modern language teaching is to enable a girl to comprehend a relatively easy French or English author, correctly to understand spoken English and French and to use the language in writing and speaking skilfully in basic everyday situations.]

The strong focus on learning about culture[3] is particularly of interest in this context: learning about culture is presented as *the* long-term aim of language teaching, which, in the curriculum quoted here, combines the utilitarian and the formalistic traditions of modern-language teaching. Moreover, this short quotation clearly illustrates that at secondary girls' schools teaching modern languages was approached using distinct didactic principles which differed substantially from those for teaching classical languages (not surprisingly, since the latter had never played a role there). A close look at school programmes (*Schulprogrammschriften*) written at and for girls' secondary schools provides further evidence: these reveal distinct characteristics for a truly original 'female' approach to English and French language teaching at private and state institutions in the final third of the nineteenth and in the early twentieth century (Doff 2002: 396ff.). As many public and private sources document (for a detailed analysis see Doff 2002: 248-54), the teacher of English and French at girls' secondary schools was often a (preferably female) native speaker, or a female teacher who had lived in Britain or France for a considerable time. In many cases, these female native speakers were not highly proficient in German.

Their poor knowledge of German was often criticized; it meant that in many cases English was not only spoken in the English lessons, but also that other subjects such as, for example, geography or history, were taught in English (Winkler 1926). This example illustrates that the methodological concept today known as 'Content and Language Integrated Learning' (CLIL) has indeed had a long tradition in Europe (cf. the contribution by Giesler in this volume).

Many of the teachers at girls' secondary schools were highly proficient in speaking modern languages; the spoken word and the training of the learners' oral skills thus prevailed in these language classrooms. This dovetailed with the principle of usefulness on which many parents, who were still not convinced as to why exactly their daughters needed a secondary education, were focused:

> Denn wollte man den Eltern fuer ihr Schulgeld sozusagen etwas Greifbares, Sichtbares, Reales liefern, dann musste man das 'Können' in den Vordergrund stellen. Deshalb ist auch schon vor der Reform in den Mädchenschule die Sprechfertigkeit immer mehr betrieben worden als in den Knabenschulen, wozu noch der Umstand nicht wenig beitrug, dass die Mädchen ihrer ganzen Natur nach für die Plappermethode besser geeignet sind als die Knaben. (Clodius 1906: 4–5).

> [Since parents had to be provided with something visible and real, practical skills had to be foregrounded. This is why oral proficiency was given a higher priority at higher secondary girls' compared to secondary boys' schools even before the reform. This was supported by the girls' nature, which the chattering method suits far better than boys.]

In the last third of the nineteenth century, however, utilitarian arguments retreated into the background, even though they did not disappear completely. Once it became important to establish girls' secondary education as equivalent to that for boys, the educational value in particular of English literature for female learners was emphasized. Reading English literature and getting to know the foreign culture better thus became key elements of English teaching at girls' secondary schools (cf. Doff and Klippel 2007); accordingly, grammar was accorded an auxiliary role.

Conclusion

The above description of the development and didactic features of a 'female' approach to language teaching in nineteenth-century Germany shows how modern this concept seems in many respects in today's light. Around the turn of the twentieth century it eventually came to combine utilitarian with formalistic elements. A possible explanation for this balancing act is that secondary education for girls, as a new strand in the national educational system, had to fulfil a double, partly contradictory, purpose. On the one hand, it had to be established as equal to secondary education for boys. On the other hand, it needed to provide a specific type of state education for female addressees who were not (yet) admitted to universities. In the late nineteenth and early twentieth centuries, the influences of this distinct approach on the curricula of modern language teaching at boys' higher secondary schools can clearly be traced. A 'female' teaching concept which awarded high

priority to the spoken word thus was turned into a success story with the strategic
support of male reformers and this finally facilitated access to language use-oriented
learning in the marketplace tradition for learners of both sexes in schools.

Bibliography

Primary sources

Centralblatt für die gesammte Unterrichtsverwaltung in Preußen. 1859–1904. Ed. by the
    Ministerium der geistlichen, Unterrichts- und Medicianlangelegenheiten (Berlin)
CLODIUS [*sic*]. (1906). 'Die höhere Mädchenschule und der fremdsprachliche Unterricht',
    Zeitschrift für französischen und englischen Unterricht, 5: 1-14
*Fremdsprachenunterricht unter staatlicher Verwaltung 1700 bis 1945: Eine Dokumentation amtlicher
    Richtlinien und Verordnungen*. 1985. Ed. by Herbert Christ and Hans-Joachim Rang, 7 vols
    (Tübingen: Narr)
KÖNIG, HANS [JOHN KING]. 1706. *A Complete English Guide for High Germans* (London:
    Frieman and Barber)
LEHMANN, RUDOLF. 1904. 'Die höheren Lehranstalten: Lehrpläne und Lehrbetrieb', in *Das
    Unterrichtswesen im Deutschen Reich*, ed. by Wilhelm Lexis, II: *Die höheren Lehranstalten und
    das Mädchenschulwesen im Deutschen Reich* (Berlin: Asher), pp. 67-165
'Lehrpläne und Lehraufgaben für die höheren Schulen vom 06.01.1892.c. Methodische
    Bemerkungen zu Französisch und Englisch'. 1985 [1892]. In *Fremdsprachenunterricht unter
    staatlicher Verwaltung 1700 bis 1945: Eine Dokumentation amtlicher Richtlinien und Verordnungen*,
    ed. by Herbert Christ and Hans-Joachim Rang, 7 vols (Tübingen: Narr), II, 69–72
PANNING, EMIL. 1898. 'Der Grammatische Lernstoff im Englischen bis zur Abschlußprü-
    fung', *Beilage zum Jahresbericht des Königlichen Realgymnasiums zu Erfurt*
REINHARDSTÖTTNER, KARL VON. 1868. *Ueber das Studium der modernen Sprachen an den bay-
    erischen Gelehrten-Schulen: Ein Beitrag zu den Ideen über die Reorganisation der Gymnasien*
    (Landshut: Thomann)
SCHOPENHAUER, JOHANNA. 1996 [1839]. 'Jugendleben und Wanderbilder', in *Erziehung und
    Bildung des weiblichen Geschlechts: Eine kommentierte Quellensammlung zur Bildungs- und
    Berufsbildungsgeschichte von Mädchen und Frauen*, ed. by Elke Kleinau and Christine Mayer,
    2 vols (Weinheim: Deutscher Studienverlag), II, 191-96
VIËTOR, WILHELM [QUOUSQUE TANDEM]. 1886 [1882]. *Der Sprachunterricht muß umkehren! Ein
    Beitrag zur Überbürdungsfrage*, 2nd edn (Heilbronn: Henninger)
WENDT, GUSTAV. 1898/99; 1900/01. 'Die Wiener Reform Thesen', *Die Neueren Sprachen*, 6:
    657-60 and 8: 61-64
WINKLER, THEOLINDE MARIA. 1926. *Maria Ward und das Institut der Englischen Fräulein in
    Bayern von der Gründung des Hauses in München bis zur Säkularisation desselben 1626–1810: Ein
    Betrag zur Geschichte der Mädchenbildung des 17. und 18. Jh.* (Munich: Seyfried)

Secondary literature

ALBISETTI, JAMES C. 1988. *Schooling German Girls and Women: Secondary and Higher Education
    in the Nineteenth Century* (Princeton, NJ: Princeton University Press)
CHRIST, HERBERT. 1987. 'Fremdsprachenlehrer im Portrait: Biographisches und Autobio-
    graphisches aus vier Jahrhunderten', in *Perspectives on Language in Performance*, ed. by
    Wolfgang Lörscher et al. (Tübingen: Narr), pp. 819-38
DOFF, SABINE. 2002. *Englischlernen zwischen Tradition und Innovation: Fremdsprachenunterricht
    für Mädchen im 19. Jahrhundert* (Munich: Langenscheidt-Longman)

———. 2007. '*Stairway to Heaven* oder *Road to Nowhere?* Wie die Lehrerinnen in die höhere Schule kamen — und was dann geschah', *Zeitschrift für pädagogische Historiographie*, 13.2: 70-77

———, and FRIEDERIKE KLIPPEL. 2007. 'Mädchen lernen fremde Sprachen: Lehrbücher und Lektüre im 18. und 19. Jahrhundert', in *Gender Studies and Foreign Language Teaching*, ed. by Helene Decke-Cornill and Laurenz Volkmann (Tübingen: Narr), pp. 47-62

HARDACH-PINKE, IRENE. 1993. *Die Gouvernante: Geschichte eines Frauenberufs* (Frankfurt am Main and New York: Campus)

HOWATT, A. P. R., and RICHARD SMITH (eds). 2002. *Modern Language Teaching: The Reform Movement*, 5 vols (London: Routledge), III: *Germany and France*

HOWATT, A. P. R., with HENRY G. WIDDOWSON. 2004 [1984]. *A History of English Language Teaching*, 2nd edn (Oxford: University Press)

HÜLLEN, WERNER. 1991. 'Der Weg durch ein Gebüsche: Analyse des Lehrwerks A royal Compleat Grammar, English and High German (1715) von John King', in *Grenzenloses Sprachenlernen*, ed. by Renate Grebing (Berlin: Cornelsen and Oxford University Press), 217-30

———. 2005. *Kleine Geschichte des Fremdsprachenlernens* (Berlin: Erich Schmidt)

JACOBI, JULIANE. 2013. *Mädchen- und Frauenbildung in Europa: Von 1500 bis zur Gegenwart* (Frankfurt am Main: Campus)

JEISMANN, KARL-ERNST. 1987. 'Das höhere Knabenschulwesen', in *Handbuch der deutschen Bildungsgeschichte*, ed. by Karl-Ernst Jeismann and Peter Lundgreen, III: *1800–1870. Von der Neuordnung Deutschlands bis zur Gründung des Deutschen Reiches* (Munich: Beck), pp. 152-80

KLIPPEL, FRIEDERIKE. 1994. *Englischlernen im 18. und 19. Jahrhundert: Die Geschichte der Lehrbücher und Unterrichtsmethoden* (Münster: Nodus)

———. 2013. 'Die neusprachliche Reform im Unterrichtsalltag: Frühe Handlungsforschung', in *Schulsprachenpolitik und fremdsprachliche Unterrichtspraxis: Historische Schlaglichter zwischen 1800 und 1989*, ed. by Friederike Klippel, Elisabeth Kolb and Felicitas Sharp (Münster: Waxmann), pp. 125-38

MCARTHUR, TOM. 1991. *Living Words: Language, Lexicography, and the Knowledge Revolution* (Exeter: University of Exeter Press)

SCHREINER, SABINE. 1992. *Sprachenlernen in Lebensgeschichten der Goethezeit* (Munich: Iudicium)

Notes to Chapter 7

1. Translations are the author's own.
2. For a detailed analysis and overview covering the nineteenth century and beyond, see Albisetti 1988.
3. For the choice of appropriate literary works see, for example, Doff and Klippel 2007.

CHAPTER 8

❖

L'allemand scolaire en Suisse romande entre langues nationales, langues internationales et dialectes (XIXe–XXIe siècles)

Blaise Extermann

The analysis presented here draws a link between language teaching and national cohesion in Switzerland and between the relative value of each language in the curriculum of secondary schools. We have adopted the viewpoint of the French-speaking part of Switzerland. The study begins with the definition of national languages in the eighteenth century and the emergence of modern languages in public education, from having long been overshadowed by Latin. It continues with the institutionalization of the national languages during the following century and then with their nationalist radicalization at the turn of the nineteenth and twentieth centuries, which led to a push in favour of Swiss German dialects. The development of international relations occurred at the same time as periods of dialect revival. However, national cohesion has never been called into question; only the appreciation of it changes over the centuries. We emphasize the role of public educational institutions as a factor of cohesion. Schools institutions have not always privileged the second national language, but it was absolutely fundamental that public education should bear responsibility for the goal of national cohesion through foreign language teaching. A comparison with Luxembourg places the results of the analysis in perspective.

Situation et problématique

Aujourd'hui en Suisse, la prééminence des langues nationales dans l'enseignement fait débat, en raison d'une double évolution: l'expansion de l'anglais comme *lingua franca* du monde globalisé et l'affirmation du dialecte comme langue principale de la partie alémanique du pays. Ce repositionnement des langues enseignées les unes par rapport aux autres est un enjeu sensible qui se manifeste dans des débats où se mêlent facilement la crainte et la passion. L'opinion publique en Suisse romande s'inquiète d'une rupture de la cohésion nationale, par le choix de plusieurs cantons alémaniques de faire précéder l'apprentissage du français par celui de l'anglais (Büchi 2015; Ammon 2015).

L'analyse présentée ici entend donner un éclairage historique à ce débat. Elle s'appuie d'une part sur une étude de l'enseignement de l'allemand en Suisse romande à partir des publications d'enseignants (revues, manuels, essais), des procès-verbaux des conférences des maîtres, ainsi que des textes officiels (programmes, lois, compte-rendu de débats parlementaires) et d'autre part sur la littérature secondaire sur l'histoire des langues étrangères en Suisse et en Europe (voir Extermann 2013). L'article retrace d'une part le lien entre enseignement des langues et cohésion nationale d'un point de vue situé, celui de la Suisse romande et d'autre part la valeur relative des langues au sein de l'enseignement secondaire. Notre parcours débute avec la définition des langues nationales au XVIIIe siècle et avec l'apparition des langues modernes dans l'enseignement public, à l'ombre du latin. Il se poursuit par l'institutionnalisation des langues nationales au cours du siècle suivant, puis par leur radicalisation nationaliste, à l'approche du XXe siècle, qui entraîne par réaction, une première poussée du dialecte alémanique. Le développement des relations internationales s'accompagne périodiquement d'un regain du dialecte. Jamais, cependant, la cohésion nationale comme finalité primordiale n'est remise en cause. Nous insisterons sur le rôle de l'institution scolaire comme facteur de cohésion. Celle-ci ne privilégie pas toujours l'enseignement de la deuxième langue nationale pour atteindre ce but, même s'il était absolument fondamental que l'instruction publique assume sa responsabilité dans l'enseignement des langues étrangères. Finalement, la comparaison avec le Luxembourg met en perspective les enjeux de l'analyse pour le temps présent.

Avant le XIXe siècle: définition des langues nationales

Le mouvement de nationalisation des langues, dans des régions européennes fortement multilingues est ancien. Il s'est effectué par l'imprimerie, par les sociétés de langues, par l'établissement de normes grâce aux travaux des grammairiens et des lexicographes, par leur adoption par les lettrés eux-mêmes et, par ailleurs, par le développement d'une philosophie de la nation (Auroux 1984; Anderson 1983). Comme le pensait le grammairien allemand Adelung (1732-1806), l'établissement d'une langue de culture (*Hochsprache*) comme langue nationale ne se justifiait pas par une référence mythique au peuple, mais pragmatiquement par un ensemble de conditions sociales et culturelles: sur le plan économique, par le développement du bien-être général et du commerce; sur le plan culturel, par le développement des sciences, de l'érudition et des arts; sur le plan moral, enfin, par la recherche collective du bon goût et de mœurs raffinés (Gardt 2000a: 169-98).

La lente élaboration des langues vernaculaires, puis leur adoption culturelle et politique comme langue maternelle et langue nationale porte à conséquence sur la perception des langues étrangères. Il existait certes depuis longtemps des ouvrages spécialisés d'apprentissage des langues étrangères et de nombreux précepteurs ont fait de cet enseignement leur métier. Dans divers établissements scolaires, la présence de plusieurs langues enseignées — soit en Suisse romande le français, l'allemand et le latin — n'avait pas encore les contours d'un enseignement spécifique bi- ou trilingue, comme nous le comprenons aujourd'hui, sur la base d'une claire distinction entre langue maternelle et langue étrangère. Jusqu'au premier tiers du XIXe siècle au moins, il s'agissait bien plutôt d'un enseignement parallèle dans les petites classes à fins d'alphabétisation des élèves dans leur propre langue, qui devait préparer à l'étude du latin. La persistance de ce modèle ancien s'explique par la confession catholique des cantons que traverse la frontière linguistique en Suisse et par le plus grand rôle qu'y joue le latin. Mais dès le début du XIXe siècle, la nécessité d'enseigner et d'apprendre les langues modernes change.

1815–1830: institutionnalisation des langues nationales et de leur enseignement

Lorsqu'en 1798 les troupes napoléoniennes abolissent les anciennes institutions pour mettre en place la République helvétique, les nouvelles autorités œuvrent à la constitution d'un État plurilingue, au nom de l'égalité des citoyens et au nom de la Nation érigée en principe fédérateur des peuples à la place des anciennes allégeances. Jusqu'ici, la Confédération helvétique se considérait comme germanophone et les territoires italophones ou francophones qu'elle comportait n'avaient pas de droits équivalents à ceux des cantons.

Relevons que l'expansionnisme bernois n'était pas un expansionnisme linguistique. Les patriciens bernois qui géraient le pays de Vaud francophone n'exigeaient nullement de leurs sujets la maîtrise de l'allemand. Bien plus, francophiles, ils s'adressaient aisément à eux en français.

Cependant, les élites suisses ont de la peine à admettre les mesures centralisatrices du nouveau gouvernement mis en place par Napoléon, et la mise sur pied d'égalité des trois langues allemande, française, italienne n'est pas conforme à leur manière de respecter les particularités et les prérogatives des uns et des autres. Aussi un projet de constitution de 1800 prévoit-il le statut de langue nationale principale (*Hauptnationalsprache*) pour l'allemand. En 1803 déjà, Napoléon met fin à la République helvétique et donne au pays un régime plus conforme aux traditions politiques du pays. À la Restauration, les territoires francophones et italophones ont certes gagné le statut de canton, mais sans que le découpage linguistique soit un critère déterminant, sans que les langues elles-mêmes obtiennent une reconnaissance politique formelle (Koller 2000: 563-609).

En 1848 encore, lorsque la Confédération se dote d'une Constitution marquée par la majorité radicale, la question linguistique n'occupe qu'une place minime dans les débats. L'article (n° 109) sur les langues dans la Constitution helvétique de 1848 est non seulement très laconique, il n'a de plus été intégré qu'au dernier moment dans le texte (Elmiger et Forster 2005). En effet, les politiciens de l'époque ont une conception avant tout politique des rapports entre les parties constitutives du pays. Or, de ce point de vue, ce ne sont pas les régions linguistiques qui constituent les entités pertinentes, mais les cantons. Et il s'agit de régler leurs rapports avec la Confédération. La culture et l'enseignement échoient aux cantons et l'usage des langues en ressort. Or, l'histoire des cantons romands présente une grande diversité de rapports avec les cantons alémaniques et au-delà, avec l'Allemagne, qui a conduit à des formes très variées de l'enseignement de l'allemand dans chacun d'entre eux (von Flüe-Fleck 1994).

C'est donc un Etat démocratique qu'il s'agit de fonder, sur le plan cantonal, comme sur le plan fédéral. L'idée nationale telle que la concevait les philosophes du XVIIIe siècle liait étroitement la langue et les institutions étatiques. Le processus de sécularisation consistait à la fois à dégager les institutions de l'emprise ecclésiastique et de renouer le lien social par une culture et une langue communes. On observe dans les textes de l'époque un usage du mot national opposé à clérical. Il peut aussi s'appliquer aux institutions cantonales lorsque celles-ci sont investies de la dimension constitutionnelle que leur donne les libéraux arrivés au pouvoir. Nationaliser revient en l'occurrence à capter la demande d'instruction — particulièrement forte pour l'apprentissage des langues étrangères — et de contribuer ainsi à renforcer le crédit encore fragile de l'instruction publique. Il s'agit d'attirer dans les établissements publics la plus grande partie de l'élite qui ne se montre pas unanimement favorable à la nouvelle institution et privilégie l'enseignement des pensionnats privés ou les formes archaïques de l'apprentissage des langues étrangères par des séjours à l'étranger, des bonnes d'enfants allophones ou des cours particuliers. Par la publication de matériel pédagogique, dans toutes les disciplines confondues, les professeurs des établissements publics affirmeront leur expertise et leur légitimité dans les questions d'enseignement.

Le terme national revêt une telle acuité dans les discours que les partisans des humanités classiques affirment à leur tour l'excellence du latin comme langue nationale, alors même que, généralement, le latin n'a plus la valeur de langue véhiculaire parmi les lettrés et les savants. L'argumentation est particulièrement visible dans les débats qui suivent l'entrée de Genève dans la Confédération helvétique, en 1815. Chez eux, la majorité germanophone de la Suisse ne constitue pas une raison suffisante pour introduire des cours d'allemand au collège. En effet, les langues modernes répondent à des intérêts particuliers, forcément divergents, estiment-ils. Elles divisent la nation en fonction des nombreux intérêts différents: pour des raisons privées, certains voudront apprendre l'allemand, d'autres l'anglais ou l'italien. Alors que le latin, également inutile et nécessaire à tous, créé les conditions, dit-on alors, d'unifier l'instruction publique ou du moins l'institution gymnasiale, dans son rôle de formation de l'élite, et ainsi d'édifier la nation (Extermann 2013: 45-52).

Longtemps encore, le latin jouera ce rôle fédérateur de l'élite du pays, même après l'introduction des langues modernes dans les plans d'études. À partir de 1880, l'étude du latin devient le critère déterminant du premier diplôme fédéral (maturité / *Maturität* ou *Matur*) qui règle l'accès aux études de médecine et à l'Ecole polytechnique de Zurich. L'allemand fait bien entendu partie du catalogue des disciplines des examens de maturité, mais joue un rôle accessoire par rapport à la langue latine (Meylan 1997).

Dans les discussions de la première moitié du XIXe siècle sur l'introduction des langues modernes, la distinction entre dialecte et langage standard ne joue pas un rôle déterminant. Dans les débats parlementaires, certains députés réticents évoquent certes la diglossie alémanique comme un obstacle gênant. Aucun partisan de l'introduction des langues vivantes ne propose cependant l'enseignement du dialecte, tant il paraît évident que le standard des langues nationales n'est pas la langue parlée mais la langue écrite. Par ailleurs, le mouvement romantique, parce qu'il exalte la communauté des peuples de même langue, incite les Suisses alémaniques à se reprocher de la *koinè* germanophone. La discussion porte davantage sur la qualité, la régularité et la stabilité des langues vernaculaires en comparaison des langues anciennes. Au début du XIXe siècle, la langue allemande est parvenue à un état d'élaboration tel que l'on peut vanter sa grammaire, ainsi que sa littérature, comme tout aussi apte à contribuer à la formation intellectuelle des jeunes gens que le grec et le latin. À cette nouvelle qualité intrinsèque de la langue s'ajoute l'attrait qu'exercent les universités allemandes par le renouvellement des *sciences* que sont à l'époque la philosophie, la théologie et la philologie (Extermann 2013: 53-59).

Deuxième moitié du XIXe siècle: affermissement de l'instruction publique

L'enseignement de la deuxième langue nationale se généralise en Suisse à partir de la fin des années 1840. Un régime radical s'implante dans la majorité des cantons, mais ni les nouvelles institutions, ni la place des langues modernes au sein des écoles ne sont encore fortement établies. Le Collège (Gymnase) de Genève, pourtant fort d'une vénérable tradition, connaît d'importantes défections d'élèves, surtout dans la nouvelle filière industrielle et commerciale sans latin. Or, une des causes de retrait dont se plaignent les autorités est le départ d'élèves en Allemagne pour y apprendre l'allemand par leurs propres moyens (Extermann 2013: 44, 54; Gyr 1989: 197-222). La place de l'allemand dans les plans d'études est remise en cause par le corps professoral, en particulier dans la filière classique. Dans les petits établissements secondaires qui se multiplient en Suisse romande, le recrutement et le financement d'enseignants qualifiés est un défi majeur. Encore l'allemand parvient-il à se maintenir, en comparaison des enseignements de l'anglais et de l'italien qui avaient été introduits en divers écoles et qui pour la plupart d'entre eux, disparaissent avant de revenir lors de la création des écoles de commerce, dans le dernier quart du XIXe siècle.

Dans cette période intermédiaire, l'allemand va s'efforcer de faire oublier l'apprentissage naturel, autrement dit les méthodes pratiques dont il est l'héritier, pour s'aligner sur les exigences d'une étude des règles, conforme à l'enseignement des langues mortes. La question du dialecte alémanique est du coup complètement éclipsée, pour deux motifs liés: sa divergence de la norme grammaticale et son aspect essentiellement oral. L'institution est occupée pour l'heure à *nationaliser* l'enseignement de l'allemand, ce qui représente déjà un effort considérable.

L'enseignement grammatical, même s'il sera fustigé par la génération suivante qui l'accusera de faire des langues vivantes des langues mortes, a rendu un fier service à leur établissement dans l'enseignement secondaire. La grammaire participe véritablement à la nationalisation des langues au travers de l'enseignement secondaire. Elle établit et confirme une norme unifiante qui n'était pas donnée a priori. L'élaboration de grammaires nationales était certes un facteur de stabilisation, mais le développement d'outils spécifiques à chacune d'entre elles conduisait à des divergences (Lauwers 2005; Auroux 1994). La tradition des humanités classiques, malgré sa vigueur, ne suffisait plus à garantir la cohérence des langues enseignées dans l'enseignement secondaire. Dès les années 1850 et périodiquement désormais, des efforts vont être entrepris au sein des établissements scolaires les plus importants pour harmoniser la terminologie grammaticale (Collège cantonal 1850).

La recherche et le soin d'une norme commune doit permettre la cohérence entre les différents enseignements nécessaire à la crédibilité de l'institution. La grammaire remplit également une fonction structurante, car elle contribue grandement au découpage des programmes scolaires, en classes, en degrés, en leçons, ce qui est une des conditions majeures du bon fonctionnement de l'école publique.

Tournant du XXe siècle — *Heimatschutz*: protéger le patrimoine national

La fin du XIXe siècle voit un nouvel essor de l'enseignement scolaire dans les pays occidentaux et ce mouvement coïncide avec la réforme de l'enseignement des langues vivantes que prônent nombre de pédagogues novateurs. Le développement des échanges économiques et des administrations publiques crée un besoin accru d'apprentissage des langues étrangères. De façon plus précise, trois mouvements au tournant du XXe siècle conduisent à une redéfinition de l'allemand scolaire: l'évolution de l'idéologie nationaliste, la valorisation des cultures populaires, la réforme de l'enseignement des langues vivantes.

La montée des nationalismes européens va aboutir à la Première Guerre mondiale et à la dissolution des empires plurinationaux. Bien qu'il exacerbe la culture nationale au détriment des cultures voisines, ce mouvement soutient cependant le développement de l'enseignement des langues vivantes, puisque l'on attend de l'apprentissage des langues étrangères une meilleure connaissance de sa langue maternelle et de ses propres caractères nationaux (Gardt 2000b).

Le nationalisme connaît également une vision pittoresque et populaire qui s'exprime au mieux lors des expositions nationales. On y forge une vision idyllique de la patrie qui imprègne les manuels d'apprentissage des langues qui sont du reste parfois primés à cette occasion. Dans ce contexte, la Suisse alémanique connaît alors ce que les historiens de la langue nomment la première vague dialectale qu'ils rattachent symboliquement à la création en 1905 du *Heimatschutz*, une association pour la sauvegarde du patrimoine national, tant de ses paysages et de son habitat, que de ses coutumes et de ses traditions. Ce mouvement touche aussi le dialecte, dont on découvre et met en valeur la richesse et la fonction identitaire (Schläpfer 1985: 90-92).

Enfin, les manuels de la méthode directe, issus de la réforme de l'enseignement des langues vivantes, tentent de répondre non seulement aux nouvelles exigences de maîtrise pratique des langues étrangères, au développement de la phonétique et de la psychologie, mais ils s'efforcent aussi de diffuser une image patriotique de la nation. La généralisation de l'enseignement de l'allemand en Suisse romande est suffisamment importante pour susciter la production de manuels locaux qui s'adaptent aux conditions particulières d'un nationalisme helvétique censé réunir une population de langues différentes. Les manuels d'histoire littéraire de Schenker et Hasler cités plus loin en sont une belle illustration. De même, pour le niveau élémentaire, les manuels du Genevois Lescaze ou un peu plus tard du Vaudois Briod qui adaptent un format méthodologique international aux exigences nationales.

Les autorités fédérales s'inquiètent en effet des nombreuses dissensions qui divisent le pays au fur à mesure que montent les tensions entre la France et l'Allemagne et interpellent les écoles, afin qu'elles contribuent à une meilleure cohésion nationale. Les professeurs, réunis en conférence, s'interrogent sur la manière de répondre à cette demande, dans chaque discipline (Falke 1914; Barth 1920; Extermann 2013: 165-69). Certains enseignants se montrent toutefois réticents: l'éducation nationale représente pour eux une finalité utilitaire voire idéologique qui s'accommode mal de l'universalisme humaniste du gymnase.

Au début du XXe siècle, les hésitations entre repli, positions partisanes et ouvertures sont bien perceptibles dans les différents secteurs de l'enseignement. Les normes linguistiques de l'allemand, le canon de la littérature scolaire, les méthodes scolaires sont remises en question. Et la période est favorable à la créativité pédagogique. Des cours facultatifs de dialecte sont instaurés, bien qu'ils soient rares. On chante, on joue à l'aide de marionnettes des pièces en dialecte (Extermann 2013: 403-05). De même des échanges scolaires sont organisés, pour permettre un contact vivant avec la langue parlée, mais ces tentatives échouent en raison des conflits. Des auteurs suisses sont inscrits désormais au programme, mais pour l'instant, on retient ceux qui, comme Keller et Gotthelf, s'expriment en allemand littéraire.

Mais dans l'ensemble pourtant, le standard culturel et linguistique ressort peu ébranlé de ces débats et de ces innovations du début du XXe siècle. Les professeurs d'allemand d'origine alémanique sont certes à présent très majoritaires dans le corps enseignant, à l'inverse de leurs devanciers un siècle plus tôt, dont le plus grand nombre venait d'Allemagne. Leur identification plus résolument helvétique ne contredit pas frontalement leur attachement à la culture allemande. Par ailleurs, l'intérêt pour les dialectes n'est pas une exclusivité alémanique. La dialectologie est une science éminemment internationale et beaucoup de professeurs d'allemand des cantons francophones contribuent avec zèle au recensement des patois de Suisse romande (Extermann 2013: 137-40)!

Le besoin de stabilité de l'institution scolaire, dans un environnement social et politique troublé, n'incite pas à des changements fondamentaux dans l'enseignement des langues nationales. Une raison majeure de ce repli est le purisme qui s'applique aux différents idiomes parlés en Suisse dans la première moitié du XXe siècle. En Suisse allemande, le souci de préservation de la pureté des langues impose une distinction nette entre les situations où se pratiquent le dialecte et l'allemand standard (à l'écrit essentiellement). En Suisse romande, le purisme consiste en revanche à se débarrasser autant que faire se peut de tout helvétisme — ou pire, de tout germanisme — dans son parler. Dans les deux cas, sous l'autorité de figures intellectuelles marquantes de l'époque (O. von Greyerz et G. de Reynold), le bilinguisme est proscrit, comme facteur de contamination des langues. On promeut alors une forme d'intercompréhension soutenue par une dialectique particulière de l'identité commune: chacun se fera comprendre de l'autre en utilisant sa propre langue et chaque Helvète apportera sa contribution à la culture nationale à condition qu'il conserve pur son particularisme culturel. Les tentatives d'initiation des élèves suisses romands aux dialectes alémaniques ne pouvaient pas, dans ce contexte, trouver un soutien politique et idéologique suffisant. L'idéal de la compréhension mutuelle par l'apprentissage de la langue de l'autre se voyait fixer une importante limite (Extermann 2013: 158-62).

1930–1950: le dialecte comme tentative d'émancipation nationale

En 1938, le romanche est érigé en langue nationale à côté de l'allemand, du français et de l'italien. Une distinction plus tranchée s'inscrit alors dans les discours entre langues nationales et langues officielles, le romanche relevant de la première et non de la seconde catégorie. Une évolution aboutit alors qui a fait passer le peuple suisse d'une conception des langues nationales jusqu'à présent assez pragmatique et institutionnelle, car subordonnée à la prérogative politique des cantons, à une conception chargée d'une plus grande valeur symbolique et identitaire. La Suisse se définit comme peuple quadrilingue, comme une alliance de minorités culturelles et linguistiques, en opposition aux totalitarismes (Widmer et al. 2004; Koller 2000: 563-609).

La politique agressive du régime nazi change la donne linguistique en Suisse alémanique qui connaît alors sa deuxième vague dialectale. Elle touche également l'enseignement de l'allemand en Suisse romande. L'opposition identitaire de la culture alémanique vis-à-vis de la culture allemande peut être illustrée par la comparaison de deux éditions du même manuel d'*Histoire de la littérature allemande* produite par deux enseignants genevois, M. Schenker et O. Hasler, l'une datant de 1917, l'autre de 1941.

En 1917, les auteurs semblent soucieux d'apaiser les tensions au sein de la Suisse entre pro-allemands et pro-français. Ils le font en montrant comment dialoguent les littératures françaises et allemandes au cours de l'histoire, et soulignent le rôle émancipateur qu'ont joué des lettrés alémaniques pour la littérature nationale allemande: Albrecht von Haller, Johann Jacob Bodmer, Johann Jacob Breitinger, contre Gottsched qui plaçait le modèle français par-dessus tout.

De même, selon les auteurs du manuel, l'existence du dialecte est un fait allemand, davantage qu'une réalité helvétique. C'est la structure politique de l'Allemagne et l'histoire de la langue allemande qui l'expliquent: le dialecte alémanique comme expression de l'*Oberdeutsch* à côté des autres dialectes du vieil allemand, dans une fédération d'États indépendants.

Bref, en 1917, la menace d'une hégémonie culturelle viendrait encore et plutôt de la France, dans la tradition du XIXe siècle allemand, et la Suisse allemande construit son identité nationale de concert avec les voisins germanophones. Tel est du moins le reflet que donne le manuel littéraire de Schenker et Hasler.

Dans le contexte de 1941, il est beaucoup plus délicat d'affirmer que Suisses et Allemands ont contribué réciproquement à la culture nationale l'un de l'autre. Les auteurs ne pratiquent pas l'autocensure en retranchant des propos de leur manuel, mais ils ajoutent des éléments qui précisent comment les mêmes Haller et Bodmer tenaient à leur particularisme helvétique.

Ils ajoutent aussi une section à leur *Histoire de la littérature allemand* consacrée aux poètes alémaniques ayant écrit en dialecte, qui n'existe pas dans l'édition de 1917. Le suisse alémanique n'est plus un dialecte parmi d'autres. Son ancienneté lui donne une légitimité supérieure à l'allemand moderne. Et ce dialecte devient *eigentliches nationales Idiom*, un idiome national de fait. Les auteurs ne nient pas l'existence d'une littérature suisse en haut allemand, mais ils insistent sur une évolution qui leur semble porteuse d'avenir, en saluant l'avènement d'une poésie dialectale.

Dans les années 1930, le débat sur la place respective de l'allemand standard met au jour trois positions. La plus radicale demande l'affranchissement du Suisse alémanique comme langue dotée de sa propre langue standard et d'une langue écrite spécifique. Emil Baer en est le partisan le plus engagé, par son adaptation de l'écriture pour la transcription des différents dialectes alémaniques. Le professeur zurichois Eugen Dieth et son mouvement *Bund Schwyzertütsch* opposent au précédent une vision plus modérée. Dieth rédige en 1938 des indications pour la transcription écrite du suisse allemand, mais garde ses distances avec l'idée de le substituer à l'allemand écrit qui conduirait à la disparition des particularités dialectales. La diglossie est perçue comme une richesse, sans qu'il faille renoncer à la pratique écrite, et même orale, de l'allemand standard.

La première position perd rapidement du terrain, mais la deuxième se voit à son tour dépassée par une troisième version plus défensive: le maintien de la diglossie fait figure de compromis, en repoussant l'allemand standard au seul registre écrit. Arthur Baur publie en 1939 une grammaire du suisse alémanique à l'attention des personnes intéressées de l'apprendre comme une langue étrangère. Les professeurs Schenker et Hedinger (un collègue lausannois) s'y réfèrent explicitement dans leur propre cours de dialecte alémanique paru en 1941: *Reded Schwîtzertütsch*. Ils lui reprennent la revendication du Suisse alémanique comme cinquième langue nationale de fait.

1945–1990: montée du dialecte et développement des langues internationales

Désormais, le dialecte alémanique a acquis un statut nouveau, par la mise au point de sa forme écrite. Des manuels pour son apprentissage sont conçus, non seulement pour les participants à des cours privés de langue, en Suisse alémanique (Baur), mais aussi pour l'enseignement publique en Suisse romande (Schenker et Hedinger). Le manuel de Baur connaît un succès remarquable jusqu'à nos jours, puisqu'il connaît sa 13ᵉ édition en 2008. Le second manuel destiné aux élèves francophones ne connaît en revanche qu'une réédition en 1949. L'évolution des prochaines décennies confirme cette tendance: des publications pour les participants à des cours de langues privés se voient rééditées, au contraire de celles qui s'adressent aux élèves de l'instruction publique.

Dans les années 60, la Suisse connaît une troisième vague dialectale. Elle est suscitée par un ensemble complexe de facteurs, qui relèvent d'une évolution mondiale: la valorisation du régionalisme, la recherche de nouveaux modes de vie et de formes d'expression alternatives, la contestation de l'hégémonie culturelle et de ses normes, le passage d'une conception patrimoniale de la culture (au moins dans les manuels) à une conception anthropologique et interculturelle de la *Landeskunde*, de la *civilisation*.

Par ailleurs, l'assouplissement des normes linguistiques et l'émergence de pratiques pédagogiques alternatives, l'ouverture des programmes scolaires semblent des facteurs favorables à une prise en compte du dialecte dans l'enseignement de l'allemand. À quoi s'ajoute la valorisation des compétences orales dans les manuels de langue étrangère depuis de nombreuses années, avec l'accès facilité à de nombreuses sources orales et audiovisuelles par les nouvelles technologies de la communication. L'enseignement de l'allemand va-t-il suivre cette tendance et redéfinir sa contribution à la cohésion nationale?

Une nouvelle fois, cette troisième vague ne constitue pas une condition suffisante pour l'enseignement durable du dialecte alémanique en Suisse romande. Il nous faut encore mieux en explorer les raisons. La coloration alémanique de l'enseignement de l'allemand en Suisse romande se manifeste surtout par la présence massive des deux auteurs phares dans les lectures des collégiens, Max Frisch (1911-1991) et Friedrich Dürrenmatt (1921-1990). Mais la langue dans laquelle ils écrivent et la stature internationale qu'ils gagnent n'ont que peu de choses en commun avec les auteurs d'expression dialectale.

L'enseignement des langues vivantes prend un développement différent. Sa contribution au lien social sera différente également. Au niveau primaire, la volonté de mettre en valeur le plurilinguisme croissant des élèves au sein des écoles du pays et de tirer parti de la capacité d'apprentissage des jeunes enfants de nombreux programmes d'initiation précoce aux langues ont pris différentes formes. De plus, des cours de 'langues et cultures d'origine' (LCO) visant à l'intégration des élèves issus de la migration ont vu le jour. Au niveau secondaire, le certificat de maturité moderne, permettant l'étude de l'italien notamment, est enfin reconnu en 1972. Ce mouvement se poursuivra à la fin des années 1990, lorsque l'espagnol deviendra à son tour une branche de maturité et lorsque des établissements toujours plus nombreux s'ouvriront à des formes d'enseignement bilingue.

Au cours de cette période, l'institution scolaire a sans doute renforcé sa dimension plurilingue en développant l'enseignement des langues, soit en étendant le catalogue des choix proposés, soit en élargissant la palette des moyens pédagogiques employés. Il faut noter que ce développement n'a pas résolu le statut des langues nationales minoritaires en Suisse (italien et romanche), qui plus que jamais craignent pour leur statut voire pour leur existence.

Actualité, mise en perspective et conclusion: le Luxembourg en comparaison

Depuis les années 1990, le mouvement de la mondialisation donne une tournure nouvelle aux rapports entre les langues dans l'espace social. Il apparaît dès lors opportun de mettre d'une part en perspective l'histoire retracée précédemment par l'évocation des questions actuelles sur l'enseignement des langues en Suisse, et par la comparaison avec un autre pays européen multilingue, le Luxembourg, d'autre part.

De façon notoire, la montée de la mondialisation renforce l'importance déjà ancienne de l'anglais comme langue mondiale. Il est vrai que par elle-même cette donnée exerce une pression sur l'enseignement des langues en général, en Suisse alémanique surtout, où l'anglais est passé dans plusieurs cantons au rang de première langue étrangère enseignée à l'école obligatoire, devant le français. Mais il y a plus: la mondialisation de l'économie et les avancées de l'intégration européenne s'accompagnent d'un mouvement de standardisation jusqu'au niveau scolaire.

Les accords bilatéraux signés dans les années 2000 ont notamment accentué l'immigration d'une population allemande en Suisse alémanique et ainsi la pratique de l'allemand standard en Suisse. Dans le même temps, les études standardisées PISA ont eu un contrecoup sur l'enseignement de l'allemand en Suisse alémanique. L'enquête PISA de 2000 révélait des insuffisances dans la maîtrise de la langue écrite chez les jeunes alémaniques. Les autorités politiques ont réagi par le renforcement de l'allemand standard à l'école obligatoire, au détriment du dialecte.

Pour augmenter l'efficience du système scolaire en Suisse, la Conférence des directeurs de l'instruction publique acceptait en 2007 le principe d'une plus grande harmonisation scolaire. Le concordat HARMOS qui en est ressorti et qui a été ratifié par une majorité de cantons préconise notamment l'avancement de l'obligation scolaire à l'âge de quatre ans. De nouveaux plans d'études intercantonaux s'alignent aussi sur l'exigence de deux langues étrangères enseignées successivement dès l'école primaire.

Or, cette double exigence s'est heurtée à une même résistance dans les cantons alémaniques. D'abord, l'introduction d'une langue étrangère supplémentaire à l'école primaire a fait craindre une surcharge des programmes: la pression sur le français comme première langue étrangère nationale a augmenté dès lors. Ensuite, la crainte de voir à son tour le *Kindergarten* devenu obligatoire, régi par des lois linguistiques conduisant à l'extension de l'enseignement du *Hochdeutsch* a amené une vague de votations pour généraliser le dialecte à ce niveau d'enseignement. L'engagement croissant d'éducatrices de langue allemande a accentué le sentiment de dépossession des dialectophones. Même si ces décisions de principes n'ont pas eu de grands effets sur les pratiques effectives dans les *Kindergarten*, toujours caractérisées par un usage souple du dialecte et de l'allemand standard, elles ont eu un impact symbolique important (Büchi 2015). Du côté suisse romand, une sensibilisation aux dialectes alémaniques a été intégrée aux cours d'allemand, dans une des filières du secondaire I à Genève. Il s'agit d'une tentative isolée. De manière générale en Suisse, le dialecte n'entre toujours pas dans les plans d'études de l'école publique ou à l'intérieur des disciplines linguistiques de façon formalisée.

L'ouverture de l'économie mondiale, la mobilité des populations au sein de l'Union européenne et les défis de l'intégration au sein de chaque société mettent en tension l'usage des dialectes, des langues nationales et internationales, défis qui se répercutent particulièrement dans les premiers degrés scolaires. En Suisse, ces tensions engendrent un débat marqué par l'inquiétude des uns et des autres. En revanche, les Luxembourgeois semblent vivre cette tension de façon plus optimiste que les Suisses, dans la mesure où aucune des langues officielles du Grand-Duché n'apparaît comme menacée, d'après l'enquête de Fehlen (2009), et que les capacités plurilingues de la population s'accroissent, avec une population étrangère encline à l'apprentissage du luxembourgeois. Il est donc opportun d'engager une comparaison entre les deux pays.

Le Luxembourg est devenu bilingue en se développant de part et d'autres de la frontière linguistique entre les aires romane et germanique par le jeu des acquisitions territoriales au gré des mariages et des alliances au milieu du XIIe siècle déjà. Pourtant, il s'agit d'un 'bilinguisme juxtaposé' (Trausch 2003) et la maîtrise des deux langues n'était l'apanage que d'une petite minorité. En cela, le Luxembourg et l'ancienne Confédération helvétique partagent les mêmes caractéristiques.

Leur situation respective commence à se distinguer au début du XIXe siècle. La Suisse moderne naît d'une part de l'entrée dans la Confédération de nouveaux territoires de langues romanes et d'autre part de l'accession de territoires autrefois subordonnés au rang de cantons de plein droit. Ainsi, en plusieurs étapes, la Suisse devient-elle officiellement un pays tri- puis quadrilingue. A l'inverse, le développement et la reconnaissance du trilinguisme luxembourgeois s'effectue à l'époque où le Grand-Duché perd ses territoires francophones. Après avoir dû céder une partie d'entre eux à la France en 1659, puis les territoires de l'Est à la Prusse, lors du Congrès de Vienne, la création de la Belgique entraîne la cession de l'actuelle province wallonne de Luxembourg, en 1838.

Dans un contexte idéologique nationaliste où les questions linguistiques sont de plus en plus politisées, le Luxembourg, indépendant depuis 1815 et dont le territoire est désormais entièrement dans l'aire germanophone, prend la décision insolite et courageuse de décréter l'apprentissage du français obligatoire à l'école primaire (loi de 1843). Sur le plan politique, il s'agissait d'affirmer son indépendance vis-à-vis des pays germaniques voisins, puisque le Luxembourg fera partie jusqu'en 1866 de la Confédération germanique. Sur le plan pratique, il s'agissait de ne pas se couper des liens ancestraux qui liaient la population du Luxembourg à celles de l'Ouest francophone. Sur le plan administratif et législatif, la plus grande aisance des juristes et de l'élite économique plaidait pour une prédominance de fait du français qui se traduira ultérieurement par un usage exclusif du français comme langue législative écrite.

Dans le monde professionnel et dans le cadre de l'Église, l'allemand est cependant privilégié par les Luxembourgeois. Ils adhèrent au *Zollverein* entre 1842 et 1918 et bénéficient d'un large espace d'échange qui, lorsque sont mis à jour d'importantes ressources minières et grâce au chemin de fer, permettra l'exportation de l'acier et l'importation du charbon qui lui manque. L'expansionnisme allemand a été certes une menace, en particulier lorsque le pays a fait l'objet d'une occupation militaire lors des deux conflits mondiaux. Cependant, les Luxembourgeois ont trouvé dans la particularité de leur dialecte l'occasion d'une résistance culturelle ayant finalement conforté leur sentiment d'appartenance nationale.

Le Luxembourg entretient donc comme la Suisse une relation en tension entre attirance et résistance vis-à-vis de l'Allemagne et de la France. Dans ce jeu identitaire, le dialecte joue aussi un rôle. Mais à la différence de la Suisse, le *Lëtzebuergesch* prend en deux siècles le développement d'une véritable langue nationale, statut qu'il acquiert formellement en 1984.

La pratique du luxembourgeois s'est renforcée au cours du XXe siècle et le gouvernement s'efforce d'en faire une langue d'intégration, sans que la société et l'école luxembourgeoises aient dû renoncer à la pratique des langues allemandes et françaises ainsi qu'à leur participation de plus en plus large aux institutions européennes. Pourtant, il est à remarquer qu'en dépit d'un plurilinguisme bien institutionnalisé, le dialecte luxembourgeois partage avec le suisse alémanique un traitement semblable, sur le plan scolaire. Le luxembourgeois sert de langue de socialisation dans les premiers degrés de scolarité et garde son rôle dans les degrés supérieurs. A partir de 1912 a été introduit une heure d'enseignement du luxembourgeois, sans que la langue soit étudiée dans toute sa spécificité, la distinction entre l'allemand écrit et parlé restant ambiguë. Entretemps, la langue et la culture luxembourgeoises sont également étudiées à l'Université du Luxembourg. Mais actuellement encore, le luxembourgeois ne fait pas l'objet d'une formalisation didactique semblable aux autres enseignements des langues, quand bien même sa plus grande homogénéité linguistique, en comparaison du suisse alémanique le lui permettrait. Pour les Luxembourgeois, la langue d'alphabétisation reste l'allemand et le gouvernement a évalué récemment l'opportunité de permettre une alphabétisation en français à la population immigrée de langue romane en croissance (Ammon 2015; Schanen 2004).

La complexité des sociétés fortement multilingues comme, parmi d'autres, le Luxembourg et la Suisse incitent les chercheurs à recourir à de nouveaux outils comme la *super-diversité* qui prennent en compte une multiplicité de facteurs sociaux (Berg et al. 2013; Vertovec 2007). De fait, le lien entre langue et nation auquel contribuait l'enseignement public des langues dites nationales pour créer de la cohésion au sein de sociétés présentant leur diversité propre semble ne plus suffire aujourd'hui. Dès lors, on observe les mêmes hésitations de l'instruction publique vis-à-vis du luxembourgeois au Luxembourg comme du dialecte en Suisse, ainsi que sur l'enseignement des langues majoritaires, nationales et internationales, dans leur articulation les unes par rapport aux autres.

Le parcours qui nous a conduits à travers deux siècles d'histoire permet ainsi de déplacer l'accent dans le débat sur l'enseignement des langues. Il importe de distinguer langue nationale et cohésion nationale. Leur lien n'est pas immédiat, il ne se mesure pas simplement à la 'bonne compréhension' des Suisses les uns avec les autres, ni à l'utilité variable des langues les unes par rapport aux autres. Ce lien est au contraire médiatisé par les institutions, scolaires, en particulier. L'instruction publique a réussi à affirmer sa place parmi les institutions politiques helvétiques. Or, au cours de son histoire, il est arrivé à l'instruction publique de favoriser d'autres langues que la deuxième langue nationale à fins de cohésion nationale: le latin, puis, d'une manière différente, la langue maternelle de chaque Confédéré. Longtemps, les langues vivantes quelles qu'elles soient ont occupé une position fragile dans les écoles secondaires. L'intégration dans l'instruction publique de plusieurs langues, simultanément ou successivement, est restée néanmoins un défi constant dans l'histoire de l'institution. Aujourd'hui, en raison de la complexité linguistique croissante de nos sociétés, cette intégration ne peut probablement plus s'effectuer par le seul élargissement de l'offre des cours de langues, mais doit se faire par une éducation plurilingue qui problématise la complexité et la richesse des phénomènes linguistiques. Cette ouverture plurilingue est propre à renforcer la vocation citoyenne dont l'instruction publique a la charge. Elle poursuit et élargit par là-même le mandat de cohésion nationale qu'avait reçu l'enseignement public au XIXe siècle.

Bibliography

AMMON, U. 2015. *Die Stellung der deutschen Sprache in der Welt* (Berlin: de Gruyter)

ANDERSON, B. 1983. *Imagined Communities: Reflections on the Origin and Spread of Nationalism* (London: Verso)

AUROUX, S. 1994. *La Révolution technologique de la grammatisation: introduction à l'histoire des sciences du langage* (Liège: Mardaga)

BAER, E. 1936. *Alemannisch: Die Rettung der eidgenössischen Seele* (Zurich: Rascher)

BARTH, A. 1920. *Les Collèges et les Gymnases de la Suisse: projets de réformes*, trans. by Charles Gilliard (Lausanne; Geneva: Payot)

BAUR, A. 1939. *Schwyzertüütsch: Praktische Sprachlehre des Schweizerdeutschen* (Zurich: Rigi)

BERG, C., M. MILMEISTER and C. WEIS. 2013. 'Superdiversität in Luxemburg?', in *Vielfalt der Sprachen — Varianz der Perspektiven: Zur Geschichte und Gegenwart der Luxemburger Mehrsprachigkeit*, ed. by H. Sieburg (Bielefeld: transcript), pp. 9-36

BRIOD, E. 1917. *Cours élémentaire de langue allemande* (Lausanne: Payot)

BÜCHI, C. 2015. *Mariage de raison. Romands et Alémaniques: une histoire suisse* (Geneva: Zoé)

COLLÈGE CANTONAL. 1850. *Principes généraux d'analyse grammaticale et d'analyse logique servant de base à une terminologie uniforme pour le français, le latin, le grec et l'allemand. Essai présenté par MM. les instituteurs du Collège cantonal et adopté par le Conseil de l'Instruction publique du Canton de Vaud, pour le Collège cantonal et les collèges communaux* (Lausanne: Genton, Luquiens)

DIETH, E. 1938. *Schwyzertütschi Dialäktschrift: Leitfaden nach den Beschlüssen der Schriftkommission der Neuen helvetischen Gesellschaft, Gruppe Zürich* (Zurich: Füssli)

ELMIGER, D., and S. FORSTER. 2005. *La Suisse face à ses langues: histoire et politique du plurilinguisme, situation actuelle de l'enseignement des langues* (Neuchâtel: IRDP)

EXTERMANN, B. 2009. 'Le Débat des langues dans l'enseignement secondaire en Suisse romande au XIXe siècle', *Documents pour l'histoire de l'enseignement du français langue étrangère et seconde*, 43: 81-98

———. 2013. *Une langue étrangère et nationale: histoire de l'enseignement de l'allemand en Suisse romande (1790–1940)* (Neuchâtel: Alphil)

FALKE, K. 1914. *Der schweizerische Kulturwille: Ein Wort an die Gebildeten des Landes*, Schriften für Schweizer Art und Kunst, 1 (Zurich: Rascher)

FEHLEN, F. 2009. *Baleine-Bis: une enquête sur un marché linguistique multilingue en profonde mutation* (Luxembourg: Sesopi)

FURRER, N. 2002. *Die vierzigsprachige Schweiz: Sprachkontakte und Mehrsprachigkeit in der vorindustriellen Gesellschaft (15.–19. Jahrhundert)* (Zurich: Chronos)

GARDT, A. 2000A. 'Nation und Sprache in der Zeit der Aufklärung', in *Nation und Sprache: Die Diskussion ihres Verhältnisses in Geschichte und Gegenwart*, ed. by A. Gardt (Berlin: de Gruyter), pp. 169-98

——. 2000B. 'Sprachnationalismus zwischen 1850 und 1945', in *Nation und Sprache: Die Diskussion ihres Verhältnisses in Geschichte und Gegenwart*, ed. by A. Gardt (Berlin: de Gruyter), pp. 247-71

GYR, U. 1989. *Lektion fürs Leben: Welschlandaufenthalte als traditionelles Bildungs-, Erziehungs- und Übergangsmuster* (Zurich: Chronos)

HELBLING, B. 1994. *Eine Schweiz für die Schule: Nationale Identität und kulturelle Vielfalt in den Schweizer Lesebüchern seit 1900* (Zurich: Cronos)

KOLLER, W. 2000.'Nation und Sprache in der Schweiz', in *Nation und Sprache: Die Diskussion ihres Verhältnisses in Geschichte und Gegenwart*, ed. by A. Gardt (Berlin: de Gruyter), pp. 563-609

LAUWERS, P. 2005. 'La Description syntaxique du français à travers le prisme des traditions grammaticales françaises et allemandes', in *Les Cultures éducatives et linguistiques dans l'enseignement des langues*, ed. by J.-Cl. Beacco et al. (Paris: PUF), pp. 47-67

LESCAZE A. 1898-1905. *Lehrbuch für den Unterricht in der deutschen Sprache auf Grundlage der Anschauung*, 3 vols (Geneva: Atar)

MEYLAN, J.-P. 1997. 'Die Maturitäts-Anerkennungs-Verordnung (MAV): Grundlage des ältesten schweizerischen Schulabschlusszeugnisses', in *La Conférence suisse des directeurs cantonaux de l'instruction publique, 1897 à 1997: sa création, son histoire, son œuvre*, ed. by Hans Badertscher (Bern: Haupt), pp. 54-59

ROUILLER, V. 2013. 'A la croisée de deux cultures, nationale et étrangère: histoire de la discipline scolaire de l'allemand en Suisse romande (1830-1990)' (unpublished doctoral thesis, University of Geneva, ERHIDIS)

SCHANEN, F. 2004. *Parlons luxembourgeois: langue et culture linguistique d'un petit pays au cœur de l'Europe* (Paris: L'Harmattan)

SCHENKER, M, and O. HASLER. 1917 [1941]. *Einführung in die deutsche Literatur* (Lausanne: Payot)

——, and P. HEDINGER. 1941. *Reded Schwîtzertütsch* (Lausanne: Payot)

SCHLÄPFER, R. 1985. *La Suisse aux quatre langues* (Genève: Zoé)

TRAUSCH, G. (ed.). 2003. *Histoire du Luxembourg: le destin européen d'un 'petit pays'* (Toulouse: Privat)

VERTOVEC, S. 2007. 'Super-diversity and its Implications', *Ethnic and Racial Studies*, 30: 1024-64

VON FLÜE-FLECK, H. P. 1994. *Deutschunterricht in der Westschweiz: Geschichte, Lehrwerke, Perspektiven* (Aarau: Sauerländer)

WIDMER, J. 2004. *Langues nationales et identités collectives: l'exemple de la Suisse* (Paris: L'Harmattan)

——, et al. 2004. *Die Schweizer Sprachenvielfalt im öffentlichen Diskurs — La diversité des langues en Suisse dans le débat public* (Bern: Lang)

CHAPTER 9

An Overview of the History of German Language Learning and Teaching in the Iberian Peninsula, with a Particular Focus on Textbooks for German as a Language for Special Purposes (LSP) in Spain

Bernd Marizzi

This chapter sheds new light on the historiography of the German language in Spain and Portugal by surveying works which have previously been neglected. The overview presented here relates to a recent project to compile and publish an analytical annotated bibliography of grammars, teaching manuals for German, and lexicographical works for Portuguese–German and Spanish–German published in the Iberian Peninsula between the end of the eighteenth century and approximately 1970, when foreign publishers expanded throughout Europe and local publication of works of this type was considerably reduced (see Marizzi and Fuentes, forthcoming). The different parts of the chapter treat, in turn: the general development of the learning and teaching of German in Spain; the growing interest in German at the end of the nineteenth century, with a special focus on materials for 'German for Academic Purposes'; German–Spanish lexicography; and a brief history of the learning of German in Portugal.

Introduction

This chapter examines the history of the teaching and learning of German in the Iberian Peninsula. One of the main goals pursued here is to fulfil, at least partially, the calls by Glück (2002: 233-44; 2013: 502) for specialized studies that offer an overview of the history of German for Spanish and Portuguese learners. I examine, in particular, the case of the teaching of German in Spain over the last two centuries, with the intention of addressing, also, the need expressed by McLelland and Smith (2014: 1) for further research into the history of language learning and teaching (HoLLT) in Europe. Although there have been some substantial investigations of

HoLLT in Spain such as Lépinette (2000) for French and the unpublished thesis by Lombardero Caparrós (2015) for English, for German there has been little research to date.

The beginnings of any substantial German learning in Spain can be found in the development of a view that German was the language of philosophy and science. The important role of Germany in certain fields (military and scientific) promoted the development of textbooks for learning German for 'special purposes' in the first half of the twentieth century, in particular. These will be focused on, together with some lexicographical publications; and the chapter ends with a brief additional discussion of the history of learning German in Portugal.

Earliest Examples of Learning German in Spain

Language contacts between the German-speaking countries and Spain existed from the late Middle Ages onwards, but the relevant secondary literature (Glück 2013: 501-16; 2014: 51) reveals that Spanish was much more frequently learned in German-speaking countries than German in Spain. Both the late entry of the German language into the circle of the important cultural languages and the political supremacy of the Spanish Empire during the sixteenth to the eighteenth centuries explain this difference. Spain's geographical proximity to France and the kinship between French and Spanish as Romance languages are undoubtedly responsible for the traditional predominance of the French language in foreign-language learning in Spain.

Up to the eighteenth century, the basic incentive for learning a foreign language was the direct benefit one could obtain from the new possibilities of understanding native speakers. In this context, one of the earliest surviving books for learning German is the *Vocaboulari molt profitos per aprendre Lo Catalan Alemany y Lo Alemany Catalan* published in 1502 by Hans Rosembach (1470-c. 1530). Rosembach was one of the first German printers established in Perpignan, which at that time belonged to the territory of the Crown of Aragon.[1] German development of new technologies at this time, for example in mercury and cinnabar mining operations in Almadén (of fundamental economic interest for Spain), did not produce textbooks or any other material for learning German. Nor were any such materials produced when, during the reign of the Bourbon Charles IV (1788–1808), German mining engineers were sent with other European experts to Peru and Mexico to provide the silver mines in the colonies with the latest technology (Puig-Samper 2010).

Beginning in the late Middle Ages, and especially during the relatively regulated wars between princes, frequently involving mercenaries, which affected Europe during the period of absolute monarchies from the Peace of Westphalia (1648) to the French Revolution (1789), one of the strongest motivations for learning a foreign language was the need to be able to communicate with other soldiers within the same army. Until the idea of a linguistically unified national army appeared from the French Revolution onwards (Glück 2013: 363), mercenaries tended to be recruited by sovereigns for their armies. In the case of Spain, during the reign of Charles V (1500-1558; r. 1516/19-1554/56), such troops included the Lansquenets (*Guardia*

Alemana); and in the War of Spanish Succession (1708–14) the Swiss Regiments (*Regimientos Suizos*). Yet this language contact did not result in the production of learning or teaching materials in Spain.

First Interest in the German Language

Dynastic change from the Habsburgs to the Bourbons as a result of the Spanish War of Succession produced an even closer relationship with France; and the first grammars for learning German were not written in Spain until the late eighteenth century. The initial publication was the *Gramática Española y Alemana. Esto es: Reglas que enseñan el leer, pronunciar, entender, y hablar el Idioma Alemán*, a manuscript from 1783 which is kept in the archives of the episcopal palace in Vic, in Catalonia. Its author was Raymundo Strauch y Vidal (1760–1823), who later became Bishop of Vic and was one of the sons of the Silesian Sergeant Franz Strauch, stationed in Tarragona with the Swiss Regiment Betschart (Marizzi 2006) and briefly chaplain of the 3rd Swiss Regiment. The first printed grammar of German for Spanish learners appeared in Madrid in 1792: the *Gramática de la lengua alemana, dividida en tres partes* by Antonio de Villa, a Dominican and the so-called 'foreigners' priest' at Madrid's General Hospital.[2] Both grammars were based on different French originals, a phenomenon which is typical for the cultural production of Spain at this time and which continued to the beginning of the twentieth century. Only in the second half of the nineteenth century did the position of France as a filter in the import into Spain of German culture change slightly.

Around the end of the eighteenth century — following the French model — some of Spain's newly founded research institutions, such as the *Jardín Botánico* and the *Gabinete de Historia Natural* (the present-day Botanic Garden and Natural History Museum) were founded in Madrid. Both of these would later make contact with researchers from other European countries — among them Saxony, thanks to the family relationships of Charles IV, son of Princess Maria Amalia of Saxony. However, this contact was still mediated through French-speaking people, as in the case of the Swiss Johann Mieg (1779–1859), whom Fernando VII invited to Madrid in 1814 as a Professor of Physics at the *Real Gabinete de Física y Química*. In the middle of the century Mieg gave German lessons at the *Ateneo Científico y Literario* of Madrid (Cáceres and Marizzi 2010: 420). Here, the liberal bourgeoisie pursued the intellectual and political renewal of Spain. One of Mieg's colleagues was Julio Kühn (1813 Berlin–1854 Madrid), who was appointed in 1845 as the first Professor of German Language at the San Isidro High School, at that time under the auspices of the *Universidad Central*. Kühn's career in Spain (Marizzi 2009) can be taken as representative of a turn in the fortunes of German in Spain: although, up to that time, French culture was still predominant in all areas, there was an increasing interest in German culture and language in the first half of the nineteenth century. In exile in Paris during the reign of Fernando VII, Spanish liberals came into contact with liberal German expatriates and on their return to Spain the *Ateneo* became a meeting point of intellectuals struggling for national regeneration.

The turn in the fortunes of German in the first half of the nineteenth century occurred, then, in parallel with attempts by the radical-liberal branch of the bourgeoisie to free themselves from the power of the military, Church and Crown and to achieve not only a democratization of access to the sciences but also a democratization of society. In 1840, Kühn founded in Madrid an *Academia Española Alemana* with the motto 'Die Wissenschaften sind wie die Sonne, leuchten für Alle. Las ciencias son como el sol, Lucen para todos' [The sciences are like the sun: they shine for all] (Kühn 1840).[3] Members of the *Academia* were leading representatives of the Spanish intelligentsia.[4]

The new interest in German literature, culture and science found expression in the textbooks of German brought into use in the secondary schools which the State began to establish from 1845 onwards. In the preface of one such work, the reason given for learning German is to get 'la llave para abrir el depósito de los tesoros que encierra'(Kühn 1844: v) — in other words, the key to the treasures of the great intellectual achievements of German literature and the results of the German inventive spirit. Thus, the declared intention of the priest Juan Jorge Braun (born Johann Georg Braun in 1828 at Gründels in Wurttemberg, died *c.* 1875 in Spain) was to publish a treatise on the 'lengua alemana científica' (Braun 1864: iii), even though the orientation of his *Nueva gramática alemana* (1864) was in fact generalist rather than aiming at the acquisition of German for academic purposes (GAP).[5]

Nevertheless, Fernández de Castroverde, whose *Gramática Alemana* included numerous texts with a scientific topic, wrote in 1868:

> los hombres de la ciencias no dudan ya de que en la época presente es indispensable estudiar la lengua alemana para poder estar al corriente de los progresos intelectuales, porque ni todo se traduce, ni las pocas obras que se vierten á otros idiomas lo son con exactitud. (Fernández de Castroverde 1868: v-vi)

> [Men of science have no doubt that at the present time it is essential to study the German language in order to be aware of intellectual progress, because not everything is translated, nor are the few works translated into other languages accurately translated.]

It is worth noting that a student of Braun's at the *Real Colegio* of *El Escorial*, Francisco García Ayuso (1835-1897), took Oriental Studies and Philology courses with Martin Haug (1827-1876) in Munich. Ayuso is considered the founder of Indo-European Studies in Spain (see Álvarez-Pedrosa 1994: 57-63) and, in the introduction to his own *Gramática Alemana* (García Ayuso 1882: xx–xxx), he presented, at the very beginning of the book, a scientific text to practice reading by Dr. Reclam, the *Gute, reine Athemluft*. This is another indication of the increasing importance of these specialized scientific GAP texts, which in some textbooks outnumber even texts on literature, arts, politics or trade.

German as the Language of Philosophy and Science

From the second half of the nineteenth century onwards, the image of Germany that prevailed in Spain was dominated by notions of science, philosophy and university organization. The success of German culture and language went hand-in-hand with the German victory in the Franco-Prussian War. The idea that Spanish intellectuals had of Germany was strongly influenced by the activity of the philosopher Julián Sanz del Río (1814-1869), who, in 1843 to 1844, had studied at Heidelberg. After his return to Spain, he promoted the philosophical system of Karl Christian Friedrich Krause (1781-1832), who remained little known in Germany. Sanz del Río's publications aided in the creation of *Krausismo*, a philosophical school of thought which advocated for the renewal of Spanish intellectual life until the Civil War and served as a kind of secular substitute for religion (Stoetzer 1998). This import of a philosophical system from Germany and the adoption of the German academic system of organization in Spanish universities (Schwinges 2001) meant that in the period before the First World War Germanophilia became very strong in Spain.

This growing Spanish interest in Germany was aided by propaganda attempts from the German Empire, an emerging great power seeking to claim, in accordance with German nationalism, a 'place in the sun' not only in geopolitics but also in the fields of science and the Humanities. As a practical consequence, more students were sent to Germany and more German was learned in Spain for academic purposes, although this does not mean that the primacy of French as the first second language came to an end at the beginning of the twentieth century. Nevertheless, from 1900 for several decades the old Humanist dictum 'Bolonia docet' [Bologna teaches] was replaced with 'Germania docet' [Germany teaches] in academic circles, and German was considered *the* language of science.[6] In 1907, with the establishment of the *Junta para Ampliación de Estudios e Investigaciones Científicas* (the JAE, or Council for the Extension of Studies and Scientific Research), visits of Spanish scientists to other countries increased considerably. After France, Germany was the most visited country and the importance of language skills was expressed in the words of Spain's most famous chemist at this time, Enrique Moles: 'Un científico que, además del suyo, no conoce como mínimo dos idiomas, es un analfabeto' [A scientist who, apart from his own language, does not know at least two languages, is an uncultured person] (cited by Pérez-Vitoria 1985: 14). Throughout the time of the boycott declared by the winning nations of World War I (1919–1926), the two nations tried to maintain academic relations (Presas i Puig 2008).

The teaching of the German language in high schools was consolidated: students had to choose between German and English in the ever-changing curricula of the scientific branches; and German was also taught at the universities.[7] Indeed, the introduction of *lenguas vivas* [modern languages] into the curriculum of secondary schools (*Institutos de Enseñanza Secundaria*) explains the fact that the production of German-learning grammars in Spain was intensified during the first half of the twentieth century. After reaching its peak in the 1940s, these efforts were maintained until the 1960s, when most of the teaching material began to be produced abroad, especially in the Federal Republic of Germany.

Focus on German as a Language for Specific Purposes (LSP) in Spain

At the beginning of the twentieth century the increasing demand for professionally and technically oriented language training produced the first textbooks of German for specific purposes. The first of these works, as might be expected, was for the military. For Military Academy cadets, Cesáreo Olavarría Martínez (1863-1947) wrote in 1900 the first of two textbooks to be used at the *Academia de Administración Militar* in Ávila, where he himself taught German. An additional novelty and a veritable curiosity of his book for advanced learners, *Deutsche Sprachübungen*, is the fact that he used the German-handwriting letters as a graphic expression of German idiosyncrasy. For foreign learners this handwriting must have presented a very big additional difficulty in learning German. The book is printed entirely in *Kurrent* handwriting with the intention of 'acostumbrarle [al alumno, B.M.] á la lectura de documentos Manuscritos Alemanes' [accustoming [the student] to read handwritten German documents] (Olavarría 1900: iii).[8]

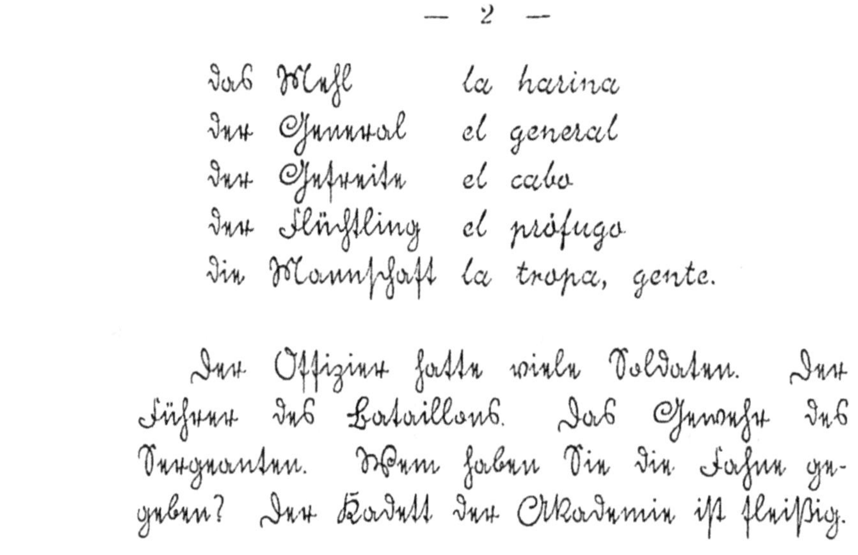

FIG 9.1. Extract from *Deutsche Sprachübungen* (1900) by Cesáreo Olavarría Martínez

The work consists of three parts — exercises, letters and war songs — but has no grammatical explanations. In the thirty exercises, a German–Spanish glossary is followed by readings on military science and different branches of the military (infantry, cavalry and artillery). This part is followed by private and commercial letters and war songs, including the nationalist song 'Wacht am Rhein'. At the end of the textbook there is a small dictionary of military expressions (*Kleines Wörterbuch militärischer Ausdrücke*), where the German words are set in the Gothic type *Fraktur* and the Spanish in Antiqua. No grammatical rules are taught; and the main focus is on military vocabulary.

The lack of grammatical rules in this textbook oriented to language for specific purposes (LSP) at the military academies led Olavarría a few years later to publish his *Gramatica Alemana Militar* (Ollavarría 1905, 1906) in two volumes. The motivation to promote German language skills among officers was not only the military supremacy of the German Empire, but also — considering the Spanish colonial disasters of loss of Cuba and the Philippines in 1898 — a desire to adapt the Prussian route from being a small German state to a European superpower as a model for a renewal of Spain:

> Sigamos el ejemplo de Alemania haciéndonos fuertes durante la paz [...] pues solamente llegando ser fuertes, es como se nos respetará. [...] Trabajemos con ahínco estudiando el idioma alemán para conocer en su verdadera fuente la organización de aquel poderoso ejército y los principios que han servido de base para su engrandecimiento. (Olavarria 1905: vii-viii)

> [Let us follow the example of Germany getting strong during times of peace [...] as only by growing strong will we be respected. [...] Let us work hard studying the German language to know in its true source the organization of this powerful army and the principles that have served as a basis for its enlargement.]

The dominance of the French language is relativized: 'Hoy no nos podemos contentar conociendo el francés, todo militar español está en la imprescindible obligación de conocer también el idioma alemán, ya que su ejército es el modelo en Europa' [Today we cannot be content knowing just the French language, all members of the Spanish military are under the imperative obligation also to know the German language, because its army is the model in Europe] (Olavarría 1905: iii).

This book presents disjointed sentences to exemplify grammar, very like the Ollendorff method, for example: 'Der Schütze hat ein Gewehr. Wo waren die Artilleristen? Sie sind nicht hier. Unsere Husaren, Ulanen und Kavalleristen' [The private has a rifle. Where were the artillerymen? They are not here. Our Hussars, Uhlans and cavalrymen] (Olavarría 1905: 39). Later on, militarily oriented translation exercises are increasingly introduced: 'In Deutschland sind die zwei Klassen der Berufsoffiziere und der Reserveoffiziere (= im Beurlaubtenstand) streng zu unterscheiden' [In Germany you must distinguish clearly between the two classes of professional officers and reserve officers (= on leave)] (Olavarría 1906: 71–72). In the last part of the second volume, the reading and translation pieces increasingly deal with the history of the Franco-Prussian War of 1870 to 1871. The appendix of this volume contains four lists: 1. Fixed expressions and idioms of the general language; 2. Commands and other military expressions; 3. Models for headings of private and official letters; 4. Military abbreviations.

As Spanish researchers' interest in German specialized texts increased, a new learner profile emerged, with new training materials being created for them. After 1916, several German for Academic Purposes (GAP) textbooks appeared in Barcelona. Their author, Richard Ratti (Berlin 1873–Barcelona 1945), had studied Japanese between 1893 and 1894 at the *Orientalisches Seminar* of the University of Berlin and, in the early years of the twentieth century, Chinese and Russian in Naples at the *Regio Instituto Orientale*. Around 1908 he settled in Barcelona where, as Richard Ratti-Kámeke,[9] he operated a language school giving classes in German, English, French and Japanese and where he wrote textbooks which together came to constitute an overall *Biblioteca Ratti* (cf. Marizzi 2011b). Apart from the inclusion of Japanese, the set was typical of the general situation of foreign-language teaching in the Spain at that time: the first foreign language across the country was French; English was the language of trade, technology and the textile industry; and German had a reputation for being the language of science (see the GAP textbooks by Ratti for Medicine: *Ejercicios de terminología Médica Alemana* (Ratti 1917b); Chemistry: *Ejercicios de terminología Química Alemana* (Ratti 1923); and Law, Economics and the Social Sciences: *Terminología Alemana de Derecho y de Ciencias Económicas y Sociales* (Ratti 1936)).

The beginning of a new orientation can be seen in the first two volumes of Ratti's series of textbooks (that is, Parts I (1916) and II (1917a) of his *Gramática y Ejercicios prácticos de Alemán*). These are grammar books with exercises (examples of *Übungsgrammatik*), but they constitute an attempt to overcome the traditional grammar-translation method. The simple German grammar in the first volume (Ratti 1916) is arranged by classes of word; and in the explanation of the verb system in the second (Ratti 1917a) all four basic skills (reading, writing, listening and speaking) are practised. Following a practical orientation, Ratti treats questions of syntax in various exercises throughout the book and not in separate theoretical sections. There is, however, a concise two-page summary of key syntax rules that appears just at the end of the second volume.

In the introductions to his LSP textbooks, Ratti highlighted — in line with the views of the *Neuphilologe* Wilhelm Viëtor (1850–1918) — the experience of many language learners that grammar learning had not hitherto produced the desired results. Specifically, Ratti complains that:

> después de haber discurrido largamente por las páginas áridas de la gramática, difícilmente pueden desentrañar el sentido del primer libro de técnica médica alemana de que quieren servirse, por desconocer, con la seguridad que se requiere, el léxico y la sintaxis especiales de la clase de ciencia que desean consultar. (Ratti 1917b: iii)

> [after having studied the arid pages of a grammar book for a long time, they can hardly unravel the meaning of the first book of German medical technology they want to understand because they do not know, with the confidence required, the vocabulary and special syntax of the type of science they wish to consult.]

As Ratti believed that the reason for this lack of understanding lay in the lack of knowledge of specific terminology and syntax, he introduced the above-mentioned LSP textbooks onto the market in which the only learning objective was LSP reading comprehension. Therefore, no dialogues are included. The author assumes that learners already have a basic knowledge of German and therefore omits any presentation of grammar. Instead he restricts himself to compiling a corpus of specialized texts of the specialist discipline in question, together with translation aids and commentary from a didactic point of view.

In these LSP text books — which constituted an innovation in the teaching of German in Spain at this time — we can see clearly that German for Academic Purposes (GAP) was associated with two basic characteristics: terminology and specific syntax. For example, in medicine, conditional clauses are not introduced by *wenn* but by the verb in sentence-initial position: 'Befindet sich das Geschwür [...], so [...]' (Ratti 1917b: 67). The objective of teaching was not grammatical knowledge, but acquiring the technical definitions, nomenclature and the linguistic structures necessary for an understanding of German specialized texts.

German–Spanish Lexicography

Dictionaries are an essential aid in the process of learning another language. Compared to French or English with Spanish, bilingual lexicographical works that combine German and Spanish emerged rather late. For the same reasons as in the field of teaching materials for German in Spain, before the early nineteenth century the German and Spanish combination rarely had a place among bilingual dictionaries. The production of such dictionaries began in the German-speaking area (Fuentes Morán 2000). There is an early Catalonian work — a vocabulary printed by Hans Rosembach in 1502 in Perpignan, already mentioned above — but this was not conceived of as a lexicographical work, but rather as an instrument to help craftsmen understand one another using the sentences provided on different themes. The first work to follow a relatively modern plan was printed in Vienna in 1670: *Diccionario muy copioso de la lengua española y alemana hasta agora nunca visto*. In contrast to Rosembach's work, this compilation, by Mez von Braidenbach, orders words alphabetically, on the grounds that the book was not conceived as a method for acquiring knowledge of the spoken language but as a resource for the resolution of problems which might arise when an author tried to express his ideas in writing. In previous books the lexical material was often organized in thematic units concerning special areas of daily life, starting with Religion, continuing with different semantically related words, and ending with easy dialogues.

The *Handwörterbuch der spanischen Sprache für die Deutschen* by Ernst August Schmid — the first Spanish–German dictionary written for German-speaking users — was published between 1795 and 1805. In the following centuries a strong German interest in learning Spanish boosted the production of bilingual dictionaries in German- speaking countries by authors like Wagner, Seckendorf, Tollhausen and Grossmann. However, up to 1931, no German–Spanish dictionaries had been produced in Spain and it was the Sopena publishing house which published the first one in Barcelona in this year (Anon. 1931). In the National Library of Madrid, however, there are galley proofs of an incomplete German–Spanish dictionary, compiled in Spain around 1790, which was never released to the public. The author of this unfinished work was Antonio de Villa, responsible for the first printed grammar of the German language in Spain (see above).

Portuguese Interest in Learning German

The teaching of German in Portugal began a little later even than in Spain when, in 1844, a reform by Minister Costa Cabral made it possible to include German as an extra-curricular discipline in the syllabus of secondary schools. A further change resulted in inclusion of German as an optional subject; and in the school year 1894 to 1895 German became compulsory (for five years of learning) for all students who wanted to go to university. This occurred as part of a reform of secondary education promoted by Jaime Moniz (1837–1917), a member of the Higher Council of Public Instruction. His ideas were based primarily on the organization and curriculum of the Prussian *Realgymnasien* (Cortez 2002). The introduction of the German language into the curricula of secondary schools resulted in serious discussions in Portuguese society. The political, economic and cultural relations of Portugal were traditionally oriented to Great Britain, so these reforms regarding the teaching of German were understood as an attack on the presence of English culture and on the relationship between the two colonial powers. Proponents of the German language countered that the increasing importance of the German Empire in industrial and technical-scientific development demanded that the German language should be studied at secondary school. Also, the strength of Germany in the Humanities served to reinforce the requirement that young people needed to know German if they wanted to have a modern university education. The result of the reform was that the hours for teaching German in secondary schools by far exceeded the number of hours dedicated to other modern languages and almost rivalled those for Latin and for Portuguese, the native language.

The controversy continued, but Jaime Moniz's overall reform lasted for ten years, as did the teaching of German in the secondary schools. As a result, there was an increase in demand for grammar and reading books; and to meet this new interest learning manuals were developed, including grammars such as those by Anstett (1863), Müffler (1890), Apell (1897), Campos (1898)[10] and Grüneberg (1903). Several of these authors also produced anthologies, such as Müffler (1894), Campos (1906) and Apell (1907). Until these books began to be published in the main cities of Portugal, that is, Lisbon, Porto and Coimbra, it had been usual in language teaching to use grammars published abroad, in France and in German-speaking countries especially.

German–Portuguese Lexicography

Just as for German–Spanish lexicographical publications, most German–Portuguese dictionaries were printed in Germany (and some in Paris). The first emerged at the beginning of the nineteenth century with the publication of the *Novo Diccionario Portuguez-Alemão e alemão-portuguez* by João Daniel Wagner (Leizpig 1811). Another interesting figure of the period was the German linguist, translator, playwright and diplomat Anton Edmund Wollheim da Fonseca (1810–1884), widower of the daughter of an important Portuguese aristocrat. He is known as the author of a *Dicionário portátil das línguas portuguesa e alemã* (Leipzig, 1844), which was reprinted several times until 1893. Among the early Portuguese production we should note the work *Dicionário alemão-português* published by João Félix Pereira in Lisbon in 1858. Also worth highlighting is the *Novo diccionário da língua portugueza e allemã* (1887, 1896), a two-volume dictionary published in Leipzig (F. A. Brockhaus) by Henriette Michaëlis, sister of the renowned Romanist and scholar Carolina

Michaëlis de Vasconcellos. Some authors of grammars also published dictionaries, as in the case of Alfredo Apell, who published his *Novo diccionário alemão-português e português-alemão* in Lisbon and Paris in 1901.

Conclusion

By establishing and describing some of the major relevant texts, this chapter has shed new light on the history of language learning and teaching of German in Spain and Portugal. Until recently there has been a great lack of basic bibliography that could serve as a basis for further analysis. By providing such a basis, the present chapter has contributed to filling a notable gap in the historiography of language teaching, in this case, that of the learning and teaching of German in the Iberian Peninsula. In a further, forthcoming publication, a group of researchers from Spain and Portugal — Teresa Fuentes Morán, Silvia Roiss and Petra Zimmermann (University of Salamanca, Spain), Teresa Alegre, Christina Carrington and Maria Teresa Cortez (University of Aveiro, Portugal), under the direction of the present author — will present further, more comprehensive, documentation of grammars and teaching manuals for German and lexicographical works for Portuguese–German and Spanish–German produced in the Iberian Peninsula (Marizzi and Fuentes, forthcoming).

Bibliography

Archives

STRÁUCH, FR. RAYMUNDO [STRAUCH Y VIDAL, RAIMUNDO]. 1783. *Gramatica / Española y Ale- / mana. / Esto es: Reglas que enseñan el leer, / pronunciar, entender, y / hablar el Idioma Alemán. / Escrita por Fr. Raymundo Stráuch. / Religioso Menor Observante. / año 1783* (Vic (Spain), Archivo y Biblioteca Episcopal, Hemeroteca, Bisbe Strauch, Caja II: Strauch, Autographa V, Gramática)

Printed material

ANON. 1502. *Vocabulari molt profitos per apendre Lo Catalan Alamany y Lo Alamany Catalan* (Perpignan: Hans Rosembach) (see Stegmann 1991 for a facsimile)
ANON. 1931. *Pequeño Diccionario alemán-español* (Barcelona: Sopena)
ANSTETT, PHILIPP. 1863. *Grammatica pratica da lingua allemã, approvada pelo Conselho Superior de instrucção publica, e offerecida á mocidade estudiosa de Portugal e Brazil* (Lisbon: Typ. da Soc. Typ. Franco-Portuguesa)
APELL, ALFREDO. 1897. *Nova grammatica theorica e pratica para o estudo da lingua alemã* (Paris & Lisbon: Guillard, Aillaud)
———. 1901. *Novo diccionário alemão-português e português-alemão* (Lisbon & Paris)
———. 1907. *Selecta allemã* (Lisbon: Ferreira & Oliveira)
BRAUN, JUAN JORGE. 1864. *Nueva gramática alemana. Curso teórico-práctico* (Madrid: Duran)
CAMPOS, AGOSTINHO CELSO DE AZEVEDO. 1898. *Grammatica allemã* (Paris & Lisbon: Guillard, Aillaud)
———. 1906. *Leituras allemãs* (Lisbon: Ferin)
CARLÓN [HURTADO], JULIÁN, and GEORG SCHIFFAUER. 1926. *Gramática alemana. Especial para juristas* (Oviedo: [Imprenta y fotograbado El Carbayón])

ESPINEY, ERNESTO H. D'. 1898. *O alemão sem mestre* (Porto: Magalhães & Moniz)

FERNÁNDEZ DE CASTROVERDE, CARLOS. 1868, ²1887. *Gramática Alemana* (Barcelona: [Tipográfica La Academia])

GARCÍA AYUSO, FRANCISCO. 1882. *Gramática Alemana* (Madrid: Academia de Lenguas)

GRÜNEBERG, EMIL. 1903. *Gramática alemã para o uso das instituições de instrução secundária* (Coimbra: Pires)

KÜHN, JULIO. 1840. *Constitución de la Academia Alemana-Española* (Madrid: [Imprenta de I. Sancha])

KÜHN, JULIO. 1844, ²1852. *Gramática alemana: precedida de un cuadro histórico del origen y progresos de esta lengua* (Madrid: Imprenta Nacional)

MEZ VON BRAIDENBACH, NICOLÁS. 1670. *Diccionario muy copioso de la lengua española y alemana hasta agora nunca visto* (Vienna: Johann Jakob Kürner) (see Messner 1999 for a facsimile)

MICHAËLIS, HENRIETTE. 1887/1896. *Novo diccionário da língua portugueza e allemã: enriquecido com os termos technicos do commercio e da industria, das sciencias e das artes e da linguagem familiar*, 2 vols (Leipzig: Brockhaus)

MÜFFLER, FRANCISCO XAVIER HUMBERTO. 1890. *Grammatica da lingua alemã* (Porto: Livraria Portuense)

———. [n. d.; approved by the authority in 1894]. *Deutsches Lesebuch* (Porto: Livraria Portuense)

OLAVARRÍA MARTÍNEZ, CESÁREO. 1900. *Ejercicios de Idioma alemán – Deutsche Sprachübungen* (Madrid: Romo y Füssel [Sondershausen: Fr. Aug. Eupel])

———. 1905/1906. *Gramática Militar Alemana*, 2 vols (Toledo: [Imprenta, escuela tipográfica y encuadernación del colegio María Cristina])

PEREIRA, JOÃO FÉLIX. 1858. *Dicionário alemão-português* (Lisbon)

RATTI-KÁMEKE, RICHARD. 1916. *Gramática y Ejercicios prácticos de Alemán*, Biblioteca Ratti, 1 (Barcelona: [Modesto Berdós])

———. 1917A. *Gramática y Ejercicios prácticos de Alemán, Segunda parte*, Biblioteca Ratti, 2 (Barcelona: [Modesto Berdós])

———. 1917B. *Ejercicios de terminología Médica Alemana*, Biblioteca Ratti, 3 (Barcelona: [Modesto Berdós])

———. 1923. *Ejercicios de terminología Química Alemana*, Biblioteca Ratti, 9 (Barcelona: [Modesto Berdós])

———. 1936. *Terminología Alemana de Derecho y de Ciencias Económicas y Sociales*, Biblioteca Ratti, 15 (Barcelona: [Modesto Berdós])

SCHMID, ERNST AUGUST. 1795–1805. *Handwörterbuch der spanischen Sprache für die Deutschen*, 2 vols (Leipzig: Schwingert)

VILLA, ANTONIO DE. 1792. *Gramática de la lengua alemana dividada en tres partes* (Madrid: Imprenta Real)

WAGNER, JOÃO DANIEL. 1811. *Novo Diccionario Portuguez-Alemão e alemão-portuguez* (Leipzig: Schwickert)

WOLLHEIM DA FONSECA, ANTON EDMUND. 1844. *Dicionário portátil das línguas portuguesa e alemã* (Leipzig: Fleischer)

Secondary literature

ÁLVAREZ-PEDROSA NÚÑEZ, JOSÉ ANTONIO. 1994. 'La lingüística indoeuropea en España hasta 1939', *Revista española de lingüística*, 24: 49-67

CÁCERES WÜRSIG, INGRID, and BERND MARIZZI. 2010. 'La Academia Alemana-Española de 1840 de Julio Kühn: relato de un proyecto de colaboración científica y cultural', *Estudios Filológicos Alemanes*, 20: 415-36

CEBALLOS VIRO, ÁNGEL. 2009. *Ediciones alemanas en español (1850–1900)* (Madrid/Frankfurt: Iberoamericana/Vervuert)

CORTEZ, MARÍA TERESA. 2002. 'As primeiras selectas para o ensino do Alemão nos liceus portugueses', in *O cieg abre as suas portas. Actas do Encontro com os Professores de Alemão da Zona Centro*, ed. by Encontro com os Professores de Alemão da Zona Centro, Coimbra, 2001 (Coimbra: CIEG), pp. 45-60

——. 2013. 'Agostinho de Campos (1870-1944). Retrato de um profesor de Alemão na viragem do século', in *Aquele século teve muitas heroínas. Festschrift für Maria de Fátima Viegas Brauer-Figueiredo zum 70. Geburtstag*, ed. by Henry Thorau et al. (Frankfurt: Lang), pp. 220-32

FUENTES MORÁN, MARÍA TERESA. 2000. 'La lexicografía bilingüe español-alemán', in *Cinco siglos de lexicografía española*, ed. by I. Ahumada (Jaén: Universidad de Jaén), pp. 381-409

GLÜCK, HELMUT. 2002. *Deutsch als Fremdsprache in Europa vom Mittelalter bis zur Barockzeit* (Berlin: de Gruyter)

——. 2013. *Die Fremdsprache Deutsch im Zeitalter der Aufklärung, der Klassik und der Romantik*, Fremdsprachen in Geschichte und Gegenwart, 12 (Wiesbaden: Harrassowitz)

——. 2014. 'The History of German as a Foreign Language in Europe (translated and with additional notes by Nicola McLelland)', *Language & History*, 57: 44–58

LÉPINETTE, BRIGITTE. 2000. *L'Enseignement du français en Espagne au XVIIIe siècle dans ses grammaires. Contexte historique. Concepts linguistiques et pédagogie* (Münster: Nodus)

LOMBARDERO CAPARRÓS, ALBERTO. 2015. 'The Historiography of English Language Teaching in Spain: A Corpus of Grammars and Dictionaries (1769-1900)' (Universitat Rovira i Virgili: Dipòsit Legal: T 1588–2015)

MARIZZI, BERND. 2006. 'Frühe Dokumente von DaF in Spanien: die erste deutsche Grammatik in Spanien (1783) und ihr Autor, Raymundo Strauch y Vidal (1760-1823)', in *Deutsch in Lateinamerika*, ed. by ALEG (Asociación Latinoamericana de Estudios Germanísticos) (La Habana and Leipzig: ALEG) <http://eprints.ucm.es/13946/> [accessed 12 May 2018]

——. 2009. 'Bemerkungen zu Julius (Julio) Kühn, dem ersten Professor für Germanistik an einer spanischen Universität, und zu seiner *Gramática Alemana*', in *Kommunikation und Konflikt: Kulturkonzepte der interkulturellen Germanistik*, ed. by Ernest W. B. Hess-Lüttich et al., Cross-Cultural Communication, 16 (Frankfurt: Lang), pp. 455-78

——. 2011A. 'Kontrastive Ansätze in der *Gramática de la Lengua Alemana* (1792) von Antonio de Villaín', in *Comparatio delectate*, ed. by Eva Lavric et al. (Frankfurt: Lang), pp. 939-52

——. 2011B. 'Deutsch als Wissenschaftssprache (DaW) in den Lehrwerken des Deutschen für Spanier von Richard Ratti-Kámeke zwischen 1916 und 1943', in *Re-Visionen. Kulturwissenschaftliche Herausforderungen interkultureller Germanistik*, ed. by Ernest W. B. Hess-Lüttich et. al, Cross Cultural Communication, 22 (Frankfurt: Lang), pp. 493-513

——. 2012. 'La Gramática de la Lengua Alemana de Antonio de Villa (1792): fuentes y correctores', *Revista española de lingüística aplicada (RESLA)*, 25: 133-45

——, MARIA TERESA CORTEZ and MARÍA TERESA FUENTES MORÁN. 2018. *Deutschlernen in Spanien und Portugal. Eine teilkommentierte Bibliographie von 1502 bis 1975* (Wiesbaden: Harrassowitz)

MCLELLAND, NICOLA, and RICHARD SMITH. 2014. 'Introduction: Building the History of Language Learning and Teaching (HoLLT)', *Language and History*, 57: 1-9

MESSNER, DIETER. 1999. *Diccionario muy copioso de la lengua española y alemana hasta agora nunca visto* (Salzburg: Institut für Romanistik der Universität Salzburg)

PÉREZ-VITORIA, AUGUSTO (ed.). 1985. *Enrique Moles: la vida y la obra de un químico español* (Madrid: CSIC)

PRESAS I PUIG, ALBERT. 2008. 'On a Lecture Trip to Spain: The Scientific Relations between Germany and Spain during the Entente Boycott (1919–1926)', *Annals of Science*, 65.4: 529–46

PUIG-SAMPER, MIGUEL ÁNGEL. 2010. 'Die Anfänge des wissenschaftlichen Austauschs zwischen Deutschland und Spanien', in *Traspasar Fronteras: un siglo de intercambio científico entre España y Alemania — Über Grenzen hinaus: Ein Jahrhundert deutsch-spanische Wissenschaftsbeziehungen*, ed. by Sandra Rebok (Madrid: CSIC), pp. 30-53

REAL ISTITUTO ORIENTALE IN NAPOLI. 1904. *Memorie. Fascicolo I. Anni scolastici 1900–1901 a 1903–1904* (Napoli: [Melfi & Joele])

SCHWINGES, RAINER CHRISTOPH. 2001. *Humboldt international: Der Export des deutschen Universitätsmodells im 19. und 20. Jahrhundert* (Basel: Schwabe)

SIEBE, DANIELA. 2009. *Germania docet: Ausländische Studierende, auswärtige Kulturpolitik und deutsche Universitäten 1870 bis 1933*, Historische Studien, 495 (Husum: Matthiesen)

STEGMANN, TILBERT DÍDAC (ed.). 1991. *Vocabulari Català-Alemany de l'any 1502 = Katalanisch-deutsches Vokabular aus dem Jahre 1502* (Frankfurt am Main: Domus)

STOETZER, O. CARLOS. 1998. *Karl Christian Friedrich Krause and his Influence in the Hispanic World*, Lateinamerikanische Forschungen, 25 (Cologne: Böhlau)

UTANDE IGUALADA, MANUEL (ed.). 1964. *Planes de estudio de enseñanza media*, Publicaciones de la revista Enseñanza Media, 425 (Madrid: Dirección General de Enseñanza Media)

Notes to Chapter 9

1. See Stegmann (1991), where a facsimile reprint is included.
2. The dates of Villa's birth and death are unknown. More about Villa can be found in Marizzi 2011a and 2012.
3. All translations in the chapter are the author's own.
4. See Cáceres and Marizzi 2010: 421-24.
5. I use the seemingly anachronistic abbreviation GAP deliberately, to highlight the fact that the apparently modern notion of teaching language for specific — in this case, academic — purposes had historical antecedents.
6. Siebe (2009) reports on foreign students in Germany and Marizzi (2011b) on the production of special works for Spaniards to learn German as a scientific language at the beginning of the twentieth century.
7. Curricula for Spanish secondary schools are summarized in Utande 1964.
8. It is logical that the printing of this work in handwritten letters took place in a specialized German company, belonging to Friedrich August Eupel, in Sondershausen (Thuringia). For more on problems of printing in Spain in *Fraktur* (Gothic type) see Marizzi 2012: 141. The expansive commercial policy of German publishers like Brockhaus and the publicity effect of the indication 'Impreso en Leipzig' led several Spanish publishers to print their books in Germany (cf. Ceballos 2009).
9. Richard Ratti soon hispanicized his name according to the Spanish standard and adopted the double name Richard Ratti-Kámeke (composed of the surnames of his father and mother).
10. The work of Agostinho de Campos (1870-1944) has been studied by Cortez (2013).

CHAPTER 10

❖

Investigating the Biographical Sources of Thomas Prendergast's (1807-1886) Innovation in Language Learning

Marjorie Perlman Lorch

Many methods of language teaching were devised in the nineteenth century by French and German educators. However, the Englishman Thomas Prendergast (1807-1886) created a system for language learning which had many original features. His first book on the subject, *The Mastery of Languages or, the art of speaking foreign tongues idiomatically* (1864), appeared following his retirement from the East India Company's Civil Service in Madras. Prendergast founded his innovative pedagogical approach for inductive oral language learning on observations of child language acquisition of both mother tongue and additional languages. This investigation of Prendergast's language-learning history contributes to an understanding of the sources of his original ideas and his motivation for his second career as a developer of foreign-language-teaching materials. It expands on the scant information previously available to provide a richer picture of the experiences that may have served as a foundation for his pedagogical notions, and examines the wider social-historical context in which he worked. New evidence is presented regarding his formal education in Britain and his life in India, with a particular focus on his language learning. It is argued that his lifetime of experience as a language learner and user in the multilingual setting of India represents a potent and distinctive context in which to develop his innovative system of language study for adults.

Introduction[1]

Thomas Prendergast (1807-1886) is an unusual figure in the history of modern-foreign-language teaching. Since the ground-breaking work on the history of language teaching by Howatt (1984), Prendergast has held a place as a minor but named contributor to the mid-nineteenth century development of reform in language teaching methods. Howatt describes Prendergast as the only Englishman in the group of Europeans who developed teaching methods at this time. Moreover,

Howatt underscores the distinctiveness of Prendergast's methodology for his use of observations of child language acquisition as a source of pedagogical rationale. Others had framed their pedagogical rationale for language teaching on notions of how children acquire their mother tongue (e.g. Dufief 1804), but one of the unique aspects of Prendergast's approach was to consider the acquisition of additional languages by children in multilingual immersion settings. In addition, he eschewed most of the principal pedagogical techniques employed by nineteenth-century language teachers.

Kirk (2018, this volume) identifies a number of properties common to teaching methods involving grammatical rules and translation employed in the nineteenth century: foreign language instruction via the mother tongue; explicit teaching of grammatical rules through the use of technical terminology and examples; bi-directional translation; bilingual vocabulary lists; instruction proceeding in a graded manner of increasing complexity; emphasis on the written text. Prendergast's 'Mastery Method' rejected all of these methodological practices. Instead, he emphasized initial learning through the practice of fluent pronunciation of long sentences, rather than the memorization of grammatical rules and vocabulary lists. These sentences were devised to be comprised of the most frequent words in the language and include grammatical variations: e.g., 'Why did you not ask him to come, with two or three of his friends, to see my brother's garden?' (Prendergast 1864: 165). Students were instructed to work for only brief periods of ten or fifteen minutes at a time, but to practise saying these sentences multiple times a day until they could be produced with fluency. He believed that the written text should only be studied after oral fluency had been gained. Prendergast was also one of the rare nineteenth-century language educators to insist that the attainment of grammatical knowledge should be an inductive rather than deductive process. In addition, he proposed that language learning should follow a 'structural syllabus' reflecting basic grammatical patterns. In this, Richards and Rodgers (2014: 8) suggest he anticipated developments in the 1920s and 1930s.

There remains a puzzle as to how Prendergast determined that this would be a sound rationale for a method of language learning in 1864, well before the Reform Movement got underway. There has been little biographical work on Thomas Prendergast that might be used to inform an account of the innovative features of his pedagogy and to understand his motivation for producing such books. There is a historiographical challenge in pursuing these issues. Prendergast did not produce any other publications beyond his initial book *The Mastery of Languages, or the Art of Speaking Foreign Tongues Idiomatically* (henceforth *Mastery*) in 1864; a *Handbook to the Mastery Series* (1868a); and five manuals for the learning of specific languages — French (1868b), German (1868c), Spanish (1869), Hebrew (1871) and Latin (1872b). Hence, evidence of the sources of intellectual influence or observations must be gleaned from the books themselves. The books regrettably do not have bibliographies or citations. They contain only a few indirect references to historical thinkers such as John Locke (1632-1704) and Dr Samuel Johnson (1709-1784), and none to contemporary scholars. Moreover, there is little in the way of direct autobiographical commentary in Prendergast's books. However, they do contain a few scattered clues as to his life history and personal experiences, which might point to the sources of his inspiration.

This investigation of Prendergast's biography is all the more important as his work was highly influential on the educators in England, America, and further afield, throughout the second half of the nineteenth century.[2] Moreover, key features of his work have enjoyed a resurgence of interest recently (e.g., Thornbury 2004): an emphasis on oral fluency; a focus on whole utterances rather than individual words from the outset; a rejection of the use of text-based grammar translation in the initial stages of language learning; and the use of a limited 'epitome'[3] of the most frequent verbs, adjectives and other grammatical words as the core vocabulary for the beginner.

The limited details given by Howatt (1984) about Prendergast and his work have since been repeated in applied-linguistics surveys and historical reviews of nineteenth-century language teaching innovators (e.g., Zimmerman 1997; Richards and Rodgers 2014; Thornbury 2004; Wheeler 2013). There are studies focused on Prendergast and his method by Tickoo (1986), Howatt and Smith (2000b), and Atherton (2010); and he was chosen for inclusion in Howatt and Smith's reprinting of works of early pioneers alongside Claude Marcel (1793-1876), Francois Gouin (1831-1896) and Lambert Sauveur (1826-1907) (Howatt and Smith 2000a). Beyond this, he has not been subject to extensive examination, even though the second edition of Howatt's history of ELT suggests that 'in spite of changing fashions, or possibly because of them, his work deserves reappraisal since it contains much that was ahead of its time' (Howatt with Widdowson 2004: 175). Tracing his personal language-learning history is a step towards this reappraisal.

The well-rehearsed story of Thomas Prendergast is that he was born in 1807 into a notable family. He spent his life working for the Honourable East India Company (henceforth HEIC) as a British civil servant in the government in Madras, India. Retiring aged fifty-two, Prendergast moved to Cheltenham, England. He lost his sight shortly after. At this time, he began writing books of instruction on language learning, which enjoyed great popularity and continued to be revised and republished for many years. He died in 1886. These details, drawn from obituaries in *The Times* (Anonymous 1886b) and *The Academy* (Anonymous 1886c) and from the *Oxford Dictionary of National Biography* (Boase 2004) can now be expanded upon through new research using contemporary newspapers and official documents as sources.[4] Through the examination of his childhood, educational experiences and professional life up to the time he published the *Mastery* in 1864, potential sources of Prendergast's innovative ideas about language learning and teaching can be traced.

Prendergast's Family Background and Early Life

Thomas Prendergast was born on 28 February 1807 in Bangalore, India, as the second of five children, to Sir Jeffrey Prendergast (1769-1856) and Elizabeth (née Dalrymple, of Scotland).[5] The family had lived in Madras since 1804, when Jeffrey joined the East India Company service.[6] We have no direct evidence of the family setting or language environment Prendergast grew up in, but there are studies of the family histories of others serving across the British Empire at this time (Cleall, Ishiguro and Manktelow 2013). Buettner (2004) explores aspects that might relate more specifically to Prendergast's childhood experiences in India, such as the advice to parents against allowing too much contact between their children and servants and risking their children picking up the 'chi-chi' Indian-English dialect.[7]

In the *Mastery*, Prendergast considers different ways an English child might be exposed to foreign languages. For example, at one point Prendergast suggests that 'every child has an irresistible impulse to imitate other children; for when separated from his own comrades, and thrown into the company of little foreigners, for three hours a day, he makes rapid progress in conversing with them' (Prendergast 1864: 246). It is unclear whether such observations are drawn on his childhood experience, that of his children, or were more theoretically motivated. However, he suggests:

> If two English boys, three or four years old, associated during play hours with two little foreigners, it seems probable that that language would obtain the ascendency which pertained to the individual who, by strength of character, could exercise supremacy over the rest. Such experiments might easily be made in any large city, and it would be interesting to observe the results. (Prendergast 1864: 247-48)

Prendergast's Language Learning at School

Prendergast was sent back to England to attend public school from the age of twelve, a typical practice for families in outposts of the British Empire (Buettner 2004). He briefly attended Harrow School, one of the old elite boarding schools of the day, entering in Term 2, 1818 and leaving after Term 3, 1819 (Welch 1911: 84).[8] In a rare comment about language practice at the time of the *Mastery*'s publication, Prendergast mentions the kind of classical education such as he might have received at Harrow:

> How to utilize that minute knowledge of Latin and Greek which we acquire in the most valuable decade of our little lives, is a point not much regarded by teachers of modern languages. The methods are generally supposed to be antagonistic and irreconcileable [sic]. (Prendergast 1864:167)

There was great emphasis on the learning of Latin and Greek at Harrow in the late 1810s and 1820s (Howson and Warner 1898). Under the Headmaster George Butler (1774-1853), who held the post from 1805 to 1829, Harrow students were seated together in a large room, working independently on their set tasks rather than being instructed collectively by a tutor. Charles Wordsworth (1806 –1892),[9] who attended Harrow from 1820 to 1825, includes details of his experience in learning the classical languages in a letter to his brother at another public school. His letter records the work he did over that week, composing Latin prose and verse, construing Juvenal and memorizing over a hundred lines of text each day (Wordsworth 1891: 18). His description gives an indication of the methods of study that more senior students used to learn the Latin and Greek classics under Butler's direction at Harrow. There is a clear emphasis on memorizing passages of text and the practice of analysing grammatical structure and parsing, which were components of common pedagogical approaches at the time. In his *Mastery*, Prendergast discusses the desirability of learning a limited number of sentences, comprising the most frequent words of the language, very well. In arguing against memorizing words in isolation, Prendergast makes the disparaging comment that: 'It is a mere schoolboy notion to try how many words can be "got by heart" in a limited time' (Prendergast 1864: 47).

However, Isaac Williams (1802-1865), who attended Harrow from 1817 to 1821, recalled that his own Latin studies under Butler and the tutor Henry Drury included intensive creative work in Latin in addition to grammar and translation work. He reminisced about his enjoyment of writing four compositions a week, motivated by the possibility of winning Latin prizes from Butler (Williams and Prevost 1892: 9). Although it appears that numerous such language prizes were awarded to students, neither the *Harrow Register* nor other accounts of students in this period note Prendergast winning any prizes, or distinguishing himself academically in any way.

Five years after leaving Harrow, in his petition to the HEIC for admission to the East India College to train as a 'Writer', i.e. clerk (Anonymous 1825), Prendergast states that the school that he had attended most recently was at Olney in Buckinghamshire, recording that his father was Lieutenant Colonel, Military Auditor General at Madras, while his mother resided at Emberton, a small village close to Olney. This school may have been one of the small educational establishments run in various private houses for small numbers of gentlemen's sons, such as Rev. John Morris's Olney House School (Knight 2014). It was quite typical for sons of elite families to attend such schools and to work on learning languages such as French and German in this period. It was also common practice to send such young gentlemen on tours of the Continent for additional educational experiences, which might include language learning. Perhaps Prendergast followed the fashion too. In the *Mastery*, he notes: 'People who go abroad to learn French or German, on the most approved principles, studying with the best masters, and living with a foreign family, seldom express themselves with facility in less than three months' (Prendergast 1864: 62). However, he goes on to state:

> It is a well-known fact that boys, who have learned to converse fluently on their travels abroad, and are under orders to keep up their knowledge of the foreign language at an English school, very frequently return to their agonized parents in the holidays, speaking spurious French or German, instead of the genuine idiomatic forms of expression, which were habitual to them before. (Prendergast 1864: 108)

He also alludes to the experience of immersion language learning in younger children:

> [A] child of six, eight or ten years of age, when suddenly transplanted to a foreign country, where he consorts chiefly with natives, immediately adopts the same course of imitation and repetition of practical sentences [...]. In three or four months he generally talks a foreign language as fluently as his own. If he never hears it spoken, except by the natives of the country, he speaks it without any adulteration; but if there are people around him who jumble together the words, or the tones, or the constructions of two languages, he always adopts their jargon. (Prendergast 1864: 15)

While this provides interesting detail of what may have been common practice amongst elite families, it is not clear whether these comments were autobiographical observations.

At the age of eighteen, Prendergast entered the East India College (later renamed Haileybury College), which he attended from1825 to 1826 (Danvers 1894). This was an elite training college in Hertford Heath (founded 1806) for young gentlemen nominated (i.e. sponsored) by its directors to 'writerships' (i.e. to become clerks) to prepare them for careers in the East India Company civil service.[10] Until the 1820s, according to Reverend Thomas R. Malthus, FRS (1766-1834), Professor of Political Economy there from 1806 to 1835,[11] candidates were required to pass an examination in Greek, Latin and Arithmetic in order to gain admission to the College (James 1979).[12] Students at the East India College at this time were required to stay for a minimum of four terms (two years) and to pass examinations in Greek, Latin, Mathematics, English, History, Geography, Paley's *Evidences of Christianity* and Moral Philosophy (Lowell 1900). The College provided a wide curriculum of subjects intended to prepare students for future overseas government career work and provide a liberal education modelled on the course in the University of Cambridge including Classics, Mathematics, Law, Political Economy and History.[13] This was alongside the Oriental Studies, which included Hindu Literature, the History of Asia, and the languages Sanskrit, Persian and Hindustani ('Hindoostanee'). These languages were compulsory, with other Indian languages optional (Lowell 1900: 12).

The East India College employed a number of professors who taught the classical languages of Arabic, Persian, Sanskrit, as well as the vernacular languages of Bengali, Telugu ('Teloogoo'), Hindi and Marathi. Some of those known to have taught at the College while Prendergast studied there were Graves Chamney Haughton (FRS, 1817-1827), who had previously taught Bengali and Sanskrit at the HEIC College in Fort St. George, Madras;[14] and Francis Johnson (1824-1855). Levels of proficiency gained in Asian languages were apparently relatively low in the decade before Prendergast's enrolment, for Fisher (2001) records that until 1814 students were not examined in the Asian languages and therefore did not take their studies seriously. A new practice was then established with an external 'visitor' who would examine the students in writing, terms of grammar, reading, translating and parsing an easy passage in these languages. One of these was Sir Charles Wilkins (1749–1836) (Danvers 1894), notable as the first translator of *Bhagavad Gita* into English and author of *Grammar of the Sanskrita Language* (1808) and a new edition of Richardson's *A Vocabulary, Persian, Arabic, and English* (1810).[15] These books were widely used by the students at the College at this time. However, language learning at the East India College in the 1820s was apparently intended to serve as only an initial foundation, with students typically obtaining little more than a beginner's proficiency. The expectation was that they would develop more knowledge of particular languages as needed once they began their foreign posting.

In the *Memorials of Old Haileybury*, Prendergast's entry in the list of alumni is notable for its brevity, solely listing the date of his attendance at the school (Danvers et al. 1894: 379). In contrast, others' entries are somewhat lengthier, detailing prizes won and the various posts they went on to hold in India. It may perhaps be inferred from this relative lack of detail that here, as at Harrow, Prendergast kept a low profile at school or perhaps failed to distinguish himself by outstanding performance.

Prendergast's Career in the Indian Civil Service

The HEIC had determined in 1801 that those sent out to India from the College must pass examinations in two Indian languages to qualify for public service. Previously, this would have been achieved by additional language tuition provided at Fort St George, Madras, after they arrived, but before their writerships were confirmed. There was a gradual transfer of teaching from Madras to the East India College over the 1820s, while language examinations for new 'writers' were still given at Fort St George (Fisher 2001). At the same time, the expected level of attainment and demonstration of fluency was raised through several revisions to the examination requirements. When Prendergast was examined, candidates were tested on oral and written translation from Hindustani into English of both literary passages and official documents. They were also required to demonstrate the ability to converse sufficiently fluently to carry on business and legal transactions with locals in their own language without an interpreter (Safadi 2012: 18).

There are varying pictures of how much or how little functional language ability these newly arrived students were expected to have and actually did possess for any of the languages spoken in Madras. Newly arrived HEIC writers' examinations results were regularly published in the *Asiatic Journal and Monthly Register*, providing a fair amount of detail. Prendergast's performance on his language examination at the College at Fort St George, Madras, in 1828 was reported in the newspaper along with five other candidates. Prendergast appears to have only entered examination in Hindustani, for which he demonstrated fair competence:

> Mr Prendergast, in his Hindoostanee examination, first translated an easy paper; but, at his own request, one of more difficulty was afterwards given him. His translations evince a degree of proficiency very creditable to him considering the short period that he has been attached to the college, and with the exception of two or three short passages, the general meaning is correctly given. He did not attempt to translate into Hindoostanee. In conversation he understood much of what was addressed to him. (Anonymous 1828: 232-33)

In contrast, the other candidates were examined in multiple languages, including the major local languages of Telugu and Tamil, and were given much higher accolades. This new evidence provides a key insight into Prendergast's language-learning competency with respect to his direct peers. This examination report suggests that Prendergast had attained a good basic level of proficiency in Hindustani but there was no demonstration of his abilities in Tamil or Telugu. It is clear that his language learning abilities were limited in comparison to his fellow trainees.

It is possible that Prendergast further availed himself of the opportunity to study the additional optional local languages at Fort St George in preparation for his post and/or attained higher fluency in Hindustani. Stephens gives the opinion that at this time 'the amount of the elements of the Oriental languages learnt [at Haileybury] formed only a slight basis for subsequent study in India' (Stephens 1900:

335). However, he may also already have begun acquiring some fluency in Indian vernacular language(s) as a child in an Anglo-Indian household in Madras. If so, the type of proficiency attained in such an informal immersion setting may not have prepared him for the formal and technical nature of the spoken and written language components of the Fort St George examination.

Prendergast returned to his childhood locale and took up a junior post in the HEIC in Madras in 1826, aged nineteen.[16] Unlike his father and several other family members, including brothers and cousins who served in the Indian military, Thomas Prendergast followed a government career. He held many administrative and judicial posts throughout Southern India, was promoted several times, and finally served as a district senior administrator in the posts of 'Collector' and 'Agent to the Governor'.[17]

At the age of twenty-one, in 1828, after two years in Madras, Thomas Prendergast married Caroline Lucy Dalrymple (aged nineteen) in Nagapatnam, Madras.[18] Their first child, Fanny Elizabeth, was born fourteen months later, followed by two sons, Hew Lindsay in 1831 and Henry North Dalrymple in 1834, all living as young children in Madras as their father had. The *Mastery* includes allusions to the experience of children in such a multilingual environment: 'A child, living in daily association with foreigners, acquires two or three languages at once, and speaks them all fluently, idiomatically, and without intermixture' (Prendergast 1864: 4). In a later passage, Prendergast states:

> [When a] child four years old, left to his own resources, [...] associates with foreign children, he does not restrict himself to single words, nor does he pick out the nouns and verbs, but he learns practical sentences, and that without the intervention of any adviser. (Prendergast 1864: 125-26)

Such comments regarding children acquiring languages in addition to their mother tongue have a ring of observer authenticity to them, and suggest that they were not second-hand.

In 1838, Prendergast was granted 'absentee allowance' from the service.[19] The likely cause was the failing health of his young wife, whom he took back to her family home in Scotland.[20] In late 1840, Prendergast returned to work in Southern India for the HEIC as a widower and remained there for the next two decades (Princep 1885: 116).[21] Prendergast's various career promotions sent him to many different locales in Madras, dealing with people who spoke a large number of different languages and dialects. Thurston (1914) reports that the languages spoken in the Madras Presidency during this period included Tamil, Telugu, Malayalam, Kannada, Oriya and Tulu, and many more local vernaculars. Prendergast's sensitivity to this complex multilingual environment is reflected in his comment in the *Mastery*:

> Every tribe, having a language of its own, has some peculiar tones and some movements of the vocal organs, which the learner has to discover and adopt. It is therefore instructive to watch, very narrowly, the manner in which our own language is uttered by a foreigner; to mark the tones, to note what words he mispronounces, and to echo those tones and sounds. (Prendergast 1864: 150)

Chapter 10 of the *Mastery* offers a thumbnail sketch of the language 'Teloogoo' with very brief details of how to begin to learn speaking it. This comes after over 150 pages of theoretical discussion on the best way to approach language learning in general, and a brief consideration of the particulars relating to learning English. In the introduction to this chapter, Prendergast provides this information on Telugu:

> This ancient language is supposed to have been introduced into Hindostan by Scythian tribes, before the arrival of the Brahmins, who gradually drove them down to the southward, where they now occupy a territory of nearly 100,000 square miles, in the Madras Presidency, with a population of about 15,000,000 souls. (Prendergast 1864: 167)

More interesting is the fact that Prendergast identified this language as belonging to the 'Turanian order'. The Oxford linguist Frederick Max Müller (1823-1900) had put forward this classification as comprising languages spoken in Asia or Europe by 'nomadic' peoples (Müller 1854). Prendergast's use of this technical linguistic term is one of the few, albeit indirect, indications of his awareness of contemporary academic literature.

Prendergast stated his intention in including this material in Telugu: 'To show the analytical character of the Mastery System, a specimen of a Teloogoo sentence, short but comprehensive and very useful, is annexed with a set of variations' (Prendergast 1864: 182). Prendergast begins by drawing analogies of grammatical form in Telugu not only with English, but also with Latin, Greek, and Sanskrit, adding an aside about the language of the North American tribes as well. While he chose to provide a practical demonstration of his method in this language for which there was a clear demand in the HEIC, the chapter on Telugu cannot be taken as proof of Prendergast's own knowledge of this language. Although one obituary does state that he had gained 'intimate knowledge' of Tamil and Telugu while carrying out his duties in the civil service (Anonymous 1886c: 345), we shall see below that the foreign-language materials in his manuals were sourced from informants.

Nevertheless, the *Mastery* also includes what might be taken as more direct autobiographical acknowledgement of Prendergast's experience of working in a foreign language context in Madras. In the chapter on Telugu, Prendergast mentions difficulties in making oneself understood in a foreign idiom:

> [R]eluctance to adopt Oriental forms of thought must be overcome at the outset, by learning long sentences, containing as many of the antagonistic forms of speech as possible. If the beginner affects conciseness he will find himself in this predicament, that orders addressed to Hindoos, with great consideration for the grammatical proprieties, will be imperfectly understood, because they are deficient in circumstantiality. He must divest himself of the habit of omitting every word which may, either classically or logically, be deemed superfluous. These standards are altogether inapplicable in the East. [...] there may be great expenditure of temper incurred in expounding his own oracular phraseology, or in witnessing the miscarriage of a project through the misapprehension of the person addressed. (Prendergast 1872a: 174)

The chapter also contains numerous other observations on intercultural and sociolinguistic aspects of communication with Telugu speakers which reveal Prendergast's attentiveness to linguistic difficulties of expression in this foreign-language setting. It is notable that the twenty-one sample variations Prendergast provides in Telugu are all explicitly framed as 'orders to domestics'.

Apart from the question of Prendergast's proficiency in Telugu or any of the other local languages of Madras, it is also not clear what his communicative practice might have been in the course of his work. It is likely that there was great individual variation in the multilingual or monolingual practices of civil servants when dealing with the non-English speaking people they were governing in the mid-nineteenth century. The British language policy for India was in transition from the 1830s onwards. In 1835, Thomas B. Macaulay (1800-1859) urged the HEIC to make English the language of education in India and called for the creation of an elite corps of interpreters for the indigenous languages (Macaulay 1965 [1835]). While some civil servants would have attained a high level of proficiency in several vernacular local languages and used them to communicate directly with their subjects and supplicants, others with lesser linguistic attainments would have resorted to communicating primarily in English in their professional sphere, relying on the assistance of native interpreters and translators. It is likely that Prendergast's various roles as a judge and magistrate would require attention to the subtleties of communication in negotiation with speakers of other languages, but how these proceedings operated with non-English speaking witnesses is difficult to determine, as the HEIC court records and other reports that have been examined do not include such details of practice.

However, in the records of the HEIC and the newspapers of the day, there are some traces of Prendergast's engagement with the local people while in Madras.[22] For example, he advised on the local government system of land exchange in his role as tax collector:

> Mr. Prendergast, the Collector, in writing to the Commissioner of the Northern Circars on March 5, 1850, considered that, although the practice had obvious disadvantages, it was quite in unison with the feelings of the people, that, when difficulties arose, it was the only method of doing strict justice and putting a stop to violent disputes, and that it was an essential part of the existing system. (Morris 1878: 314)

This demonstrates some direct engagement with the local community. Another mention of his activities in another posting indicates that he recommended that the Government prohibit the ritual practice of fire-walking (Van den Hoek 1992: 520).[23] However, most significant in relation to the present focus is that Prendergast was instrumental in founding a school that taught English to Indian boys, following the proposals set out in Macaulay's *Minute on Education*. It is recorded that: 'The Pithapuram Raja's college at Cocanada[24] was founded in 1852, as a general English and vernacular school, through the exertions of the then Collector, Mr. Prendergast, and his sheristadar,[25] M.R.Ry. Tulasinga Chettiyar. It depended entirely on private subscriptions' (Hemingway 1915: 157). According to the school's website (Anonymous [n.d.]), the Pithapur Rajah's College in Kakinada was one of the earliest institutions to provide English education to Indian boys in all of South India. It was developed initially along British public school lines to educate young boys around the age of twelve for a couple of years.[26] It is not clear whether Prendergast had any direct role in devising the curriculum of this school or took any interest in the students' language learning. It is possible that his ideas about language learning and teaching might have begun to develop or been furthered in this context.

Prendergast's Retirement in England

Aged fifty-two, Prendergast retired from HEIC service on 27 March 1858 with a pension from the annuity fund (Princep 1885). This coincided with the Government of India Act of 1858, which ended the HEIC administration of India. All biographical accounts record that he became blind shortly after returning to England (Boase 2004).[27] A studio photograph of Thomas Prendergast in a biography of his youngest son (Vibart 1914: 28), which likely dates from this period, portrays Prendergast as a moustached and grey-haired Victorian gentleman gazing blankly off into the distance.

Prendergast's activities in the early years of his retirement are not well documented. In the 1861 census, Prendergast is recorded living in his parents' house at Shoreham near Hove, Sussex. Other traces of him during this time record his address as the East India Service Club in London. He later moved into 'Meldon Lodge' in College Lawn, Cheltenham, a new, elegant detached villa, overlooking the playing field of Cheltenham College (founded 1841)[28] and across the road from the relatively new premises of the Cheltenham General Hospital (built 1849). This spa town was known to attract retired gentlemen from the Indian military and civil service from 1840 onwards due to its congenial climate (Hembry 1997; Bailey 1998) and it appears that other family relations had links to the town.

Prendergast's first publication, *The Mastery of Languages*, appeared in 1864, approximately five years after he retired to Cheltenham from Madras. While primarily taken up with explaining his pedagogical insights and rationale for his original approach, the book contains a brief chapter on Telugu (described above), and a set of sentences and variations for German and Spanish. Prendergast included these:

> for the gratification of the curiosity of those who feel disposed to make an experiment [...] the mastery of four couplets in either language will be of the greatest assistance to those who may have an occasion to go to Germany or Spain. (Prendergast 1872a: 184)

This underlines his objective, initially at least, to present a method of language learning for self-study by those who were preparing for overseas travel. In addition to those languages that Prendergast is known to have studied formally, such as Latin and Sanskrit, the *Mastery* also included examples from French, Italian, Chinese, Hebrew, Polish and Welsh. The source of these linguistic examples is unknown. Four years later, Prendergast published the *Handbook* and manuals on French and

German, on Spanish the following year, and later on Hebrew and Latin.[29] Even his authorship of these manuals may not be taken at face value as evidence of his language proficiency. In the prefaces to each of his language manuals, Prendergast openly acknowledges that others created the language materials that comprise each book. He continued to publish revised editions of these books for the next two decades.

Although intended for self-study, Prendergast's books were enthusiastically taken up by school teachers (Lorch 2016), and in new editions he included remarks regarding use in the classroom. His manuals also began to be advertised as schoolbooks in newspapers (e.g., Anonymous 1872). Prendergast appears to have had some involvement in the local schools, in part due to connections from his family and relations' children,[30] but also from his more general interest in language and education. The language materials in his Latin manual are credited to Rev. Thomas Charles Fry (1846-1930), a master at Cheltenham College from 1870 to 1873, and at his funeral one of the carriages in his cortège was filled with prefects and senior students representing the school (Senex 1887). At Cheltenham Ladies College, attended by other relatives of Prendergast, the headmistress Dorothea Beale (1831–1906) was well acquainted with Prendergast's method, and spoke highly of it in her contribution to the Government inquiry on the education of girls (Beale 1869).

Prendergast also continued to be involved in language education issues in India in retirement. He attended a meeting of the Christian Vernacular Education Society for India (founded 1858) in London as an executive committee member, under the chairmanship of the Earl of Shaftesbury (Anonymous 1868). Their purpose was to support access to literature and education in English and vernacular languages by the development of schools, teacher training and publishing in India. This commitment had begun with his founding of the Pithapur Rajah's Government College discussed above.[31]

Prendergast died in Cheltenham aged seventy-nine on 14 November 1886.[32] His obituary appeared in the *Times*; short notices appeared in *London Illustrated News*, many local and regional newspapers, and a specialist periodical, *Book Lore*. The *Academy* obituary stated: 'By the charm of his character and the dignity of his appearance, Mr. Prendergast impressed himself upon all who knew him as the ideal of an English gentleman' (Anonymous 1886c: 345). The Sunday after his funeral, The Reverend Canon Money preached a sermon from Numbers 23. 10, 'Let me die the death of the righteous, and let my last end be like His', in tribute to Thomas Prendergast as a 'bright example of earnest Christian life' (Anonymous 1886a). His legacy is the books on language teaching and learning that continued to be reprinted well into the twentieth century.

Thomas Prendergast's approach to language learning has many distinctive features (Howatt with Widdowson 2004). I have suggested here that some of these may be attributed to his language-learning education; his professional experience; to his exposure to a multilingual environment, initially as a child in Madras and later working there in roles such as tax collector, judge and magistrate which required interacting with people from many language communities. By contrast, most nineteenth-century language learning approaches were created by men who lived and travelled in Europe and typically spoke Romance and Germanic languages. In addition, most sons of gentlemen who were raised in England would have been exposed to the modern languages of French and/or German by governesses and tutors as children. This chapter has provided a fuller picture of Prendergast's quite different language-learning history. As an English gentleman headed for a career in the HEIC civil service he studied Latin, Greek, Sanskrit and the spoken languages of India. The only direct evidence of his language attainment is his writer's examination report of adequate skills in one language only (Hindustani). While an obituary credited him with 'intimate knowledge' of the Madras vernacular languages of Tamil and Telugu, no contemporary documents corroborate this. There is no mention of Tamil in any of his books;[33] and the treatment of Telugu in the *Mastery* is only a rudimentary fragment. There is a tantalizing statement contained in Prendergast's entry in the *Dictionary of Indian Biography*: '[Prendergast] [...] published *The Mastery* [...] on his system, which he had applied to the Madras vernaculars' (Anon 1906: 342), but no evidence has been found to substantiate this. As others were credited with the creation of the language materials in his five manuals, they cannot be taken as direct evidence of his proficiency in any of these other languages either.

One contemporary comment seems to reinforce the impression that the pioneer language *pedagogue* was no great language *learner*.[34] One of his publishing rivals, Richard S. Rosenthal (b. 1845), adapted Prendergast's method in a number of language-learning books published from the late 1870s onwards. In Rosenthal's French manual, he remarked:

> Prendergast, perhaps the most original mind among modern philologists, worked out a most able theory; but *being himself no linguist*, and unfortunately being totally blind, he was obliged to leave the practical part of his work to his assistants, who made — as he acknowledged himself to me — a most miserable failure in the compilation of his text-books. (Rosenthal 1885: 19) [Emphasis added]

In sum, this detailed examination of Prendergast's biography yields the picture of an individual exposed to a large number of diverse languages and interlocutors both in the classroom and in immersion contexts at various stages of his life. Either in spite of, or perhaps because of, his own language learning experiences, he was — though not a teacher — motivated to devise a new pedagogical approach to assist others in learning foreign languages. His major contribution was a theoretical and methodological one that could be applied to any language.

Bibliography

ANONYMOUS. THOMAS PRENDERGAST. In *India, Births and Baptisms, 1786–1947, India Office Records*. British Library, J/1/40. f.166

———. 1825. THOMAS PRENDERGAST. In *Committee of College References and Papers, East India Company Writers' Petitions, Records of the East India Company College, Haileybury 1749–1857*, ed. by India Office Records, 8. British Library, IOR/J/1/40/163–71

——. 1828. *Asiatic Journal and Monthly Register* (January to June): 232-33

——. 1868. Christian Vernacular Education Society for India, *Cheltenham Chronical*, p. 2

——. 1872. Book Notice, *Cheltenham Looker-On*, 14 September 1872, p. 13

——. 1875. 'The Co-operative Stores', *Cheltenham Looker-On*, 24 April 1875, p. 13

——. 1877. 'India Famine Relief Fund', *Cheltenham Looker-On*, 29 September 1877, p. 610

——. 1878. 'National Association for the Promotion of Social Science, Cheltenham Congress', *Cheltenham Chronicle*, 1 October 1878, p. 4

——. 1882. 'British Refugees from Alexandria Fund', *Cheltenham Looker-On*, 5 August 1882, p. 1

——. 1886A. *Cheltenham Chronicle*, 27 November 1886, p. 6

——. 1886B. 'Obituary of Thomas Prendergast', *The Times*, 19 November 1886

——. 1886C. 'Thomas Prendergast', *Academy*, 30: 345

——. 1906. 'Prendergast, Thomas (1806-1886)', in *Dictionary of Indian Biography* (New York: Haskell), p. 342

——. 1914. 'Foundation Stone Laying. Naunton Lane Mission Hall', *Cheltenham Looker-On*, 25 April 1914, p. 16

——. 2003-2013. 'Eton College v Harrow School in 1822', in *Cricket Archive*, ed. by Cricket Archive Oracles, Cricket Archive ascension number: misc84430 <www.cricketarchive.com/Archive/Scorecards/211/211317.html> [accessed 15 February 2014]

——. [N.D.]. 'P.R. Government College: Creating History in Education' <http://www.inkakinada.com/topstories/pr-college> [accessed 15 February 2014]

ATHERTON, MARK. 2010. '"The Globe of Language": Thomas Prendergast and Applied Linguistics in the 1870s', *Language & History*, 53: 15-26

BAILEY, EVA. 1998. 'Cheltenham and the Indian Connection', *Cheltenham Local History Society Journal*, 14: 48-51

BEALE, DOROTHEA. 1869. *Reports Issued by the Schools' Inquiry Commission on the Education of Girls* (London: Nutt)

BOASE, G. C. 2004. 'Prendergast, Thomas (1807/8–1886)', in *Oxford Dictionary of National Biography*, ed. by John D. Haigh (Oxford: Oxford University Press) <http://www.oxforddnb.com/view/article/22716> Thomas Prendergast (1807/8–1886): doi:10.1093/ref:odnb/22716 [accessed 4 July 2013]

BROWN, SAMUEL ROBBINS. 1878. *Prendergast's Mastery System Adapted to the Study of Japanese or English* (Yokahama: Kelly)

BUETTNER, ELIZABETH. 2004. *Empire Families: Britons and Late Imperial India* (Oxford: Oxford University Press)

CLEALL, ESME, LARUA ISHIGURO, and EMILY J. MANKTELOW. 2013. 'Imperial Relations: Histories of Family in the British Empire', *Journal of Colonialism and Colonial History*, 14.1: Project MUSE, doi:10.1353/cch.2013.0006, online at <https://muse.jhu.edu/article/503247> [accessed 8 June 2016]

DANVERS, FREDERICK CHARLES. 1894. *Memoirs of Old Haileybury College* (London: Constable)

DUFIEF, NICHOLAS GOUIN. 1804. *Nature displayed, in her mode of teaching language to man: Adapted to the French* (Philadelphia: Thomas L. Plowman, for the author)

FISHER, MICHAEL H. 2001. 'Persian Professor in Britain: Mirza Muhammad Ibrahim at the East India College, 1826-44', *Comparative Studies of South Asia, Africa and the Middle East*, 21: 24-32

HEMBRY, PHYLLIS. 1997. *British Spas from 1818 to the Present* (London: Athlone)

HEMINGWAY, F. R. 1915. *Madras District Gazetteers: Godavari* (Madras: The Superintendent, Government Press)

HOWATT, ANTHONY P. R. 1984. *A History of English Language Teaching* (Oxford: Oxford University Press)

——, and RICHARD C. SMITH (eds). 2000a. *Foundations of Foreign Language Teaching: Nineteenth-Century Innovators*, 6 vols (London: Routledge), III: *Thomas Prendergast*

——, and RICHARD C. SMITH. 2000B. 'General Introduction', in *Foundations of Foreign Language Teaching: Nineteenth-Century Innovators*, 6 vols (London: Routledge), I: v–xlvii

——, WITH HENRY G. WIDDOWSON. 2004 [1984]. *A History of English Language Teaching*, 2nd edn (Oxford: Oxford University Press)

HOWSON, EDMUND W., and GEORGE TOWNSEND WARNER. 1898. *Harrow School* (London: Edward Arnold)

JAMES, PATRICIA. 1979. *Population Malthus: His Life and Times* (London: Routledge)

KIRK, SONYA. 2018. 'Grammar-Translation: Tradition or Innovation?', in *The History of Language Learning and Teaching*, ed. by Nicola McLelland and Richard Smith (Oxford: Legenda), II, 000–000

KNIGHT, ELIZABETH. 2014. 'Thomas Haddon's and other schools for boys c. 1798-c. 1840' in Olney and District Historical Society website <http://www.mkheritage.org.uk/odhs/elizabeth-knights-researches/thomas-haddons-school-2/>

LORCH, MARJORIE. 2016. 'A Late 19th Century British Perspective on Modern Foreign Learning, Teaching, and Reform', *Historiographia Linguistica*, 43: 175–208

LOWELL, A. LAWRENCE. 1900. *Colonial Civil Service* (London: Macmillan)

MACAULAY, THOMAS BABBINGTON. 1965 [1835]. 'Minute by the Hon'ble T. B. Macaulay, dated the 2nd February 1835', in *Selections from Educational Records, Part I (1781–1839)*, ed. by Henry Sharp (Calcutta: Superintendent, Government Printing [1920]; repr. Delhi: National Archives of India), pp. 107-17

McLELLAN, DENNIS. 2004. 'Charles Berlitz, 90; Linguist and Author on the Paranormal', *Los Angeles Times*, 1 January, online at <http://articles.latimes.com/2004/jan/01/local/me-berlitz1> [accessed 8 February 2018]

MALTHUS, THOMAS. 1817. *Statements respecting the East India College* (London: Murray)

MORRIS, HENRY. 1878. *A descriptive and historical account of the Godavery District in the presidency of Madras* (London: Trübner) <http://books.google.com/books?id=jjoQAAAAYAAJ>

MÜLLER, FRIEDRICH MAX. 1854. 'Letter to Chevalier Bunsen on the Classification of the Turanian Languages', in *Christianity and Mankind*, ed. by Christian Carl Josias Bunsen (London: Spottiswoode)

PENNY, FRANK. 1922. *The Church in Madras, being the History of the Ecclesiastical and Missionary Action of the East India Company in the Presidency of Madras from 1835 to 1861*, 3 vols (London: Murray), II

PRENDERGAST, THOMAS. 1864. *The Mastery of Languages; or, the art of speaking foreign tongues idiomatically* (London: Richard Bentley)

——. 1868A. *Handbook to the Mastery Series* (London: Longmans, Green)

——. 1868B. *The Mastery Series. French* (London: Longmans, Green)

——. 1868C. *The Mastery Series. German* (London: Longmans, Green)

——. 1869. *The Mastery Series. Spanish* (London: Longmans, Green)

——. 1871. *The Mastery Series. Hebrew* (London: Longmans, Green)

——. 1872A. *The Mastery of Languages* (London: Longmans, Green)

——. 1872B. *The Mastery Series. Latin* (London: Longmans, Green)

——. 1875. 'To the Editor of the Educational Times', *Educational Times, and the Journal of the College of Preceptors*, 27: 11

PRINSEP, CHARLES C. 1885. *Record of Services of the Honourable East India Company's Civil Servants in the Madras Presidency from 1741 to 1858* (London: Trübner)

RICHARDS, JACK. C., and THEODORE S. RODGERS. 2014. *Approaches and Methods in Language Teaching* (Cambridge: Cambridge University Press)

ROSENTHAL, RICHARD SIGISMUND. 1885. *The meisterschaft system: a short and practical method of acquiring complete fluency of speech in the French language* (Boston: Meisterschaft)

SAFADI, ALISON. 2012. 'The Colonial Construction of Hindustani' (unpublished doctoral thesis, University of London, Goldsmiths College) <https://research.gold.ac.uk/8026/1/History_thesis_Safadi.pdf>

SENEX. 1887. 'The late Mr. Thomas Prendergast', *Harrow Notes*, 5: 6-7

STEPHENS, H. MORSE. 1900. 'An Account of the East India College at Haileybury (1806-1857)', in *Colonial Civil Service*, ed. by A. Lawrence Lowell (London: Macmillan), pp. 233-345

STORR, FRANCIS (ed.). 1899. *Life and Remains of the Rev. R. H. Quick* (Cambridge: Cambridge University Press)

THORNBURY, SCOTT. 2004. 'Big Words, Small Grammar', *English Teaching Professional*, 31: 10-11

THURSTON, EDGAR. 1914. *The Madras Presidency: With Mysore, Coorg and the Associated States* (Madras: University of Madras Press)

TICKOO, M. L. 1986. 'Prendergast and the "Mastery Method": An Assessment', *ELT Journal*, 40: 52-58

TRENCH, RICHARD CHENEVIX. 1855. *English past and present* (London: Barker)

—— — . 1994 [1851]. *On the study of words* (London: Routledge/Thoemmes)

VAN DEN HOEK, A. W., D. H. A. KOLFF, and M. S. OORT (eds). 1992. *Ritual, State and History in South Asia: Essays in Honour of J. C. Heesterman* (Leiden: Brill)

VIBART, HENRY MEREDITH. 1914. *The Life of General Sir Harry N. D. Prendergast (the Happy Warrior)* (London: Nash)

WELCH, R. COURTENAY. 1911. *The Harrow School Register, 1800–1911* (London: Longmans, Green)

WHEELER, GARON. 2013. *Language Teaching through the Ages* (London: Routledge)

WILLIAMS, ISAAC, and GEORGE PREVOST. 1892. *The autobiography of Isaac Williams, B. D., fellow and tutor of Trinity college, Oxford, author of several of the 'Tracts for the times'* (London & New York: Longmans, Green)

WORDSWORTH, CHARLES. 1891. *Annals of my early life, 1806–1846; with occasional compositions in Latin and English verse* (London: Longmans, Green)

ZIMMERMAN, CHERYL BOYD. 1997. 'Historical Trends in Second Language Vocabulary Instruction', in *Second Language Vocabulary Acquisition: A Rationale for Pedagogy*, ed. by James Coady and Thomas Huckin (Cambridge: Cambridge University Press), pp. 5-19

Notes to Chapter 10

1. The author wishes to thank the following people for their assistance: Beverly Hallam and Stephen van Dulken, Families in British India Society; Rachel Roberts, Archivist at the Cheltenham Ladies School; Gabrielle Sedita, Assistant Archivist at Cheltenham College; the staff at the Cheltenham Local and Family History Library; Joyce Cummings, Cheltenham Local History Society; Elizabeth Knight, Olney Historical Society; Argharad Meredith, Archives and Records Manager, Harrow School; and Peter Sibson. I also wish to acknowledge my gratitude for the insightful comments of Michèle Cohen, Richard Smith, and two anonymous reviewers.

2. For an extensive review of the contemporary impact and uptake of Prendergast's method by educators see Lorch 2016.

3. Prendergast uses the term *epitome* in its meaning of a condensed compendium.

4. There do not appear to be any publicly available personal papers which might shed light on his intellectual circle of acquaintances or spheres of interest.

5. There has been some confusion over Prendergast's actual year of birth. Many secondary sources cited his birth year as 1806, while his entry in the *Oxford Dictionary of National Biography* has 1807/08 (Boase 2004).

6. Jeffery Prendergast later became Colonel of the 39th Native Infantry in 1825. He was knighted for his service in the HEIC army during the Mysore War. He went on to serve as Military Auditor General in Madras in the 1850s and retired to Brighton, Sussex, in 1856. Thomas's older brother Harris became a notable QC.

7. *Chi-chi* is a nineteenth-century term which refers to someone of mixed Anglo-Indian descent.

8. He did not stay on for the senior school; neither did his elder brother, who had attended there the two years before. Thomas's first cousin and contemporary Guy Lushington Prendergast (1806-1887) also attended Harrow at this time (1818-22). There has been some confusion over the attribution of activities and achievements to the two at school and in later life. One biographical description of Thomas Prendergast states that he was a great school athlete and played for the Harrow Elevens in the 1822 cricket match against Eton at Lord's (Vibart 1914: p. 28). However, the Harrow School Register and the Cricket Archive (Anonymous 2003-2013) indicate that Guy, not Thomas, captained the cricket team in this historic match. There is no evidence of Thomas's sporting achievements otherwise.

9. Wordsworth became Master of Winchester School in the 1830s and wrote the key Greek grammar text used in all the public schools at the time, the *Graecae Grammaticae Rudimenta. In usum scholarum*, in 1839. He later became the Bishop of St Andrews, Dunkeld and Dunblane in Scotland.

10. The East India Company Military Seminary at Addiscombe, Surrey (founded 1809 and attended by Thomas's brothers) trained those headed for a military career in the HEIC.

11. Malthus wrote *An Essay on the Principle of Population* in 1798.

12. Malthus defended the College's curriculum and examination system in a public debate concerning the poor academic preparation of students entering into careers in the East India Company (Malthus 1817) that led to successively stricter standards. By 1826, new entrance requirements required candidates to demonstrate knowledge of at least two Latin classical texts, the easier parts of the Greek Testament, principles of grammar and common rules of arithmetic.

13. The last two of these subjects were taught by the Reverend Malthus.

14. Haughton went on to be a contestant for the Boden Chair of Sanskrit at Oxford in 1832.

15. Wilkins was also the creator of the first Bengali typeface.

16. The East India Company Act of 1813 asserted the sovereignty of the British Crown over the territories held by the HEIC, which included all of India except the Punjab and Sindh, while granting the Company a twenty-year renewable lease. The Company's political and administrative control of India was renewed by the Government of India Acts of 1833 and 1853.

17. 'The Collector' was the title of the most senior administrative authority in the district, somewhat like a local district governor. While in the Madras Civil Service, Prendergast was promoted and moved station every couple of years. He achieved the status of Writer in 1828, initially serving as assistant to the Principal Collector of Tanjore. He became acting Head Assistant to the Principal Collector of Nellore in 1829 and head assistant there in 1830. In 1831 he was promoted to Sub-Collector and Joint Magistrate of Nellore. Two years later, he became Assistant Judge and joint Criminal Judge at Guntoor. From 1834 to 1838 he was Assistant Judge and joint Criminal Judge of Tinnevelly. After his leave of absence and return to service in 1841, he served as Sub-Collector and Joint Magistrate in Salem. In 1844, he was promoted to Collector and Magistrate of Rajahmundry where he served for the next eleven years. In 1855 he was moved to his final post as Collector and Magistrate and Agent to the Governor in Ganjam until he retired in 1858.

18. She was a relation on his mother's side. The marriage was announced in *The Spectator* and in *Blackwood's Edinburgh Magazine*.

19. The *Asiatic Journal*, January 1838 (p. 39) announced the embarkation of Mr T. Prendergast to Europe, while the May 1838 issue of the *Asiatic Journal* (p. 57) announced the departure from Madras of Mrs Prendergast on the ship *True Briton*.

20. Caroline's death in the winter of 1839 at the age of thirty was announced in the *Gentleman's Magazine*.

21. Prendergast's daughter Fanny returned with him to Madras. She died there aged twenty-three in 1852. Prendergast's motherless sons were sent to Brighton to live with their grandfather, Major-General Sir Jeffrey Prendergast, and attend Addiscombe. Both subsequently returned to Madras to hold posts in the Army in India. Hew went on to become a General, while Henry (Harry) entered the Madras Engineers. At the age of twenty-three Harry was awarded the Victoria Cross for conspicuous bravery during the Indian Mutiny.

22. Thomas's cousin Guy Lushington Prendergast also served in the Madras Civil Service (1827-1859), based for over a decade in Malabar. Confusion over attributions to Thomas and Guy as mentioned with respect to their schooldays (see note 9 above) is also likely in their respective careers in Madras, as some documents refer to 'Mr. Prendergast' only. Attribution is additionally complicated by the fact that there was another Thomas Prendergast in India at this time, possibly a distant relation, who was an apothecary surgeon in the HEIC. In all, there appear to have been at least seven individuals called Thomas Prendergast active in this period.

23. One lasting monument of Prendergast's time in Madras was the Grand Godavery Anicut (dam) and the significant irrigation works associated with it. With General Sir Arthur Cotton (1803–1899), Prendergast facilitated the construction of this major infrastructure building project (Vibart 1914). A more personal legacy attests to his Christian beliefs. Prendergast was a major contributor to the building of two churches: 'The year 1850 saw the beginning of Church building in the District. Mr. T. Prendergast, of the Madras Civil Service, occupied the office of Judge at Rajahmundry. He is not known to have left any record of his good deeds, however Prendergast appears to have paid for the majority of the building expenses for the church out of his own pocket' (Penny 1922: 179).

24. The town of Cocanada is today known as Kakinada.

25. This is the chief administrative officer to the court.

26. It later expanded to a high school (1866) and then became a college (1926). It is now known as the Pithapur Rajah's Government College.

27. There are no details of how or why he became blind, but his older brother Harris Prendergast (1805-1878) also lost his sight in middle age (Welch 1911).

28. Cheltenham College was one of the first newly established public schools in the Victorian period. Cheltenham Ladies College (founded 1853) was also a new educational initiative. The town was also home to a teachers' training college and several other significant schools.

29. In 1868, Prendergast also re-married, to Theresa Charlotte Drummond (1820-1890) of London.

30. Prendergast's grandsons attended Cheltenham College between 1872 and 1886.

31. His support for charitable works linked to India is recorded in donations to the India Famine Relief Fund (Anonymous 1877) and the British Refugees from Alexandria Fund (Anonymous 1882). He also supported cultural activities and other town developments such as the establishment of the Co-operative Stores (Anonymous 1875).

32. Prendergast was buried in the Cheltenham Cemetery adjoining Christ Church. There is no headstone for Prendergast there now [Section H; plot no. 203].

33. One of Prendergast's immediate predecessors, Charles Philip Brown (1798-1884), served in the HEIC and was a Judge in Rajahmundry until 1834. He appears to have produced language-learning books for Telugu and Hindustani in the 1850s.

34. The example of Charles Berlitz (1914-2004) runs contrary to that of Prendergast. While Berlitz also developed a method of language-learning that was subsequently applied to numerous languages, he was said to have gained fluency in thirty-two languages himself (McLelland 2004).

CHAPTER 11

❖

Modern Foreign Languages Get a Voice: The Role of Journals in the Reform Movement

Andrew R. Linn

This chapter investigates the significance of specialized journals for the development of modern language teaching. It begins by explaining the development of language journals up to the point at which language teaching reform really took off with the emergence of the so-called Reform Movement in the 1880s. The principal journal for this movement was *Phonetische studien* [*Phonetic Studies*], founded in 1888 and renamed *Die neueren Sprachen* [*Modern Languages*] in 1894. The style of the early issues of this journal allows modern readers an insight into the discourse practices of that community of language scholars and teachers, the opportunity to hear its characteristic 'voice' and recreate the means by which modern-foreign-language teaching became an independent discipline.

Introduction

Any community needs what Swales (1990: 25) calls 'mechanisms of intercommunication', and these are all the more important to the community when it is a dispersed one. 'The participatory mechanisms will vary according to the community', writes Swales, 'meetings, telecommunications, correspondence, newsletters, conversations and so forth'. Such means of remaining in touch are typically online in the twenty-first century, but those of us who lived in the pre-digital age will remember the satisfaction in finding a newspaper from home when travelling overseas. It would be several days late and also exorbitantly expensive, but it provided not just information but familiar forms of discourse and a physical link with home. There are plenty of examples throughout history of the community-bonding function afforded by shared texts and documents. For nineteenth-century scholars the primary mechanism of intercommunication was the journal, and in this chapter I shall investigate the emergence of specialized journals to support the study and teaching of modern languages, and their role in the development of the field of language teaching and of the community which worked in that field.

In the second section I shall introduce the scientific journal as a genre and consider its development up to the second half of the nineteenth century, when the journal which is our main focus, *Phonetische studien*[1] [*Phonetic Studies*], began to be published. In the third section attention turns to the first journals to deal with the study of the modern foreign languages, albeit prior to the reforms — nay revolutions — in thinking about language teaching which characterize the 1880s. In the fourth section I present the community whose work and interaction resulted in the establishment of *Phonetische studien* and take the opportunity to expose a few deep-seated myths about the linguistic work of the decades around the turn of the twentieth century. Finally, in the fifth section I look closely at some features of *Phonetische studien* and its subsequent incarnations up to the end of the century in order to seek to understand more about the nature of this community of modern linguists via its discourse as revealed in its principal surviving forum. In short, the aim of this chapter is to seek to reconstruct the voice of the Reform Movement (although see the fourth section for a critique of that label).

Journals in the History of Science

Various infrastructural developments have been key to the professionalization of science. These developments have had a symbiotic relationship with the discipline itself (or disciplines) in that they have both enabled and sprung from the changing goals and ambitions of science. The foundation of the Royal Society in England in 1660 (Royal Society 2015), for example, was both a means by which scientific work could be advanced and an outcome of the enthusiasm and commitment of its founders. Morrell (1990: 982-84) identifies six '"stages" of professionalization' which resulted in science gradually developing from an amateur to a professional pursuit during the nineteenth century. These were: more full-time employment opportunities; specialist qualifications; improved training especially through the universities; increased technical complexity; growing group solidarity; and new reward systems. Underlying all this was the increased and constantly increasing opportunity for that community of scholars to communicate with one another and with interested parties outside their immediate ranks in the pages of the new, specialized journals.

The scientific journal is usually regarded as having been born in 1665 in the form of the French *Journal des Sçavans* (Manten 1980: 1) and the Royal Society's *Philosophical Transactions*. More specialized medical journals began to appear soon after, and with the eighteenth century we find the appetite for specialized professional publications becoming increasingly insatiable. This development was fired by the emergence of privately published journals and the involvement of independent publishers to supplement the more general journals of the established learned societies (Lowood 2003: 430). As the eighteenth century, with its coffee houses and shared bourgeois hunger for the consumption and generation of knowledge, turned to the nineteenth century, 'the specialization of knowledge made it increasingly difficult to maintain the notion of a unitary public sphere' (Dawson, Noakes and Topham 2004: 4).

The 1860s were a decade 'characterized by a very great expansion in the field of periodical publishing' (Ellegård 1957: 1), so the Reform Movement of the 1880s was born just as the specialized scientific periodical was achieving its pre-eminence as the primary means for professional debate. Several new journals (see below) provided natural fora for their adherents to drive forward their radical ideas about language teaching and related applied-linguistic interests, not least because 'periodicals thrived on controversy and intellectual disputes like no other nineteenth-century mode of cultural production' (Cantor et al., 2004: xix).

The 1840s had witnessed the advent of journals for general linguistics, and the modern-language journals of the 1870s and 1880s continued on the way they had paved. The Philological Society of London started to publish its *Proceedings* with effect from its first meeting in 1842 (Marshall [n.d.]). This periodical came out monthly following each meeting and consisted of the papers read at the meeting in question. The topics addressed were as wide-ranging as the interests of the members. The very first communication to be read and published in the *Proceedings* was a letter from James Yates (1789-1871), Fellow of the Royal Society and Unitarian minister, on the subject of reform in the orthography of English. This is interesting because the topic is clearly applied rather than historical or theoretical and also because orthographic reform had similarly exercised the founder members of the Royal Society in the 1660s (Scragg 1974: 98-99). The list of original members of the Philological Society (*Proceedings*, 1 (1842): 1-5) reveals the same mixture of professional scholars, ordained ministers and interested laypeople that would later characterize the contributors to *Phonetische studien*. A distinction between professional linguists and 'others' has not yet been fixed: language is a topic for all educated people and there is no formal constraint on what passes as appropriate material for discussion. By 1854 the *Proceedings* had been renamed the *Transactions*, the title which remains in use to this day, although in the 1850s it still reads more like a series of meeting reports than a collection of scholarly articles.

The next journal in this field more resembled the later conception of a journal as a collection of discrete research outputs. In 1846 the first issue of the *Zeitschrift für die Wissenschaft der Sprache* [*Journal of the Science of Language*] was published by the publishing house of Georg Reimer under the editorship of Orientalist Albert Höfer (1812-1883) of the University of Greifswald. Unlike the journal of the Philological Society, the new German journal was short-lived (four volumes), victim of what was undoubtedly a precarious market, rendered all the more so by this new periodical being the work of an individual enthusiast rather than a society with subscribing members. Although the first article proper was by the leading light of historical-comparative language study, Jacob Grimm (1785-1863) — 'Über das finnische epos' [On the *Kalevala*] (Grimm 1846) — the first issue contained several articles either written by, or translated by, the editor. The journal sought to be as wide-ranging in its understanding of the science of language as possible; and this openness to all forms of language study (not only the historical-comparative) and all languages, ancient and modern, is set out in the opening manifesto (Hoefer [*sic*] 1846). The two journals just discussed typify the general content of the first generation of periodicals in a particular field. Linguistic journals were the product of the nineteenth century and the period of 'very great expansion' in periodical publishing; and, as journals became more focused in their scope, it was inevitable that these general journals would soon be joined by ones catering for the burgeoning interest across Europe in questions relating specifically to the study and teaching of modern languages.

The First Journals for Modern Foreign Languages

The modern languages began to enter the curricula of schools across Europe around the middle of the eighteenth century (Howatt and Smith 2014: 79), bringing to an end the 'so-called quiet period' (Hüllen 2005: 63-72) in which foreign languages were not studied in the schools in any consistent way. Which languages were offered and how much teaching was available depended very much on local conditions and priorities. It was typically in response to curricular reforms at school level that university positions in modern languages were created, in order to prepare would-be school teachers for their new profession (see the papers in Engler and Haas 2000; Haas and Engler 2008). The philology of the modern languages which began to blossom as a result was, however, rather more traditional in its object of study and in its methods than the 'philology of the ear instead of the eye' (Jespersen 1962: 839) pursued by the subsequent Reform Movement.

The pages of *Englische Studien* [*English Studies*], the first journal for English, launched in 1877, thus evidence a traditional interpretation of philology, embracing both language and literature but with a strong historical emphasis. *Englische Studien* was founded by medievalist Eugen Kölbing (1846-1899), professor at the University of Breslau and editor of the new journal until his death (Utz 2006 [n.pag.]). According to Utz (2006), Kölbing was anxious about the sustainability of his project, given the very limited size of the community of English philologists in Germany. Despite these misgivings, *Englische Studien* prospered and each of its first four volumes ran to over five hundred pages. Each issue of the new periodical was divided into three sections, as was common practice: original articles; reviews of recently published literature; and 'miscellaneous'. The emphasis was firmly on Old and Middle English literature, although there were more squarely linguistic pieces, not least two very brief notes by the leading English linguist of the day, Henry Sweet (1845-1912) (Sweet 1879a; Sweet 1879b) in the second volume, and a more polemical article by the language-teaching reformer and English scholar Wilhelm Viëtor (1850-1918) (Vietor [*sic*] 1880) in Volume 3. *Englische Studien* is a good example of the diversification of the periodical literature in the mid-to-late nineteenth century as it sought to speak to an increasingly specialist audience. The project, like the *Zeitschrift für die Wissenschaft der Sprache*, was the work of an individual pioneer rather than a collective, but this time the specialist interest was what made the project marketable. Its audience was a rapidly growing one, such that in 1880 the publisher was pleased to propose the launch of a parallel journal, *Französische Studien* [*French Studies*], and within a year there was room for another journal in the same field.

Anglia: Zeitschrift für englische Philologie [*Journal of English Philology*] was founded the following year by Richard Paul Wülcker (1845-1910) in collaboration with Moritz Trautmann (1842-1920) as reviews editor. Wülcker was an Anglo-Saxonist and the contents of *Anglia* tended to focus more on Old English language and literature than *Englische Studien*, whose emphasis was more on the subsequent period. Despite this partial complementarity of coverage, there blew up 'a flurry of heated exchanges about the priority, value, and quality of both ventures during the first few years of their existence' (Utz 2006). Trautmann, professor at Bonn, was an Old English specialist too, but also author of a comparative practical phonology of English, French and German (Trautmann 1886). The inclusion on the editorial board of Sweet and also the Leipzig phonetician Eduard Sievers (1850-1932) was probably thanks to Trautmann engaging his extended 'discourse community' (see Linn 2008); and Sweet wrote several pieces in the earliest volumes of *Anglia. Anglia*, still going strong today, takes pride in being the longest-standing continuous journal publication dedicated to English. Today its sub-title appears in both English and German guise and English has become the language of publication.

The last journal I shall mention here, dedicated to the traditional philology of the modern languages (see Storost 2000: 1260 for journals dealing with German), is the *Zeitschrift für romanische Philologie* [*Journal of Romance Philology*]. This was founded in the same year as *Englische Studien* under the editorship of Gustav Gröber (1844-1911), professor at the University of Breslau and so a colleague of Kölbing. It was published by the Max Niemeyer Verlag, publisher of *Anglia*, which demonstrates both a real commitment to the field of modern-language philology by the academic publishers and something of a cartel amongst editors and publishing houses. Like *Anglia* it is still in print; and also like *Anglia* it has now been taken over by the de Gruyter publishing house. As with its sister periodical, the early issues covered the full range of philological topics, although there was greater emphasis on the language than was the case in the English journals. In Volume 2 of 1878, for example, six of the nine articles are on language, including 'Die Negation im Altfranzösischen' [Negation in Old French] by Friedrich Perle and 'Ueber die vocalisirten Consonanten des Altfranzösischen' [On the Vocalized Consonants of Old French] by Oscar Ulbrich. This is, however, philology of the most traditional sort. There appears to have been no real interest in more practical linguistic questions or applied methods, such as those which would have faced these scholars in the classroom and would have been pressing issues for their students as they prepared to go out into the schools. In fact they signal an interest in language which, with its historical emphasis and focus on narrow phonological and morphological points, looks firmly backwards towards the first half of the century. The time was right for a revolution.

The Reform Movement and the Journal Genre

The journals discussed thus far supported the professionalization of language study in the nineteenth century as characterized above by Morrell. In the canon of the history of linguistics — the version of that history propagated through the principal textbooks in the field, thus defining its boundaries for new generations of its students — the professional field during the nineteenth century emerges with certain standardized characteristics. First, it was dominated by German science and German scholars, a view expounded, for example, in R. H. Robins's *A Short History of Linguistics*:

> after 1800 [...] one is brought face to face with a remarkable continuity of scholarship focused on a specialized field of theory and practice, in which generations of scholars, mostly from Germany or from other countries trained in Germany, built up their subject on the basis of what had been done by their predecessors or earlier contemporaries. (Robins 1997: 190)

The second canonical characteristic of the nineteenth century is that it was one of historical-comparative studies which continued unabated until the Saussurean revolution in the second decade of the twentieth century, as set out in Seuren's *Western Linguistics: An Historical Introduction*: 'In the 19th century, the most obvious and spectacular progress was made in historical linguistics' (Seuren 2004 [1998]: 51); and '19th century comparative philology, which led straight to 20th century structuralism and hence to the gamut of modern theories of grammar' (Seuren 2004 [1998]: 104).

I do not deny this version of history, but such a view of the development of linguistics fails to take into account the applied-linguistic work carried out in the final three decades of the century by scholars from across Europe, with England and the Nordic countries leading the way. The proponents of this work, inspired by the advances made in the field of phonetics, turned their focus onto what they called 'the living language', wherever that may be found. Henry Sweet, in his presidential address to the Philological Society in 1877, wrote of the importance of 'phonetics and pronunciation' in bringing the language scholar 'face to face with the ultimate facts of all linguistic investigation, viz. the living language' (Sweet 1879c: 7).

Many of these language scholars were or had been foreign language teachers and so they had a strong interest in language-teaching reform and have thus been identified as members of the *Reform Movement* (Howatt and Smith 2002; Howatt with Widdowson 2004: Ch. 14). However, their commitment to investigating the living language drew them to other issues as well, such as spelling reform and dialectology. As Howatt and Smith (2014: 82) note, the term 'Reform methods' was not used in the 1870s and 1880s to describe the activities of this community of applied linguists. They referred to themselves by a variety of other names; and labels were applied freely as linguistics moved ahead at a tempo almost too quick for those who sought to define the various new philologies (Toy 1885). The leading Danish linguist, Otto Jespersen (1897-1899: 55) writes of 'the Anglo-Scandinavian School', a label I have found helpful for historiographical purposes (Linn 2008), as it shines the light away from the trope of German dominance. Paul Passy preferred the label 'les jeunes phonéticiens' [the young phoneticians] (e.g. Passy 1887: 4), emphasizing the unifying influence of phonetics as well as their radicalism by suggesting a link to 'die Junggrammatiker', the 'young philologists' (Neogrammarians) of the previous generation. Later on, looking back at their achievements, Hans

Raudnitzky (Raudnitzky 1911) wrote of *Die Bell-Sweetsche Schule* [the Bell–Sweet School], emphasizing the role of key pioneers in the field. A fully adequate label may prove elusive, but 'Reform Movement', linked as it is specifically to reform in language teaching, does not do justice to the full range of this group's ambitions for the science of language (see next section), although I shall continue to use it here since the focus of this book is on teaching. The fact remains — in surviving correspondence; evidence of visits to each other's homes; encounters at conferences and on dialect field trips, etc. — that the pioneers of this new approach to language study and teaching communicated with each other enthusiastically and incessantly and they constituted a textbook example of a 'discourse community':

> a set of individuals who can be interpreted as constituting a community on the basis of the ways in which their oral or written discourse practices reveal common interests, goals and beliefs, i.e. on the degree of institutionalisation that their discourse displays. The members of the community may or may not be conscious of sharing those discourse practices. (Watts 1999: 43)

I do not have the space to discuss the 'set of individuals' in detail here or to explore the full range of means by which they interacted and how their vision of the living language developed (see Linn 2008). Here I shall concentrate on the journal they made their own, *Phonetische studien*, the forum in which language teachers from school and university came together around a common cause and made their voice heard. Borg, following Swales (1990), defines a prototypical discourse community as 'a society of stamp collectors scattered around the world but united by a shared interest in the stamps of Hong Kong': 'The collectors never gather together physically; instead a newsletter, that has a particular form of text organization, making it a genre, which they use to pursue their goals, unites them' (Borg 2003: 398). The group of teachers and scholars and other interested parties we are discussing here did meet, and it is clear that their discourse was both oral and written. As their oral practices do not survive, we are limited to studying their written discourse in order to help us to understand the processes by which modern foreign languages became a discipline and so we now turn to the genre in question, their 'newsletter'.

Phonetische studien (1888–)

The journals explored above gave proponents of the linguistics of the modern languages a means to talk to one another in a scholarly environment as the modern languages established their *bona fides* as university disciplines. In the same way, *Phonetische studien*, renamed *Die neueren sprachen: Zeitschrift für den neusprachlichen unterricht* [*The Modern Languages: Journal of Modern Language Teaching*] in 1894, provided the discourse forum for the Reform Movement. It was not, in fact, the first journal to seek to bridge the gap between school and university, between the study of foreign languages and their teaching. In the same year as the short-lived *Zeitschrift für die Wissenschaft der Sprache* was established, Ludwig Herrig (1816-1889) and Heinrich Viehoff (1804-1886) had published the first volume of their *Archiv für das Studium der neueren Sprachen* [*Archive of Modern Language Studies*]. The editors did not represent a self-styled school, nor did they have the sense of purpose and of independence of the later movement. Content remained 'old' philological. They explain that their focus is on historical-comparative grammar and onomastics; literary history; metrics; poetics and prosody; the interpretation and criticism of texts; and the teaching of those topics (Herrig and Viehoff 1846: 3). There is little interest in methodology, although the early volumes do contain reviews of new teaching materials. But in an account of the means by which the community of modern-language scholars and teachers came to exchange ideas, the *Archiv für das Studium der neueren Sprachen* is a landmark in the pre-history of the Reform Movement. A complete investigation of the role of the journals in the establishment of modern-language teaching as a field would call for a more intensive study of this journal and its predecessor, the *Archiv für den Unterricht im Deutschen* [*Archive of German Teaching*] (1843–44) than our current focus allows.

    Phonetische studien appeared in 1888 with the subtitle *Zeitschrift für wissenschaftliche und praktische phonetik mit besonderer rücksicht auf den unterricht in der aussprache* [*Journal of Scientific and Practical Phonetics with Particular Regard for the Teaching of Pronunciation*]. The title was a work in progress, as we shall see in due course; and its fluidity tells us much about the journal and the community it served. The style of the title was clearly calqued on that of the journals we have already surveyed above (*X studien*) and it served to position the newcomer amongst them as a serious contribution to the philological literature. By the 1880s journals had come to 'represent the most important single source of information for the scientific research community' (Meadows 1979: 1); and any self-respecting scholarly endeavour needed one to give it credibility as well as serving 'to create and solidify a bonding sense of community for scholars who might otherwise have remained isolated individuals or small cadres' (Christie 1990: 17). *Phonetische studien* appeared two years after the Scandinavian philologists' meeting in Stockholm in 1886, attended by Passy, which led to the formal statement of the four key principles of language teaching reform (see Linn 2002). This meeting, and indeed the other philologists' conferences which were by now a regular fixture in the annual calendar, must have been an invigorating and empowering experience for the phonetically minded language-teaching reformers; and the new journal was a way of keeping the community together and focused between times. Regular reports on efforts to put reform measures into practice provided a source of encouragement to those who felt themselves to be lone voices against a chorus of traditional methods. However, those lone voices were joining forces rapidly to form a new chorus of reforming zeal. Writing in 1893, and looking back over the previous years, Viëtor charts the dramatic development of this community of scholars and teachers dedicated to applying the insights of phonetics to language teaching reform. He notes that 'this rather insignificant germ of reform literature has meanwhile grown to very considerable dimensions' (1893: 353) and that the community is coming together in significant numbers:

> The [...] *Verband der Neuphilologen Deutschlands* [German Association of Modern Philologists] now numbers about one thousand members, and may be said to be

thoroughly representative. [...] Between five and six hundred modern language
teachers of different countries have joined [the Phonetic Teachers' Association].
(354)

The founding editor of *Phonetische studien* was Wilhelm Viëtor himself, 'the main
initiator of the late 19th century Reform Movement' (Smith 2007), its *primus motor*
via his famous reform pamphlet (Quousque Tandem 1882), but the involvement
of the wider community of scholars and teachers is clear from the title page on
which the members of the editorial board are listed. Volume 1 was published
'unter mitwirkung von' [with the collaboration of] fifty-one leading names in the
interlinked fields of phonetics and language teaching, although the fifty-one were
evidently only the most noteworthy, as the list concludes 'u.a.' [amongst others].
The group numbers seventy-seven 'u.a.' in Volume 2 and this is an ever-growing
army of supporters, such that the list is replaced from Volume 3 onwards by the
statement 'unter mitwirkung zahlreicher fachgenossen' [with the collaboration of
numerous colleagues]. Amongst the list of names are: Henry Sweet; the leading
Norwegian linguist of the day Johan Storm (1836-1920); Otto Jespersen; the Swedish
phonetician and reformer J. A. Lundell (1851-1940); and the Norwegian teacher and
grammarian August Western (1856-1940). These are joined by *éminences grises* of the
older generation of phonetics such as Alexander Melville Bell (1819-1905) and A. J.
Ellis (1814-1890). The new journal was crucially showing itself to have the authority
to take on its role.

It was not unusual for new journals to open with a 'manifesto', setting out the
agenda for the new publication, siting it within the market and clarifying what
readers could expect. This was the case for the two new journals of 1846 discussed
above (*Zeitschrift für die Wissenschaft der Sprache* and *Archiv für das Studium der neueren
Sprachen*). Indeed, the editors of *Archiv* open their preface thus:

> Wenn man von dem Herausgeber jeder periodischen Schrift mit Recht
> verlangen darf, daß er sich beim Beginn derselben über Gegenstand, Zweck
> und Umfang eines Unternehmens ausspreche, wovon er zunächst nur schwache
> Anfänge und kleine Fragmente dem Publikum zur Ansicht vorlegen kann: so
> erscheint diese Forderung bei einer Zeitschrift, wie die hier angekündigte,
> welche sich ein neues Feld zur Bearbeitung ausersehen hat und so in gewisser
> Hinsicht als die erste ihrer Art gelten kann, doppelt gerechtfertigt. (Herrig and
> Viehoff 1846: 1)

> [If it can reasonably be expected of the editor of every periodical that he
> pronounce at the beginning of the same on the object, goal and reach of the
> endeavour, of which he can at first only present weak beginnings and small
> fragments to the public, so the challenge seems doubly justified in a journal,
> like the one presented here, which has chosen to develop a new field and so in
> a sense can be considered the first of its kind.]

Phonetische studien does not open with a statement by the editor but with an article
from the pen of one of the first to hold a university position in phonetics and
the architect of the teaching reform principles elaborated at the 1886 Stockholm
meeting, J. A. Lundell. It is, however, a rhetorically daring manifesto for the new
journal and the ambitions of the community it served.

Lundell's enthusiasm and his sense of being involved in a paradigm shift are palpable. His manifesto, with the seemingly innocuous tile 'Die phonetik als universitätsfach' [Phonetics as a University Subject], opens with a clear statement of that shift. The article starts with quotations from William Dwight Whitney (1827-1894) and from Sweet, predicting a bright phonetic future and immediately marshalling two of the leading linguists on either side of the Atlantic to the cause:

> [Phonetics] will also become by itself a definite science, or department of study, having its close and important relations to physiology and acoustics, as well as to philology. (Whitney 1875)

> I have little doubt that before many years there will be professors of phonetics and elocution at many of the Continental universities. (Sweet 1882)[2]

With these giants looking forward, Lundell looks back to the previous generations, both the early nineteenth-century pioneers of historical-comparative linguistics and the Neogrammarians, as 'yesterday's men':

> Die begründer der vergleichenden sprachforschung in der ersten hälfte dieses jahrhunderts, BOPP, GRIMM und die übrigen vertreter der historisch-antiquarischen richtung, kehrten sich bekanntlich an die eigentliche natur der sprachlaute nicht viel. [...] Nicht nur BOPP und GRIMM, sogar SCHLEICHER und CURTIUS sind schon antiquirt. (Lundell 1888: 3-4)

> [The founders of comparative linguistic research in the first half of this century, Bopp, Grimm and the other representatives of the historical-antiquarian direction, as is generally known did not give much to the actual nature of the sounds of language. [...] Not only Bopp and Grimm, but even Schleicher and Curtius are already old-fashioned.]

The thirty-six-year-old 'Young Turk' Lundell does soften his dismissal of his forebears by acknowledging that 'die jüngere generation steht eben auf den schultern der älteren und hat deshalb einen weiteren horizont' [the younger generation just stands on the shoulders of the older one and therefore has a wider horizon] (1888: 4). His enthusiasm for what phonetics can achieve is almost unbounded. He makes the case for the role of phonetic insights in historical-comparative language study, but he also maintains that phonetics will revolutionize orthographies, the teaching of reading, the education of the deaf and dumb [die taubstummenbildung], speech pathology, the study of metrics, rhetoric and the art of singing. As if this list of beneficiaries from the science of phonetics were not long enough, he finally erupts: 'Also auch hier mehr phonetik!' [So here too more phonetics!] (1888: 6).

While Lundell's manifesto is a clarion call for the increased study of phonetics, as might well be expected at the start of a publication entitled *Phonetic Studies*, reform in language teaching is the focus of many of the articles and reports which fill the pages of the early volumes. In fact it feels as though the journal cannot quite make up its mind what its role is, as witnessed by the constantly changing title in the early volumes. The constantly changing title is indicative of a community in a hurry, acting first and then thinking later, wanting to get on with what they believed to be important reforms. The first volume of 1888 was entitled *Phonetische studien. Zeitschrift für wissenschaftliche und praktische phonetik mit besonderer rücksicht auf den unterricht in der aussprache* [*Journal of Scientific and Practical Phonetics with Particular Regard for the Teaching of Pronunciation*]. So, to begin with phonetics was in the foreground with the teaching of pronunciation listed as a particular focus. The titles of subsequent volumes are as follows. Volume 2 is *Phonetische studien. Zeitschrift für wissenschaftliche und praktische phonetik mit besonderer rücksicht auf die phonetische reform des sprachunterrichts* [*Journal of Scientific and Practical Phonetics with Particular Regard for the Phonetic Reform of Language Teaching*], such that it is not only the teaching of pronunciation that is in the spotlight now but reform in language teaching more broadly. Volume 3 is *Phonetische studien. Zeitschrift für wissenschaftliche und praktische phonetik mit besonderer rücksicht auf die REFORM des sprachunterrichts* [*Journal of Scientific and Practical Phonetics with Particular Regard for the REFORM of Language Teaching*], the phonetic element of the reform being no longer specified but with reform upgraded via the use of upper-case letters; reform has now become more overtly visible. Volume 7 is effectively Volume 1 of *Die neueren sprachen. Zeitschrift für den neusprachlichen unterricht mit dem beiblatt Phonetische Studien* [*Modern Languages. Journal of the Teaching of Modern Languages with the Supplement Phonetische Studien*], so by 1893 phonetics has drifted into the background, with the former journal described as a 'beiblatt' [supplement]. Ernst von Sallwürk explains in his introduction:

> Die *Phonetischen Studien* erweitern sich zu einer zeitschrift für den gesamten neusprachlichen unterricht, soweit derselbe in den gesichtskreis unserer höheren schulen fällt. Sie bezeichnen durch diese vergrösserung ihres gebietes den fortschritt, den seit ihrem bestehen der neusprachliche unterricht selbst gemacht hat. (Sallwürk 1893: 1)

> [*Phonetische Studien* has been expanded into a journal for the whole of modern languages teaching, in so far as it falls within the scope of our higher schools. Via this expansion of its field it indicates the advance that modern-language education has itself made since it was founded.]

Volume 6 of *Die neueren sprachen* (1899) simply describes itself as a 'fortsetzung [continuation] der phonetischen studien' and by the new century the rhetorical shift is complete, from a journal of phonetic studies to a journal of modern-language teaching, appearing in ten annual instalments. On the front of Volume 10 for 1902/1903 phonetic studies are no longer mentioned at all.

Another manifestation of the fact that the journal is a 'work in progress' is that reviews and replies to those reviews could appear in the same volume. The discourse is ongoing. In Volume 1 Willem Sijbrand Logeman of Newton School, Rock Ferry, Birkenhead, and subsequently Professor of Modern Languages at the South African College (later the University of Cape Town), published a series of 'remarks' on Passy's views on the phonetics of French in June 1887 and these were immediately followed by Passy's response of August 1887. This exchange was good-natured, although Logeman did take the opportunity to have a swipe at the 'enthusiasm for dealing with "living realities"' (Logeman 1888: 170) and at the opinion of Western and others that teachers should teach their own dialect: 'Would Mr Western like a Lancashire or Dorsetshire man to teach the dialect of his county as "English"? or that of Alsace or say dep. Puy de Dôme as French?' (Logeman 1888: 170). Logeman was a future professor and a textbook author, so it would be wrong to characterize this sort of disagreement as one between scholars and practitioners, but the roster of contributors is one which does not discriminate between academic linguists and those dealing with language matters from a practical point of view. One of the strengths of the Reform Movement, I maintain (see Linn 2011), was precisely that practice and theory were undifferentiated; there was just the 'living language'. This was a journal of 'wissenschaftliche <u>und</u> praktische phonetik'.

However, given the immediacy of response allowed this discourse community by the availability of a journal with regular issues, real arguments could blow up, as when R. M'Lintock of Liverpool published a review of Sweet's *Elementarbuch des gesprochenen englisch* in Volume 2 of *Phonetische studien* in which he objected in the strongest possible terms to Sweet's version of London English, 'wie er in gebildeten kreisen gesprochen wird' [as spoken in educated circles] (Sweet 1885: iii). For M'Lintock this was a variety which 'the cultured — and even the half-cultured — of three fourths of the kingdom can scarcely hear without a feeling of somewhat scornful displeasure tempered with amusement at the curious combination of (apparent) mincing affectation and (real) slovenliness displayed by it' (M'Lintock 1889: 212). Sweet's 'Reply to Mr Maclintock's Review' was characteristically explosive:

> Mr M'Lintock's review [...] shows such utter and complacent ignorance of the elements of phonetics and philology, and involves so many gross misunderstandings of plain statements in my book that I shall not stop to discuss details, but content myself with a few general remarks. (Sweet 1890: 114)

M'Lintock's mournful response, published straight afterwards, notes that, regarding the 'prejudices' of which Sweet accuses him, he has 'no interest in them whatsoever' (M'Lintock 1890: 115). (R. J. Lloyd would later (Lloyd 1895: 52) recommend that the student of English should 'choose a sound *via media*, and speak an English which will be recognised as pure and good everywhere'!) Academic fights make for amusing reading, but there are some serious points here about the nature of the discourse community as it exchanges ideas in the journal: it brought all those committed to the 'living language' together, regardless of their status or views; it was one of immediacy, of 'speak now and worry about the consequences later'; it was made up of passionate people for whom language and language teaching were something important.

The activity reflected in the pages of this journal gives the lie to the assumption that nothing new was happening in the world of linguistics between historical-comparative philology and Saussure, contrary to Seuren (2004 [1998]), cited above. The fact that the Association Phonétique des Professeurs de Langues Vivantes (later the International Phonetic Association) boasted 743 members by 1896 would further support this line. The *Phonetische studien* community also demonstrates that this was no uniquely German endeavour. In his report on the activities of the Association Phonétique, Viëtor (1897: 60) lists the national background of that Association's members. The largest contingent is from Germany (202), but ninety-two are from Sweden, seventy-eight from Denmark, seventy-one from France and fifty-four from England. Twenty-two nationalities are represented, making phonetics and its application in the language classroom a truly international commitment. Contributors to the discourse of *Phonetische studien* are similarly international. Some of the more regular contributors include: Rudolf Lenz (1863-1938), director of the Instituto Pedagógico at the University of Chile; Sylvester Primer (1842-1912) from Charleston, South Carolina, later at the University of Texas at Austin, whose contributions dealt with the dialect of Charleston; József Balassa (1864-1945) from Székesfehérvar, Hungary; Romeo Lovera (Salò, Italy, 'un personnage clé, dont le profil reste à tracer' [a key personality, whose profile remains to be drawn] (Galazzi 2002: [n.pag.]).

Conclusion

In 1994 Konrad Schröder wrote an overview of the twentieth-century history of *Die Neueren Sprachen* (Schröder 1994), focusing on the impact of the history of ideas and of developments in German society on its contents. In the following year (1995) the journal seemed to enter its final issue (94.6 (December 1995)), although it started to appear again in 2010, this time as a yearbook rather than in monthly instalments. On page 589 of the issue of December 1995 the journal was described as having been a 'reformfreudiges Organ, das die Verbindung von Schule und Hochschule, Praxis und Wissenschaft auf hohem Niveau zu thematisieren versuchte' [reform-minded organ which tried to address the link between school and university, practice and science, at a high level]. It had certainly been that; and the connection between school and university, practice and science, had characterized it from the very outset, indeed had been one of its major strengths. However, this somewhat laconic backward glance does not capture the great significance of the journal, notably during its years as *Phonetische studien*, as the key forum for the development of the Reform Movement in language teaching as well as for the wider Anglo-Scandinavian School.

Over the course of two centuries the journal genre had become the academic and professional forum par excellence, a position it retains to this day; and this pre-eminent position was fully arrived at by the time of the Reform Movement. It was inevitable that the new movement would seek to establish a journal as part of its programme of expansion and development, but *Phonetische studien* was more than just a signal that modern-language teaching had come of age. It had a title which placed it alongside the other serious philological journals and it had an extensive international editorial board to give its contents the necessary imprimatur. From the historiographical point of view it allows us to see the Reform Movement in operation, to hear its voice. That voice is one of urgency and enthusiasm, exemplified above all in the ever-changing title but also in the way in which debate is actively taking place in its pages. This is no dry academic publication, but rather a hot-house of impassioned views about the importance of phonetics and the need for a revolution in language teaching based on the study and application of phonetics. Given this, it is noteworthy how quickly phonetics slips into the background in terms of how the journal presents itself. Scientific journals had become specialized forums; and another journal for phonetics was established at the same time. In May 1886 the first issue of *Dhi Fonètik Tîtcer* was published by Dhi Fonètik Tîtcerz' Asóciécon as the brainchild of Passy (MacMahon 1986). This journal also underwent a name change, becoming *Le maître phonétique* in 1889 (before later morphing in 1970 into the *Journal of the International Phonetic Association*); and further research is called for in order to understand the relationship between these journals, their contributors, their readers and the subsequent development of both phonetics and the theory and practice of modern-language teaching. The 1880s were heady times; and the air of excitement, infecting those within and beyond academia, the sense that language learning is important, is one of enduring value.

Bibliography

BORG, ERIK. 2003. 'Discourse Community', *ELT Journal*, 57: 398–400

CANTOR, GEOFFREY, ET AL. 2004. 'Introduction', in *Culture and Science in the Nineteenth-Century Media*, ed. by Louise Henson et al. (Aldershot & Burlington, VT: Routledge), pp. xvii–xxv

CHRISTIE, JOHN R. R. 1990. 'The Development of the Historiography of Science', in *Companion to the History of Modern Science*, ed. by R. C. Olby et al. (London: Routledge), pp. 5–22

DAWSON, GOWAN, RICHARD NOAKES, and JONATHAN R. TOPHAM. 2004. 'Introduction', in *Science in the Nineteenth-Century Periodical: Reading the Magazine of Nature*, ed. by Geoffrey Cantor et al. (Cambridge: Cambridge University Press), pp. 1–34

ELLEGÅRD, ALVAR. 1957. 'The Readership of the Periodical Press in Mid-Victorian Britain', *Acta Universitatis Gothoburgensis*, 63.3: 1–41

ENGLER, BALZ, and RENATE HAAS (eds). 2000. *European English Studies: Contributions towards the History of a Discipline* (Leicester: The English Association)

GALAZZI, ENRICA. 2002. 'Echos phonétiques en Sicile entre XIXe et XXe siècles', *Documents pour l'histoire du français langue étrangère ou seconde* <http://dhfles.revues.org/2626> [accessed 5 June 2015]

GRIMM, JACOB. 1846. 'Über das finnische epos', *Zeitschrift für die Wissenschaft der Sprache*, 1: 13–55

HAAS, RENATE, and BALZ ENGLER (eds). 2008. *European English Studies: Contributions towards the History of a Discipline II* (Leicester: The English Association)

HERRIG, LUDWIG, and HEINRICH VIEHOFF. 1846. 'Vorwort', *Archiv für das Studium der neueren Sprachen*, 1: 1–4

HOEFER, A. 1846. 'Andeutungen zur Eröffnung der Zeitschrift', *Zeitschrift für die Wissenschaft der Sprache*, 1: 1–12

HOWATT, A. P. R., and RICHARD C. SMITH (eds). 2002. *Modern Language Teaching: The Reform Movement*, 5 vols (London: Routledge)

——, WITH H. G. WIDDOWSON. 2004 [1984]. *A History of English Language Teaching*, 2nd edn (Oxford: Oxford University Press)

——, and RICHARD SMITH. 2014. 'The History of Teaching English as a Foreign Language, from a British and European Perspective', *Language and History*, 57: 75–95

HÜLLEN, WERNER. 2005. *Kleine Geschichte des Fremdsprachenlernens* (Berlin: Erich Schmidt)

JESPERSEN, OTTO. 1897–1899. *Fonetik: En systematisk fremstilling af læren om sproglyd* (København: Schubothe)

——. 1962. 'Farewell Lecture at the University Given on 25th May 1925', in *Selected Writings of Otto Jespersen* (London: Allen & Unwin; Tokyo: Senjo), pp. 835-45

LINN, ANDREW R. 2002. 'Quousque Tandem: Language-Teaching Reform in 19th-Century Scandinavia', *The Henry Sweet Society Bulletin*, 38: 34-42

——. 2008. 'The Birth of Applied Linguistics: The Anglo-Scandinavian School as "Discourse Community"', *Historiographia Linguistica*, 35: 342-84

——. 2011. 'Impact: Linguistics in the Real World', *Histoire Epistémologie Langage*, 33: 15-27

LLOYD, R. J. 1895. 'Standard English', *Die neueren sprachen*, 2: 52-53

LOGEMAN, WILLEM S. 1888. 'Remarks on Paul Passy's French Phonetics', *Phonetische studien*, 1: 170-71

LOWOOD, HENRY. 2003. 'Journal', in *The Oxford Companion to the History of Modern Science*, ed. by J. L. Heilbron (Oxford: Oxford University Press), pp. 429-31

LUNDELL, J. A. 1888. 'Die phonetik als universitätsfach', *Phonetische studien*, 1: 1-17

M'LINTOCK, R. 1889. 'Review of Henry Sweet, *Elementarbuch des gesprochenen englisch*', *Phonetische studien*, 2: 212-16

——. 1890. 'On Mr Sweet's Reply', *Phonetische studien*, 3: 115

MACMAHON, M. K. C. 1986. 'The International Phonetic Association: The First 100 Years', *Journal of the International Phonetic Association*, 16: 30-38

MANTEN, A. A. 1980. 'Development of European Scientific Publishing before 1850', in *Development of Scientific Publishing in Europe*, ed. by A. J. Meadows (Amsterdam, New York and Oxford: Elsevier), pp. 1-22

MARSHALL, FIONA. [N.D.]. 'History of the Philological Society: The Early Years' <http://www.philsoc.org.uk/includes/Download.asp?FileID=39> [accessed 18 May 2015]

MEADOWS, A. J. 1979. 'Introduction', in *The Scientific Journal*, ed. by A. J. Meadows (London: Aslib), p. 1

MORRELL, J. B. 1990. 'Professionalisation', in *Companion to the History of Modern Science*, ed. by R. C. Olby et al. (London: Routledge), pp. 980-89

PASSY, PAUL. 1887. *Le phonétisme au Congrès philologique de Stockholm en 1886: Rapport présenté au Ministre de l'Instruction publique* (Paris: Delagrave & Hachette)

QUOUSQUE TANDEM. 1882. *Der Sprachunterricht muss umkehren! Ein Beitrag zur Überbürdungsfrage* (Heilbronn: Henninger)

RAUDNITZKY, HANS. 1911. *Die Bell-Sweetsche Schule: Ein Beitrag zur Geschichte der englischen Phonetik* (Marburg: Elwert)

ROBINS, R. H. 1997 [1967]. *A Short History of Linguistics*, 4th edn (London and New York: Longman)

ROYAL SOCIETY. 2015. 'History' <https://royalsociety.org/about-us/history> [accessed 18 May 2015]

SALLWÜRK, E. VON. 1893. 'Zur Einführung', *Die neueren sprachen*, 1: 1-4

SCHRÖDER, KONRAD. 1994. '100 Jahre Fremdsprachendidaktik. 100 Jahre *Die Neueren Sprachen*', *Die Neueren Sprachen*, 93: 6-44

SCRAGG, D. G. 1974. *A History of English Spelling* (Manchester: Manchester University Press; New York: Barnes & Noble)

SEUREN, PIETER A. M. 2004 [1998]. *Western Linguistics: An Historical Introduction* (Oxford and Malden, MA: Blackwell)

SMITH, RICHARD C. 2007. 'Wilhelm Viëtor's Life and Career' <www2.warwick.ac.uk/fac/soc/al/research/collect/elt_archive/halloffame/vietor/life> [accessed 4 June 2015]

STOROST, JÜRGEN. 2000. 'Die "neuen Philologien", ihre Institutionen und Periodica: Eine Übersicht', in *History of the Language Sciences / Geschichte der Sprachwissenschaften / Histoire des Sciences du Langage*, ed. by Sylvain Auroux et al., 3 vols (Berlin: Mouton de Gruyter), II, 1240-72

SWALES, JOHN M. 1990. *Genre Analysis: English in Academic and Research Settings* (Cambridge:

Cambridge University Press)

SWEET, HENRY. 1879A. 'Some of the Sources of the Anglo-Saxon Chronicle', *Englische Studien*, 2: 310-12

——. 1879B. 'Old English Etymologies', *Englische Studien*, 2: 312-16

——. 1879C. 'The Work of the Philological Society, from May, 1876, to May, 1877', *Transactions of the Philological Society*, 1877/88/89: 1-122

——. 1885. *Elementarbuch des gesprochenen englisch (grammatik, texte und glossar)* (Oxford: Clarendon Press)

——. 1890. 'Reply to Mr Maclintock's Review', *Phonetische studien*, 3: 114-15

TOY, C. H. 1885. 'The New Philology', *Science*, 6: 366-68

TRAUTMANN, MORITZ. 1886. *Die Sprachlaute im allgemeinen und die Laute des Englischen, Französischen und Deutschen im besonderen* (Leipzig: Fock)

UTZ, RICHARD. 2006. 'Medieval Scholarship in *Englische Studien*, Part 1: Eugen Kölbing and the Foundational Period (1877-1899)', *Erfurt Electronic Studies in English*, 12 <webdoc.sub. gwdg.de/edoc/ia/eese/artic26/Richard/textfield.html> [accessed 5 May 2015]

VIETOR [*sic*], W. 1880. 'Die wissenschaftliche grammatik und der englische unterricht', *Englische Studien*, 3: 106-24

——. 1893. 'A New Method of Language Teaching', *Educational Review*, 1893: 351-65

WATTS, RICHARD J. 1999. 'The Social Construction of Standard English: Grammar Writers as a "Discourse Community"', in *Standard English: The Widening Debate*, ed. by Tony Bex and Richard Watts (London: Routledge), pp. 40-68

——. 2008. 'Grammar-Writers in Eighteenth-Century Britain: A Community of Practice or a Discourse Community?', in *Grammars, Grammarians and Grammar Writing*, ed. by Ingrid Tieken-Boon van Ostade (Berlin: Mouton de Gruyter), pp. 37-56

Notes to Chapter 11

1. It did not adopt upper-case letters word-initially in nouns.
2. As cited in Lundell 1888: 1.

CHAPTER 12

❖

Technology and Pronunciation Teaching, 1890–1940

Michael Ashby and Joanna Przedlacka

This chapter considers the relationship between experimental phonetics and pronunciation teaching in the period 1890–1940, a period when phonetics was very influential in modern language teaching. It is shown that although the founders of the Reform Movement were 'ear-phoneticians', there were throughout the period attempts to apply the instruments and techniques of the phonetics laboratory in language teaching. In fact, utility in language teaching was one of the justifications for the foundation and funding of phonetic research laboratories. We review some of the devices which were available, their capabilities and limitations, and the linguistic and pedagogical assumptions which underlie the attempts to use them. We give a critical evaluation of their likely effectiveness in teaching, and review the way in which these efforts were rather sensationally documented in the popular press.

Phonetics and the Reform Movement

Almost all of the leading figures who guided and inspired the Reform Movement — Henry Sweet, Paul Passy, Wilhelm Viëtor and Otto Jespersen, for example — were phoneticians, but the kind of phonetics they practised required no laboratories and no instruments. They were concerned with the development of practical skill in listening and sound production, and with phonetic transcription as a means of representing natural conversational speech. True, Viëtor gave ample space to experimental work by others in *Phonetische Studien*, the journal he produced from 1887, and himself gave first-hand reports of the main techniques (Viëtor 1894). Jespersen also tried out various instrumental methods (Jespersen 1995: 96–97), but neither made contributions to scientific phonetics themselves. Passy did no experimental work, while Sweet spoke of a 'natural antagonism' between linguistic and experimental approaches:

> At present there is a natural and indeed, unavoidable antagonism between the practical linguistic phonetician and the physico-mathematical instrumental phonetician. [...] It cannot be too often repeated that instrumental phonetics is, strictly speaking, not phonetics at all. It only supplies materials which are useless

till they have been tested and accepted from the linguistic phonetician's point of view. The final arbiter in all phonetic questions is the trained ear of a practical phonetician. Differences which cannot be perceived by the ear — and many of the results of instrumental phonetics are of this character — must be ignored; and what contradicts a trained ear cannot be accepted. And it must not be forgotten that the utility of instrumental phonetics as a means of research does not necessarily imply a corresponding utility as a help in acquiring a practical mastery of sounds which, as we have seen, is the only sound foundation of the science. As yet, instrumental phonetics, so far from being a help in the practical study of sounds, has been rather a hindrance, by diverting the learner's attention from that patient cultivation of the organic and acoustic sense which is the indispensable basis. (Sweet 1908: 109-10)

The most important twentieth-century successor of these phoneticians, Daniel Jones (1881–1967), was also an ear-phonetician rather than a scientist, as was his influential associate Harold Palmer (1877–1949) (Collins and Mees 1999; Smith 1999). Nevertheless, we shall argue in this chapter that the attempt to apply a 'scientific' kind of phonetics in language teaching was present all along. We examine what devices and techniques were available and look critically at their possible effectiveness.

Experimental Phonetics

The techniques and instruments of experimental phonetics began to be settled from about 1890 onwards, particularly under the leadership of the Abbé Rousselot (1846–1924) in Paris. Rousselot began to publish from 1891; his *Principes de phonétique expérimentale* appeared in 1897; and he set up a dedicated laboratory of experimental phonetics at the Collège de France in 1898. Similar laboratories soon followed elsewhere in Europe and around the world.

By 1916, one estimate (Barrows 1916: 62) put the number of phonetics laboratories worldwide at 'something more than twenty-five [...] most of which are in Europe'. Unfortunately, Sarah Barrows does not give a list, mentioning by name only Rousselot's laboratory in Paris and the much more modern laboratory in Hamburg to which her visit was the occasion for the report. Some idea of the proliferation of laboratories can be reconstructed from the retrospective notes in a much later survey (Pop 1956). In France alone, for example, laboratories soon followed at Grenoble (1904), under the direction of Théodore Rosset (Boë and Vilain 2010), and in the same year at Montpellier under Maurice Grammont.

Rousselot's original motivation had been the study of dialectology (Rousselot 1891), but generally two purposes came to dominate the justification of experimental work in phonetics. They were (1) to help in the treatment of those with speech disorders, including the deaf; and (2) the teaching of foreign languages. At Grenoble the juxtaposition of a well-equipped laboratory with practical work on the teaching of pronunciation was particularly explicit, since the laboratory was partly funded by sales of Rosset's book of pronunciation exercises for foreign learners of French (Rosset 1905). The Grenoble institute attracted the favourable attention of Daniel Jones (1909), then at the very beginning of his career, and probably exerted an influence on the form of the phonetics department that Jones was soon to develop in London.[1]

Instruments and Techniques of the Phonetics Laboratory

Within a few years of the establishment of Rousselot's laboratory in Paris, the equipment he had assembled was being described to the lay reader as 'machinery for teaching pronunciation'. In a detailed article in *The Strand Magazine*, Grace Ellison (1905) describes a visit to Rousselot's laboratory.[2] The various instruments and techniques of the phonetics laboratory are discussed in some detail and illustrated with photographs which show them being applied in teaching pronunciation.

Ellison deals first with the techniques of palatography and kymography, which were the two cornerstones of experimental phonetics at this period.[3] Palatography was devised by an English dentist, James Oakley Coles (1845–1906) with the express purpose of teaching remedial speech. His original technique (Coles 1872) was 'direct', in that he painted the palate and other inside surfaces of the mouth (he used a mixture of flour and gum) and observed the contact patterns resulting from an articulation by noting the removal of flour from the palate and its transfer to the tongue (Abercrombie 1957). By Rousselot's time, an 'indirect' method was in vogue. A dark-coloured artificial palate was dusted with chalk and inserted to cover the hard palate. Following an articulation, the artificial palate was removed and the tongue contact pattern recorded by drawing or photography. Indirect palatography has the advantage that the withdrawn palate can be viewed from directly above for drawing or photography, but the disadvantages that a palate must be made for each speaker (a lengthy and relatively expensive procedure), and that the palate may interfere with articulation.

Ellison (1905: 457) reproduces three palatograms showing the successive attempts of 'an English girl' to pronounce 'the French CH' — i.e., the voiceless palato-alveolar fricative [ʃ] as in *chat* (cat). First the contact made by the tongue is too far forward; the initial correction moves the tongue too far back; and at the third attempt the pattern is 'correct'.

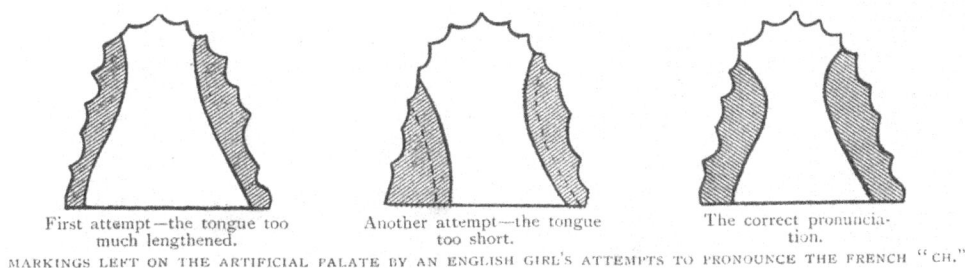

First attempt—the tongue too much lengthened.   Another attempt—the tongue too short.   The correct pronunciation.

MARKINGS LEFT ON THE ARTIFICIAL PALATE BY AN ENGLISH GIRL'S ATTEMPTS TO PRONOUNCE THE FRENCH "CH."

FIG. 12.1. Palatograms reproduced by Ellison (1905) showing successive attempts of 'an English girl' to articulate French [ʃ] correctly. All figures in this paper are digital photographs made by the authors from originals which are believed in every case to be out of copyright. The authors assert their moral right to be identified as the creators of the digitized and enhanced images.

C. F. PALMER (LONDON) LIMITED.   135

THE PHONETIC KYMOGRAPH.

FOR GRAPHICALLY RECORDING SPEECH.

Fig. 1.   **A24.**

THE Phonetic Kymograph illustrated above has been designed to record the vibrations produced in the air, and other variations of pressure involved in speech by the human voice. The name Kymograph is derived from two Greek words, meaning "wave" and "writing." It consists essentially of two parts :—

(1) A surface to be recorded on, and
(2) Sensitive recording points.

The surface consists of a moving endless band of highly glazed paper, on which is deposited, by means of a special gas (Fig. 2) or Kerosene (Fig. 3) burner, a thin layer of soot.

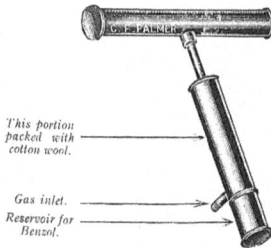

This portion packed with cotton wool.

Gas inlet.
Reservoir for Benzol.

Fig. 2.   **A291.   A292.**

The number of writing points, and the means of moving them, vary according to the nature of the problem. In all tracings it is necessary to know the time in which

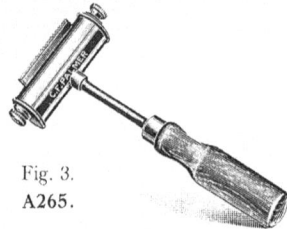

Fig. 3.
A265.

certain phenomena occur. For this purpose the high speed time-marker (Fig. 4) is used. It is electromagnetic in action, having a very light armature, and is worked in

Fig. 4.   **B25.**

circuit with a battery and an interrupter which takes the form of a vibrating fork (Fig. 5), giving 100 cycles per second. Time, therefore, to 1/200 of a second can be

FIG. 12.2. The phonetic kymograph manufactured and sold by
C. F. Palmer Ltd. from the 1920s.

Ellison illustrates the kymograph (1905: 458), and gives a creditably clear account of its operation, although in this case she does not give a specific instance of its application in teaching pronunciation.

The kymograph[4] was a device which made acoustic, aerodynamic and articulatory representations of speaking activity on smoked paper wrapped around a rotating drum (see Figures 12.2 and 12.3). The traces it produces are called kymograms. The durations of vowels, consonants, aspiration of voiceless plosives, etc., can be measured against a timing trace provided by a tuning fork. The traces are drawn by fine levers actuated by air pressure. Air pressure variations collected by a mouthpiece, and by other devices applied to the larynx and nose, are conveyed to the drum by rubber speaking tubes.

The kymograph (German *Kymographion*, formed from Greek elements meaning 'wave writer') had been developed by Carl Ludwig (1816–1895)[5] and was widely used for physiological and medical research from the mid-nineteenth century. In the phonetics laboratory, it was pressed into service to record not only the relatively slow movements of the articulating organs (for which it was quite well adapted) but also the rapid fluctuations of air pressure in the speech signal itself. This latter role it never fulfilled very successfully, though the device was to remain a standard piece of equipment for the phonetics laboratory into the 1950s and beyond (MacCarthy 1956: 47). It was cumbersome in operation, and required the ministrations of a dextrous technician (Suddard 1917).

Although some small portable kymographs were manufactured, those employed in phonetics laboratories were commonly very large. From the 1920s a British firm, C. F. Palmer,[6] manufactured and sold around the world a large phonetic kymograph (Figure 12.2) designed at University College London (C. F. Palmer 1934). For a generation, the large drum of the kymograph was the most conspicuous piece of 'machinery' visible in any phonetics laboratory and indeed was almost a symbol of the whole enterprise. This may render a little less surprising Daniel Jones's uncharacteristic and implausible attempts — which continued into the mid-1920s — to emphasize the value of the kymograph in pronunciation teaching.

Figure 12.3 shows Masao Kanehiro (a UCL phonetics alumnus) pictured with his brand new Palmer kymograph in Japan's first phonetics laboratory, founded in Osaka in 1921 (Ashby and Ashby 2009). The aim was certainly not disinterested scientific research, but to analyse — and teach — the pronunciation of English and other languages. Kanehiro (1933), for example, covers all the usual topics in English phonetics to be found in any handbook for students, but is illustrated at every step with relevant kymograms.[7]

Application to Teaching

Ellison (1905) reports on Rousselot's ideas about foreign accent and its correction, though these take the form of anecdotes about individuals rather than a systematic theory. Rousselot's basic idea seems to have been that the visible records from instruments could somehow assist the development of auditory discrimination in the learner, though exactly how this was to happen was not spelled out — and like

FIG. 12.3. Masao Kanehiro with a Palmer kymograph in
Japan's first phonetics laboratory in Osaka. The frontispiece from Kanehiro (1933).

many other pedagogical proposals of the time, its effectiveness was not subjected to any empirical test.

Rousselot had already published a book aimed at the foreign learner of French (Rousselot and Laclotte 1902). It begins conventionally enough with a consideration of the best pronunciation model to follow; and a whole final section is devoted to fairly conventional practical pronunciation exercises. The chapters in between deal with vowels, consonants, accent, liaison, etc., but with palatograms and kymograms as appropriate, as well as photographs of lip-positions, instead of mere verbal description. In all, the work has some eighty-three illustrations.

The first kymograms which the authors introduce (p. 52) deal with the weak or absent pre-voicing of voiced stops in English (as initially in the word *goal*), which is contrasted with the regular pre-voicing typical for French (as in *gant* (glove)). Interestingly, four varying English attempts are compared. One can see that in the hands of a teacher with the necessary production skills to improvise ear-training exercises, such diagrams might well support auditory training that would give the learner insight.

Before examining any of the other devices covered in Ellison (1905), it is worth considering in what ways instruments might in principle be of value to the language learner. Barrows (1916) is very thoughtful on the mode in which they might work and on the immediacy of their effect:

> Thus we see that while Experimental Phonetics has no immediate effect upon the pronunciation of the experimenter, he obtains an insight into the nature of speech sounds and how they influence each other and are related to the organs of speech, he gains a keenness of ear perception, so that his efforts to improve his own pronunciation have more rapid and more satisfactory results, while the drudgery of teaching pronunciation is transformed into a pleasure. (1916: 74)

There are at least two assumptions here which continue to be debated by researchers of pronunciation teaching — that 'insight' into the production of speech sounds can influence perception, and that an improvement in perception will be linked with an improvement in production. Barrows is aware that not all learners can themselves make direct use of experimental techniques:

> In these days we are demanding in all callings and professions efficient methods of work, and in my opinion, which is based on my experience, training in Experimental Phonetics adds to the efficiency of the teacher and student of language to an extent which quite justifies the time and exertion devoted to it. And while we can not [*sic*] all of us become experimental phoneticians, we can all of us make use of the facts revealed by the experiments, as far as they will lighten our labors in the learning or teaching of pronunciation. (1916: 75)

The 'facts revealed by the experiments' are not here aspects of the learner's faulty pronunciation, but rather characterizations of the target pronunciations to be aimed at. Barrows's own work (e.g., Barrows 1922), was published by the Division of Immigrant Education for California as part of the 'Americanization' programme then at its peak. She herself makes use of palatograms[8] to illustrate the differences between /l/ and /r/, and between /s/ and /ʃ/. Of all the graphical representations provided by experimental phonetics, palatograms are probably the simplest and most directly understood.

One use of experimental phonetics was thus to provide pictures of articulations to be aimed at by learners. A palatogram was to be used not by the learner making palatograms of his own, but by imagining and sensing what a palatogram of his own articulation *would* look like if it could obtained.

Another type of use is possible if the learner *does* — at least briefly — 'become an experimental phonetician'. The graphic record can then furnish a diagnosis of the learner's error. The feasibility of this depends on the time and expense required —

it would certainly seem to entail an extended course of pronunciation instruction and the opportunity for one-to-one tuition. Although the palatograms reproduced by Ellison (1905) are indeed those of a student, Rousselot and Laclotte do not, for example, suggest that their readers should have artificial palates made in order to monitor their pronunciation progress. The application of palatography in teaching was always chiefly imaginary, one supposes.

The kymograph was even further out of the reach of the ordinary learner. Even if he or she were to enrol in an institute where the instrument was in principle available, it operated so ponderously that only extended individual tuition could have provided any one learner with adequate feedback, even on a handful of pronunciation points.

A third possibility is that a device might furnish what we would now term interactive feedback. For this, the device must function in real time, providing the learner with an easily interpreted visual indication, which can be monitored and used to control speech output. Interestingly, several of the photographs in Ellison (1905) show devices from Rousselot's laboratory which provided exactly that.

MISTRESS SHOWING LITTLE GIRL WITH A SPIROMETER EXACTLY HOW MUCH BREATH OUGHT TO BE EXPIRED IN ORDER TO PRONOUNCE CORRECTLY THE ENGLISH CONSONANTS
From a]   AND THE SAME IN FRENCH.   [*Photograph,*

FIG. 12.4. Interactive monitoring of breath flow using a spirometer (Ellison (1905)).

In Figure 12.4 both teacher and student are watching the indicator dial of a spiro-graph, which is being used to indicate to a student the supposedly correct breath flow to use — different amounts were specified for English and for French. In another picture, nasal airflow is collected from the student's nostrils and caused to move a large indicator across a scale. There is a reason, of course, why these feedback devices do not figure in Rousselot and Laclotte (1902). Unlike palatography and kymography, they do not produce any permanent graphical output and hence are of no value to the student working from a book, who has no access to the device itself.

In the days before electronics, feedback had to be accomplished mechanically or by utilizing the sound sensitivity of gas flames. The Victorians noticed that the gas flames used for lighting were sometimes responsive to sounds (Tyndall 1867). With experiment and adjustment, a flame could be made selectively sensitive to certain sounds and not others. For example, a flame could be made to dip in response to a sibilant [s] but show no response to a dental fricative [θ], thus offering the possibility of visual feedback in an attempt to distinguish *think* and *sink*.

FIG. 12.5. A sensitive flame, showing (at right) dipping of the flame, probably in response to a sibilant fricative (Still frames from the film described in Ashby 2011).

Work along these antiquated lines continued up until the Second World War (Fry 1938).

A distinct application of gas flames was in the flame manometer, devised by Rudolph Koenig in 1862 (Pantalony 2009: 58). A speaking tube conveys air pressure variations from a mouthpiece to a small gas flame, the height of which is thus modulated to follow the input. When the flickering flame is viewed in a rotating mirror arrangement (so as to spread it out along the time dimension) an approximation to the speech waveform becomes visible. The flame manometer is shown in use for teaching in another of the photographs in Ellison (1905).

Apart from the flame manometer, throughout most of the period under consideration in this paper there was no simple way of displaying the acoustic waveform of speech — still less of producing a permanent record for inspection. It is a task we now accomplish easily by speaking into a microphone connected to our laptops. The lioretgraph — or more properly, the 'lioretgraphe inscripteur' (Anton 2006) — plotted waveforms laboriously by using a system of levers to enlarge the groove on a gramophone record, drawing the result on smoked paper in the same manner as the kymograph. Of course, the sound had first to be recorded on disk and plotting was then performed very slowly. Nevertheless, as noted below, UCL boasted of the possession of a lioretgraph as an attraction to its Vacation Course in English for foreign learners. Unsurprisingly, no specific example of its useful application in teaching seems to be documented.

The cathode-ray oscillograph, a general purpose scientific instrument which, when coupled with a microphone, provided a real-time display of the speech waveform and the first practical electronic feedback device for speech, was cutting-edge technology in the mid-1930s and had only just begun to appear in phonetics laboratories at the end of our period (Curry 1936).

Weird and wonderful devices proliferated. The 'strobilion' (Scripture 1913) aimed to teach pitch and intonation. A speaking tube conveys air pressure variations from a mouthpiece to a gas flame, following the same principle as the manometric flame. The pulsating flame illuminates the markings on a stroboscope disc which is being rotated at a known rate. The particular band on the disc which appears stationary gives an indication of the voice pitch.

FIG. 12.6. The 'strobilion', a motor-driven stroboscope lit by a gas flame modulated by the voice, for teaching control of voice pitch.

Reasonably accurate real-time extraction of voice pitch, resulting in an immediately displayed intonation curve, did not become possible — even in the research laboratory — until the late-1930s (Obata and Kobayashi 1937) and relied on special-purpose electronics linked to a cathode-ray oscillograph display.

Assumptions

On the whole, as has been seen, laboratory phonetics came up with very much the same ideas for teaching the foreign learner as for teaching the deaf. There was a great emphasis on visual displays, particularly on static pictures of articulatory configurations. The learner must therefore be imagined as able to make use of pictures to control his or her articulation, though whether a picture could be expected ever to guide a learner to more than a rough approximation to the required output went largely unquestioned (and certainly untested).

Further unquestioned assumptions of the day were that speech can be adequately characterized as a sequence of static 'postures'; and that individual speakers are sufficiently alike that precise positions determined for one speaker can be directly copied by another. Rousselot even arrived at specifications of tongue positions for French vowels expressed in millimetres of spacing between tongue and palate. The values are reproduced in the Appendix to Rousselot and Laclotte (1902: 209–10). It is not explained how learners were supposed to adjust their tongues to the nearest millimetre to match the specifications.

Though he had started with the view that experimental phonetics was potentially of great benefit to the language learner (Jones 1917), by the early 1920s Daniel Jones had reached the conclusion that visual representations of articulations had very limited value in teaching: 'A most accurate diagram of the tongue-position obtained by X-ray photography will not of itself enable the student to pronounce the sound correctly' (Trofimov and Jones 1923: 25). Instead, auditory comparison with sounds already known to the learner was the method to follow. This realization guided Jones's own practice, but was not widely shared. In laboratories around the world, work continued on more and more accurate specification of 'the positions' of the speech sounds of various languages.

Languages of Empire

The focus fell not only on the major and familiar modern foreign languages of Europe. The hundreds of little-studied languages of colonial empire were seen as a powerful argument for the ambitious expansion of phonetic research and teaching. One of the best-equipped laboratories was at the Kolonialinstitut in Hamburg, under the direction of Giulio Panconcelli-Calzia (1878-1966), which Daniel Jones and a nucleus of his early staff visited in April 1914 (Collins and Mees 1999: 133). Colonial competition with Germany became an impetus to Daniel Jones in Britain, and led to an ambitious scheme for a vast Institute of Phonetics that was to be established in London. Plans were drawn, a site was selected, and the scheme very nearly went ahead — failing only from ultimate lack of funding and Jones's breakdown suffered from overwork in his attempt to raise money. Even though German colonial ambitions were effectively ended by the Treaty of Versailles in 1919, Jones maintained the same stance well into the 1920s.

It is interesting to note that the reasons urged in favour of studying the languages of the Empire were every bit as practical as those which might motivate an Englishman to take up a European language such as French or German. The ability to train people in the relevant local languages would permit the efficient commercial development of the Empire. Indeed, the cynical focus on commercial advantage appears particularly shocking, since in Europe, at least, businessmen presumably competed on equal terms, whereas the relationship with the peoples of the Empire was openly portrayed as exploitative, with a background assumption that native cunning and dishonesty had to be overcome. An article in *The Observer* (1919), reports an interview in which Sir Edward Denison Ross (1871–1940), Director of the School of Oriental Studies in London (1916–37) is quoted, speaking in support of Jones's grand scheme for an Institute of Phonetics:

> Many big banks and business houses are sending their representatives to evening classes here in order that before they go to the East they may get an introduction to the vernacular. They realise how important it is for a man to break the back of a language before he goes abroad. [...] [I]f he is armed with some knowledge of the language he is at least saved a great deal of trouble on his arrival, and it is of the utmost advantage to him, particularly where commerce is concerned, to know what the natives are saying with whom he is to do business. Talking amongst themselves to their own people in their own language they may be saying that the article he is showing them is worth £10, but they will offer him £5. Unless he knows something of their language he must inevitably be at a disadvantage.

So, if language teaching was one of the main justifications for experimental phonetic research, and commerce one of the main drivers of language teaching, the rather improbable conclusion appears to follow that the ultimate motivation behind scientific pursuits such as palatography and kymography was the hope of commercial gain. It seems that a measure of scepticism may be in order in considering language scientists' own articulations of the motivations for their work.

Sound Recording and Reproduction

The phonograph was included among the instruments of the phonetics laboratory from the outset, and the gramophone was added when it appeared. From 1902, with the appearance of mass-produced commercial recordings, the application of sound recording in language teaching (and in education generally) grew very rapidly (Driesen 1913). Innovations in the systematic management and exploitation of recorded language materials — developments which subsequently led to the 'language laboratory' — took place mostly in the United States. According to Roby (2004: 524), Frank C. Chalfant, a former Grenoble student, set up a phonetics laboratory at Washington State College in Pullman during the academic year 1911 to 1912: 'Pictures of this installation in use show students listening via networked earphones. This lab also had a phonograph-recording machine so that students could compare their pronunciation with the native-speaker models'. Similar facilities were established by Ralph H. Waltz (1930, 1931), first at the University of Utah and a few years later at Ohio State. He offers a detailed description:

> As many as forty students could use a single unit or machine at one time. However, for our purposes we have fixed on a table seating 16 students. [...] The table is divided into compartments by a thin 18 inch board running down the center and boards of the same material running at right angles.
>
> The transcribing machine is placed at the end of the table and connected by its flexible tube to a nickeled brass pipe running the length of the table. This pipe has soldered into it a sufficient number of small nipples to feed the listening tubes. The listening head sets can be bought or made up in the laboratory. They are connected to the main tube by means of the small nipples. It is apparent that the entire set-up is mechanical. (1930: 28)

Though it did not come to fruition, Daniel Jones's planned Institute of Phonetics in London was also to have state-of-the-art listening facilities including a 'Phonographic Class Room' accommodating forty students and '40 phonograph receivers connected to the phonograph at the head of the table' (Collins and Mees 1999: 264). A number of similarities between Waltz's description and Jones's 1919 plans, such as the mention of forty possible simultaneous users and the seating of users around a single table, suggest, perhaps, that both are derived from a preceding source that has not been identified, possibly Rosset.

The use of recorded materials in pronunciation teaching had enthusiastic advocates, but there were also thoughtful and sceptical critics. Schenck (1930) and Levin (1931) point out problems such as poor sound reproduction, wear and deterioration of the recordings, inadequate sound insulation between students, and lack of motivation. Though the fidelity of commercially produced material improved dramatically following the introduction of electrical recording in 1926, there were no comparable advances in the means for students to record their own voices until the introduction of magnetic recording after the Second World War. Used alone, pre-recorded materials can support only the training of listening, not directly of pronunciation. At University College London, for example, a collection of several hundred gramophone records was amassed in the inter-war years (the bulk of this has since been accessioned into the British Library Sound Archive as 'The UCL Phonetics Collection'), but it is unclear whether they were intended as a pronunciation training resource, or simply formed a reference collection. In her account of the department, Ward (1928: 54) mentions gramophones among her list of laboratory instruments, but she is vague as to their purpose: 'A gramophone library has been started and it is hoped to make a special feature of this in the future'.

The Publicity Value of Technology

A feature of almost all the laboratory devices considered above is their cumbersome and laborious operation. It is not inconceivable that a French learner of English, or an English learner of French, might learn something useful from the kymograph about — say — the aspiration of voiceless plosives in the target language. But probably a whole classroom hour, and an experienced technical assistant, would be needed to set up the equipment and obtain a handful of satisfactory traces from one speaker. This raises the question of whether the technology was actually of much practical use, or whether its real value was in adding a sort of impressive scientific cachet to otherwise conventional teaching.

It is noticeable that many of the accounts of the use of technology in language teaching appeared in popular press reports rather than academic forums. *The Straits Times* (an English-language Singapore newspaper) in 1923 carried an article ('London's Hall of Babel' (1923)) on the University College London Summer Course in English Phonetics, designed for learners of English from around the world. (The course began in 1919 and continues to the present day.) Along with an account of the students and the predictable stereotyped representation of phonetics as being concerned with vocal gymnastics and strange noises are awed mentions of the kymograph and the lioretgraph:

> Mechanical aids are invoked by the instructors. There is a kymograph, or instrument for registering waves of sound. Or, by the aid of the lioretgraph — named after the inventor — which enlarges 300 times the groove of a gramophone record, an expert can learn the most remarkable things.

In quite what way the mechanical aids were 'invoked' is not made clear. The phrasing rather suggests a reporter — and presumably also a clientele for the course — ready to be impressed by the mere availability in principle of these devices. They establish the prestige of the institution and of the instructors, even if they are put to no practical use on the course.

Of course, a single press report may mean little; but there are others — and indeed it looks as if Daniel Jones most uncharacteristically sought out publicity and did not discourage what seem like exaggerated claims for the technology. In an article from 1919 in the *The Daily Chronicle* under the heading 'Empire language "factory". Institute as guide to 1000 tongues. Wonderful devices', we find:

> Explaining some of the remarkable features of the institute [i.e., the planned Institute of Phonetics] and the work now being done in the Gower Street laboratory, the principal [i.e., Jones] produced an instrument known as a kymograph.
> When a language quite untranslated is spoken into the kymograph by a native the voice vibrations move a needle, which writes the language down on a revolving drum upon smoke paper. The continuous curves thus drawn can then be translated into phonetic English, and step by step can ultimately be produced in book form. (*Daily Chronicle* 1919)

One wonders whether Jones was given any opportunity to revise this copy before it went to press, and whether he sanctioned the naïve (or deliberately deceptive?) simplification it incorporates. The suggested parallel between tracing a curve on the kymograph and 'writing down' a language is also hinted at in Ellison (1905: 457), where the photograph of a kymograph has the caption 'The machine for writing speech'.

A report in *The Sunday Times* (1925) again carries rather extravagant claims about the value of the kymograph in teaching attributed to Jones. The grand Institute has been forgotten, and the emphasis is now on teaching English pronunciation to foreign learners:

> An instrument by means of which you can see yourself speaking, and so, with a little practice, can correct errors in pronunciation, is to be seen in a small laboratory at the back of London University. [...] Prof. Daniel Jones, head of the Phonetics Department of University College, who showed the machine to the SUNDAY TIMES yesterday, said that, exceedingly useful as it was at present, there were even greater possibilities before it.
>
> By its means, at present, the pronunciation of even the most difficult foreign languages was made possible [...] and correct pronunciation would be much more readily obtained, he said, than was ever thought possible before the invention of the Kymograph.
>
> Similarly, for foreigners learning English, the machine was of inestimable value.
>
> 'Among our students here learning English,' he continued, 'are men and women from Japan, China, Georgia, India, Switzerland, Africa, Poland, Hungary, Esthonia, France, Germany, Italy, Holland, Denmark, Sweden, Rumania, Russia, Spain, and Czecho-Slovakia, and to these the Kymograph has been of greatest use. Each can see his own errors of pronunciation and, in time and by practice, correct them.'

If Jones's claim were literally true, it would imply something of the order of twenty individual programmes of study completed in the small basement laboratory (where tuition was generally on a one-to-one basis), none of which were reported in the academic literature or left any other historical footprint. And the implication that the kymograph was a recent invention is bizarre. By this time it had been a commonplace of the phonetics laboratory for nearly thirty-five years.

Conclusion

We have attempted to show that rather than scientific phonetics developing independently and then finding application in language teaching, the relationship was entirely the other way around: the requirement to teach pronunciation was one of the main justifications given for establishing laboratories and undertaking programmes of research. As each item of apparatus became available, improbable claims were advanced about its value in teaching pronunciation, and the kymograph in particular enjoyed a reputation as a 'machine for teaching'.

Pronunciation teaching — however effective or ineffective it may really have been — has since the late-nineteenth century wished to promote itself as having a scientific basis; and practitioners did not hesitate to adopt the superficial trappings of science even when they were presumably forced to rely in the main on traditional classroom techniques.

Bibliography

ABERCROMBIE, DAVID. 1957. 'Direct Palatography', *Zeitschrift für Phonetik*, 10: 21–25

ANTON, JULIEN. 2006. *Henri Lioret: un horloger pionnier du phonographe* (Condé-sur-Noireau: CIRES)

ASHBY, MICHAEL. 2011. 'Film from a Phonetics Laboratory of the 1920s', *Proceedings of the 17th International Congress of Phonetic Sciences* (Hong Kong: City University of Hong Kong), pp. 168–71

——, and PATRICIA ASHBY. 2009. 'The London Phonetics Training of Masao Kanehiro (1883-1978)', *Journal of the English Phonetic Society of Japan*, 13: 21–37

BARLOW, WILLIAM HENRY. 1874. 'On the Pneumatic Action Which Accompanies the Articulation of Sounds by the Human Voice, as Exhibited by a Recording Instrument', *Proceedings of the Royal Society of London*, 22: 277–86

BARROWS, SARAH T. 1916. 'Experimental Phonetics as an Aid to the Study of Language', *The Pedagogical Seminary*, 23: 63–75

——. 1922. *English Pronunciation for Foreigners* (Sacramento: California State Printing Office)

BOË, LOUIS-JEAN, and CORIANDRE-EMMANUEL VILAIN (eds). 2010. *Un siècle de phonétique expérimentale, fondation et éléments de développement: hommage à Théodore Rosset et John Ohala* (Lyon: École Normale Supérieure)

C. F. PALMER (London) Ltd. 1934. *Research and students' apparatus for physiology, pharmacology, psychology, bacteriology, phonetics, botany, etc. manufactured by C. F. Palmer (London) Ltd* (London: C. F. Palmer)

COLES, JAMES OAKLEY. 1872. 'On the Production of Articulate Sound (Speech)', *British Medical Journal*, 17 February: 181–82

COLLINS, BEVERLEY, and INGER MEES. 1999. *The Real Professor Higgins: The Life and Career of Daniel Jones* (Berlin: Mouton de Gruyter)

CURRY, ROBERT OSWALD LEONARD. 1936. 'The Cathode-ray Oscillograph in Speech Recording, with Special Reference to the Study of the Modern Northern English Dialects', in *Proceedings of the Second International Congress of Phonetic Sciences, London, 1935*, ed. by Daniel Jones and Dennis Butler Fry (Cambridge: Cambridge University Press), pp. 194–98

Daily Chronicle. 1919. 'Empire language "factory"', *The Daily Chronicle*, 19 November

DRIESEN, OTTO. 1913. *Das Grammophon im Dienste des Unterrichts und der Wissenschaft* (Berlin: Deutsche Grammophon-Aktiengesellschaft)

ELLISON, GRACE. 1905. 'Teaching French Pronunciation by Machinery', *The Strand Magazine* 30: 456–61

FRY, DENNIS. 1938. 'On the Behaviour of Sensitive Flames and their Application to Speech Training', in *Proceedings of the Third International Congress of Phonetic Sciences*, ed. by Edgard Blancquaert and Willem Pée (Ghent: Laboratory of Phonetics of the University), pp. 118–24

HOFF, HEBBEL. E., and LESLIE ALEXANDER GEDDES. 1959. 'Graphic Registration before Ludwig: The Antecedents of the kymograph', *Isis* 50: 5–21

JESPERSEN, OTTO. 1995. *A Linguist's Life: An English Translation of Otto Jespersen's Autobiography with Notes, Photos and a Bibliography*, ed. by Arne Juul, Hans Frede Nielsen and Jørgen Erik Nielsen (Odense: Odense University Press)

JONES, DANIEL. 1909. 'Phonetics at Grenoble', *Le Maître Phonétique*, 24 : 143–46

——. 1917. 'Experimental Phonetics and its Utility to the Linguist', *Proceedings of the Royal Institution of Great Britain*, 20: 8–21

KANEHIRO, MASAO. 1933. *The Experimental Phonetics of English* (Tokyo: Taibundo)

LEVIN, LAWRENCE M. 1931. 'More anent the phonetic laboratory method', *The Modern Language Journal*, 15: 427–31

MacCarthy, Peter Arthur Desmond. 1956. 'The Department of Phonetics, University of Leeds (1948)', in *Instituts de phonétique et archives phonographiques*, ed. by Sever Pop, Publications de la commission d'enquête linguistique, 7 (Leuven: Commission d'enquête linguistique), pp. 47–51

Marichelle, Hector. 1897. *Phonétique expérimentale: La parole d'après le tracé du phonographe* (Paris: Delagrave)

Millet, Adrien. 1933. *Les grammairiens et la phonétique: ou l'enseignement des sons du français depuis le XVIe siècle jusqu'a nos jours* (Paris: Monnier)

Obata, Jûichi, and Ryûji Kobayashi. 1937. 'A Direct-reading Pitch Recorder and its Applications to Music and Speech', *The Journal of the Acoustical Society of America*, 9: 156–61

The Observer. 1919. 'Gramophone and the Empire', *The Observer*, 23 November

Pantalony, David. 2009. *Altered Sensations: Rudolph Koenig's Acoustical Workshop in Nineteenth-Century Paris* (Dordrecht & New York: Springer)

Pop, Sever (ed.). 1956. *Instituts de phonétique et archives phonographiques*, Publications de la commission d'enquête linguistique, 7 (Leuven: Commission d'enquête linguistique)

Roby, Warren B. 2004. 'Technology in the Service of Language Learning: The Case of the Language Laboratory', in *Handbook of Research on Educational Communications and Technology*, ed. by David H. Jonassen (Mahwah, NJ: Erlbaum), pp. 523–41

Rosapelly, Charles-Léopold. 1876. 'Inscription des mouvements phonétiques', in *Physiologie expérimentale: travaux du laboratoire de M. Marey*, ed. by Etienne-Jules Marey (Paris: Masson), pp. 109–31

Rosset, Théodore. 1905. *Exercices pratiques d'articulation et de diction, composés pour l'enseignement de la langue française aux étrangers* (Grenoble: Gratier)

Rousselot, Pierre-Jean. 1891. *Les Modifications phonétiques du langage, étudiées dans le patois d'une famille de Cellefrouin (Charente)* (Paris: Welter)

——. 1897. *Principes de phonétique expérimentale* (Paris: Welter)

——, and Fauste Laclotte. 1902. *Précis de prononciation française* (Paris: Welter)

Schneck, Erna H. 1930. 'Practical Difficulties in the Use of the Phonetics Laboratory', *The Modern Language Journal*, 15: 30–32

Scripture, Edward Wheeler. 1913. 'The Strobilion: Control of Pitch by Means of Sight', *The Volta Review*, 15: 76–80

Smith, Richard. 1999. *The Writings of Harold E. Palmer: An Overview* (Tokyo: Hon-no-Tomosha)

The Straits Times. 1923. 'London's Hall of Babel', *The Straits Times* (Singapore), 15 November, p. 11

Suddard, Edward F. E. 1917. 'The Starting of a Phonetic Laboratory', in *Estudis fonètics*, ed. by Pere Barnils (Barcelona: Institut d'Estudis Catalans), pp. 237–63

The Sunday Times. 1925. 'Machine to Teach English', *The Sunday Times*, 8 November

Sweet, Henry. 1908. *The Sounds of English: An Introduction to English Phonetics* (Oxford: Clarendon)

The Times. 1935. 'Miss Grace Ellison', *The Times*, 4 October, p. 16

Trofimov, Michael V., and Daniel Jones. 1923. *The Pronunciation of Russian* (Cambridge: University Press)

Tyndall, John. 1867. *Sound: A Course of Eight Lectures Delivered at the Royal Institution of Great Britain* (London: Longmans, Green)

Viëtor, Wilhelm. 1894. 'Kleine Beiträge zur Experimentalphonetik', *Phonetische Studien*, 7: 25–36 (=*Die neueren Sprachen*, 1, Supplement)

Waltz, Ralph H. 1930. 'The Laboratory as an Aid to Modern Language Teaching', *The Modern Language Journal*: 15: 27–29

——. 1931. 'Language Laboratory Administration', *The Modern Language Journal*, 16: 217–27

WARD, IDA CAROLINE. 1928. 'The Phonetics Department, University College London', *Revue de Phonétique*, 5: 47–54

Notes to Chapter 12

1. Jones's only complaint about Rosset is that the latter failed to use the alphabet of the International Phonetic Association. Rosset joined the IPA in 1910, and from 1912 editions of his book do utilize IPA representation.
2. Grace Mary Ellison (1880–1935) was a journalist and travel writer with a particular interest in the culture of Turkey. Some details of her life are given in a *Times* obituary (1935). No other publications concerned with phonetics or language teaching have been located in her writings.
3. The great French physiologist Etienne-Jules Marey (1830–1904), in the preface that he contributed to Marichelle (1897), characterizes Rousselot's contribution as the bringing together of these two existing techniques. Rousselot's protégé Millet gives a similar assessment (1933: 93–94).
4. Film showing the operation of a kymograph, and of the sensitive flame, was discovered and digitized in 2010. It is accessible at <https://youtu.be/cXp7jfgRNVA> (See Ashby 2011).
5. Ludwig is generally credited with the invention of the device, although there are antecedents extending back at least to the seventeenth century (Hoff and Geddes 1958). The application of the kymograph to speech is generally attributed to Rosapelly (1876), though the earliest kymograms of speech appear to be those published by Barlow (1874).
6. The firm had no connection with H. E. Palmer.
7. The title of the book is in English, though the text is in Japanese.
8. Interestingly, the palatograms are drawn to include the teeth and hence resemble direct palatograms in appearance. There is no indication of how they were obtained. According to the title page, the drawings in the book are by Miss Olive Johnson, State Teachers College San Francisco.

CHAPTER 13

❖

A Utilitarian Subject:
The Introduction of Spanish Language in British Schools in the Early Twentieth Century

Luis G. Martínez del Campo

This chapter offers the first overview of the historical development of Spanish as a foreign language in British secondary education from its beginnings in the nineteenth century to its first crisis during the late 1930s. It explores why Britons became interested in learning Spanish in the early twentieth century. Special attention is paid to economic and political motives that encouraged the study of the language in Britain. On the one hand, the growth of British trade in Latin America in the late nineteenth century emphasized the importance of a good knowledge of Spanish and fostered its study. On the other hand, the British government promoted the teaching of Spanish for strengthening ties with Spanish-speaking countries during the Great War. Nevertheless, both factors lost importance in the 1930s and the development of Spanish language teaching suffered a setback in the UK.

Introduction

> When Latin and Greek were almost the only written languages of civilized man, it is manifest that they must have furnished the subjects of all liberal education. The question, therefore, is wholly changed since the growth of a complete literature in other languages.
>
> THOMAS ARNOLD[1]

Before the eighteenth century in Britain the only two universities (Oxford and Cambridge) and the majority of secondary schools barely offered any languages other than Latin and Greek. However, the emergence of nationalism, the strength of vernacular literatures and the implementation of national systems of education prompted the teaching of modern foreign languages in different European countries. As a result of these changes, the study of French was extended among British schools in the Georgian era. German had an inferior status compared to French, but it also started to be taught in many institutions all over Great Britain in this period. Moreover, both languages were included as subjects in public examinations in the late 1850s (McLelland 2014: 128).

In the early nineteenth century Spanish appeared in the curricula of only a few English schools, as shall see below. However, three historical events set the scene for the spread of Spanish language teaching in the British Isles. The first was initiated with the second restoration of Ferdinand VII to the Spanish throne in 1823, forcing many Spanish liberal intellectuals and politicians to seek refuge in London. The cultural and literary activities of these exiles gave Londoners a taste of Spanish culture (Muñoz and Alonso 2011). The second event was the constant flow of British writers and travellers who visited Spain and returned with romantic descriptions of an exotic country. They helped produce positive stereotypes of Hispanic culture (Robertson 1988). The third was the independence of the Spanish colonies in America in the 1810s and 1820s. These Latin American movements for emancipation were supported by Britons, who took advantage of the situation in order to increase their commercial and political influence over the region. Towards the end of the century a large number of British companies were established in Spanish-American countries, exploiting mining resources, controlling commercial shipping, building infrastructures and organizing financial systems (Bethell 1989: 1–24).

These new circumstances heralded a change in the development of Spanish language teaching in the UK in the early twentieth century, as entrepreneurs and politicians began to support initiatives to promote the learning of Spanish all over Great Britain. As we shall see below, it was thought that Spanish would be useful for those who went into business with Latin America; and British companies interested in trading with Spain's former colonies donated large amounts of money to establish professorships of Spanish (such as the Gilmour Chair at Liverpool University in 1908 and the Cowdray Chair at Leeds University in 1918) and lobbied for the introduction of Spanish in many schools. After the outbreak of the Great War, politicians were also engaged with the spread of Spanish language teaching. The British government wanted to win the Spanish-speaking countries to the Allied cause and its foreign policy encouraged Britons to learn Spanish (Martínez del Campo 2015: 11–36). Nevertheless, the stimulus given to the study of Spanish was lost in the 1930s. The outbreak of the Spanish Civil War marked a setback for Spanish in British secondary education.

In the first half of the twentieth century, the geographical distribution of Spanish language teaching in Britain was uneven. The majority of schools offering Spanish were concentrated in England rather than in other parts of Britain. In Wales, Spanish was taught in a very limited number of schools before the 1930s. By 1922, only two Welsh cities (Bangor and Barry) had grammar schools where Spanish was taught. There is no evidence to say that the situation of Spanish language education was better in Scotland. Although we do not have exact figures, it seems that very few Scottish schools included Spanish in their curricula during this period. This chapter, therefore, largely concentrates on the introduction of Spanish in English secondary schools.

In the Beginning...

> For its linguistic, literary, and commercial value, Spanish should be included in the curricula of the schools of this commercial nation.
>
> E. A. Woolf[2]

In the nineteenth century, the vast majority of British schools did not offer modern foreign languages other than French and German. Nevertheless, a few technical colleges and commercial institutes included lessons in elementary Spanish as a part of their curricula. In the beginning Spanish was introduced into schools for commercial purposes, frequently related to the rise of the Latin American market. This economic origin helps explain why the language was first taught in industrial and commercial centres of Great Britain such as Liverpool, London and Manchester.

There is evidence that Spanish was taught on the banks of the Mersey from 1833. 'Mr De Lara' was the teacher in charge of Spanish, Italian and Portuguese lessons in the evening courses of the Mechanics' Institute of Liverpool, a centre founded by the Royal Institution in 1825 (Tiffen 1935: 35). After a few years, De Lara was replaced by Lorenzo Lucena Pedrosa (1807-1881), a Cordovan Protestant pastor who arrived in England in 1849 (Memory 2001: 213-26). Lucena worked as a teacher of Spanish at the Mechanics' Institute, later known as the Liverpool Institute and School of Arts. His classes were attended by few students, but it seems that at least two of them developed outstanding linguistic skills in Spanish (Tiffen 1935: 35-36). Other modern foreign languages were taught in this institute but, with the exception of French classes, they were not well attended. Perhaps it was this experience that encouraged Lucena to apply for a position of Taylorian Teacher at the University of Oxford, where he began teaching Spanish in 1858 (Edwards 2001).

In the nineteenth century, Spanish was taught at different levels in London. Various Spanish exiles worked in language-teaching to make a living. In fact, the first professorship of Spanish language and literature established in Britain was held by one of these exiles, Antonio Alcalá Galiano (1789-1865), at University College London from 1828. Three years after, a Chair of Spanish was also founded at King's College London. Furthermore, it is well documented that a number of London institutions and schools offered Spanish lessons in this period. For instance, Ricardo Ramírez, who was the last holder of the Chair in Spanish at King's College before it was abolished in 1910, had taught Spanish at secondary level in London since 1881. He worked as a teacher of Spanish at the City of London School, the Young Men's Christian Association (Aldersgate Street) and the Aldenham Institute (St Pancras). It seems that his classes were well attended, with thirty or forty students every year. However, Spanish was not well established in British education, and this instability kept Ramírez continuously on the lookout for a new post.[3]

In addition to Liverpool and London, another English industrial city, Manchester, had secondary education institutions in which provision was made for the teaching of Spanish. In the late nineteenth century, Colombo Angelo Toledano (1859-1920) was teacher of Spanish and Italian at various schools in Manchester, including the

Manchester Grammar School and the High School for Girls. Moreover, it seems that he taught Spanish at the Manchester College of Commerce from 1890 onwards (Rubenstein et al. 2011: 984; and *Vida Hispánica*, 5 (1952): 1).

Thus, Spanish had appeared on the curricula of various schools in the nineteenth century, but its teaching was not extended to the whole of England in this period. It can be argued that the slow spread of Spanish language teaching was partly connected with the problems of the British secondary education system (Gillard 2011). However, other factors should be considered, given that French and German were widely spread in Great Britain in the Victorian era. According to Breul, Spanish was taught in only six secondary schools for boys at the end of the nineteenth century, but 345 offered French and 217 taught German. This disproportion indicates that French and German were much more prestigious languages than Spanish, which only improved its status with the growth of British trade in Latin America (McLelland 2015: 78).

Spanish Language and British Commerce

> The belief that Spanish was a 'commercial' language had been vigorously and repeatedly attacked by those who knew better, but it died hard. When, at one university, a lecturer announced a course on Spanish literature, a colleague, in perfectly good faith, enquired: 'Literature? Has it any?'
>
> 'I suppose you're going into business', was the usual comment when a schoolboy, or an undergraduate, expressed a desire to specialize in Spanish rather than in French or German. French 'got you everywhere'; German you needed for plumbing the mysteries of science; Spanish merely helped you to be a high-grade shopkeeper.
>
> EDGAR ALLISON PEERS[4]

The belief in Spanish as a commercial language existed already in the eighteenth century. In 1718, a manual to learn the language, *Spanish and English Dialogues*, pointed out that Spanish had 'become much more necessary than formerly' to ensure the development of British trade (cited in Watson 1971: 487). Although emphasis was also laid on the practical value of other languages, too (German, Russian, etc.), Spanish was labelled 'in the popular mind as a commercial subject'. This process was accelerated by the independence of Latin American countries, which affected British perceptions of the Spanish language: it was believed that it would be useful in the world of business with the newly independent nations (Peers 1944: 1).

During the Victorian era, many British firms were successfully established in the former Spanish colonies in America. These companies required well-qualified professionals able to speak Spanish, which became an essential skill for those who went into business with Latin America. Thus, local institutions advocated the study of Spanish language and culture. For instance, the London Chamber of Commerce provided Spanish evening courses and issued certificates of proficiency in the language. As we shall see below, there is evidence that school teachers attended those courses because they were in charge of teaching Spanish at their own education centres, so these evening classes had an impact on secondary education.

These local organizations of business were pioneers in the promotion of the Spanish language, also supporting the study of Spanish in secondary schools. In 1895, for instance, Spanish was introduced in the Whitechapel Foundation School on the advice of the London Chamber of Commerce. A three-year course in Spanish was provided for those interested in taking a second foreign language in addition to French. About seventy students attended the Spanish lessons, which took three hours per week. For seventeen years, Spanish was taught at this school, until it was dropped from the curriculum in the 1910s. The head of the school explained the reason for the decision:

> We have attracted a good deal of attention as being the only Secondary School in London that takes Spanish as a class subject, but we have attracted no boys by it, neither do I think that it has proved useful to more than a few of our boys. Intending teachers drop it in favour of Latin or extra French and no boy takes it as a subject for the Matriculation Examination.[5]

It was widely assumed that French and Latin helped pupils to develop an 'elevated tone' (Slee 1986: 11), but the reputation of Spanish was exclusively linked to commercial activities. Students who attended Spanish classes were those who wanted to go into business. The Whitechapel Foundation School illustrated this particularity pointing out the high number of Jewish students who took the subject:

> During the years (1895-1912) that Spanish was taught, the number of Jews in the School increased from 50% to more than 80% and it was found that though most of these boys went into commerce, they very rarely entered offices where Spanish was useful. (ED12/226: S. 631)

Accordingly, Spanish was dropped from the curriculum of the Whitechapel Foundation School in 1912. Paradoxically, the change coincided with the promotion of the language elsewhere in Great Britain in the 1910s. For instance, the Hampton Grammar School (London) and the George Watson's College (Edinburgh) introduced Spanish lessons before the outbreak of the Great War (*Vida Hispánica*, 5 (1952): 1).

The UK government began to promote the introduction of Spanish in British schools on the assumption that knowledge of it would help British companies to trade with Latin America. A few English entrepreneurs (George Gilmour) and commercial institutions (London Chamber of Commerce) who had supported the study of Spanish in Great Britain since the late nineteenth century encouraged politicians to take action. On 7 August 1913, the situation of Spanish language teaching was discussed in the House of Commons. The financier and MP Joseph King (1860-1943) put the following question:

> To ask the President of the Board of Education, whether he is aware that Spanish is only taught in five secondary schools on the grant list, but is taught in 77 evening schools; and, having regard to the commercial importance of the Spanish tongue, especially in connection with our expanding trade in South American, he will urge the teaching of Spanish in secondary schools. (ED12/226: S. 454)

In the early twentieth century, the number of pupils who took Spanish was still very small, and the Board of Education planned strategies to promote the extension of its teaching in England and Wales. The guidelines of this plan were described in the *Memorandum on the Teaching of Modern Languages in Secondary Schools,* issued by the Board in 1912 (ED12/226: S. 454). What they did was very simple, but effective. Firstly, inspection visits were organized to ascertain how Spanish was taught at British schools. Secondly, the Board's inspectors advised school authorities in order to improve the teaching of the language. During the academic year 1913–14, for instance, Fernando de Arteaga and other university lecturers visited evening institutes in various London boroughs, including Camberwell, Lambeth and Paddington. Although Spanish was taught competently in the majority of those centres, inspectors warned about the lack of manuals and books to study languages in these institutes. They suggested that teachers should take into account the professional usefulness of Spanish, but that the classes should not be focused exclusively on Spanish commercial correspondence. They also observed that some sessions took too long, reducing the students' motivation (ED12/226: A. Kahn, HMI, F. de Artega).

After this initial timid promotion of Spanish for commercial purposes by local institutions and the UK government, its study was also fostered for political reasons after the outbreak of the Great War.

The Linguistic Boom

> The idea that it was possible for schools to teach other languages than French and German was one of the small-sized bombs dropped during the War. It produced a minute shock but caused only minor damage and few — very few — casualties. (Edgar Allison Peers)[6]

With the outbreak of World War I, a period of the development of Spanish language education began in some Western countries. From 1914 to 1945, scholars and social actors campaigned for the extension of Spanish teaching in the USA. Their advocacy of Spanish linked knowledge of the language to US geo-political and economic interests in Latin America (Bale 2011, but see also Bale's contribution in Volume III of this History). As a result, the American Association of Teachers of Spanish was founded during the war (1917) and Spanish was introduced as a subject in American universities and schools. A similar process occurred in Britain after 1914.

During World War I, the British Foreign Office had designed a special policy to counteract German influence over the Hispanic World. The strategy included the promotion of Spanish language and culture all over Great Britain. British diplomats assumed that knowledge of Spanish would help Britons to become closer to both Spain and Spanish-American countries, and to win the propaganda battle. Therefore, many schools and universities started to offer Spanish lessons as a form of patriotic service for their country.

In this context, one campaign called for German to be replaced with Spanish as the second foreign language in British schools. The promoter was H. Holford Bottomley, 'a publicity specialist' who served as 'director of special publicity and propaganda for the National War Savings Committee and the National War Bonds

Campaign' (Simmons 2007: 190; and *The Times*, 5 March 1920, p. 11). In October 1915, *The Times* published his call to start a patriotic movement for the substitution of Spanish for German as a second language in schools and public examinations (Bottomly 1915: 9). Holford Bottomley's proposal became very popular. The English press contributed to this movement publishing every letter of support. E. J. Carroll welcomed the idea as follows:

> I have read with great interest and pleasure Mr. Holford Bottomley's admirable letter [...] advocating the substitution of Spanish for German as a second language in schools and public examinations. Spanish is not only infinitely more useful commercially, but it is a language with a charm which no Saxon tongue can approach, and it reveals the soul of a people more delightful than any to be found without the circle of our Allies. (Carroll 1915: 9)

Before this campaign, Spanish was already offered as an alternative to German in a few schools. In 1914, for instance, Northampton Boys School had introduced Spanish as a second foreign language. In this school, all boys studied French, but they had to choose a second language from three options: German, Spanish and Latin. It seems that many students took up Spanish (ED12/226: S. 169).

Undoubtedly, Holford Bottomley's campaign had an impact on British secondary education. It was estimated that twenty-five schools dropped German as a subject during the Great War (McLelland 2014: 140). At the same time, Spanish began to be taught in various educational institutions. For instance, the Ilford County High School for Boys (Greater London) introduced Spanish in its curriculum in 1915 (ED12/226: S. 268). While a number of schools offered Spanish as an alternative to German, few replaced German with Spanish, and the motivations for such a change varied. For example, Morpeth Grammar School (Northumberland) carried out the substitution, but it seems that Spanish lessons were not particularly popular — only five students took the language, one of them the son of a merchant based in Newcastle and doing important business in South America. An education inspector of the school noted that the commercial potential of the language was not a factor in the switch. Rather:

> The substitution of Spanish for German was partly on account of the war, but partly due to the fact that the new modern language Master appointed in January 1915 has a predilection for Spanish and is less well qualified for German. (ED12/226: S. 269)

Whatever the real motivations, attendance was far from satisfactory. In June 1916, the Barnard Castle School (County Durham) offered Spanish as an alternative to German. Six students took up Spanish, but only three attended classes to the end (ED12/226: S. 275). In that year, two pupils of the Haberdashers' Aske's Boys' School (Deptford, South London) took Spanish because they wanted to go into business. These two students represented 1% of the total of the school's pupils. Although Spanish-language teaching was extended in the wartime, the number of students who took the subject remained very low and the status of German in British secondary education remained higher than that of Spanish (ED12/226: S. 624).

This weak demand determined a poor supply. Teachers of Spanish normally offered other modern foreign languages too; were usually specialists in French or German; and had barely studied Spanish, which only first appeared on the curricula of the majority of the British universities in the First World War. For instance, Miss Sanders, who was the teacher of Modern Foreign Languages at Sydenham High School (an independent school for girls in London), had gained a Bachelor's degree in French, but she also had to teach Spanish, which was offered as an alternative to Science and German. The low number of pupils taking Spanish (dropping from nineteen girls in 1915/16 to nine in 1916/17) made it impossible to hire a specialist teacher. Sanders first attended an evening course at the London Chamber of Commerce, where she passed an intermediate Spanish exam; she continued taking private lessons with the Spaniard who had taught the course and attained a certificate in Advanced Spanish from the National Union of Teachers. Ultimately, she was able to teach her students about Spanish literature (such as *La dama errante* by Pío Baroja or *El sí de las niñas* by Leandro Fernández de Moratín) (ED12/226: S. 628).

In addition to this, Spanish was often considered a complement of other subjects. In many schools, those students who wanted to take Spanish were expected to have previous knowledge of another language. Since 1915/16, the Reading School (Berkshire) offered four hours of Spanish classes per week, but students who wanted to take these lessons had to have learnt French and Latin for two years (ED12/226: S. 629).

Although the low number of students interested in learning Spanish, its teaching was extended in British secondary education during the Great War, promoted by various political institutions in accord with British foreign policy. For example, London County Council managed the funds that businessmen, banks and commercial institutions made available to promote the study of Spanish in London; and this alliance between the interests of trade and politics supported the introduction of Spanish in many schools after the outbreak of the War. Moreover, British companies and banks offered grants to encourage pupils attending London schools and evening institutes to study Portuguese and Spanish (ED12/226: S. 170):

> Now more than ever before a knowledge of foreign languages is essential to the young man entering the world of commerce. We welcome, therefore, the offer of £50 to the London County Council by the British Bank South America as prizes in order to encourage students, British born of British born parents, and engaged, or intending to engage, in a banking or commercial occupation, to acquire a practical working knowledge of the Portuguese language. The Banco Español del Río de la Plata has offered to the Council a sum of £10 10s as prizes to encourage the study of Spanish language. (British Chamber of Commerce for Spain 1919: 23)

Besides prizes, London County Council and commercial firms engaged in trade with Latin American countries also provided classes in Spanish language. All those activities were pursued to create a pool of British candidates qualified for jobs in commercial companies, which were interested in well-qualified staff to conduct business in Spanish-speaking countries.

The British ruling classes were also involved in the promotion of Spanish. Before 1914, the UK Parliament had already discussed how to spread the learning of Spanish throughout Britain, but after 1914 politicians showed particular interest in fostering its study in line with British foreign policy, which included a plan to win the Spanish-speaking countries to the Allied cause. Furthermore, Westminster and the economic elite understood that a knowledge of Spanish would help promote British trade links with the Hispanic world at a time when the USA dominated the Latin-American market (Bale 2011). On 21 March 1917, Arthur Fell (1850–1934), a Conservative MP, tabled questions in Parliament about how Spanish-American culture was taught in state-aided schools. The President of the Board of Education summarized what had been done:

> The metric system of weights and measures is taught in all State-aided Secondary and Technical Schools. The money systems of the South American States are not generally taught in State-aided Secondary Schools, but they are taught in a considerable number of Day and Evening Commercial Classes. The Faculties of Commerce at most of the Universities make arrangements for the study of foreign systems of weights and measures and currencies. Spanish has been taught for some years past in a few Secondary Schools, and in many others arrangements are now being made for its introduction. It is taught in a considerable number of Evening Schools and Classes; Portuguese is taught in a few only. The question of extending the provision for the teaching of these languages is now being actively considered by many Local Education Authorities; and it is too soon to say whether the supply of competent teachers will be adequate. Instruction in Spanish is provided at the Universities of Oxford, Cambridge, London (King's College), Durham (Armstrong College), Birmingham and Liverpool, and at the University Colleges of Nottingham and Southampton. (ED12/226: S. 204)

Much still remained to be done, but the British government had already started to promote the study of Spanish in the UK. In 1917, the General Committee of The Modern Language Association circulated a memorandum that explicitly suggested that Spanish should appear as second foreign language on the curricula of the majority of the British secondary schools. It was also recommended that Spanish be made the first foreign language in those schools located in regions where commercial links to the Hispanic world were strong, such as Liverpool, Bristol or Southampton:

> The importance of Spanish as a school study is being increasingly demonstrated. Many of the leading schools in London and the provinces have included the study of Spanish in their curricula (City of London, Hackney Downs, St. Olave's, St. Dunstan's, Liverpool Institute, Manchester High School, Sedbergh, Cheltenham, Bradford, Bristol, George Watson's, etc.), either as an alternative to German or as a separate subject, while several education authorities (Manchester, Lancashire, Liverpool) are advocating the inclusion of the study in the curriculum of secondary schools. In every Commercial Institute in London and in the vast majority of Commercial Institutes in the provinces Spanish forms a part of the curriculum, and from information received is attracting an increasing number of students. (General Committee 1917: 52–54)

Although there was strong support from the ruling classes for the study of Spanish, its situation in British education was only marginally improved during the First World War. But all these initiatives had a real impact after 1918.

A Time of Hope: The Teaching of Spanish in the Interwar Period

> Many of the pledges made in government reports had not come to fruition, although there had been a period of high hopes between 1921 and 1936. In this decade and a half, there had been an expansion of Spanish teaching in secondary schools. (Nicholas Bowen)[7]

After the Great War, the promotion of Spanish continued, but the motivations changed. With the conflict over, the Foreign Office was no longer interested in influencing public opinion in Spanish-speaking countries. In the post-war period, German was still sometimes replaced by Spanish in a few British schools, but this change pursued a commercial agenda rather than political aims. In 1919, for instance, Abbeydale Secondary School for Girls (Sheffield) dropped German from its curriculum and introduced Spanish as second foreign language. This change was justified by Sheffield's commercial links with Latin America:

> German will not be taught, but in view of the fact that Sheffield has important trade relations with South America, the second foreign language will be Spanish. This second foreign language will not be begun until the Girls have completed two years' work in French. (ED12/226: S. 24)

In the 1920s, Spanish was winning a place in British education on the grounds of its perceived usefulness as a commercial language. From 1920 to 1922 the Board of Education validated the introduction of Spanish language lessons in a large number of educational institutions, such as Portsmouth Grammar School, Manchester Central High School for Girls, Hampstead University College School, Westminster Grey Boat Hospital School, and Atkinson Road Girls Secondary School in Newcastle upon Tyne. In the academic year 1921–22 there were 139 evening schools in which Spanish was taught, with an estimated 365 classes in the subject. These numbers demonstrate that the British government was still supporting the spread of Spanish language teaching (ED12/226: S. 454/18).

On 16 February 1923, William Joynson-Hicks (1865-1932), a Conservative politician and at the time Secretary for Overseas Trade (Development and Intelligence), sent a letter to Edward Frederick Lindley Woods (1881-1959), who was in charge of the Board of Education. They agreed that the teaching of Spanish should be promoted on the grounds of the British commercial links to Latin America:

> You will remember that I spoke to you the other day about the growing importance of Spanish and Portuguese. The point is that, Europe being economically prostrate and likely to provide few and poor markets for our exports for some time to come, it is, outside English speaking countries overseas, largely to South America that we have to look for the necessary expansion of our foreign trade. Hence the importance to this country of a plentiful supply of business men, commercial travellers, agents, etc. familiar

with the Spanish and Portuguese tongues. I am inclined, for instance, to think that it will pay us better in the long run if the linguistic side of our commercial education could be concentrated in this directions rather than on German. (ED12/226: S. 454/3)

This letter sparked considerable debate in the Board of Education. Woods and other members discussed the importance of Spanish for British trade. The teaching of Spanish had been extended over commercial regions, but it seems that the demand for Spanish classes had been overestimated, for although it was included in the curricula of many schools, it was frequently dropped after a few years due to low student numbers. In a letter to the Board of Education, E. J. W. Jackson, who apparently acted as an inspector of secondary schools in England, reported changes in student numbers:

Hull, of course, as a port has its own Spanish problem and last year it had about 35 students in 3 classes. Huddersfield had 24 students in 3 classes. Halifax, Leeds and Sheffield usually run 2 classes and Newcastle and York manage one. Wakefield had one class in the boom years 1918-20, but it died a natural death last session [1921-22]. (ED12/226: S. 454/3)

It was argued that Spanish had to be introduced in British secondary schools to supply well-qualified clerks to companies operating in Latin America, but in practice Spanish language teaching had a modest impact on British–Spanish commercial relations. Employers preferred people with a good knowledge of Spanish, but it was not an essential requirement. According to Jackson's report, many companies received letters in Spanish, but they generally sent these documents to a professional translator:

There are always a few people in a town who can read Spanish and most firms send their correspondence to these people for translation. Of course, they would consider the ability to deal with such correspondence an asset in any clerk they employed, but as far as I am able to gather it is an asset that they are not prepared to pay for. (ED12/226: S. 454/3)

Nevertheless, Spanish language teaching was still promoted exclusively for commercial purposes after 1918. Before the Great War, only five state-aided schools had offered Spanish lessons in Great Britain. In the academic year 1922 to 1923, Spanish was taught at sixty-eight state-funded schools in England and two in Wales. Other educational institutions had also included Spanish in their curricula. For instance, the number of evening schools offering Spanish increased from 77 in 1913 to 139 in 1922. The expansion of Spanish language learning continued on the grounds of its commercial utility and, consequently, it was mainly introduced in those schools located in industrial cities, such as the Alsop High School in Liverpool and the King Edward VII School in Sheffield (1923) (ED12/226: S. 454/16 and S. 454/18).

The Board of Education made a full list of state-aided schools offering Spanish language in England around 1925. According to this list, Spanish was taught in seventy-six state-aided schools, 6.4 % of all the grant-earning schools (there were 1187 state-aided schools). Fifty of those seventy-six schools were for boys, sixteen for girls and ten for both sexes. In those seventy-six schools, 3266 pupils (2791 boys and 475 girls) took Spanish (ED12/226: 98). The geographical distribution of those pupils is shown in Table 1:

Local Education Authority Area	Number of schools	Number of pupils	Local Education Authority Area	Number of schools	Number of pupils
Bath	1	7	London	11	307
Bedfordshire	1	10	Manchester	3	192
Berkshire	1	10	Middlesex	6	186
Birkenhead	1	35	Newcastle-upon-Tyne	1	6
Birmingham	1	33	Norfolk	1	56
Blackburn	1	18	Northamptonshire	1	61
Bootle	1	40	Northumberland	2	13
Bradford	3	227	Nottinghamshire (Nottingham)	3	175
Cheshire	2	122	Salford	1	8
Croydon	2	107	Sheffield	2	125
Essex	4	321	Somerset	1	44
Hampshire	1	80	Southend-on-Sea	2	93
Kent	3	154	Surrey	3	86
Lancashire	8	359	York (West Riding of Yorkshire)	1	7
Leeds	2	35	*Totals:*		
Leicestershire (Leicester)	1	12		76 schools	
Liverpool	5	337		3,266 pupils	

TABLE 1. Position Of Spanish In Grant-Earning Secondary Schools In England (1925) (ED12/226: 98)

This list suggests that the provision of Spanish was particularly strong in port cities like Liverpool, where 337 students took the language. Although Spanish was taught in eleven London schools, the number of pupils who studied it in the capital was low in comparison with other, smaller cities. For instance, 227 students took Spanish in three state-funded schools in Bradford, a small city with trade links to Spanish America (ED12/226: 98).

In 1925, Spanish was taught in only three Welsh schools and the number of students who took this subject was very small. Friars School in Bangor, one of the oldest schools in Wales, offered lessons in Spanish, but only five boys learnt the language by then. Monmouth Grammar School included Spanish in its curriculum, although there is no information about attendance. In Barry Grammar School, Spanish and Latin were taught to 'suitable pupils' after their first two years. Barry was probably the largest coal port in Great Britain at that time (ED12/226: 454/19).

There is evidence that scholars and companies promoted the teaching of Spanish in Scotland in the 1920s. After World War I, the Spanish Society of Scotland was founded to advocate Spanish language education. Branches of this association were established in Glasgow, Edinburgh, Aberdeen and Dundee. Spanish classes were given at the Glasgow office. These lessons focused on literary and commercial uses of the language. The number of students increased quickly, from eight to eighty pupils. In 1919 a lectureship in Spanish was established at the University of Edinburgh; and the University of Glasgow founded the Stevenson Chair of Spanish in 1924 (Martínez del Campo 2015: 33–35). Although we do not have exact figures, a few Scottish schools included Spanish in their curricula after World War I. In fact, William James Entwistle, who was the first holder of the Stevenson Chair, 'spent much time as Inspector of Spanish' in Scottish secondary schools in the late 1920s (Michael 1999). In 1935, however, a report by the Spanish Committee of the Modern Language Association stated that Spanish had made the greatest progress in the North and North Midlands of England, where over twenty schools offered the language. Although the report did not include an exhaustive list of secondary schools where Spanish was taught, the authors only included one Scottish school in their report (Chaytor et al. 1936).

While belief in Spanish as a commercial language determined the geographical expansion of its teaching, Spanish classes were not exclusively dedicated to commercial vocabulary or topics related to trade. Many testimonies pointed out that it was also taught with academic and cultural aims in view: 'It is the claim of many [teachers of Spanish] that even when taught for commercial purposes in Secondary Schools the study of the language must be distinctly cultural' (IAAMSS 1929: 214).

However, its supposed commercial usefulness was the excuse to promote its study. During the inter-war period, the situation of Spanish language teaching improved rapidly thanks to the governmental support. In the year 1930–31, there were 118 state-aided secondary schools in England teaching Spanish and nine in Wales. Thus, the number of grant-aided secondary schools in which provision was made for the teaching of Spanish had increased from seventy in 1922/23 to 127 in 1930/31(ED12/226: Q&A. House of Commons. 02/06/1932). From 1928 onwards, there was also a considerable increase in the number of pupils who offered Spanish in the School Certificate and Higher Certificate Examinations (see Figure 13.1):

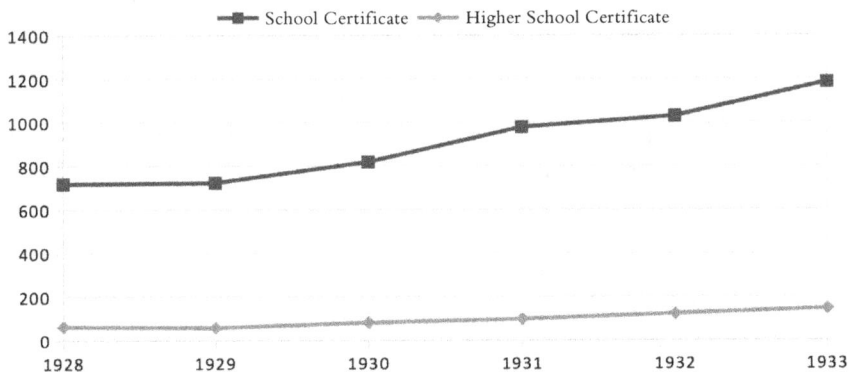

FIG. 13.1. Number of Candidates for Spanish at School Certificate and Higher School Certificate (1928-33) (ED12/226: S. 454/25)

In the academic year 1933–34, 197 grant-aided secondary schools offered Spanish classes, an increase of 100% in comparison with the figures of the immediate post-war years. But although Spanish was winning its place in secondary education, there was still work to be done. In 1930, only 819 pupils took Spanish in the School Certificate, a ludicrously low figure in comparison with German (4600) and French (55,900). Edgar Allison Peers calculated that approximately ninety children were 'learning French in school for every one learning Spanish' around 1930 (Peers 1932).

Spanish was still a second-rate subject in the 1930s, losing the battle for the status of second foreign language to the more prestigious German. The British government had promoted the study of the language on the grounds of its practical usefulness. However, changes in patterns of British trade and another period of war (1936-45) undermined the belief in Spanish as a commercial language. From 1936 onwards, Spanish began to be dropped from the curricula of many schools.

The Collapse of the Belief in Spanish as a Commercial Language

During the interwar period, many British secondary schools included Spanish in their curricula. In the UK, however, the growth in the teaching of this language was stopped by the outbreak of the Spanish Civil War. From 1936 to 1939, only four British schools introduced Spanish lessons. Moreover, a few schools decided to drop this language as subject and, consequently, the number of students taking Spanish decreased significantly (*Vida Hispánica*, 5 (1952): 1).

World War II exacerbated this crisis. The teaching of Spanish suffered interruptions in many British schools for various reasons: some Spanish teachers were sent to the war, causing difficulties in teacher supply. Evacuations also provoked important disruptions in many educational institutions. In the 1950s, the Association of Teachers of Spanish and Portuguese in Great Britain, which was founded in 1947, estimated that forty-three schools had serious problems in providing Spanish classes and had to face breaks of continuity in the teaching of this language (*Vida Hispánica*, 5 (1952): 1).

The staffing problems were partly solved by the presence of Spanish exiles. During the Spanish Civil War, many intellectuals and writers left Spain and sought refuge in the UK. They frequently taught their mother tongue for a living. For instance, the famous poet Luis Cernuda worked as Spanish assistant at Cranleigh School, an independent boarding institution in Surrey, from September 1938 to January 1939, when he resigned his post to become lector at Glasgow University (Harris 1973: 8).

It was not just the wars that caused setbacks in the teaching of Spanish, but also changes in trade, as in the 1930s many British companies had lost interest in the Latin American market, which was strongly dominated by the USA. This new situation called into question the usefulness of Spanish for commercial activities (Bethell 1989: 1-24).

Conclusion

This chapter has shown that the history of Spanish language teaching in Great Britain is not linear. It was a long process with many setbacks. Although Spanish was widely taught at British secondary schools in the 1920s and 1930s, it remained a second-rate subject in comparison with French and German. From the outbreak of the Great War onwards, Spanish competed with German for the status of second foreign language after French, but German held that position for a long time. Spanish only overtook German in the first decade of the twenty-first century (McLelland 2015: 194).

We have also seen that the belief in Spanish as a commercial language determined its geographical expansion. The secondary schools located within commercial and industrial areas were usually pioneering institutions in the teaching of Spanish. The majority of students who took Spanish lived in Liverpool, Bradford and other cities involved in trade with Latin American countries. Moreover, Spanish was learnt by students interested in going into business. However, Spanish was also taught with academic and cultural aims in view.

After the outbreak of the Great War, political motives were also involved in the promotion of Spanish language teaching. However, the importance of British trade in Latin America was the main excuse to promote its teaching in Great Britain. When British firms turned away towards other markets in the 1930s, it did not make sense to foster the study of Spanish for commercial motives. This change and the Spanish Civil War caused a considerable decrease in the number of schools offering Spanish. After World War II the situation of Spanish-language teaching improved. From 1940 to 1952 ninety British secondary schools made provision for Spanish lessons. However, Spanish was not taught for commercial purposes any more (*Vida Hispánica*, 5 (1952): 1). In the second half of the twentieth century Spanish was probably winning more pupils for its status as a useful 'holiday language' than on the basis of the solid economic or political purposes (McLelland 2015: 194).

Bibliography

BALE, JEFF. 2011. 'The Campaign for Spanish Language Education in the "Colossus of the North", 1914-1945', *Language Policy*, 10: 137-57

BETHELL, LESLIE. 1989. 'Britain and Latin America in Historical Perspective', in *Britain and Latin America: A Changing Relationship*, ed. by Victor Bulmer-Thomas (Cambridge: Cambridge University Press), pp. 1-24

BOTTOMLEY, H. HOLFORD. 1915. 'Spanish for German', *The Times*, 2 October, p. 9

British Chamber of Commerce for Spain, The. 1919. 'Studying foreign languages', *Monthly Report*, 9: 23

BOWEN, NICHOLAS. 1979. *A History of Canning House* (London: The Hispanic and Luso-Brazilian Council)

BREUL, KARL. 1899. *The Teaching of Modern Foreign Languages in our Secondary Schools* (Cambridge: Cambridge University Press)

CARROLL, E. J. 1915. 'Spanish for German', *The Times*, 4 October, p. 9

CHAYTOR, H. J., et al. 1936. 'The Teaching of Spanish in Secondary Schools', *Bulletin of Spanish Studies*, 13: 61-79

EDWARDS, JOHN. 2001. 'Both Catholic and Anglican: Lorenzo Lucena (1807-81): Priest, Translator and Teacher', in *Culture and Society in Habsburg Spain: Studies Presented to R. W. Truman by his Pupils and Colleagues on the Occasion of his Retirement*, ed. by Nigel Griffin et al. (London: Tamesis), pp. 181-200

FITCH, JOSHUA. 1897. *Thomas and Matthew Arnold: Their Influence on English Education* (London: Heinemann)

General Committee of The Modern Language Association. 1917. 'Memorandum on Spanish', *Modern Language Teaching*, 13: 52-54

GILLARD, DEREK. 2011 [1998]. *Education in England: A Brief History* <www.educationengland.org.uk/history>

HARRIS, DEREK. 1973. *Luis Cernuda: A Study of the Poetry* (London: Tamesis)

Incorporated Association of Assistant Masters in Secondary Schools. 1929. *Memorandum on the Teaching of Modern Languages* (London: University of London Press)

McLELLAND, NICOLA. 2014. 'French and German in Competition in British Schools, 1850-1945', in *French, English and German: Three Languages in Competition between 1850 and 1945*, ed. by Marcus Reinfried (= *Documents pour l'histoire du français langue étrangère ou seconde*, 52), pp. 125-51

———. 2015. *German through English Eyes: A History of Language Teaching and Learning in Britain, 1500–2000* (Wiesbaden: Harrassowitz)

MARTÍNEZ DEL CAMPO, LUIS GONZAGA. 2015. *Cultural Diplomacy: A Hundred Years of History of the British-Spanish Society* (Liverpool: Liverpool University Press)

MEMORY, JAIME. 2001. 'Lorenzo Lucena Pedrosa (1807-1881): recuperando una figura señera de la Segunda Reforma española', *Anales de Historia Contemporánea*, 17: 213-26

MICHAEL, IAN. 1999. 'Afterword: Spanish at Oxford, 1595-1998', *Bulletin of Hispanic Studies*, 76: 173-93

MUÑOZ, DANIEL, and GREGORIO ALONSO (eds). 2011. *Londres y el liberalismo hispánico* (Madrid and Frankfurt am Main: Iberoamericana-Vervuert)

PEERS, EDGAR ALLISON. 1932. 'Spanish in Schools', *The Times*, 23 September, p. 13

———. 1944. *Spanish-now* (London: Methuen)

———. 1948. 'Twenty-five Years', *Bulletin of Spanish Studies*, 25: 199-206

PUBLIC RECORD, '(Spanish). Extent of teaching. Representations from Department of Overseas Trade, 1913–1935'. The National Archives of the United Kingdom. Reference: ED12/226

ROBERTSON, IAN. 1988. *Los curiosos impertinentes: viajeros ingleses por España desde la accesión de Carlos III hasta 1855* (Madrid: Serbal)

RUBINSTEIN, WILLIAM D., et al. 2011. *The Palgrave Dictionary of Anglo-Jewish History* (London and New York: Palgrave Macmillan)

SIMMONS, DEIDRE. 2007. *Keepers of the Record: The History of the Hudson's Bay Company Archives* (Montreal and Kingston: McGill-Queen's University Press)

SLEE, PETER R. H. 1986. *Learning and a Liberal Education: The Study of Modern History in the Universities of Oxford, Cambridge and Manchester, 1800–1914* (Manchester: Manchester University Press)

TIFFEN, HEBERT J. 1935. *A History of the Liverpool Institute Schools, 1825 to 1935* (Liverpool: The Liverpool Institute Old Boys' Association)

The Times. 1920. 'Mr. Holford Bottomley', 5 March, p. 11

Vida Hispánica. 1952. 'Editorial', 5: 1

WATSON, FOSTER. 1971. *The Beginning of the Teaching of Modern Subjects in England* (Wakefield: S. R. Publishers)

WOOLF, E. A. 1917. 'The Place of Spanish in School Curricula', *Modern Language Teaching*, 13: 91-92

Notes to Chapter 13

1. This quotation is taken from Fitch 1897: 32-34. Thomas Arnold's words were originally published in the *Journal of Education* in 1834.
2. Woolf 1917.
3. King's College London Secretary in correspondence comprising letters regarding the successful application of Ricardo Ramírez for the Chair of Spanish Language and Literature (University of London, King's College Archives, KA/IC/R76).
4. Peers 1948: 199-206.
5. 'Spanish at Whitechapel Foundation School' (File's former reference S. 631) in Public Record: '(Spanish). Extent of teaching. Representations from Department of Overseas Trade, 1913-1935', The National Archives of the United Kingdom, ED12/226. The main archival source of my chapter is this record (ED12/226), which belongs to those issued by the Modern Languages Committee (Board of Education) and is held in the National Archives in Kew. This record includes various files about Spanish language education in British schools from 1913 to 1935. Among other files, this record contains Board of Education minute papers on Spanish teaching; reports of H. M. Inspectors on the classes in Spanish; letters from the Department of Overseas Trade, etc. As will be seen below, the data that this record provides have been verified with other archival sources such as newspapers, reports, etc. The reference ED12 contains a sub-series of files on the teaching of various Modern Foreign Languages in the UK. Henceforth, references in the text to this record will be given in the form (ED 12/226: S...). S is the former reference given to every document that this record contains. S will be used to identify the record's document or file that is quoted. Where an S reference is not available, names, page numbers or other references are used to identify the document.
6. Peers 1944: v.
7. Bowen 1979: 3-4.

CHAPTER 14

❖

Teaching Second Languages at Pre-School Age: The Russian Experience

Ekaterina Protassova

The history of foreign language teaching to the very young in Russia is interrelated with the need of society to organize a better linguistic education at school which yields people who are able to read important sources in other tongues. Formally, the declared goal is communication with foreigners as equals in their languages. In reality, very few foreigners were allowed to enter the USSR and only nominated reliable citizens of the Soviet Union crossed its borders, mostly on their way to other Socialist countries. Politics influenced the selection, the volume and the ways of teaching languages in education. In the nineteenth century, when Russia was an integrated part of Europe, the natural approach was used for the most-taught contemporary languages, to the detriment of mother-tongue teaching. Soviet rule reversed this tendency: as autarchy advanced, contacts with other countries were cut; speakers of foreign tongues became suspect. Authorities mistrusted those who could read without censorship. The interest in an early start in the teaching of foreign languages in the Soviet Union and Russia peaked in the 1960s (the period of Khrushchev's *Thaw*) and the second half of the 1980s up until the mid-1990s (*Perestroika* and democratic development). In the 2000s, the situation changed again: the very rich sent their children abroad or invited native speakers to teach them while they were brought up in Russia; the less well-off paid for additional lessons. During Soviet times, most of the contents of the foreign-language-teaching materials referred to life in the Soviet Union; they supposed that foreigners would arrive to learn how well everything was going on there. From life abroad, only old texts could be taken, or those connected with the fight of the working classes for their rights. The specific Russian approach underlines the importance of conscious learning and the use of the mother tongue in the study of foreign languages, as well as the major role of Russian as the state language in teaching the indigenous languages to the national minorities. The role of one's own and of others' thought connected to language is one of the topical discussions throughout the history of foreign-language teaching.

Introduction

The image of children and their role in society has changed throughout history. Sometimes they were regarded as small adults; sometimes as abnormal creatures that had to be instructed at every stage of their development; and sometimes as innocent angels from whom adults had to learn and who would be defiled by contact with the contemporary world. Thus, the role of a foreign language and culture was considered to be either a sin or a blessing, a benefit or a danger. A foreign language could be condemned as an alien way of thinking, as an imported cultural influence or as an antagonistic picture of the world; consequently, it had to be banned. Yet it was also important to penetrate the thought of the enemy through his language. Russia is no exception.

The history of teaching a second language in Russia can be divided into (i) teaching classical languages such as Greek and Latin; (ii) teaching the language of religion (Church Slavonic, Old Church Slavonic and others); (iii) teaching modern languages like German, French and English; and (iv) teaching Russian to minorities inside Russia. Only (iii) and (iv) apply to the pre-school age. The methods of teaching influenced each other, but the ideology has differed and changed over the years. One had to decide what the reasons for selecting the languages were. Then the order, periods and intervals for introducing languages had to be discussed. The optimal order, according to tradition, is to start with German, to proceed to French, and finally to learn English, if there is enough time: German as the language of discipline and science that controls the brain and develops the variety of sounds; French as language of culture that enables one to perceive nuances; and English as the language of literature, business, style and thought. At the beginning of the twentieth century, people believed that English pronunciation could hamper the sounds in other languages, so it should be acquired after German and French (information from my interviews; see below).

Pre-school age is specific in many respects. Children acquire almost perfect pronunciation. On the one hand, small children are believed to be more receptive to foreign languages than adults; on the other hand, they can forget everything that they have learned, apart from songs and poems. Proponents of the early start have accentuated its outcome: almost all pupils who started at pre-school age spent less time studying later, had very good results and showed high cognitive development. Its opponents still consider the learning of languages to be money- and time-consuming, a hard and painful task which is not worth trying (Lomakina and Laer 2014; and numerous websites for parents).[1]

The question of the teachers' competence arises. In the nineteenth century, teachers were native speakers of the language. After the October Revolution, in the first years of Soviet rule, almost everybody who was competent in foreign languages on a high level had left the country with the White emigration. Those who remained became teachers of languages without development: their language fossilized; their pupils never left the country and were even less competent than their teachers were. The general competence declined. A knowledge of the alien culture supposed an acquaintance with dangerous values like religious festivities that were banned from education in the USSR.

This chapter presents the views of famous Russian educators on the effects of early language education and traces the brief history of teaching methods from the end of the nineteenth century up to the present. It demonstrates the interdependence between methods for *adults* and those for *children*. There will be a special focus on 'Russian' approaches. The goal is to show the discrepancy between the home-made image of the culture connected with the foreign language, grammatical drill, and the uneven availability of such education depending on social class. Parallels in the ideology of the past and present of language teaching will be noted, notwithstanding new technological possibilities. I also offer an example of one teaching technique used from the nineteenth century to the present day in teaching languages to young children in Russia: lotto.

Foreign-Language Teaching in Russia

The growing necessity to know foreign languages can be traced back to the times of Tsar Peter the Great (r. 1682-1721), who introduced Dutch and German as the languages of his 'teachers'. He was interested in learning new things through languages. His daughter Elisabeth, whilst on the throne (r. 1741-1762), supported French. Inspired by Peter the Great, the etiquette manual *Yunosti chestnoe zerkalo* [*The True Mirror of Youth*] (Anon: 1819 [1717]) says that those who are able, besides other talents, to speak foreign languages can become courtiers:

> [T]he young lads should speak among themselves in foreign languages in order to be acquainted with them; especially in case they happen to say something secret, so that the servants and housemaids are unable to find out what it is about, and in order to distinguish them from ignorant blockheads, because every merchant praising his goods sells as he can.[2]

In the middle of the eighteenth century, the first ABCs and grammars of Latin, French, Italian and German were published; English came some years later and in 1773 was introduced as a compulsory subject at the Academic Gymnasium in Saint Petersburg, for example (Surina 2008).

In Russian history, there were three ways of becoming bilingual. One could be born to bilingual parents, which was rather common in a country where even today there are more than 160 indigenous languages spoken. Next, one could grow up in a family where another language was spoken or in a foreign country. Third, the family could invite a family teacher to speak to the children in his language. According to the fine literature of the nineteenth century, the last variant was common practice in well-to-do families, where teachers of French and German were invited (Rjeoutski and Tchoudinov 2013). French had the reputation of being the language of social encounters and the arts, whereas German was the language of education. By the end of the nineteenth century, as in the family of the Russian writer Vladimir Nabokov, English became more widely spoken (Nabokov 1989). Society copied the way of speaking in the Tsar's family, who changed their habits according to the political situation (Zimin 2011). When a foreign language was taught at schools, it was German rather than French; in gymnasiums (grammar or upper secondary schools), Latin and Ancient Greek were taught as well.

According to Russian historians of language teaching (Rahmanov 1972; Miro-liubov 2002; Gal'skova 2003; Nikshikova 2007), the methodological periods in Russia can be delineated as follows:

⋆ 1860-1920. Direct, or natural, method: family tutors and teachers of language spoke to children. The educated strata of society introduced three languages to their children in early childhood. The manuals of mother and foreign tongues did not differ much from each other and books in original language were used to study. State schools became affordable for all and many more people gained access to education.

⋆ 1920-50. Characterized by the search for Socialist ways of teaching (e.g., at some point Esperanto became popular), and by a lack of competent teachers. The dead languages were rejected; the teaching of German was reinforced as the language of Communist predecessors Marx and Engels, of the German proletariat. The grammar-translation method dominated. Lexis was divided into active and passive use of vocabulary. Every syllabus started with an introductory phonetic propaedeutic course, the teaching sets developed (including teachers' and pupils' textbooks and additional materials, not only the schoolbook). Only one foreign language was taught, usually German.

⋆ 1950-90. Lowering of the age for starting foreign-language learning in schools; experiments with schools and kindergartens specializing in foreign-language teaching (in small numbers, for the elite strata of society). The English language began to dominate. Consciousness and comparison in the acquisition of language grew. Programmed and intensive methods grew. Home-made textbooks, classical and Socialist literature were used for all languages taught. A second foreign language, usually French or German, was introduced in some schools by the end of the period.

⋆ 1990-. An increasing need to know foreign languages in view of the openness of the newly democratic Russian society. More effective and varied methods of language teaching; opportunities to travel abroad and study in other countries. Emergence of a wide group of parents who teach languages at home. The introduction of imported methods of language teaching, the use of foreign textbooks. Native speakers became teachers in nurseries and pre-schools. The implementation of computer- and internet-based methods. Language teaching started to be planned throughout the lifespan (including minority and state languages). Since 2004, English (more rarely other languages) is taught from the age of eight to nine in all schools.

The teaching of Russian to the national minorities became obligatory before the Second World War; the generations that started school later grew up more competent in Russian than in their mother tongue. A reverse tendency of national mobilization and de-Russification started in the late 1980s and different types of bilingual kindergartens are still emerging in Russia: for example, in 2015 there were more than 160 pre-primary groups where German is taught both as a foreign language and as a minority language of the Russian Germans in eight regions of Russia, mostly near Omsk and in Altai, according to information from the Russian-German House (<http://drh-moskau.ru; www.rusdeutsch.eu>). They use the method 'Deutsch mit Schrumdi' developed in cooperation between Russian and German educators.

Teaching Languages to pre-School Children in the Past

The age for starting school varies from country to country at different epochs. In Russia in the eighteenth and nineteenth centuries, children started school between eight and twelve years; after the Second World War the age was first seven and is now between six and eight years of age.

The first nurseries and pre-schools started to function in the 1860s, so organized teaching goes back to that period. There were two tendencies: kindergartens for the children of the intelligentsia or cultured people; and kindergartens for the children of workers. The first were designed for socialization and for teaching different subjects, among other things foreign languages; the latter were more to keep children safe while their parents were working and to teach them the basics of behaviour. It is necessary to add that at that time dialects were spoken in the countryside that differed in many aspects from the literary language. Indeed, it was a triglossic situation because children whose education was provided by the Russian Orthodox Church alone had to acquire Church Slavonic as the language of their literacy. The mother tongue of children differed from Russian in the national areas where a significant part of the local population had another ethnicity; and in some regions (such as the Caucasus, Tatarstan, Bashkiria, Middle Asia, Siberia) they might have a different religion, and be using a different language and a different script as well.

In the nineteenth century textbooks for children often consisted of grammar rules, texts and sometimes lists of words; they evolved with time (Miroljubov 2002: 48–63). The natural teaching of languages was based upon an understanding of the ways of speaking to children, oriented towards everyday communicative situations. Children wanted to express their thoughts in a foreign language because they had no other option.

The journals for kindergartens that were published in the nineteenth century mentioned certain topics that are still relevant to this day: for example, the natural character of teaching that can be achieved if we start early. Mrs Okorokova (1873) proposed not to translate, but to use visual aids and actions with objects, to start with words and then go on to phrases and sentences. First, children had to analyse the sound composition and afterwards the letter composition of words. Next, children had to learn to interpret. Oral language and translation should take priority. An anonymous opponent, using only the initials N. I. (1874: 317), wrote:

> The teaching of foreign languages must contribute to the general intellectual development of the child, to teach them to overcome difficulties, to develop their independence, to serve, so to speak, as gymnastics for the mind. However, the teaching of languages with the sole goal of grasping how to speak will be a one-sided training of memory, leaving all other sides of the mind completely untouched.

This discussion continued over the years. Some believed that communication while teaching languages must not be conducted in the foreign language only, as it could hamper the ease and the genuineness of self-expression by the child, who is thinking in Russian anyway. An anonymous author (Anon. 1877: 414) wrote that 'the learning of foreign languages must start at an early age, when the mechanical memorizing function is simpler, when the brain is suppler and the ear is softer; but the stage for this is seven years'. At this stage, children at that time were not yet at school and had not learned their alphabet.

Some thinkers in Europe turned to patriotic ideas, romanticizing the traditional way of life and trying to form a national consciousness. The famous Russian educator Konstantin Ushinskiy (1873: 11) stated that a child can learn a foreign language in a few months to a level that adults can only reach through years of hard work. He and other renowned educators — Elizaveta Vodovozova and Elizaveta Tiheeva in particular — stressed that children should speak their own language well first and that it was unpleasant to listen to children who can speak different foreign languages but stumble in their mother tongue. The national culture should precede other cultures. A foreign language must be started only once the mother tongue is deeply rooted, wrote Tiheeva (1981: 122-23); and one or two hours per day are enough. These were democratic principles because the elite should not be separated from their own people through the lack of a common language; and these ideas won after the Revolution of 1917. Unfortunately, they still influence pre-primary teaching today, even though the situation in the country has changed completely.

From the 1920s until the 1950s the general teaching of a second language besides Russian as the state language started rather late. The intelligentsia and the new bourgeoisie during the times of the New Economic Policy continued to teach foreign languages at pre-school age in private, for groups of children or individually. I have collected personal testimonies (through personal interviews with old people from the 1970s to 1990s, all of whom could remember learning a foreign language in their childhood) that German, French and English were all taught; and it was not a rare practice, but rather a must in educated society. In the 1930s a certain Emma Fjodorovna and Magda Arturovna (of German origin; their names were adapted to Russian tradition through patronymics) used to gather children to take them on a group stroll to learn some songs and poems, which was quite normal practice at the time. For women of the former higher social stratum, teaching modern languages was a question of earning money. The methods described were reading and discussing books, doing exercises, playing games, singing songs.

Olga Tolstaya-Voeikova (2005; 2012) describes her practice with her grand-children, who spoke three foreign languages (besides Russian) — French, German, English — alternating between them; she tried to organize play sessions with their peers to make them communicate in the language acquired (Jobert 2013). The same books were re-read many times until all the vocabulary could be understood; all the grammatical forms remembered; all the expressions learned by heart; and until all the conversations ran smoothly. The old books by the Comtesse de Ségur, née Rostopchine, were still very popular. Regularity of lessons had to be observed. Three foreign languages and the reading of foreign literature in the language of origin were a must in the educated layers of society. This method continued until the mid-1930s in families where intellectual values dominated and was treated much like the ability to dance, as a social accomplishment.

Not everyone knows that Lev Vygotsky formulated most of his pedagogical ideas while teaching foreign languages to children. In 1928 he wrote that there are no general rules to judge bilingualism as a propitious or a hampering factor under any possible circumstances, always and everywhere, independently of the concrete conditions under which this development happens and of the regularities of this development, which change at each age level. The solution to this question, according to Vygotsky, is very difficult and depends on the age of the children, on the character of the encounter of both languages, and on the pedagogical impact on the development of one's own and others' speech (Vygotsky 1982: 334).

Under the autarchy of the Soviet Union, new books, new teaching methods and new native speakers were difficult to come by. Those who could speak foreign languages at a native-like level were simply dying out or in exile. Still, a thin stratum of intelligentsia continued to employ people who could teach any foreign tongues to their children. According to my interviews, English began to predominate in the 1960s as the language of science and fine literature. One of the teachers famous in Moscow was Ida Moiseevna, half Jewish and half Afro-American, who came to the USSR in the 1930s in search of her Communist husband, who perished in the GULAG; she did not learn Russian but taught a group of children English, giving them an American accent, which some considered insulting (Protassova and Rodina 2011: 77–78). A certain Maria Teodorovna taught English too; Maria Grigorievna (in the 1960s) and Madam Agnes (in the 1980s) taught French. They gathered groups of children with whom they repeated the same phrases, made pictures and learned new words, poems, songs and dialogues. Parents were involved too: they had to rehearse the phrases etc. at home with their children.

During the Thaw period after the Stalin's death, the Communist Party issued a resolution that the teaching of foreign languages had to be improved, e.g. through an earlier start. Experts immediately started to publish programmes for the teaching of languages. Most of them contained phrases; thematically organized lexicology; question–answer situations; songs and poems for children. Besides using original folklore, the authors composed texts themselves, but there were no native speakers to check the quality of the language, just as there are not enough competent proof-readers even now. In the 1960s Bekker, Braginskiy, Carapkina and others published materials for young learners (e.g. Chistiakova et al. 1964). Another source was the manuals imported from other Socialist countries, such as *Mała Mozaika*, a magazine from Poland for those who studied foreign languages, and the monthly children's magazine *Bummi* from the German Democratic Republic, as well as imports of English-language children's books from China and later from India.

The practice of teaching foreign languages in kindergarten had demonstrated that every child aged four or five could learn a foreign language. To be communicative meant to be able to construct phrases, to ask questions, to issue commands, to describe pictures and situations, to understand short stories told by the teacher. All these phrases could be put together into a longer utterance. The model played an important role. The contents had to be familiar to the child, while the environment should be distinct from that connected with other activities, so that the child would concentrate upon the foreign language and not confound it with the mother tongue. The early start had a positive influence on school studies. Sometimes one could believe that it is a question of enthusiasm, but it was much more a question of motivation and quantity of input.

The next step in the development of the methodology was taken by Mateckaya (1971) who introduced activity in the foreign language in congruence with other children's activities. It was similar to the theory of total physical response popular at that time. For her, children acquired different speech qualities for their character while speaking during dramatization (such as tempo, intonation, voice, individual characteristics, etc.). The culture of speaking consisted of the ability to listen, to pronounce the endings of words and phrases, and to gain a better command of the mother tongue by comparing it with the foreign language. Klimentenko (1976) conducted experiments with six-year-old children. She highlighted the importance of imprinting, imitation, concrete objects and actions, and learning whole set phrases, arranged thematically. Semantization was based on images and translations. She also wanted children to switch their attention from external control to internal control. Testing was based on translation. Futerman (1984) and Natal'ina (1982) worked along the same lines.

In the 1980s the most popular method was formulated by Negnevickaya (1986), a structural linguist who based her theory on the typological differences between languages on all levels (differences in phonetics, grammar, semantics, syntax became motivated through play and games: the child wished something in play, therefore a certain grammatical or lexical unit should be used). The research was based upon the psychological theories of Vygotsky (especially his zone of proximal development); Leontiev's motivation of each language action; Slobin's and Shahnarovich's theories of child language development from word to utterance; and Bakhtin's theory of the addressee of every speech act. Negnevickaya motivated each part of the sentence by play and games, which she considered the most appropriate way for a child to acquire something. The basis of her most influential approach is: understanding before acting; learning language together with action; the need to formulate any part of the sentence or text according to the goal; the combination of verbal actions and step-by-step growth of utterances in all domains of human speech activity (Negnevickaya and Shahnarovich 1981). Each construction started with imperatives; going on to differences between singular and plural, third and later first and then second person; adding nouns and prepositions; and everything was accompanied with the handling of real objects. Parents played an important role in teaching because they were present during the lessons and practised the words and constructions with the children at home. After three years of visiting lessons twice a week, children could produce orally, read and write small texts in English (Negnevickaya 1986).

Negnevickaya worked mostly with English and Russian. Androchnikova (1988) and others expanded these principles to French, German and Spanish. A group of educators and researchers in the Soviet national republics transferred this system to the teaching of Russian as a second language. I personally took part in all these developments and report here what was happening. In 1987, the Collegium of the Ministry of Education of the Russian Federal Republic started experiments in teaching foreign languages to children aged four in kindergartens and six at primary schools. These large-scale experiments were conducted in Belarus, Estonia, Georgia, Latvia, Lithuania, the Russian Federation and Ukraine; their purpose was to prove that foreign languages could be included in the general programmes of pre-primary and primary education. Tens of thousands of children and hundreds of school and pre-school teachers participated in them throughout the country and made Negnevickaya's methods very popular. The pre-schools organized lessons twice a week with a group of twenty children who proved to have good memory skills and to be able to imitate sounds very well. At the same time, the practice found that the children shouted loudly, they soon became tired and could not listen to each other. For such children, a special tradition of rituals was necessary: when they heard the same phrases at the beginning, they were happy. Some movement and etiquette rules were also set at the beginning. Extrapolation to the national republics often led to a situation where about fifty children in a group with only one teacher and using several minority languages were expected to learn the Russian language by immersion.

I made protocols of such encounters at that time and keep these records. The typical lesson in a pre-primary was as follows: children sat on chairs in a circle or at a table; the teacher used many visual aids and alternated activities; no parents were present; combining words with movements was a widely used technique. In a couple of years children learned the seasons and the times of the day; could ask and speak about domestic and wild animals; about what they liked and did not like; about the colours of their toys; about themselves; their families; their clothing; their house; toys; colours; what they could and could not do. They learned many poems; could count; organized gymnastics; sang songs. The crucial part of the method was to start by naming actions and carry them out in reality: go, run, jump, sit, stand, count, see, sleep, sing, dance, fly, swim, climb, wash, play, etc. (from 'Tigers, swim!' to 'Tigers, swim two times across the river!' to 'Six yellow tigers and three black monkeys are swimming across the big blue river'). Imagination was used even in the teaching of grammar rules. Phonetic exercises were explained in a playful manner; the games were based on contrasts between sounds. Children repeated English phrases and inserted English words into their Russian phrases in their free play. They counted in English for all their games outside the classroom.

According to my notes, parents supported the learning of languages as they thought that their children would develop special intellectual characteristics and acquire communicative initiative. They stated that the children looked forward to the lessons and were not tired. They played the same games at home with their toys. Parents received instructions from the teacher, to ask their children what the lesson was about, what was learned there; they also received a copy-book with all the words and phrases so that the children could study at home as well. They were invited to festivities in English. Books in English were recommended. However, not all of the children joined in the games; some were too shy to speak.

Audio and television materials were also created for the three most popular foreign languages: German, French and English. Teachers emphasized the role of foreign languages for the general development of the child: memory, attention, stability, linguistic conjecture, edification, discipline, activity, collectivism, intellectual curiosity. Artistic and dramatic, cognitive and aesthetic abilities were formed. The special capabilities of talented children can be found even at that age; but all the children were found to be much better prepared for school through lessons in a second language (Leont'ev 1986; Negnevickaya 1987; Gal'skova and Nikitenko 2004; Utehina 2013). In 1989 to 1992, the TV program *Detskiy chas* [*Children's Hour*] showed its own lessons of English, German and French for children and included fragments of the BBC series *Muzzy in Gondoland* (1986) and *Muzzy Comes Back* (1989), directed by Richard Taylor, from 1990 onwards.

The Current State

The relevance of the pre-school age for teaching foreign or second languages has long been a subject of discussion. The usual themes discussed are the Critical Period Hypothesis and the optimal age to start (e.g., Krashen et al. 1982; Johnson and Newport 1989; Birdson 1999; Flege et al. 1999; del Pilar García Mayo and Lecumberri 2003; DeKeyser 2013); the relationship between value and quality; the scope of the possible achievement targets; the evident advantages of different approaches; the stability and the duration of results (Marinova-Todd et al. 2000; Murad 2006; Nikolov 2009; Rich 2014; Salzmann 2014). Other related questions are: who can be a teacher for the very young (a native speaker only?); what his/her professional qualification should be (pre-school teacher, school teacher, foreign-language, mother-tongue teacher?); how the group should be organized; what additional materials can be used (specially prepared; authentic for mother-tongue or second-language learners?); what the size and the composition of the group must be (all ability or matched levels/ages/backgrounds?); how beneficial or injurious this can be for children with a language impairment or other special needs; in which areas specific benefits can be found; what the age-appropriate and fruitful methods of teaching are (Brumfit et al. 1991; Vale and Feunteun 1995; Rixon 1999; Cameron 2001). The increase in the various methods of foreign-language teaching to the very young has produced a large amount of interdisciplinary research data and a number of recommendations (Edelenbos et al. 2006; Enever et al. 2009; Mourão and Lourenço 2015). Nevertheless, not everyone gives a definition of what a young learner is; there are some difficulties with restricting language teaching to classroom use only; therefore, it is sometimes difficult to compare the learning environments of learners and their families' influence. All the above-mentioned subjects and concerns are discussed by Russian educationalists as well.

Several hundred publications and dissertations concerning foreign-language teaching at pre-school age in Russia appeared in the years between 1992 and 2015, after the collapse of the Soviet Union. For this particular analysis we have chosen only some of the most representative. Theoretical questions interest, for example,

Sulin 2000; Gorlova 2003; Markosian 2004; and Nikolaeva 2011. Questions reflecting particular Russian concerns that differ from prevailing Western views include the following: how detrimental is the learning of foreign languages to the national identity of the Russian citizen? To what extent must a foreign language be learned so that it cannot harm the first language, Russian? Should foreigners, who have other values, be allowed to teach our children? It is still widely believed that a foreign language takes up some place in the mind to the detriment of one's own language, consciousness and picture of the world, so the theoreticians have to fight for the very idea of the early language teaching.

Many researchers also discuss what should be taught as culture related to the language (Mahneva 2001; Danilova 2009); what kind of personality is formed ideologically; and what the teacher's attitude towards the foreign culture should be (Kartashova 2002). In many cases where authentic materials cannot be found, the decision is to teach the local culture decoded into a foreign language (everything can be said in a foreign language). The contents of the teaching (Logunova 1997), the visual stimuli (Voroncova 1999), integration with other activities and the development of the first language (Yacenko 1994; Bahtalina 1998) and the development of cognitive and linguistic abilities (Yudovina 2000; Zhigaleva 2009) are also discussed. The musical (Achkasova 1997; Nevezhina 2000), symbolic (Bludova 1997), playful and fairy-tale (Ponimatko 1991; Snegova 1994) methods are underlined as suitable for pre-schoolers; however, it is difficult to measure the effectiveness of the materials applied. Studying a foreign language is still regarded as a special activity among other educational activities (Shaverneva 2003; Spiridonova 2010). The geography of investigations is very large; these processes are studied all over Russia.

Some scholars study how children learn foreign languages 'artificially': in families where no one speaks these languages as a native speaker, still one of the parents chooses to speak English to the child and the child succeeds in acquiring it (Chernichkina 2007; Chirsheva 2012). Most of the research is dedicated to English-language learning (Tarasiuk 1999; Vronskaya 2015), but some papers concern German, French or Spanish (Hlybova 2000; Tkachuk 2001). Sometimes international experience is taken into account (Gainutdinova 2005). Protassova and Rodina (2009; 2010) combine the two approaches, namely, organized activities and immersion: they build the inclusion of play into the motivation scheme while teaching a second language during specially organized lessons; other activities throughout the day can be accompanied by the second language. Kantelinen et al. (2008) observe that a commodification of foreign languages has occurred in the last decades. There are special programmes at many universities all over Russia that prepare teachers of foreign languages for kindergartens. The Federal Standard does not prescribe the language of education,[3] but takes into account the ethno–cultural situation of the child's development. Some programmes propose teaching a second language for children as a component of the core curriculum. Teaching foreign languages takes place on a fee-paying basis in pre-primary institutions, each lesson lasting between fifteen and twenty-five to thirty minutes.

FIG. 14.1. (a) Language lotto in the nineteenth century. No bibliographical data.
<http://bit.ly/2QRZ2pd>
(b) Language lotto, reproduced from an old set from nineteenth century.
Example from the reverse side of a small card:
Пробочникъ. Der Korkzieher. Le tire-bouchon.
Starinnoe loto. 2002 (Moscow: Museum of Moscow)

FIG. 14.2. Language lotto in the 1950s-1970s. Example from the reverse side of a small card: *Платье La robe A dress Das Kleid*. Painters: D. V. Brodskaya and A. M. Savchenko

In multilingual Russia and in the states that emerged after the collapse of the Soviet Union a foreign language is often not a second but already a third language for young learners (Iliasov 1991; Sidorova 1992; Fomin 1998). The national republics and regions within Russia have started programmes for the revitalization of the indigenous languages from pre-school on, attempting to reverse the language shift.

A Teaching Technique across the Decades: Lotto

Lotto in four languages (Russian, French, English and German, in this order) was one of the main materials for teaching for many years (see Figures 14.1-4). It is like bingo, although bingo itself was never popular. In lotto sets, a large card has a big picture in the middle (called subject or plot picture in Russian pedagogy). On three or four sides around it (on the margins) are smaller pictures representing objects to be found in the main picture (called object pictures in Russian pedagogy). Inscriptions in four languages are on the reverse side of the picture (the Russian tradition is to put an article before the noun). Small cards double the pictures put on the sides of the big picture.

There are several ways of playing lotto. The leading player may put small cards in front of the players and ask them 'What is this?'. If s/he answers successfully, s/he may keep the card; if not, the leader places it under the pack. The next player takes his or her turn. The winner is the one who has collected more cards than the other players. Or, if the big cards are distributed, the players fill the slots by matching the small cards and the winner is the person who covers all the slots first. In another variant, players must ask the leader for the small cards by naming the objects represented upon them. The most difficult variants are based upon discussing parts of the big picture. It is widely held that lotto contributes to enlargement of vocabulary, knowledge of the game rules (a person who can follow the rules is seen as an organized person who can pay attention to many things at the same time), and acquisition of elementary discussion skills.

The usual themes for lotto sets were the family, meals, transport, fruit and vegetables, the countryside, the seashore, children's occupations, wild and domestic animals. Lotto has been widely used in foreign-language teaching for young learners from the nineteenth century to the present day. Changes to the contents and layout have coincided with peaks of interest in the early start of foreign-language learning. The earliest set I have found dates from the nineteenth century (Figure 14.1a); the characters and circumstances are, to my mind, typical of any middle-class European family of that time. Another set from the nineteenth century, recently reproduced, has no big pictures and only three languages (Figure 14.1b).

The earliest lotto set from the Soviet period that I have found dates from 1956, the latest from 1977. The author of all Soviet language sets (Figures 14.2, 14.3a, 14.3b) was Anna I. Kreshchanovskaya (who also developed materials for teaching German). The first set was published in Moscow by *Bumagootdelochnaja fabrika Upravlenija poligraficheskoj promyshlennosti i kul'ttovarov*. Later, *Moskovskiy kombinat igrushek* and the publishing house Malysh also issued sets.

The set in Figure 14.2 reflects the typical Russian/Soviet culture of the time, idealizing family, food, transport etc. As in the schoolbooks, everyone lived in the USSR and had to describe his or her life in different languages. The set was revised again only in the late 1980s and early 1990s (Figure 14.3); the same pictures were updated, but lost their charm. Today, those who learned languages through this aid cherish the pictures as a monument to the epoch. In the 2000s, when everybody had access to internet photos and Photoshop, the old idea was redesigned once again, with gaudy colours and no style; the scales of the images do not correspond to each other; the composition is poor; some pictures are unrecognizable; and there is a mistake on the cover (Figure 14.4). There may well have been millions of these lotto sets: on the cover of my copy, reference is made to an edition of 100,000 copies.

In parallel, other lotto sets in four languages, renewed periodically, covered themes of animals (Zoological Lotto) and plants (Botanical Lotto).[4] In 2013 a lotto set with inscriptions in the Russian, English, Arab (with transcription) and Tatar languages was published, treating the usual themes (i.e. how people are dressed, what their usual meals and occupations are), but from the point of view of Islam.[5]

FIG. 14.3. (a) Language lotto in 1986. Painter V. Riabchikov
(b) Language lotto in 1991. Painter M. Trubkovich

FIG. 14.4. Language lotto in the 2000s. Designer L. I. Tolmacheva.
Moskovskiy kombinat igrushek

Conclusion

The objectives of foreign-language teaching have changed from that of providing an unquestioned marker of belonging to the pan-European culture and society among elite members in the past, to teaching a common language for the working classes all over the world in the twentieth century, to supplying an accessible instrument for gaining economic profits today. Characterizing the development of pre-school teaching methods, Lukina (1999) traces its steps as the imitation of adults' speech in the 1950s to the mid-1960s; psychological and educational research in the late 1960s and 1970s; the conscious formation of practice in the 1980s to the mid-1990s; interest in authentic materials, foreign civilization and adequate language; the integration of language studies with all sorts of physical activities from the mid-1990s to the present.

Today, lessons revolve around certain themes (the lesson is like a play with a plot, a fairy tale in development, changing under the children's eyes); they rely on the flexible use of the children's mother tongue for explanations; and use various visual and sensory aids. Rhymes, songs and dramatizations are still used, but teachers are conscious of employing different activities, play and games. The teaching methods differ from the ways in which language is taught at school, especially because there are no manuals; nonetheless, it is expected that parents will help their children to make progress, otherwise they do not advance. The pragmatism of modern people is oriented towards communication and the practical use of language, so that less grammar is taught consciously. The problem of transition from pre-primary to school still remains: how continuity between pre-school and school teaching should be ensured; whether to start to study a second language in the second year and not in the first; how to take into account the knowledge already acquired and to manage multilevel classrooms. Pre-primary teachers discussed these questions at their meetings where I was present in 2015 to 2016.

The world is growing smaller and needs more speakers who are proficient in different languages. The opportunities to study or work abroad have opened up to Russian citizens in recent times and offered new horizons, in contrast to the Soviet times when all foreign-language teaching was restricted to the reading of books and some Communist newspapers and journals (see, e.g., Shelestiuk 2013). Parents who missed out on early support in learning foreign languages and who, therefore, suffer from insufficient knowledge are longing to put their children into a pre-school providing foreign-language teaching in order to ensure a challenging linguistic environment for their offspring (the same idea and tendencies are relevant, for example, for Turkey: cf. Deneme et al. 2011; Kocaman and Kocaman 2012). In Russia, where the glamour of Tsarist times has been revived in the last decades, everyone imagines himself or herself as being part of the well-educated aristocracy, which meant foreign language skills. Russian classical literature of the nineteenth century (Pushkin, Tolstoy, etc.), which is an obligatory subject at school, provides enough evidence of the advantages of employing a governess or an au pair to speak to the child in a foreign language.

Bibliography

ACHKASOVA, NATALIA N. 1997. *Metodika postroeniya propedevticheskogo kursa po angliyskomu yazyku dlia detei 5 let na muzykal'noj osnove* (Moscow: Moscow Pedagogical State University)

ANDROCHNIKOVA, GALINA M. 1988. 'Nuzhno li doshkol'nikam izuchat' inostrannyj yazyk', *Narodnoe obrazovanie*, 2: 15-17

ANON. 1819 [1717]. *Yunosti chestnoe zerkalo* [*The True Mirror of Youth*] (St Petersburg: n. pub.)

ANON. 1877. 'Zametka ob izuchenii inostrannyh yazykov', *Detskiy sad*, 9: 411-20

BAHTALINA, ELENA Y. 1998. *Integrirovannoe obuchenie angliyskomu yazyku v detskom sadu* (Petrozavodsk: Karelian State Pedagogical University)

BIRDSON, DAVID (ed.). 1999. *Second Language Acquisition and the Critical Period Hypothesis* (Mahwah, NJ: Erlbaum)

BLUDOVA, TATIANA P. 1997. *Ispol'zovanie uslovnyh znakov v obuchenii detei doshkol'nogo vozrasta angliyskomu yazyku* (St Petersburg: Gerzen Russian State Pedagogical University)

BRUMFIT, CHRISTOPHER J., JAYNE MOON, and RAY TONGUE (eds). 1991. *Teaching English to Children: From Practice to Principle* (London: HarperCollins)

CAMERON, LYNNE. 2001. *Teaching Languages to Young Learners* (Cambridge: Cambridge University Press)

CHERNICHKINA, ELENA K. 2007. *Iskusstvennyj bilingvizm: lingvisticheskiy status i harakteristiki* (Volgograd: Volgograd State Pedagogical University)

CHIRSHEVA, GALINA N. 2012. *Bilingvizm* (St Petersburg: Zlatoust)

CHISTIAKOVA, TATIANA A., ELENA M. CHERNUSHHENKO, and GALINA I. SOLINA. 1964. *Obuchenie inostrannym yazykam v detskix sadax* (Moscow: Prosveshhenie)

DANILOVA, MARIA V. 2009. *Formirovanie osnov inoyazychnoj kul'tury u detei doshkol'nogo vozrasta* (Moscow: Moscow Pedagogical State University)

DeKEYSER, ROBERT M. 2013. 'Age Effects in Second Language Learning: Stepping Stones toward Better Understanding', *Language Learning*, 63: 52–67

DEL PILAR GARCÍA MAYO, MARÍA, and MARÍA LUISA GARCÍA LECUMBERRI (eds). 2003. *Age and the Acquisition of English as a Foreign Language* (Clevedon: Multilingual Matters)

DENEME, SELMA, SELEN ADA, and KUTAY UZUN. 2011. 'Teaching a Foreign Language and Foreign Culture to Young Learners', *International Journal of Business, Humanities and Technology*, 1: 152–64

EDELENBOS, PETER, RICHARD JOHNSTONE, and ANGELIKA KUBANEK. 2006. *The Main Pedagogical Principles Underlying the Teaching of Languages to Very Young Learners: Languages for the Children of Europe: Published Research, Good Practice and Main Principles*, Final Report of the EAC 89/04, Lot 1 study, European Commission Education and Culture, Culture and Communication, Multilingualism Policy <http://ec.europa.eu/dgs/education_culture/repository/languages/policy/language-policy/documents/young_en.pdf>

ENEVER, JANET, JAYNE MOON, and UMA RAMAN (eds). 2009. *Young Learner English Language Policy and Implementation: International Perspectives* (Reading: Garnet)

FLEGE, JAMES E., GRACE H. YENI-KOMSHIAN, and SERENA LIU. 1999. 'Age Constraints on Second-Language Acquisition', *Journal of Memory and Language*, 41: 78–104

FOMIN, MIHAIL M. 1998. *Obuchenie inostrannomu yazyku v usloviyah mnogoyazychiya (dvuyazychiya)* (Moscow: Mir knigi)

FUTERMAN, ZINOVIY Y. 1984. *Inostrannyj yazyk v detskom sadu* (Kiev: Radian'ska shkola)

GAINUTDINOVA, MARINA Y. 2005. *Vozmozhnosti ispol'zovaniya opyta rannego obucheniya detei inostrannomu yazyku vo Francii v praktike otechestvennyh obrazovatel'nyh uchrezhdeniy* (Yaroslavl: Ushinskiy Yaroslavl State Pedagogical University)

GAL'SKOVA, NATALIA D. 2003. *Sovremennaya metodika obucheniya inostrannym yazykam* (Moscow: Arkti)

——, and ZINAIDA D. NIKITENKO. 2004. *Teoriya i poraktika obucheniya inostrannym yazykam. Nachal'naya shkola* (Moscow)

GORLOVA, NATALIA A. 2003. 'Sostoyanie metodiki rannego obucheniya inostrannym yazykam', *Inostrannye yazyki v shkole*, 4: 11–17

HLYBOVA, TATIANA B. 2000. *Osobennosti obucheniya nemeckomu yazyku v detskom sadu* (Moscow)

ILIASOV, ILIAS O. 1991. *Osnovy obucheniya inostrannym yazykam v usloviyah mnogoyazychiya* (Makhachkala: Daguchpedgiz)

JOBERT, VÉRONIQUE. 2013. 'Pratique du multilinguisme dans une correspondance privée russe au XXe siècle: formes et fonctions', *Mosaïque slave: communications de la délégation française au Congrès international des slavistes*, 84: 123–36

JOHNSON, JACQUELINE S., and ELISSA L. NEWPORT. 1989. 'Critical Period Effects in Second Language Learning: The Influence of Maturational State on the Acquisition of English as a Second Language', *Cognitive Psychology*, 21: 60–99

KANTELINEN, RITVA, EIJA L. SOKKA-MEANEY, and VICTORIA POGOSIAN (eds). 2008. *Seminar on Early Language Education* (Joensuu: University of Joensuu)

KARTASHOVA, VALENTINA N. 2002. *Formirovanie lingvogumanitarnoj kul'tury uchitelia v sfere rannego inoyazychnogo obrazovaniya: nauchnaya monografiya* (Moscow: Prometei)

KLIMENTENKO, ANNA D. 1976. 'Eksperimental'noe obuchenie angliyskomu yazyku detei s shesti let', *Inostrannye yazyki v shkole*, 2: 37–47

KOCAMAN, ORHAN, and NURGÜL KOCAMAN. 2012. 'Age Factor in Foreign Language Education at Preschool Level', *Procedia — Social and Behavioral Sciences*, 55: 168–77

KRASHEN, STEPHEN D., MICHAEL H. LONG, and ROBIN C. SCARCELLA (eds). 1982. *Child–Adult Differences in Second Language Acquisition* (Rowley, MA: Newbury House)

LEONT'EV, ALEKSEI A. 1986. 'Rannee obuchenie inostrannym yazykam', *Russkiy yazyk za rubezhom*, 5: 50-53

LOGUNOVA, SVETLANA V. 1997. *Metodika formirovaniya grammaticheskih konstruiruyushhih umeniy v rannem obuchenii angliyskomu yazyku (u shkol'nikov 6 letnego vozrasta)* (Tambov: Tambov State University)

LOMAKINA, GUL'NARA R., and ANNA A. LAER. 2014. 'Rannee obuchenie inostrannomu yazyku: pliusy i minusy', *Molodoi uchionyi*, 20: 597-99

LUKINA, MARINA M. 1999. *Stanovlenie i razvitie teorii i metodiki rannego obucheniya inostrannym yazykam v otechestvennoi pedagogike vtoroi poloviny XX veka* (Murmansk: Murmansk State Pedagogical Institute)

MAHNEVA, IRINA A. 2001. *Integrirovannaya igrovaya tehnologiya oznakomleniya s inoyazychnoj kul'turoi detei doshkol'nogo vozrasta* (Ekaterinburg: Southern Ural State University)

MARINOVA-TODD, STEFKA H., D. BRADFORD MARSHALL, and CATHERINE SNOW. 2000. 'Three Misconceptions about Age and L2 Learning', *TESOL Quarterly*, 34: 9-34

MARKOSIAN, AIDA S. 2004. *Ocherk teorii ovladeniya vtorym yazykom* (Moscow: Psihologiya)

MATECKAYA, ELENA I. 1971. *Rechevaya igra na zaniatiyah angliyskim yazykom v detskom sadu* (Moscow: USSR Academy of Pedagogical Sciences)

MIROLIUBOV, ALEKSANDR A. 2002. *Istoriya otechestvennoi metodiki obucheniya inostrannym yazykam* (Moscow: Stupeni)

MOURÃO, SANDIE, and MÓNICA LOURENÇO (eds). 2015. *Early Years Second Language Education: International Perspectives on Theory and Practice* (London and New York: Routledge)

MURAD, JASMINA. 2006. *Age as a Factor in Second Language Acquisition* (Berlin: Grin)

N. I. 1874. 'Kritika i bibliografiya', *Detskiy sad*, 7: 31-23

NABOKOV, VLADIMIR V. 1989. *Speak, Memory: An Autobiography Revisited* (New York: Vintage)

NATAL'INA, SVETLANA A. 1982. *Soderzhanie obucheniya angliyskomu yazyku detei doshkol'nogo vozrasta* (Kiev)

NEGNEVICKAYA, ELENA I. 1986. *Psihologicheskie usloviya formirovaniya u doshkol'nikov rechevyh navykov i umeniy na vtorom yazyke* (Moscow: USSR Academy of Pedagogical Sciences)

——. 1987. 'Inostrannyj yazyk dlya samyh malen'kih: vchera, segodnya, zavtra', *Inostrannye yazyki v shkole*, 6: 20-26

——, and ALEKSANDR M. SHAHNAROVICH. 1981. *Yazyk i deti* (Moscow: Nauka)

NEVEZHINA, IRINA I. 2000. *Obuchenie inostrannomuyazyku detei 5-8 let na muzykal'no-ritmicheskoj osnove: na materiale angliyskogo yazyka* (Moscow: Moscow Pedagogical State University)

NIKOLAEVA, MARINA N. 2011. *Sovremennye tendencii v obuchenii inostrannym yazykam i mezhkul'turnoj kommunikacii* (Elektrostal: New Humanitarian Institute)

NIKOLOV, MARIANNE (ed.). 2009. *The Age Factor and Early Language Learning* (Berlin: de Gruyter)

NIKSHIKOVA, LANA Y. 2007. *Istoriko-pedagogicheskie osnovy prepodavaniya inostrannyh yazykov v Rossii XIX — nachala XX vv* (Nizhny Novgorod: State University of Architecture and Building in Nizhny Novgorod)

OKOROKOVA, A. 1873. 'O pervonachal'nom prepodavanii inostrannyh yazykov', *Sem'ya i shkola*, 11: 93-100

PONIMATKO, ALEKSANDR P. 1991. *Obuchenie doshkol'nikov inostrannomu yazyku na osnove igrovogo modelirovaniya inoyazychnogo obshheniya* (Moscow: Lenin Moscow Pedagogical State University)

PROTASSOVA, EKATERINA Y., and NATALIA M. RODINA. 2009. *Little by Little. Obuchenie doshkol'nikov inostrannomu yazyku* (Moscow: Sfera)

——, and NATALIA M. RODINA. 2010. *Metodika obucheniya doshkol'nikov inostrannomu yazyku* (Moscow: Vlados)

——, and NATALIA M. RODINA. 2011. *Mnogojazychie v detskom vozraste* (St Petersburg: Zlatoust)

RAHMANOV, IGOR' V. (ed.). 1972. *Osnovnye napravleniya metodiki prepodavaniya inostrannyh yazykov v XIX–XX veke* (Moscow: Pedagogika)

RICH, SARAH (ed.). 2014. *International Perspectives on Teaching English to Young Learners* (New York: Palgrave Macmillan)

RIXON, SHELAGH (ed.). 1999. *Young Learners of English: Some Research Perspectives* (Harlow: Pearson)

RJEOUTSKI, VLADISLAV, and ALEXANDRE TCHOUDINOV (eds). 2013. *Le Précepteur francophone en Europe XVIIe–XIXe* (Paris: L'Harmattan)

SALZMANN, KEVIN. 2014. *Do Children Learn Second Languages Easier Than Adults? A Comparative Analysis of Child and Adult Second Language Acquisition* (Berlin: Grin)

SHAVERNEVA, JULIYA Y. 2003. *Metody i sredstva kul'turno-kommunikativnogo razvitiya detei starshego doshkol'nogo vozrasta v usloviyah rannego izucheniya inostrannogo yazyka* (Maykop: Adyg State University)

SHELESTIUK, ELENA V. 2013. 'Vesternizatsiya v SSSR i Rossii: analiz nekotoryh prichin', in *Inostrannyi yazyk v sisteme srednego i vysshego obrazovaniya* (Prague: Sociosfera), pp. 71–79

SIDOROVA, LIUDMILA V. 1992. *Rannee obuchenie inostrannym yazykam: iz opyta raboty detskih sadov i shkol Chuvashii* (Cheboksary: Chuvash Republican Institute for Professional Development)

SNEGOVA, SVETLANA V. 1994. *Ispol'zovanie angliyskoj skazki v obuchenii angliyskomu yazyku na nachal'noj stupeni obucheniya* (Moscow: Lenin Moscow Pedagogical State University)

SPIRIDONOVA, ANNA V. 2010. *Obuchenie detei rannego vozrasta inostrannomu yazyku v processe dopolnitel'nogo obrazovaniya* (Chelyabinsk: Chelyabinsk State Pedagogical University)

SULIN, MIHAIL A. (ed.). 2000. *Rannee obuchenie inostrannomu yazyku: opyt, problemy, perspektivy* (Veliky Novgorod: Yaroslav Mudryj University)

SURINA, OKSANA P. 2008. 'Inostrannye yazyki v sisteme obrazovaniya Rossii XVIII veka', *Narodnoe obrazovanie. Pedagogika*, 3: 74–84

TARASIUK, NATALIA A. 1999. *Inostrannyj yazyk dlia doshkol'nikov: uroki obshheniya (na primere angliyskogo yazyka)* (Moscow: Flinta)

TIHEEVA, ELIZAVETA I. 1981 [1925]. *Razvitie rechi detei (rannego i doshkol'nogo vozrasta)* (Moscow: Prosveshhenie)

TKACHUK, GALINA D. 2001. *Obuchenie doshkol'nikov inostrannomu yazyku na osnove sochinitel'stva skazochnyh istoriy: na materiale francuzskogo yazyka* (Nizhny Novgorod: Dobroliubov Russian State Linguistic University)

TOLSTAYA-VOEIKOVA, OLGA A. 2005. *Russkaja sem'ya v vodovorote 'Velikogo pereloma'. Pis'ma 1927–1929 gg* (St Petersburg: Nestor-Istorija)

——. 2012. *Kogda zhizn' tak deshevo stoit... Pis'ma 1931–1933 gg.* (St Petersburg: Nestor-Istorija)

USHINSKIY, KONSTANTIN D. 1873. *Chelovek kak predmet vospitaniya* , vol. I. (St Petersburg: Kotomin)

UTEHINA, ALLA N. 2013. *Inostrannyi yazyk v doshkol'nom vozraste. Teoriya i praktika* (Moscow: Flinta)

VALE, DAVID, and ANNE FEUNTEUN. 1995. *Teaching Children English: A Training Course for Teachers of English to Children.* (Cambridge: Cambridge University Press)

VORONCOVA, EKATERINA A. 1999. *Ispol'zovanie sinteticheskoj i analiticheskoj naglyadnosti v obuchenii angliyskomu yazyku detei starshego doshkol'nogo vozrasta* (St Petersburg: Gerzen Russian State Pedagogical University)

VRONSKAYA, IRINA V. 2015. *Metodika rannego obucheniya angliyskomu yazyku* (St Petersburg: Karo)

VYGOTSKY, LEV S. 1982 [1928]. 'K voprosu o mnogoyazychii v detskom vozraste', *Sobranie sochineniy*, 3 (Moscow: Pedagogika), pp. 329–37

YACENKO, NATALIA A. 1994. *Puti metodicheskoi integracii razvitiya rechi i obucheniya inostrannym yazykam v usloviyah detskogo sada* (Moscow: Lenin Moscow Pedagogical State University)

YUDOVINA, YULIYA B. 2000. *Razvitie intellektual'nyh sposobnostei rebenka doshkol'nogo vozrasta pri ovladenii angliyskim yazykom v processe igrovoj rechevoj deyatel'nosti* (St Petersburg: Gerzen Russian State Pedagogical University)

ZHIGALEVA, KSENIA B. 2009. *Metodika formirovaniya lingvisticheskoj kompetencii doshkol'nikov na osnove sistemno-orientirovannogo modelirovaniya processa obucheniya inostrannomu yazyku* (Nizhny Novgorod: Dobroliubov Russian State Linguistic University)

ZIMIN, IGOR V. 2011. *Detskiy mir imperatorskih rezidenciy* (Moscow: Centrpoligraf)

Notes to Chapter 14

1. For example: <http://www.imho24.ru/answers/children/detail/1770/; http://detsky-mir.com/blog/psychology/4525/anglijskij_s_rannego_vozrasta_pljusy_i_minusy>; or <https://otvet.mail.ru/question/46438516>.
2. All English translations are by the author.
3. Order of the Ministry of Education of the Russian Federation № 1155, dated 17 October 2013, 'Concerning the Confirmation of the Federal State Standard of pre-primary education', which came into effect on 14 January 2014, sets requirements, organizational frameworks and educational directions for the operation of pre-primary institutions.
4. The author was again Anna I. Kreshchanovskaya; different painters, e.g. V. Trofimov for the *Zoologicheskoe loto 'V mire zhivotnyh'* (1989), N. Kniaz'kova for *Botanicheskoe loto 'Zelionyy drug'* (1985); Russian-French-German-English order of inscriptions; the same publishing houses and thirty years of publication. One version holds inscriptions in five languages (Spanish was added).
5. Authors A. Abdrahmanov and Y. Zamaletdinova, *Loto dlia detei i vzroslyh* [*Lotto for Children and Adults*], Detskaya yazykovaya laboratoriya (without place of publication).

CHAPTER 15

❖

La place de l'écrit dans la méthode structuro-globale audiovisuelle (SGAV)

Marie-Odile Hidden

Because the structuro-global audio-visual method (SGAV) (1960s–1980s) gives priority to oral skills and especially to mastering pronunciation, it was criticized for not giving enough relevance to teaching how to read and write. The main criticisms were the following: within the SGAV method, written text is confused with written form (orthography); written code specificities are not taken into account; and reading means reading aloud and in a linear fashion. In order to confirm whether these criticisms are justified, this chapter analyses several French teaching handbooks: two SGAV handbooks and two other handbooks which are dedicated to learning how to write and which were published in the 1970s. The analysis shows an evolution between handbooks, and even between different editions of the same handbook: although the teaching of written skills remains delayed, the handbooks give increasing importance to it. The comparison of the two handbooks dedicated to written expression also highlights the methodological approaches each one of them has adopted.

La méthode[1] structuro-globale audiovisuelle (fin des années 50 – début des années 80[2]) dénommée aussi 'méthode Saint-Cloud – Zagreb' parce qu'elle est le fruit d'une collaboration entre une équipe de l'Ecole Normale Supérieure de Saint-Cloud (autour de G. Gougenheim et P. Rivenc, l'amorce du futur CREDIF) et une équipe de l'Université de Zagreb (autour de P. Guberina), revêt une importance particulière dans l'histoire de l'enseignement des langues en France, comme le montre l'ouvrage de H. Besse publié en 1985 qui lui consacre une place de choix.[3] Comme on le sait, elle s'inscrit en continuité avec la méthode directe (Besse 1985; Puren 1988) et donc en rupture avec la méthode grammaire-traduction (Germain 1993) et d'autre part, elle est née dans un contexte bien précis: aux lendemains de la deuxième guerre mondiale, le ministère de l'Education nationale français, voyant que l'anglais était en train de devenir une langue internationale, voulait en effet redynamiser la diffusion du français à l'étranger. Or, cette méthode SGAV se caractérise notamment par le fait qu'elle donne la priorité à l'oral (Galisson et Coste 1976: 57) et ce, d'une manière sans doute encore plus radicale que la méthode directe.[4] Dans son ouvrage de 2003, P. Rivenc reconnaît lui-même que le SGAV des premières années 'ne s'était pas encore sérieusement attaché à construire une méthodologie de l'entraînement à l'expression écrite digne de celle qu'il avait su imposer pour l'oral' (p. 107). Toutefois, il estime que certaines critiques adressées à la méthode dans ce domaine étaient exagérées et récuse notamment celle selon laquelle le SGAV se serait exclusivement intéressé à l'oral (p. 94): si l'écrit est différé, il n'est pas pour autant totalement absent. Les autres reproches formulés à l'encontre de la méthode étaient les suivants: confondre écrit et graphie, ne pas respecter la spécificité du code écrit et privilégier une lecture à voix haute et linéaire de textes fabriqués (Galisson 1980: 78, 79). Ces critiques, émises à une époque marquée au niveau méthodologique par de grands espoirs, des désillusions et donc de vifs débats (Coste 1972), méritent, il nous semble, un examen approfondi: sont-elles réellement fondées? Concernent-elles toute la période SGAV ou plutôt ses débuts? Certes, les principaux manuels SGAV ont fait l'objet de nombreuses analyses détaillées,[5] mais elles portaient avant tout sur le cœur de la méthode (l'enseignement de l'oral, le rapport image/son, les différents moments de la classe, les relations enseignant/ apprenants, etc.) et donc peu sur l'enseignement de l'écrit. Adopter un angle d'analyse inhabituel sur cette méthode devrait en faire ressortir certains aspects peu soulignés jusqu'à présent qui, s'ils existent dans d'autres méthodes, peuvent constituer des points de continuité entre ces méthodes et la méthode SGAV, ce qui présenterait un intérêt historiographique évident.

Afin donc d'évaluer la place de l'écrit dans cette méthode, nous avons analysé les deux ensembles SGAV du CREDIF *Voix et images de France* première partie (désormais: *VIF*) (1ère édition en 1958) et *De vive voix* (*DVV*) première partie (1972) ainsi que deux manuels publiés dans les années 70 qui ont pour objectif déclaré d'enseigner à rédiger en langue étrangère: *Initiation à l'expression écrite,* élaboré au CREDIF en 1972 pour être utilisé conjointement à *VIF* ou *DVV* d'une part, et *Passage à l'écrit* (1975) qui fait partie de l'ensemble pédagogique de *C'est le printemps* (désormais: *CLP*).[6]

Dans un premier temps, nous nous intéresserons à la notion de 'passage à l'écrit', caractéristique de la méthode SGAV, en cherchant à en cerner les tenants et les aboutissants. Puis, nous verrons comment en ce qui concerne l'écrit, on observe une évolution entre les différents manuels audiovisuels et même entre les différentes éditions d'un même manuel. Enfin, nous nous emploierons à présenter les deux manuels consacrés à l'écrit afin d'en comparer les options méthodologiques.

Le 'passage à l'écrit'

On l'aura compris: notre objectif n'est pas ici de présenter la méthode structuro-globale audio-visuelle de façon complète,[7] mais de nous focaliser sur la place qu'elle a accordée à l'enseignement de l'écrit, en compréhension et en production. Afin de comprendre pourquoi, dans cette méthode, l'écrit est systématiquement différé et comment il faut comprendre la notion de 'passage à l'écrit' présente dans les préfaces des manuels,[8] nous allons nous référer à deux articles de P. Guberina (1974 et 1984) dans lesquels il explique les fondements du SGAV.

Il écrit: 'Le SGAV est fondé sur la linguistique de la parole' (Guberina 1984: 86). Comme le précise bien l'auteur, il n'est pas question ici de la 'parole' au sens saussurien, car celle-ci ne saurait être un acte individuel: il s'agit bien d'un fait social. Cette parole comprend des 'moyens lexicologiques' (phonétique, morphologie et syntaxe) et des 'moyens non lexicologiques' très variés: intonation, rythme, intensité, tension, pause mimiques, gestes, position du corps et états émotionnels, situation, ambiance sociale, aspects psychologiques, mobiles des sujets parlants (dont affectivité). Etant donné que ces moyens non lexicologiques sont également dénommés 'valeurs de la langue parlée', on pourrait penser que la linguistique de la parole se limite à la langue orale, mais Guberina ajoute qu'elle prend aussi en compte le langage intérieur et la langue écrite, car 'tous les emplois du langage doivent être étudiés' (1984: 87). C'est d'ailleurs la raison pour laquelle il se refuse à remplacer la dénomination 'linguistique de la parole' par 'linguistique de la langue parlée'.

Cependant, si l'enseignement de l'écrit n'est pas évacué des fondements de la méthode SGAV, il doit céder le pas, dans un premier temps du moins, à l'enseignement de l'oral car 'c'est la langue parlée qui représente le mieux tous les procédés d'expression humaine [...] qui font partie d'un système linguistique donné' (Guberina 1974: 50). Plus concrètement, 'une importance prépondérante doit être accordée [...] au côté acoustique de la parole' (Guberina 1984: 96) aussi bien en compréhension qu'en production. Pour ce faire, les auteurs de la préface à la première édition de *VIF* (1960) préconisent une 'méthode entièrement orale' en début d'apprentissage: non seulement l'élève n'a aucune tâche d'écriture, mais il faut éviter à tout prix qu'il ait sous les yeux la graphie du français qui, en raison de son caractère conventionnel, peut nuire à une bonne prononciation. De plus, l'écrit 'invite à un excès d'analyse' et 'fait donc perdre de vue l'essentiel qui est la perception globale du sens' (p. 43). En conséquence, le livre de l'élève ne comprend pas la transcription des dialogues entendus en classe, mais seulement les images du film fixe qui ont été visionnées en même temps.[9]

Comment et quand l'écrit est-il introduit? On note une différence entre *VIF* et *DVV*. Alors que dans le premier, les élèves sont d'abord amenés à faire des dictées (à partir de la leçon quinze, soit après une soixantaine d'heures de cours) et seulement plus tard à lire des textes (après la leçon vingt-deux), l'initiation à l'écriture et à la lecture sont concomitantes dans *DVV* et commencent à la leçon cinq,[10] afin que la lecture puisse alimenter la production écrite, comme on le verra plus loin.

Selon F. Debyser (1972: 11), le modèle de langue orale proposé est 'de nature à permettre sans trop de difficultés le passage à l'écrit', car il s'agit d'une langue 'neutre ou non marquée' qui peut donc être facilement transcrite. Il en vient même à parler de 'code unique'. De même, L. J. Calvet remet en cause la pratique qui consiste à 'allouer au même texte le double statut de langue écrite et de langue parlée' (1972: 146). En d'autres mots, il semblerait que la notion de 'passage' ne signifie pas seulement que l'introduction de l'écrit est retardée, mais que les différences entre l'écrit et l'oral sont très fortement atténuées. Comme le dit R. Galisson, 'on sait qu'oral et écrit constituent deux codes différents, mais pour faciliter le passage de l'un à l'autre, on transcode artificiellement l'oral en écrit' (1980: 78).

On comprend dès lors que l'entrée dans l'écrit se fasse sous la forme d'une dictée,[11] car si l'écriture peut s'apparenter à une simple transcription de l'oral, la principale difficulté de cette activité réside sans aucun doute dans la maîtrise de l'orthographe et de la ponctuation. Les pages consacrées au 'passage à l'écrit' dans la préface de 1960 de *VIF* donnent donc avant tout des conseils sur la façon de faire les dictées, en commençant par ce qui 's'écrit phonétiquement': chaque son est présenté dans un mot-clé écrit au tableau, puis des mots ou phrases contenant ce son sont dictés avec le rythme et l'intonation adoptés au cours des leçons; ils sont ensuite relus par l'enseignant et par l'élève 'qui doit bien associer ce qu'il entend et dit, avec ce qu'il a écrit sur sa feuille' (*VIF* 1960: 44); après la correction au tableau, les apprenants relisent à nouveau le texte de la dictée à haute voix. Ces relectures à voix haute du texte dicté ont sans doute pour fonction de vérifier que l'élève continue à prononcer adéquatement les sons transcrits. Concernant la ponctuation, elle ne doit pas être dictée, 'c'est à l'élève d'apprendre à la mettre lui-même' (ibid.), probablement en se basant sur les pauses faites par l'enseignant ainsi que sur son intonation. Comme on le voit, la référence à l'oral reste prégnante même dans l'exercice écrit de la dictée.

En ce qui concerne les activités de lecture, les indications pédagogiques se font beaucoup plus rares dans la préface de 1960. A partir de la leçon douze, on fait lire à l'apprenant des récits élaborés à partir des thématiques de chaque leçon, mais aucune réelle démarche d'enseignement n'est proposée pour l'aider à comprendre ces textes. De plus, l'activité préconisée est l'oralisation des textes, puisque l'enseignant est invité à 'enseigner les rythmes et les intonations propres à la langue de la lecture, apprendre à ménager les pauses [...], à faire les liaisons' (p. 46).

Une évolution au profit de l'écrit

L'introduction de textes écrits dans les manuels

Parmi les évolutions repérées par C. Puren entre ce qu'il appelle 'les cours audiovisuels' de première (*VIF*) et de seconde génération (*DVV*, *CLP*[12]), il indique notamment 'l'introduction dès les premières leçons de situations d'écrit et de documents écrits' (1988: 254). En effet, si le livre de l'élève de *VIF* et de la version de 1972 de *DVV* ne contiennent aucun texte, on en trouve en revanche dans la version de 1975 de *DVV*: des questions à partir de la leçon trois et de petits textes fabriqués (souvent illustrés) dès la leçon cinq.[13] Dans *CLP 1* (1972), l'apprenant est confronté dès la leçon un à des documents écrits, souvent authentiques qui plus est: statistiques, petites annonces, bandes dessinées, etc.

Quelle(s) fonction(s) ces textes sont-ils amenés à jouer dans la classe de langue? En ce qui concerne *CLP 1*, il semble que ces documents écrits aient surtout pour objectif de préparer en petits groupes[14] des dialogues ou discussions étendus ensuite à toute la classe (Avant propos du livre du professeur 1976: 9). Dans *DVV* également, la lecture des textes a pour but de nourrir les échanges en classe, mais pas exclusivement. On trouve en effet dans le livret du professeur (1975) des réflexions plus développées sur l'activité de lecture: il s'agit d'orienter l'apprenant vers 'une compréhension globale du texte', grâce notamment aux illustrations[15] qui lui permettent de reconstituer le contexte et donc de reconstruire le sens sans se perdre dans le mot à mot. Pour ce faire, il est conseillé à l'enseignant de laisser tout d'abord l'apprenant essayer de comprendre seul le texte proposé et de n'apporter des explications que dans un deuxième temps (*DVV* 1975: 14). Ajoutons que contrairement à ce qui était préconisé dans *VIF* (cf. *supra)*, il n'est plus question de faire lire l'apprenant à haute voix: 'ils [les textes] ne sont pas faits pour être dits mais principalement pour être lus, c'est-à-dire compris' (ibid.). Le changement est de taille: la lecture n'est plus un moyen pour vérifier la bonne prononciation des mots et devient une activité à part entière.

DVV comprend également d'autres textes fabriqués (toujours en lien avec la thématique de chaque leçon) qui ne figurent que dans le livret du professeur. Ces textes 'qui dépassent légèrement le potentiel linguistique de l'étudiant' (p. 14) remplissent une double fonction: d'une part, ils doivent contribuer à fixer davantage certaines constructions abordées lors des exercices de production écrite; d'autre part, ils constituent une sorte de réservoir de procédés linguistiques nouveaux dans lequel l'apprenant pourra puiser au moment de rédiger un texte. Les activités de lecture et d'écriture se nourrissent donc mutuellement.

Quels exercices d'écriture?

Le livret du professeur de *DVV* (1975) consacre une partie non négligeable à l'expression écrite. De plus, il ne s'agit plus de transcrire les textes des dialogues ou même le récit oral que l'apprenant fait mais, comme l'explique très justement H. Besse, de 'le recomposer en fonction des contraintes propres à la discursivité écrite' (1985: 126). Cette recomposition se fait par étapes: tout d'abord, en s'aidant des questions présentes dans son manuel, l'apprenant fait un récit écrit de ce qui se passe dans le dialogue de la leçon et interprète la situation en fonction de ce que disent les personnages, de leur attitude et de leur psychologie: il est donc amené à utiliser le discours indirect, le discours rapporté et à traduire par écrit le comportement et l'état d'esprit des personnages; enfin, il porte toute son attention sur la cohésion et sur l'organisation des idées au sein de son texte. Grâce à ce dernier travail, il se familiarise avec 'les divers procédés ou possibilités d'arrangements et les éléments de liaison mis en œuvre pour regrouper les idées' (Besse 1985: 11), ainsi qu'avec des constructions syntaxiques caractéristiques d'un texte écrit, par exemple l'apposition, certains cas d'inversion du sujet ou encore les phrases complexes. Ainsi à partir de ces trois 'idées' permettant de raconter la fin de l'épisode où Pierre et Mireille vont au cinéma:

— Pierre est gêné par le chapeau d'une dame
— Il ne voit rien
— Pierre et Mireille décident de s'en aller

on peut composer le mini-texte suivant: 'Pierre et Mireille ont décidé d'aller voir un film. [...] Pierre, gêné par le chapeau d'une dame, ne voit rien; aussi décident-ils de s'en aller' (livre du professeur: 42). Ajoutons que le livre du professeur de *DVV* propose à chaque fois plusieurs corrigés qu'il ne faut pas considérer comme des modèles à imposer, mais comme des ressources à mettre à la disposition des apprenants afin qu'ils puissent diversifier leurs textes et s'initier aux particularités de la langue écrite.[16] On pourra objecter que ce type d'exercice est peu créatif dans la mesure où l'apprenant est tenu de raconter et de décrire ce qui se passe dans le dialogue de la leçon, mais il a le mérite d'attirer l'attention de ce dernier sur certains aspects qui distinguent le discours écrit du discours oral.

Voyons à présent quelles démarches méthodologiques sont préconisées dans deux manuels d'expression écrite publiés à la même époque que *DVV*, l'un associé à ce manuel et l'autre à *CLP*, afin notamment de voir si on y trouve des points de continuité avec d'autres méthodes d'enseignement des langues.

Comparaison de deux manuels consacrés à la production écrite

Première description[17]

Initiation à l'expression écrite est un matériel complémentaire du CREDIF qui peut être utilisé en même temps que *VIF* ou *DVV*. La proximité avec ce dernier manuel est tangible, puisqu'il a été réalisé en collaboration avec Marie-Thérèse Moget, auteur de *DVV*.[18] Nous utiliserons donc l'abréviation *IEE-DVV* pour nous y référer. *Passage à l'écrit* fait partie de l'ensemble pédagogique de *CLP*,[19] mais comme il se présente sous la forme de livres indépendants, il peut être utilisé avec d'autres manuels (cf. livre du professeur de la partie 1); son titre sera abrégé en *PE-CLP*. Chaque manuel est constitué de deux parties avec à chaque fois un livre du maître et un livre de l'élève. De plus, excepté *PE-CLP 2*, chaque partie comprend une bande magnétique et *IEE-DVV 1* dispose également de quatre films fixes.

Cette première description matérielle nous montre que chaque manuel se présente en fait comme une sorte d'ensemble pédagogique, ce qui souligne déjà l'importance accordée par les auteurs à l'expression écrite. Toutefois, ces manuels ne dérogent pas à la règle selon laquelle, dans un cours audiovisuel, l'écrit doit être différé.[20] Autres points communs aux deux manuels: ils soulignent tous deux l'importance d'enseigner à rédiger et présentent chacun une véritable démarche pédagogique pour le faire. Afin de comparer ces démarches, nous allons analyser les deux manuels sous les trois aspects suivants: le rapport oral/écrit, l'entrée dans l'écrit, c'est-à-dire comment l'apprenant est amené à rédiger, et enfin les relations lecture/écriture.

Oral/écrit

Le but premier du manuel *IEE-DVV* est 'de supprimer la confusion trop souvent rencontrée chez l'étudiant entre expression écrite et expression orale' (préface, livre du maître, première partie: 6). Les auteurs de *PE-CLP* pointent également cette difficulté inhérente à un cours audio-visuel où la priorité est donnée à l'oral et où l'apprenant a donc tendance à utiliser à l'écrit des énoncés propres à une situation de communication orale. Comment faire pour éviter ce travers? Les démarches des deux manuels divergent. Dans *IEE-DVV*, on procède par confrontation: on se propose de faire mesurer à l'apprenant l'écart existant entre discours écrit et discours oral en lui faisant produire les deux discours et en lui montrant ensuite ce qui dans son texte ne convient pas et comment il peut l'améliorer. Dans *PE-CLP 1* en revanche, 'on ne propose à l'étudiant que des structures et du lexique qu'il pourra utiliser dans certaines situations d'écrit' (livre du professeur: 9) Autrement dit, on évite de lui fournir des énoncés qui seraient caractéristiques de la langue parlée.

D'autre part, toujours parce que l'on se trouve dans un contexte de méthode audiovisuelle, les auteurs de chaque manuel éprouvent le besoin de justifier l'enseignement de la production écrite. Selon ceux de *IEE-DVV*, oral et écrit étant imbriqués dans la vie réelle, il n'est pas justifié d'en dissocier l'apprentissage. Ainsi, dans la deuxième partie du manuel, l'écoute d'une situation à l'oral (par exemple, les commentaires de passants suite à un accident de la rue) débouche sur une activité de production écrite (rédiger le rapport d'accident). Dans *PE-CLP* au contraire, le document déclencheur qui amène l'apprenant à rédiger est toujours un document écrit, par exemple une petite annonce à laquelle il faudra répondre.[21] Pour expliquer le bien fondé de l'enseignement de l'écrit, le livre du professeur de *PE-CLP 2* souligne la diversité des besoins et motivations des apprenants en matière de lecture et écriture: dans le cadre des études, d'un travail professionnel ou encore pour des raisons personnelles, etc. Cette nouvelle façon d'envisager l'écrit annonce sans aucun doute l'approche communicative.[22]

Entrée dans l'écrit

La démarche pédagogique adoptée par *IEE-DVV* est fidèle aux principes du SGAV, puisqu'elle donne un rôle-clé à la *situation:*[23] on fait passer l'apprenant d'une 'situation de locuteur' à une 'situation de scripteur' (préface, livre du maître, première partie: 6) afin de lui faire comprendre que son message devra varier selon la situation. Dans la première partie, on fait visionner aux apprenants des images du film fixe et on leur demande d'imaginer un dialogue (situation du locuteur), par exemple entre une mère de famille et sa femme de ménage; puis, on leur dit que finalement la mère de famille ne sera pas chez elle quand la femme de ménage arrivera et on les invite donc à rédiger le billet qu'elle va lui laisser (situation de scripteur). Dans la deuxième partie, les images sont remplacées par un bref dialogue enregistré qui comprend les informations qui seront à transmettre dans un message oral, puis écrit. Si la méthodologie reste la même dans les deux parties du manuel, on observe une progression: on passe d'un travail sur la phrase[24] (1ère partie) à un travail sur le paragraphe (2ème partie). L'objectif de chaque leçon est de familiariser l'apprenant avec certains procédés syntaxiques dont plusieurs sont caractéristiques de l'écrit, par exemple: l'énumération de verbes sans répétition du sujet, l'emploi du participe présent pour expliquer, *aussi* suivi de l'inversion verbe-sujet (expression de la conséquence), etc. Comment la familiarisation avec ces différents procédés se fait-elle? On corrige au tableau le texte d'un des apprenants puis on fournit à tous un 'modèle' de phrase ou de paragraphe qui comprend la construction syntaxique à acquérir.[25] L'apprenant peut ensuite s'entraîner à réutiliser la nouvelle construction en rédigeant d'autres mini-textes à partir des autres situations de communication proposées par le manuel: il s'agit donc d'un apprentissage par imitation.[26]

En ce qui concerne *PE-CLP,* les deux parties du manuel ne suivent pas la même méthodologie, notamment parce que la deuxième partie (intitulée *Compréhension et expression*) comprend également des activités de lecture,[27] ce qui n'est pas le cas de la première qui est consacrée exclusivement à la rédaction. D'autre part, comme les auteurs de *CLP* ont écarté l'exercice de la dictée[28] contrairement à ceux de *VIF* et *DVV* (cf. *supra*), *PE-CLP* I inclut des activités permettant à l'apprenant d'acquérir l'orthographe du français. Chaque exercice de production écrite à proprement parler est précédé de deux 'séances d'acquisition du code'. Ces séances sont elles-mêmes divisées en trois étapes, les deux premières se faisant avec un support enregistré: on commence par des exercices de reconnaissance (suivre des yeux dans son livre des phrases pendant qu'on les écoute au magnétophone) et de discrimination (choix entre deux formes proches) dont le but est de permettre à l'apprenant de 'faire la liaison entre les formes orales qu'il connaît et leur représentation graphique' (livre du professeur: 4). S'ensuit une étape de 'conceptualisation de règles graphiques' (ibid.: 6) au cours de laquelle l'apprenant est amené à induire des règles orthographiques et morpho-syntaxiques, puis à les vérifier. Enfin, lui sont proposés des exercices de transformation[29] lui permettant de systématiser les règles qu'il vient de découvrir. Contrairement à *IEE-DVV*, l'accent n'est pas mis — à ce niveau de l'apprentissage du moins — sur des constructions syntaxiques qui seraient spécifiques à l'écrit.[30] D'autre part, comme dans l'autre manuel, il n'existe pas encore de véritable réflexion sur la construction textuelle: après avoir fait faire à l'apprenant une batterie d'exercices comprenant exclusivement des phrases isolées,[31] on lui demande de rédiger un texte sans vraiment lui montrer comment enchaîner les phrases. Concernant les consignes de rédaction, elles permettent des productions un peu plus libres que celles proposées dans *IEE*: certes, le thème et la situation sont donnés, mais pas le contenu précis du message.[32] Autre différence, il existe souvent un texte déclencheur et celui-ci est parfois un document authentique. Enfin, dans le livre du professeur, l'auteur du manuel insiste sur l'importance d'actualiser les activités d'écriture afin qu'elles correspondent à des besoins réels des apprenants: il conseille par exemple à l'enseignant de remplacer certains documents déclencheurs par d'autres, plus en lien avec leurs préoccupations du moment.

Lecture/écriture

Dans *De vive voix*, les activités de lecture et d'écriture peuvent s'alimenter mutuellement et notamment, l'observation de textes peut constituer une aide précieuse à la rédaction. Lorsqu'on analyse la méthodologie adoptée par un manuel consacré à l'expression écrite, il est donc justifié de se demander si ce manuel a recours ou non à une telle aide. Dans le cas de *IEE-DVV*, la réponse est clairement négative: le manuel ne comprend aucun texte de lecture, pas même dans la deuxième partie. Les seuls textes présents sont les phrases-modèles (partie 1) ou les paragraphes-modèles (partie 2) qui présentent aux apprenants les nouveaux procédés syntaxiques à acquérir. Dans *PE-CLP* I, on trouve en revanche quelques textes écrits, les documents déclencheurs des activités de production écrite (cf. *supra*). Mais on a vu que ces textes permettent surtout de donner une thématique et de créer une situation d'écriture et ne fonctionnent donc pas vraiment comme des lieux d'observation de procédés à réemployer.

Il en va tout autrement avec PE-CLP 2 dont l'objectif affiché est triple: le développement de la compréhension écrite, celui de l'expression écrite et l'acquisition du code qui sont considérés comme trois 'niveaux' interdépendants permettant d'assurer une bonne maîtrise de l'écrit (cf. présentation du livre du professeur). Chaque dossier du livre de l'élève propose donc des activités permettant de travailler à chacun de ces 'niveaux'. Comme dans *PE-CLP 1*, 'l'acquisition du code' consiste en des exercices d'analyse puis de systématisation de certaines règles orthographiques et morpho-syntaxiques. Cependant, ces exercices ne doivent pas forcément précéder les activités de production écrite: cette partie est plutôt conçue comme un 'self-service' d'exercices auxquels l'apprenant peut avoir recours quand il en éprouve le besoin.[33] La même souplesse d'utilisation caractérise d'ailleurs l'ensemble du manuel qui contrairement à *IEE-DVV* et *PE-CLP 1*, ne suit pas une progression stricte.[34] En revanche, les auteurs préconisent d'opérer un 'va-et-vient constant' (livre du professeur: 7) entre les trois 'niveaux' du passage à l'écrit.

A la différence de *IEE-DVV*, *PE-CLP 2* comprend un grand nombre de textes, pratiquement tous authentiques, parfois longs et complexes et en tout cas très variés: ils sont souvent issus de la presse, mais on trouve également d'autres documents comme des publicités, un constat d'accident, un télégramme, etc.[35] Comme dans *DVV*, la démarche préconisée est 'la compréhension globale du document' mais cette fois-ci, des indications précises sont données à l'enseignant et aux apprenants pour y parvenir: dans le livre de l'élève, chaque texte est accompagné de consignes très précises de lecture et le livre du professeur contient des explications et des suggestions supplémentaires. Il s'agit d'une part de montrer à l'apprenant comment 'se servir d'éléments connus pour accéder au sens de ce qui n'est pas connu' (livre du professeur: 7) et d'autre part, de l'amener à repérer certains éléments dans un texte: son organisation et/ou les principales informations véhiculées ou encore la position de l'auteur, etc. Ce travail de recherche se fait souvent sur plusieurs textes: par exemple, on fait comparer à l'apprenant la façon dont trois articles de presse issus de journaux différents relatent un même fait (dossier 2). Une autre stratégie de la compréhension globale consiste à faire découvrir à l'apprenant 'les moyens linguistiques mis en jeu pour transmettre telle ou telle intention langagière' (ibid.). En conséquence, l'activité de lecture permet à l'apprenant de réfléchir au fonctionnement de la langue ('acquisition du code') et lui fournit également des procédés langagiers qu'il pourra ensuite réemployer au moment de rédiger un texte (expression écrite). De plus, contrairement à la démarche adoptée dans *IEE-DVV*, les procédés linguistiques ne lui sont pas présentés dans un court paragraphe, c'est à lui de les chercher dans plusieurs textes; il a donc une attitude plus active qui contribue sans doute aussi à une meilleure compréhension des textes. Le fait de devoir repérer certains procédés dans différents textes présente un autre avantage: cela permet à l'apprenant de repérer par exemple les différents procédés pour exprimer la cause, puis en confrontant les textes dans lesquels ils apparaissent, de comprendre comment chacun doit être utilisé: en fonction de la syntaxe (*Pour* + infinitif passé; *parce que* + verbe conjugué), mais aussi en fonction du genre discursif;[36] ainsi, les prépositions *à la suite de* ou *en raison de* ne conviennent sans doute pas à tous les contextes. Alimentées par les activités de lecture et d'analyse de la langue, les activités d'expression écrite présentent une grande variété: d'une part, l'apprenant est amené à transformer ou reconstituer des énoncés non seulement au niveau phrastique (reformulation d'une phrase), mais surtout au niveau textuel (résumé de texte ou au contraire extension; rétablir la ponctuation d'un article de presse, etc.). D'autre part, il lui est demandé de produire des textes avec des consignes lui laissant une marge variable de liberté.[37]

Conclusion

Un trait remarquable de la méthode SGAV, c'est qu'elle a su évoluer au fur et à mesure de l'expérimentation du matériel pédagogique sur le terrain et en fonction des nouvelles situations offertes par les stages de formation d'enseignants (Rivenc 1984: 135). Concernant l'apprentissage de l'écrit, nous avons vu en effet que les manuels ont tendance à lui accorder une importance croissante, même si cet apprentissage reste différé. Les principaux changements que nous avons pu constater sont les suivants: l'introduction de textes écrits dans le livre de l'élève et le fait de commencer les activités de lecture plus tôt dans l'apprentissage (*DVV*); le passage d'une lecture linéaire et à voix haute à une lecture silencieuse et globale (*DVV*); l'élaboration d'une véritable méthodologie pour la compréhension de texte (*PE-CLP 2*). En ce qui concerne la production écrite, même si la notion de 'passage à l'écrit' est toujours employée dans le manuel du même nom, la démarche pédagogique n'est plus du tout la même que dans *VIF*: alors que dans ce dernier manuel, l'accent est mis sur la dictée, donc surtout sur la graphie, dans les autres manuels, on cherche à initier l'apprenant à la rédaction de textes: en lui fournissant les procédés langagiers caractéristiques de l'écrit afin qu'il puisse les réemployer (*DVV, IEE-DVV*), en cherchant à lui faire rédiger des textes qui correspondent vraiment à ses besoins (*PE-CLP 1*), en lui faisant analyser des textes authentiques et en lui faisant transformer ou reconstituer toutes sortes de textes (*PE-CLP 2*). Il apparaît donc que les critiques que nous avions évoquées en introduction (confusion écrit/graphie; non-respect des spécificités de l'écrit; lecture linéaire et à haute voix) ne peuvent s'appliquer qu'aux débuts de la période SGAV (*Voix et images de France*). Si la méthode SGAV donne la priorité à l'oral, l'intérêt pour l'acquisition de l'écrit n'en est pas pour autant absent, comme l'atteste l'élaboration de deux manuels consacrés à la production écrite. Qui plus est, ces deux manuels proposent chacun une véritable démarche pédagogique pour apprendre à rédiger en langue étrangère. L'analyse de ces manuels permet de mettre à jour une facette moins connue de cette méthode et montre qu'il faut se garder de la présenter comme un bloc monolithique, comme on est parfois tenté de le faire pour mieux la distinguer des autres méthodes d'enseignement des langues.

D'autre part, il ressort de la confrontation entre les deux manuels de production écrite que l'introduction d'activités de lecture — d'autant plus s'il s'agit de textes authentiques — permet d'enrichir les activités d'écriture. A cet égard *CLP*, en utilisant des textes authentiques et en soulignant la nécessité de prendre en compte les besoins des apprenants, apparaît comme un manuel charnière entre la méthode audio-visuelle et l'approche communicative. Sans doute du fait de l'évolution qu'a connue la méthode SGAV au cours des années, elle présente donc des points de continuité avec l'approche d'enseignement qui lui a succédé, ce qui revêt un intérêt indéniable d'un point de vue historiographique.

Bibliography

Language manuals

Initiation à l'expression écrite. Première partie. Livre du maître. Thérèse Delporte, sous la direction pédagogique de Marie-Thérèse Moget, avec la collaboration de Martine Farinaux-Salomé, Nicole Riottot et Charles de Margerie, Ecole normale Supérieure de Saint-Cloud, Paris : Didier/CREDIF, 1972.
——. 1971. *Initiation à l'expression écrite. Première partie. Livre de l'élève* (Paris: Didier/ CREDIF)
Initiation à l'expression écrite. Deuxième partie. Livre du maître. 1973. Charles de Margerie, avec la collaboration de Marie-Thérèse Moget, Ecole normale Supérieure de Saint-Cloud (Paris: Didier/CREDIF)
——. 1973. *Initiation à l'expression écrite. Deuxième partie. Livre de l'élève* (Paris: Didier/ CREDIF)
Passage à l'écrit 1. Orthographe et expression. Livre du professeur. 1975. Christian Lavenne (Paris: Clé international)
——. *Passage à l'écrit 1. Orthographe et expression. Livre de l'élève.* 1975. (Paris: Clé international)
——. *Passage à l'écrit 2. Compréhension et expression. Livre du professeur.* 1980. Christian Lavenne and Evelyne Bérard-Lavenne (Paris: Clé international)
——. 1979. *Passage à l'écrit 2. Compréhension et expression. Livre de l'élève* (Paris: Clé international)

Secondary literature

BESSE, HENRI. 1985. *Méthodes et pratiques des manuels de langue* (Paris: Didier/Crédif)
CALVET, LOUIS JEAN. 1972. 'Les Problèmes de la compréhension et de l'expression écrites', in *Le Niveau 2 dans l'enseignement du français langue étrangère*, ed. by R. Nataf (Paris: Hachette), pp. 145-56
COSTE, DANIEL. 1972. 'Le Renouvellement méthodologique dans l'enseignement du français langue étrangère: remarques sur les années 1955-1970', *Le Français dans le monde*, 87: 12-21
——, and EDDY ROULET. 1976. *Un niveau-seuil: systèmes d'apprentissage des langues vivantes par les adultes*, Conseil de la coopération culturelle du Conseil de l'Europe (Paris: Didier)
DEBYSER, FRANCIS. 1972. 'L'Enseignement du français langue étrangère au niveau 2.', in *Le Niveau 2 dans l'enseignement du français langue étrangère*, ed. by R. Nataf (Paris: Hachette), pp. 4-22
——. 1973. 'La Mort du manuel', *Le Français dans le monde*, 100: 63-68
GALISSON, ROBERT, and DANIEL COSTE (eds). 1976. *Dictionnaire de didactique des langues* (Paris: Hachette)
——. 1980. *D'hier à aujourd'hui la didactique générale des langues étrangères: du structuralisme au fonctionnalisme* (Paris: Clé international)
GERMAIN, CLAUDE. 1993. *Evolution de l'enseignement des langues: 5000 ans d'histoire* (Paris: Clé International)

GOUGENHEIM, GEORGES, et al. 1964. *L'Elaboration du français fondamental (1ᵉʳ degré)* (Paris: Didier)

GUBERINA, PETER. 1974. 'La Parole dans la méthode structuroglobale audio-visuelle', *Le Français dans le monde*, 103: 49-54

——. 1984. 'Bases théoriques de la méthode audio-visuelle structuro-globale (méthode Saint-Cloud-Zagreb): une linguistique de la parole', in *Aspects d'une politique de diffusion du français langue étrangère depuis 1945: matériaux pour une histoire*, ed. by D. Coste (Paris: Hatier), pp. 85-99

MOIRAND, SOPHIE. 1974. '"Audio-visuel intégré" et communication(s)', *Langue française*, 24: 5-26

PORQUIER, RÉMY, and ROBERT VIVÈS. 1974. 'Sur quatre méthodes audio-visuelles: essai d'analyse critique', *Langue française*, 24: 105-22

PUREN, CHRISTIAN. 1988. *Histoire des méthodologies de l'enseignement des langues* (Paris: Clé international)

RENARD, RAYMOND. 1963. *Une révolution dans l'enseignement des langues vivantes: la méthode audio-visuelle et structuro-globale de Saint-Cloud-Zagreb* (Mons: Fonds Raoul Warocqué)

RIVENC, PAUL. 1984. 'Contributions à une histoire subjective du CREDIF: premiers engagements, premiers défis. 1951-1965', *Aspects d'une politique de diffusion du français langue étrangère depuis 1945: matériaux pour une histoire*, ed. by D. Coste (Paris: Hatier), pp. 128-37

—— (ed.). 2003. *Apprentissage d'une langue étrangère/seconde. 3. La Méthodologie* (Brussels: De Boeck)

Notes to Chapter 15

1. On entend ici par *méthode*: 'un ensemble raisonné de propositions et de procédés [...] destinés à organiser et à favoriser l'enseignement et l'apprentissage d'une langue naturelle' (Besse 1985: 14).
2. Nous proposons ces dates en nous basant sur les années de publication des trois principaux manuels SGAV: *Voix et Images de France*, ébauché en 1955, a été publié pour la première fois en 1958; *De Vive Voix*, après une première version dans les années 1964-65, a été diffusé dans sa version définitive en 1972; *Archipel* dont les premiers essais datent de la fin des années 70, est paru en 1982 et 1983 (Besse 1985).
3. Après avoir passé en revue en les caractérisant les différentes méthodes d'enseignement des langues en commençant par la 'méthode naturelle', l'auteur s'emploie à analyser par le menu trois manuels SGAV afin d'en dégager des pratiques pédagogiques qui lui semblent transférables à d'autres situations de classe (autres manuels ou même sans manuel).
4. D'après Puren (1988), l'élève participant à un cours selon la méthode directe était au moins confronté à la forme écrite des nouvelles acquisitions à la fin de chaque leçon, car il les retrouvait dans son manuel. Or, ce n'est plus le cas avec les premiers manuels SGAV qui ne comprennent aucune trace écrite, comme on le verra plus loin dans cet article. Il serait d'ailleurs intéressant d'analyser de plus près la place de l'écrit dans la méthode directe.
5. Notamment Debyser 1973, Moirand 1974, Porquier et Vivès 1974. Les deux derniers articles analysent les quatre manuels suivants: *Voix et Images de France 1ᵉʳ degré*, *De vive Voix*, *La France en direct 1* et *Le Français et la Vie 1*.
6. Même si dans l'avant-propos à *C'est le printemps,* les auteurs se démarquent des manuels SGAV en en critiquant notamment les thématiques abordées et la progression adoptée, ils définissent malgré tout leur méthode comme 'de type audiovisuel' et 'donnant la priorité à l'oral' (livre du professeur 1976: 14 et 20).
7. Pour cela, le lecteur pourra se reporter à la bibliographie et notamment à l'ouvrage de H. Besse (1985).
8. 'Passage à la langue écrite' dans la préface de 1960 de *VIF* (42); 'passage à l'orthographe et à l'expression écrite' dans celle de *DVV* (X).

9. A cet égard, on observe une évolution avec *CLP* où l'élève peut retrouver, à la fin de son livre, les textes des dialogues enregistrés, 'ce qui le rend plus autonome dans son apprentissage'. Toutefois, les auteurs du manuel n'ont pas fait figurer les dialogues des deux premières unités afin de favoriser 'une approche uniquement orale du français' en tout début d'apprentissage (livre du professeur: 10).

10. Cette prise en compte plus rapide de l'écrit s'accompagne d'autres modifications comme l'allongement des énoncés associés à chaque image.

11. C'est le cas dans *VIF* et *DVV*, mais plus dans *CLP*, comme on le verra plus loin.

12. Egalement *Le Français et la vie* et *La France en direct*.

13. *DVV* première partie comprend également des petits poèmes qui sont très souvent des poèmes-dialogues et qui sont donc faits pour être dits.

14. *CLP 1* préconise en effet 'une pédagogie de groupe' et conseille même d'aménager l'espace de la classe de façon à permettre un travail en tandems ou trios (Avant propos du livre du professeur: 8).

15. Comme on l'a dit plus haut, les textes proposés à la lecture sont en effet illustrés.

16. Concernant l'exemple ci-dessous, les deux reformulations suivantes sont proposées:

'Pierre et Mireille ont décidé d'aller voir un film. [...] Pierre ne voit rien parce qu'il est gêné par le chapeau d'une dame. Ils décident alors de s'en aller.

Pierre et Mireille ont décidé d'aller voir un film. [...] Gêné par le chapeau d'une dame, Pierre ne voit rien, si bien qu'ils décident de s'en aller' (livre du professeur: 42).

17. Les références précises des deux manuels consultés se trouvent en bibliographie.

18. De plus, les images sont de P. Neveu, comme dans *DVV*.

19. Il a donc lui aussi été expérimenté au Centre de Linguistique Appliquée de Besançon.

20. Selon la préface de *IEE-DVV*, l'apprentissage de l'écrit peut commencer après 200 à 250h de pratique de la langue orale en cours intensif et d'après *PE-CLP*, après 120h de cours.

21. Bien que la différence puisse sembler mineure, elle est importante au point de vue de la conception de l'écrit: les auteurs de *CLP* conçoivent l'écrit comme un monde en soi.

22. Les auteurs font d'ailleurs explicitement référence aux travaux du Conseil de l'Europe et au *Niveau Seuil*.

23. Selon P. Guberina, la base de l'enseignement est en effet 'la parole en situation' (1974: 53). Comme l'explique H. Besse (1985: 40), présenter la parole étrangère 'en situation' signifie 'dans des conditions plausibles d'usage', d'où le recours à l'image afin que l'apprenant puisse reconstituer une partie des circonstances dans lesquelles certaines répliques peuvent être prononcées et ainsi accéder au sens. Car cette méthode 'présuppose que le sens [...] naît des rapports qui s'instaurent entre les circonstances de l'échange et les mots utilisés' (ibid.).

24. Il s'agit très vite de phrases complexes comprenant des coordinations et/ou subordinations.

25. Ainsi, après avoir demandé à l'apprenant de rédiger pour la presse le compte-rendu d'une réunion syndicale, on lui propose le texte suivant: 'Après avoir fait un bref résumé du conflit qui oppose les ouvriers à la direction de l'usine, le délégué syndical a fait le point de la situation; **la position de la direction n'ayant pas changé** au cours de la réunion qui a eu lieu dans la matinée, les ouvriers ont décidé de poursuivre la grève' (*Initiation à l'expression écrite* deuxième partie, livre du maître: 3; c'est le manuel qui souligne le procédé nouveau).

26. Toutefois, dans la partie 2, les exercices d'écriture à faire à la maison exigent aussi de l'apprenant un effort de composition: par exemple, à partir d'un dialogue entre deux locataires qui se plaignent d'une fuite d'eau, on demande à l'apprenant de rédiger la lettre écrite par l'un d'eux pour signaler cette fuite au propriétaire.

27. *PEP-CLP 2* sera donc analysé dans la partie 3.4 qui traite des relations entre lecture et écriture.

28. L'auteur du manuel se livre à un réquisitoire sans doute excessif contre la dictée qui est décrite comme un exercice 'non motivant, facteur d'inattention, ne provoquant pas l'acquisition d'habitudes scripturales, donnant des résultats catastrophiques dès que l'étudiant se trouve en situation d'expression et non plus de transcription du code oral' (PE-CLP *1*, livre du professeur: 6).

29. Parfois aussi des exercices d'extension consistant à compléter librement un début de phrase.

30. Ainsi, le contenu prévu pour l'écrit 4 est le suivant: 'Opposition masculin/féminin; Verbes: *chercher/connaître* (1ère personne); Présentatif *c'est*' (livre du professeur: 12).

31. Par exemple, dans l'étape de conceptualisation de règles de la leçon 1, l'apprenant doit compléter des phrases du type: 'Jean a .... qui est étudiante. (un ami/une amie)' (livre de l'élève: 7).

32. On a vu que dans *IEE-DVV*, les consignes de rédaction précisent également les principales informations du texte à produire: le contenu d'un message, d'un rapport etc.

33. Ce qui correspond à l'évolution des années 1976 et 1978.

34. Rappelons que le respect d'une progression rigoureuse est caractéristique de la méthode SGAV qui prévoit de n'introduire qu'un nombre limité d'unités linguistiques nouvelles à chaque leçon. Comme on le sait, le choix de ces unités nouvelles repose sur les listes lexicales et grammaticales du *Français fondamental* qui résultent d'enquêtes statistiques sur la fréquence relative des mots dans les échanges du quotidien (cf. Gougenheim et al. 1964).

35. Notons en revanche qu'il n'y a pas de texte littéraire.

36. Problématique en germe à l'époque.

37. Contrairement à *IEE-DVV*, les informations principales ne sont pas toujours imposées à l'apprenant. Par exemple, à partir de la photo d'une ville, il doit rédiger une lettre où il explique pourquoi la vie y est agréable ou non.

CHAPTER 16

❖

The Spread of Communicative Language Teaching: ELT in Italy in the 1980s and 1990s

Luciana Pedrazzini

Not much research has previously been carried out into the recent history of English Language Teaching (ELT) in Italy, and this chapter aims to shed light, specifically, on ELT in the 1980s and 1990s. On the basis of contemporary sources, interview data and an analysis of secondary school textbooks published locally, the investigation aims to explore how a communicative approach made its way into the Italian school context and was both supported and reinterpreted from a local perspective. The chapter is divided into three parts. In the first part, I provide a general overview of the Italian cultural and pedagogical context of the early 1970s, which prepared the ground for a radical renewal of the teaching of foreign languages and paved the way for the so-called 'communicative' period. In the second part, I examine how Communicative Language Teaching (CLT) orientations were boosted by school reforms and teacher-training initiatives. In the final part, I report on the preliminary findings of a small-scale study aimed at exploring how communicative teaching principles were interpreted and applied in the design of secondary school textbooks by Italian authors in the 1980s and 1990s.[1]

Introduction

From the end of the 1970s Communicative Language Teaching (CLT) reached the Italian foreign-language teaching context, in which English and French were the main languages taught in schools. Since then, the label 'communicative' has found great favour among most Italian foreign-language teachers and is still used with a positive connotation in relation to teaching activities and types of materials. The main implication of this new perspective on language teaching was the identification of 'a rationale for relating form and meaning to the real world of language use' (Howatt with Widdowson 2004: 326). This was a great challenge to the Italian tradition of language teaching based on classical languages and still mainly imbued with the grammar-translation method. A break with the old grammar-translation tradition and a general renewal of language teaching methodology were strongly supported by a number of language teacher associations. They called for more authentic language in textbooks, to be presented through dialogues based on real-life situations, and for language skills to be practised in micro-situations (Crisari 1972). Their bottom-up activities were eventually successful in promoting a reform of the national lower-secondary school syllabuses, which took place at the end of the 1970s. These events, together with the first experiment in institutional training for secondary foreign language teachers, contributed to a gradual process of change constituting a 'communicative turn' in foreign language teaching, as will be outlined in the first and second parts of this chapter.

The investigation reported in this chapter was carried out using different methods. A large set of data was gathered from the journals of the major associations of language teachers in Italy in the 1980s and 1990s. These journals supplied accounts of conferences and seminars, petitions and other documents in support of educational reforms, textbook reviews, checklists for textbook evaluation and articles on second language teaching methods. In addition, among the leading figures in the ELT field of the period, I was able to interview Luciano Mariani and Maria Cecilia Rizzardi, both of them authors of best-selling textbooks in the early 1980s and 1990s and of methodology books for language teachers. The questions for their interview touched upon several issues: the cultural and educational context of these two decades; their involvement in teacher training activities; and the coursebooks they authored, with a focus in particular on the design process that led them to introduce communicative features. Finally, the analysis of a small corpus of selected ELT secondary-school textbooks published in Italy in the 1980s and 1990s supplied further data on the contributions of Italian materials writers to the spread of communicative teaching principles. The analysis — preliminary findings of which are reported in the third part of this chapter — was aimed at gauging how the new principles were actually interpreted and applied according to the needs of the Italian educational context.

Before Communicative Language Teaching

Since the early 1970s, critical reflection on the way languages were taught in the Italian context had been encouraged by several teacher associations (e.g. ANILS — *Associazione Nazionale Insegnanti Lingue Straniere*, the oldest association for language teachers, which was founded in 1947) as well as by local groups of language teachers.[2] A case in point is *Lingua e Nuova Didattica* (LEND), which was originally founded as an informal group of foreign-language teachers in 1971. The association was distinctive for its overall left-leaning nature. True to the combination of the terms 'language' and 'new teaching' in its name, the association became a driving force for radical innovation of language teaching in Italy. In its first public document, the state of foreign language teaching in Italy is described as being characterized by an overt contradiction between the need to learn a language as a means of communication on the one hand and the prevailing unsuitable conditions of schools and outdated syllabuses on the other (LEND 1972: 17-18). In effect, the majority of foreign language teachers did not use a proper 'coursebook' or any audio-visual aids, but still relied on some kind of grammar-translation approach, as Luciano Mariani points out:

> In the 1970s, most language teachers used to adopt a grammar book, which was used not as a reference book as we would expect, but as the main coursebook itself. Often, the grammar book was supplemented by a textbook with reading passages on cultural and geographical topics.[3]

Mario Papa (2004), one of the best-selling authors of ELT materials published in Italy, reports what typically happened in an English lesson:

> The focus of the lesson was only on rules and the translation of sentences. The oral language was considered too difficult so it was totally ignored. Classroom activities were repeated with the same routine: after the roll call, a student was asked to explain the rule that was studied and read out the sentences he or she had translated at home; the teacher then explained a new rule and assigned further translation exercises.[4]

The grammar-translation method was seen as one of the main obstacles to the hoped-for radical renewal — hence there were calls to 'eradicate' it to implement teaching practices in which the four language skills (listening, speaking, reading and writing) would be taught in a wide range of situations (Crisari 1972). While the activities of associations such as ANILS and LEND involved teachers of various languages, including Italian as a mother tongue, specific initiatives for the innovation of ELT were promoted by TESOL Italy, an off-shoot of the international TESOL (Teachers of English to Speakers of Other Languages) organization, which was founded by Mary Finocchiaro and Renzo Titone in 1975.

A parallel action for a renewal of foreign language teaching was undertaken by a number of journals supported by associations of language teachers and official institutions of foreign languages and cultures. Journals such as *Scuola e Lingue Moderne* (1963), *Lingua e Civiltà* (1969), *Rivista Italiana di Linguistica Applicata* (1970), *Lingua e Nuova Didattica* (1972) and *Lingue e Didattica* (1973) gave voice to teachers' experiences and practices concerning textbook evaluation, the use of teaching techniques and visual aids, testing, and so on; and hosted contributions by Italian scholars and teacher trainers as well as renowned applied linguists, who brought theoretical issues to the fore. Many Italian ELT teachers also attended seminars offered by the British Council and consulted teaching materials, catalogues and bibliographies in its English language information centres. Donn Byrne, who was English Language Officer at the British Council in Rome during the 1970s, worked very closely with language-teacher associations to help set up seminars and workshops. The British Council (together with the Bureau Linguistique and the Goethe Institute) also supported the publication of *Lingua e Nuova Didattica* — the journal of LEND. TESOL Italy joined the ELT debate through the publication of a regular newsletter and a journal (*Perspectives*), which was published twice a year and has included papers from TESOL Italy's annual convention since 1975.

In contrast to traditional teaching, the new orientations to foreign language learning and teaching pointed towards more contextualized teaching procedures. In her editorial in the first issue of *Lingua e Nuova Didattica*, D'Addio (1972: 8) argues that 'language proficiency goes beyond the mere mastery of grammatical structures. Language does not take place *in vacuo*, but is a communicative act with individual, cultural and social relevance'. Despite the focus here on communication, D'Addio (1972: 9) favours a 'situational approach', as she says, 'to place any language activity within a communicative domain, that is, within a situation'. Throughout the 1970s, the whole debate over the need for a new approach to the teaching of foreign languages was also enhanced by a flurry of methodology books authored by Italian scholars (for example, Freddi 1970; D'Addio 1974; De Angelis and Bertocchini 1978; Siani 1978; Titone 1978). Both journals and methodology books, supported by intense activity on the part of teachers' associations, provided foreign language teachers with necessary methodological support for renewal.[5]

Journals, in particular, played a key role in guiding second language teachers critically to evaluate coursebooks then in use in Italian schools and supplied them with the necessary tools for the analysis of new 'situational' materials. In the early 1970s, textbooks such as *First Things First* (Alexander 1967) and *Hello There!* (Burnand and Crisari 1971) were considered good examples of the way the situational method could be applied because they featured all the supposed necessary ingredients: a gradual presentation of grammatical structures through 'authentic' everyday dialogues; a controlled use of vocabulary; practice of language structures in 'micro-situations'; pictures to illustrate the situations introduced; essential grammar rules aimed at encouraging inductive learning; supplementary audio material; and detailed teacher's notes (Bizzoni and Di Giuliomaria 1972: 5-12). *First Things First* in particular, which had borrowed a format introduced from the French 'Audio-Visual Method' (Howatt with Widdowson 2004: 249; see also Hidden, in this volume), was adapted and published in different versions to suit the needs of the Italian lower- and upper-secondary school market (*Language and Life* by Alexander and Evangelisti 1970; *Link Up* by Alexander and Evangelisti 1972; and *Way In* by Alexander et al. 1978). Other successful situationally oriented series, such as *Access to English* (Coles and Lord 1974), began to be adopted in some classes of the Italian upper secondary. As Mariani argues (interview): '[A]lthough this choice by Italian ELT teachers was not always supported by a full awareness of the new methodological principles, it can certainly be viewed as an attempt to make a break with the grammar-translation tradition and move forward'.

Towards Communicative Language Teaching

How did the transition from a situational approach to communicative language teaching actually take place in the Italian context? The new paradigm shift did not occur as a sudden and unexpected phenomenon, but rather was locally and gradually prepared. A number of co-occurring events, which will be outlined in this section, may be said to have contributed in different ways to this transition.

First of all, in 1978 the LEND national conference had as the key theme 'Communicative competence and the teaching of languages' (*Competenza comunicativa e insegnamento delle lingue*) and this served as a springboard for the ideas that inspired

Communicative Language Teaching in Italy. Fifteen hundred teachers from all over Italy attended the conference. One of the main aims was to present the Threshold Level Project (van Ek 1975/1980) established by the Council of Europe and coordinated by J. L. M. Trim, with its specification of Wilkins's syllabus of semantic and functional categories for the description of language use. As Howatt with Widdowson (2004: 249) point out:

> what was needed was a more analytical approach which accepted that 'situations' were made up from smaller events: asking for things, expressing likes and dislikes, making suggestions, and so on. These were the categories which were to provide the functional 'bridge' between language use and linguistic form that came to play a key role in the next, communicative, phase of ELT after 1970.

During the conference a number of key ideas at the heart of the communicative movement such as 'language needs' and 'communicative competence' were placed at the centre of the debate. These ideas, which had just begun to spread through some ELT textbooks published in Italy, still needed to be refined and adapted to the specific needs of the Italian school scenario.

While the idea of identifying learners' language needs, as in threshold-level syllabuses, seemed to work well for the specification of objectives for special/specific purpose language teaching, it did not seem equally suitable for the design of school syllabuses, whose contents also required specifications in terms of general educational language needs. It was also argued that the concept of 'communicative competence' needed further specification of skills and competences for school learners. As Ciliberti (1979: 5) reports, the conference also aimed 'to provide teachers with the necessary tools to evaluate textbooks more critically as publishers have sometimes transferred the results of the Council of Europe project superficially and hastily'. Issues such as 'application' and 'applicability' of the notional-functional syllabus still needed to be addressed. In effect, one of the risks of adopting a notional-functional syllabus was that sets of language functions with their language exponents would be inserted into coursebooks without any specific criteria and be simply 'practised' as 'a collection of situationally sensitive phrases like "Can I help you?" or "How do you do"' (Howatt with Widdowson 2004: 337).

The initiatives for a radical revision of the school syllabus for languages supported by the main teachers' associations in the 1970s eventually led to new National Syllabuses for lower secondary schools (*I Nuovi programmi per la media inferiore* 1979) and, after more than ten years, also led to proposals for a revised syllabus for upper secondary schools (Pozzo and Quartapelle 1992). It is interesting to note that after the publication in 1979 of the new syllabuses, the whole process of change involving foreign language teaching took more than ten years. It was approached from a general perspective of *educazione linguistica* [language education], a term which first appeared in the ground-breaking document *Dieci tesi per l'educazione linguistica democratica* (GISCEL 1975), which presented ten theses for a 'democratic' language education. The theses were set forward by a group of linguists and teachers and defined the main theoretical assumptions and lines of action for a comprehensive project targeted at *all* languages learnt at school, Italian included. The project was aimed at highlighting both similarities and differences among languages and encouraging the implementation of shared aims and procedures of language education both at school and in teacher training (cf. for example Bertocchi et al. 1981). However, as Mariani recalls:

> Although most second language teachers ideally agreed with this idea of cross-curricular learning, they did not consider it a priority in their teaching. In fact, they were literally overwhelmed by the newness the communicative principles brought along and more interested in trying out communicative-based materials.

The very first effect of the spread of communicative principles can be traced in the National Syllabuses for the lower secondary school, in which the foreign language is defined as 'a means of communication' and learning aims are specified in terms of 'acquisition of skills of spoken and written comprehension and production'. Learners are therefore expected to learn how 'to use the foreign language' in 'meaningful contexts of communication' and teachers will use procedures and set up activities aimed at the acquisition of the foreign language according to specific 'communicative functions'. The terms 'communication, language use, functions, skills' in official documents can certainly be interpreted as a clear sign of transition from the traditional Italian teaching scenario. As Howatt and Smith (2014: 88) point out, when these labels began to be applied in different contexts in Europe:

> [t]he basic common purpose of the changes was clear enough, namely to shift the aims and priorities of language teaching away from the acquisition of well-rehearsed skills in their own right and towards the confident use of those skills in the attainment of purposes and objectives of importance to the learner in the 'real world'.

The new Italian syllabuses required a comprehensive teacher-training plan that involved a large number of foreign language teachers.

Institutional training of both pre-service and in-service foreign language teachers in Italy was indeed one of the key issues still waiting for practical and long-term solutions. While no institutional pre-service training was yet available, the existing forms of teacher training were considered insufficient and inadequate. A survey carried out by the International Association for the Evaluation of Student Achievement in 1977 pointed out the low levels of foreign language competence of Italian students, the main cause of which was considered to be the lack of specific training of practising teachers. In effect, neither hiring procedures nor a university degree were able to provide prospective foreign language teachers with the necessary preparation. In order to respond to these shortcomings, the Ministry of Education decided to set up a training programme that would involve secondary school teachers of English, French and German in different areas of the country. The programme, called *Progetto Speciale Lingue Straniere* (PSLS), was started in 1978 and was the first attempt to address the professional needs of in-service foreign language teachers in an institutionalized way. The programme had indeed very 'special' and innovative features due to its methodology and investment. In the decade 1978 to 1987, around one thousand courses were run on a regular basis and attended by half of the foreign language teachers in service. The training course required weekly attendance at a local centre, for a total number of one hundred hours training in a school year.

Locally prominent teachers who had been trained on a six-week course in the USA sponsored by the American Embassy led the PSLS programme. Maria Cecilia Rizzardi, one of the first PSLS trainers to attend the course, reports on her experience:

> Groups, especially at a very first stage, were mixed in terms of language competence and teaching experience. The training provided was essentially focused on the teaching of the four language skills but we were not taught how to be 'trainers' and deal with groups of teachers. Therefore, once back to Italy, most of us had to work hard to prepare the materials for our PSLS course.[6]

In the 1970s, Ealing College in London also provided advanced training courses for Italian teachers in language, literature and methodology sponsored by the British Council. It is notable how many of the lecturers on such courses were also UK textbook authors whose books became popular in Italy. It is also worth mentioning the Distance Training Foundation Module (DTFM) set up in Italy by the British Council, which ran its first course in 1981. Several PSLS and non-PSLS trainers tended to attend these courses as well.

The PSLS training programme was aimed at improving both the teachers' language competence and teaching skills. The trainer first showcased a lesson; the trainees had to analyse it in groups and prepare the materials for a similar lesson, which was then evaluated. As underlined in the final report on the PSLS experience:

> Trainers were not supposed to illustrate a variety of approaches and methods to the teaching of a foreign language but they had rather to insist on the aims and procedures of 'communicative language teaching' or 'The Communicative Approach' as it came to be known. (*Ufficio Studi e Programmazione* 1988: 34)

This approach was deemed the most suitable for providing teachers with a new rationale for the definition of their language syllabuses and new techniques to reshape their teaching.

Finally, mention must be made of the TESOL Italy and British Council annual conferences in the 1980s and 1990s, which not only played a key role in the dissemination of communicative language teaching ideas and innovative teaching methods, but also provided additional training opportunities for a large number of English-language teachers. Italian trainers and material writers increasingly took part as speakers in the sessions on EFL teaching in Italy. The conferences were also seen by both UK and Italian publishers as a major marketing opportunity and provided not only a field of competition but of 'cross-fertilization' for teaching and publishing ideas as well.

'Communicative' ELT Secondary School Textbooks Published in Italy in the 1980s and 1990s

In the early 1980s, communicative language teaching seemed to find its way into the Italian ELT classrooms through the publication of a number of coursebooks specifically designed to address the needs of Italian school learners. In most cases, they were written by teachers and teacher trainers actively involved in teacher associations and in in-service training. Labels such as 'communicative' and 'functional' started to crop up in titles and prefaces and gradually replaced the old labels of 'situational' and 'structural'. However, this was not always evidence of a new approach to coursebook design. The whole process of change took longer. As Rizzardi and Barsi (2005: 169) argue, 'the oral-situational method merged into the communicative method in a nonconflictual way [...]. The two methods coexisted in Italian textbooks, [...] influencing each other'. A case in point is *Learning to Communicate* (Di Giuliomaria and Carra 1977, 1982): both its editions seem to embrace the new philosophy in the book's subtitle *A Functional Approach to English* but a closer look inside mostly reveals features of situational teaching, with a structural syllabus and contexts for practice in the form of pictures, dialogues and situations.

In this section, I will report on some preliminary findings of a small-scale study aimed at exploring how communicative teaching principles were interpreted and integrated in the design of secondary school ELT textbooks written by Italian authors in the 1980s and 1990s. For the purpose of this study, I identified a number of textbooks that not only claimed to be 'communicative', but also in fact appeared to present new and innovative features. In particular, the selection included textbooks which, while applying the principles of communicative language teaching, made an attempt to find original solutions in relation to specific educational needs in the Italian school context. The selection on these principles resulted in a small sample of ten textbooks in total for lower and upper secondary schools (Tables 1 and 2, respectively).

Year of publication	Title	Author (s)	Publisher
1982	*Communication Tasks*	Iantorno & Papa	Zanichelli
1982	*Got the Message?*	Elviri, Rizzardi & Bertocchi	Principato
1982	*Ready, Steady, Go!*	Angeletti Meirano, Fox & Fugiglando Cumino	Paravia
1988	*Adventures in English*	Whitney & Dandini	La Nuova Italia / Oxford University Press
1990	*Keyword*	Radley, Sharley, Massari & Redaelli	Edizioni Scolastiche Bruno Mondadori/ Heinemann/ The British Council

TABLE 1. Italian ELT textbooks (1980s-1990s) for the lower secondary school

Year of publication	Title	Author (s)	Publisher
1986	*Skills and Meanings*	Papa	Zanichelli
1989	*Performance*	Cumino & Iantorno	La Nuova Italia/ Oxford University Press
1991	*Choices*	Mariani & O'Malley	Zanichelli
1994	*Review*	Dodman	Archimede Edizioni
1999	*Up to You*	Pavoni, Pozzo & Priesack	Loescher Editore

TABLE 2. Italian ELT textbooks (1980s-1990s) for the upper secondary school

The selection also accounts for the following specific criteria:

- textbooks by Italian authors who sometimes shared the writing process with English native speaker material writers;
- textbooks mainly published by Italian companies and in some cases with UK publishers;[7]
- textbooks which turned out to be a 'landmark' in the Italian ELT teaching context in providing innovative and alternative examples of teaching materials: indeed, a few of them became best-selling titles (for example, *Communication Tasks*; *Got the Message?*; *Choices*).

The sample does not include textbooks that are adaptations of original versions published for an international market. This happened, for example, with the successful series *Strategies* (Abbs and Freebairn 1975 onwards) which, according to the authors, became surprisingly popular in secondary schools and led to commissions for further coursebook series for younger learners such as *Discoveries* (1986 onwards) (Rixon and Smith 2012). In the early 1980s, such adapted versions began to make their way into the Italian marketplace. In most cases, the adaptation simply involved an added section with essential grammatical notes and a bilingual glossary and neither the original syllabus nor the teaching sequence of the teaching activities was altered. An example is the bestselling title *Communicating Strategies* (Abbs et al. 1980), which was targeted at upper-secondary learners and was essentially an Italian compact version of *Starting Strategies* and *Building Strategies* (Abbs and Freebairn 1975 and 1979 respectively), the first two volumes of the breakthrough *Strategies* series. *Flying Start* (Abbs, Freebairn and Mariani 1987), another bestselling title aimed at Italian ten-to-fourteen-year-old lower-secondary learners, was an offshoot of the well-known *Discoveries* series (Abbs and Freebairn 1986). However, as Mariani — the Italian author in the team — explains:

> it did involve a process of co-authoring rather than adaptation. The grammatical component I was asked to write was indeed meant to address the specific needs of Italian EFL teachers who wanted additional work on the language. Keeping in mind the age of the learners, I designed simple grammatical tasks according to an inductive learning approach.

It may be argued that the careers of several Italian authors of EFL materials were 'kick- started' by their experience as writers of supplementary materials or adaptations.

The analysis of the sample considered here will address the following questions in particular: what were the emerging innovative features in terms of syllabus design and types of learning tasks? What features of previous methodologies were preserved? What alternative 'local' solutions were implemented? In keeping with an approach to the history of ELT aimed at emphasizing continuity rather than sudden breaks (Hunter and Smith 2012; Howatt and Smith 2014), the analysis is thus intended to uncover a number of features that not only marked a break with the past but also continuity or possibly evidence of alternative options. In this respect, both Mariani and Rizzardi (interviews) seem to agree on the fact that in the 1980s and early 1990s authors were granted more freedom to try out their ideas compared to recent years, in which the creation of ELT materials has increasingly become market-driven.

Italian ELT textbooks published in the early 1980s claimed to be and were, in fact, designed according to a renewed syllabus. Grammatical and situational-based syllabuses were replaced by syllabuses built around a selection of functional or communicative objectives such as introducing people, asking and saying the time, describing objects and so on. The functional objectives were listed next to the corresponding structures and lexical items to provide the majority of teachers with an additional and more familiar resource for the planning of their lessons. As Howatt and Widdowson (2004: 339) argue, 'the new semantic syllabuses did not, however, discard the familiar structures and patterns altogether, though they did reorganize them somewhat'. In only one textbook examined (*Adventures in English*) were topics related to school subjects also added in an attempt to address learners' cross-curricular needs. In the 1990s, a 'multi-syllabus' approach became a common feature and was made evident by the use of more detailed contents pages. This type of syllabus involved the integration of functions, grammar, topics and skills through a 'spiral' approach. Additionally, two of the textbooks considered (*Choices*; *Review*) combine their communicative-oriented syllabus with a metacognitive component aimed at developing learners' awareness of language and language learning through strategies and study skills. As Mariani underlines:

> the strong point of *Choices*, which had as a subtitle 'An integrated course in language and learning strategies', was indeed its metacognitive slant. However, it seems to me that this component was perceived by most teachers as something 'separate' and was not fully exploited in the classroom activities.

A learner-based approach to language learning was another highly innovative feature in the Italian ELT context and contributed to the introduction of new types of activities focused on the use of English to learn. As also specified in the subtitle of *Review*, this was not only about 'learning English' but also 'learning through English'.

The spread of communicative language teaching generated a flurry of learning activities and tasks unseen before and this was perceived in the Italian ELT context as one of the main innovations, indeed, as a real revolution:

> For many teachers what was attractive about the communicative approach in this form was not so much the novel syllabuses as the refreshing sense of freedom that followed the end of the over-rigid structural syllabus and the welcome variety of classroom activities that accompanied the new approach. (Howatt with Widdowson 2004: 339)

In most of the textbooks considered, communicative language teaching techniques are exploited in the so-called 'weaker' version of communicative approach, which was primarily aimed at providing learners with opportunities to use their English for communicative purposes (Howatt and Smith 2014: 91). The new textbooks must have appeared rather eclectic, if not confused, especially to those teachers who felt more comfortable with a straightforward and gradual presentation-and-practice-lesson sequence. While in the textbooks published in the 1980s the presentation phase mainly consists of a dialogue followed by a task, those published in the 1990s prefer a more dynamic presentation with 'preparation' and 'leading-in' activities. Moreover, in most of the books considered, the boundary between practice and production is not always made clear, in the sense that a number of activities targeting specific communicative objectives and language skills are provided throughout. A plethora of labels is used to identify the focus of the different types of activities ('Skills Work'; 'Communication Strategies'; 'Project'; 'Game'; 'English for your Curriculum'; 'Story Time', etc.). Nevertheless, from the early 1980s onwards three main types of activities came to replace the traditional practice exercises — role-play and simulation activities; problem-solving activities and games; and skill-training activities (Howatt with Widdowson 2004: 256-57). For example, *Got the Message?* features at least ten activities of these types in each unit. As Rizzardi recalls:

> [W]e wanted to provide learners with a broad range of activities that would actively involve them in a communicative use of the language. This also gave teachers the chance to choose which game or role-play was best for their learners.

Finally, despite the great potential provided by communication-based learner-centred activities, the priority accorded to them over grammar practice was a constant concern for Italian second language teachers, partly on account of the rooted and pervasive tradition of grammar-translation teaching, which was still alive and well in most school contexts (see also Nava in this volume). During the 1980s and 1990s, Italian coursebook writers seemed particularly sensitive to this concern. In continuity with a structural approach to language learning, a number of textbooks simply added a section — usually at the end of the teaching unit — which included grammatical notes, tables and a battery of drills and exercises (for example, *Communication Tasks*; *Skills and Meanings*; *Up to You!*). Other textbooks (*Got the Message?*; *Ready, Steady, Go!*; *Adventures in English*; *Choices*; *Review*) turned to alternative procedures which would involve learners in a process of self-discovery of specific language features. By starting from the analysis of a short meaningful context provided by a text, learners are led through questions to notice specific language features, collect examples, fill in tables and diagrams, and eventually use the language features in similar contexts. In the late 1990s, though, 'grammar' sections began to be expanded, at the expense of the wealth of communicative activities that had brought a change in most Italian EFL textbooks.

Conclusion

This chapter has aimed to shed light on the history of ELT in the Italian context in the 1980s and 1990s. In keeping with an approach that highlights not only breaks but also continuity with the past (Hunter and Smith 2012; Howatt and Smith 2014), the chapter has tried to provide an account of the way communicative language teaching orientations were supported and reinterpreted from an Italian perspective.

In the mid-1970s a number of circumstances and initiatives in the Italian cultural and educational context provided fertile ground for the spread of communicative methodologies. In addition to these, the dissemination of communicative language teaching ideas and innovative teaching methods in general was greatly supported through local TESOL and British Council seminars and annual conventions. The preliminary findings of a small-scale study aimed at exploring how communicative teaching principles were interpreted and integrated into Italian secondary school ELT textbooks have shown that in the early 1980s the grammatical and situational-based syllabuses adopted by most textbooks gave way to functional and communicative syllabuses and these to multi-syllabuses in the 1990s. A variety of communication-based activities became prominent in most textbooks, which made the traditional 'presentation and practice' lesson sequence more dynamic and provided learners with additional opportunities for language production.

Although communicative textbooks created high expectations in terms of improvement of the learners' communication skills, many teachers perceived a continuing need for more explicit work on language and viewed the lack of it as a problem. This was addressed by Italian ELT coursebook writers according to two co-existing methodological approaches to language learning and teaching: the first was a continuation of the structural approach of the past, while the latter was more learner-centred and forward-looking. However, the first approach was to prevail in the late 1990s.

In responding to Howatt and Smith's (2014: 93) call for 'further decentering and localization of ELT history', this chapter has aimed to provide an account of a period of ELT history in Italy in which a reinterpretation of the main ideas of communicative language teaching gave impulse to local teaching proposals and solutions. The investigative methods used involved not only documentary and textbook analysis but also interviews with two of the leading figures in the Italian ELT field, who provided their personal perspectives on the cultural and educational context of the period. I hope that my account will contribute to increasing awareness among a younger generation of teachers about the main circumstances that made Italian ELT history in the 1980s and 1990s and helping them use the legacy of this period as a point of reference in their future work.

Bibliography

ALEXANDER, L. G. 1974. 'Operation and strategie', *Lingua e Nuova Didattica*, 3: 6
———. 1976. 'Incantations', *Lingua e Nuova Didattica*, 5: 3
BALBONI, PAOLO (ed.). 2016a. Bibliografia dell'educazione linguistica in Italia. BELI. Parte I (1960–1999) <http://www.itals.it/sites/default/files/docs/Bibliografia_Educazione_Linguistica_in_Italia_1960–1999.pdf> [accessed 8 February 2018]
BALBONI, PAOLO (ed.). 2016b. Bibliografia dell'educazione linguistica in Italia. BELI. Parte II (2000–2015) <http://www.itals.it/sites/default/files/docs/Bibliografia_Educazione_Linguistica_in_Italia_2000–2016.pdf> [accessed 8 February 2018]
BERTOCCHI, D., ET AL. 1981. *Educazione linguistica e curricolo* (Milan: Edizioni Scolastiche Bruno Mondadori)
BIZZONI, F., and S. DI GIULIOMARIA. 1972. 'La scelta del libro di testo per l'insegnamento dell'inglese: scuola media inferiore', *Lingua e Nuova Didattica*, 1: 5-12
CILIBERTI, ANNA. 1979. 'Competenza comunicativa e insegnamento delle lingue', *Lingua e Nuova Didattica*, 8: 5-11
CRISARI, MAURIZIO. 1972. 'Il metodo situazionale', *Lingua e Nuova Didattica*, 1: 19-21
D'ADDIO, WANDA. 1972. 'Metodi e scelta di un metodo', *Lingua e Nuova Didattica*, 1: 7-9
———. 1974. *Lingua straniera e comunicazione: problemi di glottodidattica* (Bologna: Zanichelli)
DE ANGELIS, FRANCA, and PAOLA BERTOCCHINI. 1978. *Didattica delle lingue straniere* (Milan: Edizioni Scolastiche Bruno Mondadori)
DI GIULIOMARIA, SIRIO. 1978. *Scuola e lingue straniere* (Florence: La Nuova Italia)
FREDDI, GIOVANNI. 1970. *Metodologia e didattica delle lingue straniere* (Bergamo: Minerva Italica)
GISCEL. 1975. *Dieci tesi per un'educazione linguistica democratica* <http://www.giscel.it/?q=content/dieci-tesi-leducazione-linguistica-democratica> [accessed 8 February 2018]
HOWATT, A. P. R., and RICHARD SMITH. 2014. 'The History of Teaching as a Foreign Language, from a British and European perspective', *Language and History*, 57: 75-95
———, WITH H. G. WIDDOWSON. 2004 [1984]. *A History of English Language Teaching* (Oxford: Oxford University Press)
HUNTER, DUNCAN, and RICHARD SMITH. 2012. 'Unpackaging the Past: "CLT" through ELTJ Keywords', *ELT Journal*, 66: 430-39
LINGUA E NUOVA DIDATTICA. 1972. 'Per un profondo rinnovamento dell'insegnamento delle lingue straniere nella scuola italiana', *Lingua e Nuova Didattica*, 1: 17-18
MINISTERO DELLA PUBBLICA ISTRUZIONE. 1979. 'I Nuovi programmi per la media inferiore. Decreto Ministeriale 9 febbraio 1979', *Gazzetta Ufficiale*, 50: 4–23, online at <http://www.gazzettaufficiale.it/eli/gu/1979/02/20/50/so/0/sg/pdf>
PAPA, MARIO. 2004. *A modo mio: un'autobiografia professionale* (Bologna: Zanichelli) <http://www.mariopapa.eu/34/Biografia.html?551275619> [accessed 8 February 2018]
POZZO, GRAZIELLA, and FRANCA QUARTAPELLE (eds). 1992. *Insegnare la lingua straniera: dalla teoria alla pratica didattica nel nuovo biennio* (Florence: La Nuova Italia)
RIXON, SHELAGH, and RICHARD SMITH. 2012. 'The Work of Brian Abbs and Ingrid Freebairn', *ELT Journal*, 66: 383-93
RIZZARDI, MARIA CECILIA, and MONICA BARSI. 2005. *Metodi in classe per insegnare la lingua straniera* (Milan: LED)
SIANI, C. (ed.). 1978. *Glottodidattica. Principi e realizzazioni. Antologia di 'Lingua e Nuova Didattica'* (Forence: La Nuova Italia)
TITONE, RENZO (ed.). 1978. *Didattica delle lingue straniere in Italia (1957–1977)* (Milan: Oxford Institutes)
UFFICIO STUDI E PROGRAMMAZIONE. 1988. *Il progetto speciale lingue straniere*, Studi e Documenti degli Annali della Pubblica Istruzione (Florence: MPI-Le Monnier)

VAN EK, J. A. 1975. *The Threshold Level in a European Unit/Credit System for Modern language Learning by Adults* (Strasbourg: The Council of Europe); republished as *Threshold Level English*, with L. G. Alexander (Oxford: Pergamon, 1980)

WIDDOWSON, HENRY. 2004. 'A Perspective on Recent Trends', in A. P. R. Howatt, with H. G. Widdowson, *A History of English Language Teaching* (Oxford: Oxford University Press), pp. 353-72

WILKINS, DAVID. 1972. *The Linguistic and Situational Content of the Common Core in a Unit/ Credit System* (Strasbourg: Council of Europe)

———. 1976. *Notional Syllabuses* (Oxford: Oxford University Press)

Textbooks

ABBS, BRIAN, and INGRID FREEBAIRN. 1975. *Starting Strategies* (Harlow: Longman)

———, and INGRID FREEBAIRN. 1979. *Building Strategies* (Harlow: Longman)

———, and INGRID FREEBAIRN. 1986. *Discoveries* (Harlow: Longman)

———, INGRID FREEBAIRN, and LUCIANO MARIANI. 1987. *Flying Start* (Harlow: Longman)

ABBS, BRIAN, et al. 1980. *Communicating Strategies* (Bologna: Zanichelli; Harlow: Longman)

ANGELETTI MEIRANO, GRAZIELLA, FOX, GWYNETH and FUGIGLANDO CUMINO, MARGHERITA. 1982. (Turin: Paravia)

CUMINO, MARGHERITA, and GIULIANO IANTORNO. 1989. *Performance* (Florence: La Nuova Italia / Oxford: Oxford University Press)

DI GIULIOMARIA, SIRIO, and FIORELLA CARRA. 1977. *Learning to Communicate* (Florence: La Nuova Italia; Oxford: Oxford University Press)

DODMAN, MARTIN. 1994. *Review* (Milan: Archimede Edizioni)

ELVIRI, FIORELLA, MARIA CECILIA RIZZARDI and DANIELA BERTOCCHI. 1982. *Got the Message?* (Milan: Principato)

IANTORNO, GIULIANO, and MARIO PAPA. 1982. *Communication Tasks* (Bologna: Zanichelli)

MARIANI, LUCIANO, and KAIRAN O'MALLEY. 1991. *Choices* (Bologna: Zanichelli)

PAPA, MARIO. 1986. *Skills and Meanings* (Bologna: Zanichelli)

PAVONI, MARIA CARLA, GRAZIELLA POZZO and TIM PRIESACK. 1999. *Up to You* (Torino: Loescher Editore)

RADLEY, PAUL, ALAN SHARLEY, , ADRIANA MASSARI, and ADRIANA REDAELLI,. 1990. *Keyword* (Edizioni Scolastiche Bruno Mondadori/ Heinemann/ The British Council)

WHITNEY, NORMAN, and MARIA GRAZIA DANDINI. 1988. *Adventures in English* (Florence: La Nuova Italia / Oxford: Oxford University Press)

Notes to Chapter 16

1. I am very grateful to Luciano Mariani and Maria Cecilia Rizzardi for agreeing to be interviewed and for supplying some of the textbooks analysed in this chapter. Thanks also to the anonymous reviewer whose insightful comments and suggestions helped me improve the first draft of this chapter.

2. A similar debate went on within general associations for teachers (e.g. OPPI — *Organizzazione per la Preparazione degli Insegnanti* — and CIDI — *Centro di Iniziativa Democratica degli Insegnanti*), which set up training courses for foreign language teachers as well as for teachers of other subjects.

3. Quotes by Luciano Mariani are from an interview recorded with him in April 2015 and presented here in my translation.

4. The quotation is from the online version of Papa's autobiography (no page numbers) and

is provided here directly in my translation, as are all quotations from Italian sources in the chapter.

5. A useful attempt to trace the wealth of publications in the field of foreign language learning and teaching in Italy since the 1960s is the bibliographical inventory compiled by Paolo Balboni (2016a and 2016b).

6. Quotations by Maria Cecilia Rizzardi are from her interview recorded in April 2015 and supplied here in my translation.

7. UK publishers forged close alliances and joint ventures with Italian publishers in the 1980s and 1990s (in particular, Oxford University Press/La Nuova Italia; Longman/Zanichelli; Heinemann/Bruno Mondadori). These relationships led to the publication of several best-selling textbooks.

CHAPTER 17

❖

A Return to Grammar amid the Communicative 'Revolution': Italian Pedagogical Grammar Books for EFL Students (1980–2000)

Andrea Nava

A comprehensive history of modern English grammaticography is still far from being written. The late 1980s and the 1990s saw a surge of academic interest in the investigation of English grammar writing, yet the main thrust of these inquiries was the analysis of English descriptive grammars. The realm of recent English *pedagogical* grammar writing, however, is still largely unexplored. The aim of this contribution is to analyse Italian-produced pedagogical grammar books for English as a Foreign Language (EFL) students. This genre became extremely popular in Italy between the mid-1980s and the early 1990s, when the communicative approach was starting to become mainstream. Pedagogical grammar books for EFL students filled a gap in the market, as teachers and students were often puzzled by the apparent lack of grammar in the new 'all-singing, all-dancing' coursebooks. After sketching the Italian language-teaching background in the 1980s, the chapter presents the findings of a grammaticological analysis of a corpus of pedagogical grammars published in Italy in the last two decades of the twentieth century. The analysis aims to ascertain the extent to which the views on grammar and grammar teaching underlying communicative language teaching were taken up in Italian-produced pedagogical grammars for EFL students; and ponders the role that local educational and language teaching traditions played in shaping this grammaticographical genre.

Introduction

The history of recent English pedagogical grammaticography is still to a large extent uncharted territory. Grammaticological[1] inquiries (Leitner 1986, 1991; Graustein and Leitner 1989) have mainly focused on English descriptive grammars: academic works written by linguists and aimed at scholars or university students. A few exceptions notwithstanding (e.g. Chalker 1994; Ellis 2002; Linn 2006; Nava

2008), recent English *pedagogical* grammar writing has not yet received adequate scholarly attention, particularly the output of pedagogical grammar authors outside the UK and the USA.

The focus of this chapter is on the genre of 'pedagogical grammar books for EFL [English as a Foreign Language] students' in its Italian incarnation. Pedagogical grammars for EFL learners are books meant to accompany (not replace) language teaching coursebooks; to be dipped into for reference or to be read from cover to cover; to be used in class or for self-study; and featuring explanations, examples and exercises. While pedagogical grammar books for EFL students have been published since at least the first few decades of the twentieth century (e.g. Palmer 1924), the genre had its heyday in several European countries in the 1980s and 1990s (notably in the form of *English Grammar in Use* (Murphy 1985), which became a bestseller and has gone through several editions, published by Cambridge University Press). In Italy, at the time of the so-called 'communicative revolution', a plethora of home-grown pedagogical grammar books for EFL students was published and they went on to enjoy huge commercial success. The genre is alive and well to this day in Italy, so much so that new editions of 'classics' published in the 1980s and 1990s are regularly issued and constantly top the bestseller lists for school books.

The grammaticographical corpus analysed in this chapter consists of a sample of Italian pedagogical grammar books for EFL learners published between 1980 and 2000. Before presenting the findings of my grammaticological study of this corpus, I provide an overview of the Italian language teaching background, in particular in relation to grammar teaching, at the time of the communicative turn in language teaching.

Tradition and Innovation: Language Teaching in Italy at the Time of the Communicative Turn

In Italy the effects of the communicative turn in mainstream foreign-language teaching started to be felt towards the latter part of the 1970s. At the time communicative textbooks published in the UK (such as the *Strategies* series by Abbs and Freebairn (1977-82)) had begun to be used in Italian secondary schools; and local offices of the British Council were extremely active in spreading the new communicative 'gospel' (cf. Pedrazzini, in this volume). By the mid-1980s the call for a 'return to grammar' that began to be heard throughout Europe as teachers and students were faced with what many viewed as 'grammarless' language-teaching materials (Cook 1989: 2) resonated strongly in Italy. The Italian language-teaching context had indeed been mainly characterized by a long-standing tradition of both Italian as a mother tongue and foreign-language teaching being modelled upon the teaching of classical languages. This placed a premium on the teaching of grammar, which usually involved a deductive approach consisting of the explicit presentation of grammar rules, grammar parsing exercises (in mother-tongue teaching) and translation (in foreign language teaching). In the 1970s this tradition had somewhat been shaken by local developments in educational linguistics, such as the concept of *educazione linguistica* [language education] (GISCEL 1975), which was the result of years of theoretical reflection by academics such as Tullio De Mauro and Raffaele Simone (e.g. De Mauro 1972; Simone 1979) and practical experimentation in schools by teachers and teacher educators, who were supported by a recently established professional association, *Lingua e Nuova Didattica* (*LEND*).[2] Although originally intended to refer only to the teaching of Italian as a mother tongue, *educazione linguistica* soon came to be viewed as an all-encompassing philosophy of school-based language teaching, including foreign and classical languages as well as the teaching of Italian as a national language and of mother tongues different from standard Italian (regional dialects and minority languages) (Balboni 2009).

One of the cornerstones of *educazione linguistica* was a shift in focus from the teaching of grammar as an inventory of prescriptive rules concerning orthography, morphology and syntax to grammar teaching as instrumental to the development of abilities in language use. The process of *riflessione sulla lingua* [reflection on language], as grammar teaching was renamed, was to start from the implicit knowledge that learners already had or had acquired through engaging in meaning-based tasks and gradually lead learners to become aware of features and regularities in language use, as instantiated in oral as well as written texts, that might help them become more skilled communicators (Lugarini and Rizzardi 1988). This emphasis on language in use was, of course, in keeping with what appeared to be advocated by the communicative approach in the foreign-language-teaching field (e.g. Widdowson 1978). However, the process of *riflessione sulla lingua* entailed that language features were eventually to be 'raised to consciousness', in other words, explicit attention was to be drawn to them. This contrasted with the *perception* that many teachers in Italy had of the communicative approach, which, in their eyes at least, was all about 'grammarless' implicit teaching. It should be pointed out that despite initial enthusiasm fuelled by the progressive climate of the 1970s, by the mid-1980s the actual impact of the *educazione linguistica* movement on grassroots language teaching in Italian schools had still been negligible, as witnessed (in the teaching of Italian as a national language), for example, by Gensini (1985), who detected little evidence of the new 'philosophy' in the most widely used textbooks for Italian as a mother tongue.

Given the central role that grammar had played for decades in mainstream language teaching in Italy as well as its recent incarnation as *riflessione sulla lingua* in the *educazione linguistica* movement, it is little surprise that those Italian applied linguists who had been relatively open to the proposals of methodological innovation coming from abroad soon started to question the apparent lack of grammar and grammar teaching in communicative language teaching. In her plenary speech at the 1985 annual *Lingua e Nuova Didattica* conference, devoted to the issue of 'Grammar and Communicative Teaching', Wanda D'Addio, Professor of Language Teaching Methodology at the University of Rome, stated that, amid the various attempts at implementation of the communicative approach in Italy, a return to grammar was in the air (Giunchi 1986). D'Addio pinpointed two trends this 'comeback' seemed to have spawned: firstly, a more 'innovative' one, which viewed the communicative approach as an opportunity to extend the traditional remit of grammar analysis to include language in use (semantics/pragmatics/discourse) and language variation (register and genre analysis), and called for a revamp of grammar teaching in line with the *riflessione sulla lingua* approach associated with *educazione linguistica*, as the traditional, deductive approach hardly seemed to suit the learning of semantic, text-based phenomena; secondly, a trend branded 'reductive/traditional', which called for a reinstatement of grammar analysis and structural practice alongside work on functions and communicative activities, without necessarily going the way of reassessing the traditional ways of conceiving of and teaching grammar — pragmatics and grammar were thus to co-exist in this approach, but they were hardly to influence each other.

During the conference, D'Addio, who, as one of *LEND*'s founding members, was a supporter of the 'innovative' trend alongside other conference presenters (Anna Ciliberti, Maria Teresa Prat Zagrebelsky), also raised the issue of what forms and functions pedagogical grammar might have within the new Italian communicative-language-teaching context. The debate about pedagogical grammar (centring on questions such as 'Is pedagogical grammar an application of linguistic grammar?'; 'Can theoretical eclecticism be justified in pedagogical grammar?'; 'How do pedagogical grammar rules differ from 'linguistic' rules?', and so on), which had already occupied applied linguists in several European countries (UK, France, Germany; e.g. Corder 1972, 1974; Noblitt 1972; Mindt 1981) in the previous decade, had not had much of an echo in Italy. Pedagogical grammar was, however, to be the subject of a number of publications in Italy during the 1980s which, taking up and developing the 'innovative' point of view, called for a reappraisal of grammar and grammar teaching in communicative language teaching along the lines of the *riflessione sulla lingua* approach and according to the principles of *educazione linguistica*. These publications shared a strong orientation to *ricerca didattica*, that is, 'research on teaching', and aimed to bridge the gap between research findings and the day-to-day practice of the ordinary language teacher. The field of Italian as a mother tongue was the first to be investigated (e.g. Ambel 1982), while the foreign-language domain took a few years to catch up (Prat Zagrebelsky 1985; Ciavatta et al. 1987; Giunchi 1990). Except for Prat Zagrebelsky's *Grammatica e lingua straniera* (1985), publications in this area tended to take the form of edited collections of papers (often reports of *ricerca didattica*), which made them relatively unappealing to teachers, who were not necessarily familiar with this kind of academic genre. However, Prat Zagrebelsky (1985) had a more reassuring organization as a 'teaching handbook' and succeeded in raising the main issues stemming from recent research relating to the teaching of grammar within a communicative orientation while at the same time providing practical ways of dealing with these issues in the Italian secondary school context. Among the various facets of the learning/teaching of foreign languages in Italian schools covered in Prat Zagrebelsky (1985), I shall summarize a few here that are particularly pertinent to the focus of this chapter:

- *Grammar Teaching and the National Syllabuses*. Prat Zagrebelsky reviews the syllabuses for the different types of secondary schools existing in Italy. While the syllabuses for lower secondary schools had just been revamped (1979) and seemed to have taken on board the proposals of the *educazione linguistica* movement for the teaching of both Italian and foreign languages, other types of secondary school relied on syllabuses dating to the 1960s or in some cases to the 1920s. The syllabuses' old-fashioned nature and the fact that they tended to provide only very general guidelines about contents and methodology had meant that teachers were often dependent on the choices made by textbook authors;

- *The Role of the 'Pedagogical Reference Grammar for Students'*. Prat Zagrebelsky devotes a section of her handbook to the analysis of 'reference grammars', introducing the now familiar distinction between 'descriptive' and 'pedagogical' grammars. She points out that pedagogical grammar books for students written in Italian were still few and far between, and that those in existence had a very traditional outlook and organization and were often new editions of older books modelled on those used for the teaching of classical languages (e.g. Grasso and Bottalla 1958). According to her, this state of affairs contributed to the fallacy that grammar is 'one' and does not change over time but also seemed to point to the need for up-to-date grammar books as complements to the new communicative materials being used in intermediate and advanced level language teaching (Prat Zagrebelsky 1985: 26);

- *A Contrastive Approach in Grammar Description*. Prat Zagrebelsky notes that, unlike other countries (the Netherlands, Poland) which had a long-standing tradition of contrastive pedagogical grammars based on the analysis of learner errors, in Italy contrastive analyses were still 'parziali' [partial] (ibid.: 51). Prat Zagrebelsky suggests that a contrastive approach to grammar description need not focus exclusively on areas of difference between two languages but may also highlight similarities. In the latter case, what is focused on are universal aspects of languages or areas that are common to both languages with a view to building on knowledge that students already have;

- *Difficulties in the Implementation of Communicative Grammar Teaching*. Prat Zagrebelsky does not shy away from the difficulties inherent in the implementation of com- municative grammar teaching in the Italian secondary school context. She points to the patchy nature of available descriptions of discourse/pragmatic aspects of language use, and the complex relationship between discourse/pragmatics and language exponents. More relevant to the Italian context is the preoccupation that the newer language teaching approaches might have brought about a lessening of students' cognitive engagement. Hence, the 'ambiguo rimpianto' [ambiguous longing] expressed by many teachers for the times when foreign- language teaching was more akin to the teaching of classical languages (ibid.: 94);

- *A 'Cognitive' Approach to Grammar Teaching within Communicative Language Teaching*. Prat Zagrebelsky stresses the importance of including *riflessione sulla lingua* activities at different stages of a communicative language-teaching sequence. The focus of such activities should extend, to the extent that this is feasible, to discourse/pragmatic aspects of the language and to analysis of the processes of language use. The suggested activities include a preliminary stage, where targeted features of the language are made salient to the students, and guided questions, which should lead students to compare, analyse and formulate hypotheses about language data.

It could be argued that in the mid-1980s and for at least a decade the Italian language-teaching context was characterized by a highly vocal minority of 'innovators' and a (relatively) silent majority of 'traditionalists'. While applied linguists (and some teachers and teacher educators) were engaged in a flurry of scholarly activity resulting in theoretical proposals and attempts at practical experimentation aimed at promoting an 'innovative' solution to the issue of grammar in communicative language teaching, many ordinary teachers, although aware that communicative language teaching was not going to go away, viewed it as complementary to traditional deductive grammar teaching practices, of which they were not willing to let go. Surveys such as the one carried out by Anna Giacalone Ramat (1983) among foreign language teachers in the Pavia province showed that the majority of those teachers polled strongly supported the explicit teaching of grammar using a deductive approach.

Against this backdrop, Italian educational publishers did not stand still and from the mid-1980s began to issue pedagogical grammar books for EFL students which were touted as a practical solution to the grammar-in-communicative-language-teaching conundrum. The findings of the analysis of a sample of Italian pedagogical grammar books for EFL students will be presented next.

Italian Pedagogical Grammar Books for EFL Students: A Corpus

The sample selected for the study consists of eleven pedagogical grammar books for Italian students of English published in Italy mainly between the mid-1980s and the late-1990s. The selection was based on the findings of an informal survey of Italian English-language teachers and teacher educators, who were asked to single out the most influential Italian pedagogical grammars for EFL students published in the period between 1980 and 2000. It should be pointed out that the items in the corpus are essentially five books together with variations issued, in different versions, at later dates:

ANDREOLLI, MARIA GIOVANNA. 1998. *A Reference Grammar for Italian Students* (Turin: Petrini)
ANDREOLLI, MARIA GIOVANNA, MARGHERITA LEVI FIORETTO, and ORNELLA GARIO. 1986. *English Grammar for Italian Students* (Turin: Petrini)
ANDREOLLI, MARIA GIOVANNA, MARGHERITA LEVI FIORETTO and ORNELLA GARIO. 1992. *English Grammar for Italian Students. New edition* (Turin: Petrini)
BONOMI, MAURETTA, GIUSY PESENTI BASILI, LILIANA SCHWAMMENTHAL, and ELISABETTA STROHMENGER. 1988. *The Grammar You Need* (Milan: Principato)
BONOMI, MAURETTA, GIUSY PESENTI BASILI, and LILIANA SCHWAMMENTHAL. 1994. *Grammar Matters* (Milan: Principato)
CAMESASCA, EMMA, IPPOLITA MARTELLOTTA, and ANGELA GALLAGHER. 1993. *Working with Grammar* (Milan: Longman)

CAMESASCA, EMMA, ANGELA GALLAGHER, and IPPOLITA MARTELLOTTA. 1998. *New Working with Grammar* (Milan: Longman)

DE DEVITIIS, GUIDO, LUCIANO MARIANI, and KIERAN O'MALLEY. 1984. *Grammatica inglese della comunicazione* (Bologna: Zanichelli)

DE DEVITIIS, GUIDO, LUCIANO MARIANI, and KIERAN O'MALLEY. 1989. *Grammatica inglese della comunicazione. Seconda edizione* (Bologna: Zanichelli)

PALLINI, LELIO. 1996. *Grammar Alive* (Rapallo: CIDEB)

JEFFRIES, DAVID, and LELIO PALLINI. 1999. *Talking Grammar* (Rapallo: CIDEB)

The aim of the analysis is to ascertain how Italian pedagogical grammar books for EFL students tackle the issue of grammar in communicative language teaching. Do they take on board the calls for an extension of the remit of grammar to include semantic and pragmatic aspects of language in use, and language variation? In this analysis, the paratexts (introductions, prefaces etc.) and the explanatory and illustrative sections of the books (descriptions and examples) were scrutinized from a qualitative standpoint.

I shall not dwell on the general structure and organization of the books. A more detailed presentation of the general features of Italian pedagogical grammar books for EFL students can be found in Nava (2014). It is, however, of interest for the purposes of the present study to mention that the books in the corpus claim to be 'complete' grammar books — in the sense that they are meant to cater for the needs of upper secondary school students throughout their five years of schooling. We shall see that the term 'complete' also hints at the actual use that has been made of the books in Italian schools. On the whole, as stated in the introductions/prefaces, self-study as well as classroom use of the books is envisaged. However, classroom use is obviously what the books are mainly designed for as many of the texts do not provide keys to the exercises in a form easily accessible to students (e.g. keys are collected in separate booklets).

The authors of the books in the corpus claim to be practising teachers. Except in one case (Luciano Mariani), they do not appear to have had a direct role in the flurry of teacher-training activities, seminars, discussions and refresher courses about the principles and practices of the communicative approach that took place in Italy during the 1980s.

Grammar and/or Communication?

As will be shown in more detail below, the books in the corpus seem to take a stand overall on the relationship between 'communication' and 'grammar', siding as a rule with the 'traditional' camp. (Partial) exceptions are the two editions of De Devitiis et al. (1984, 1989), Andreolli (1998), and the two editions of Andreolli et al. (1986, 1992).

Thus, the introductory parts of several books feature references to the perceived shortcomings of notional/functional approaches in the area of grammar teaching. In Bonomi et al. (1988: 5), for instance, it is mentioned that the notional/functional coursebook, which is acknowledged to be 'the most modern and widespread solution',[3] lacks 'a clear and detailed presentation of grammar rules'. By the same token, communicative exercises, while suitable for 'the practice and integration of the four main skills', turn out to be unsuited to the 'memorization and consolidation of morphosyntactic structures'. As a result, teachers often have to supplement the information provided by the coursebook, resorting to 'dictating or handing out notes' and preparing suitable exercises (ibid.). Camesasca et al. (1993: 5) touch on similar issues and also point out that 'teaching experience has shown how difficult it turns out to be for beginners to make sense of the different uses and structures if they are not illustrated clearly and systematically'. The need for 'systematicity' and 'exhaustiveness' is in keeping with the Italian tradition of studying classical and modern languages, whereby grammar is viewed as an area of knowledge that is valuable in itself, irrespective of its role in facilitating the actual practical mastery and spontaneous use of the target language by the learner. As such, the more exhaustive and detailed the presentation of this area of knowledge is, the more highly regarded the material that features it may tend to be.

The quotation above from Camesasca et al. (1993) exemplifies the way calls for a return to grammar are often claimed to be warranted by the authors' long-standing classroom experience. Several communicative textbooks — in particular, the earlier ones (e.g. Elviri et al. 1982) — were written by applied linguists based in universities, and this was thought to be one of the reasons why such materials were often felt to be out of touch with teachers' needs and preferences. By casting themselves as 'classroom teachers', it appears that the authors of many Italian pedagogical grammar books are marking their distance from academia and reclaiming their role as 'experts', at the same time implicitly rejecting the value of research developments in the area of language learning and teaching in favour of time-honoured on-the-job experience.

While refraining from referring explicitly to the *riflessione sulla lingua* approach, a few books in the corpus highlight the advantages of 'cognitive learning' (Andreolli et al. 1986: iii) to complement implicit learning, associated with the communicative approach, particularly in view of different 'learning strategies' (De Devitiis et al. 1984: v) favoured by students.

Despite their ambivalent attitude towards communicative language learning and teaching, when it comes to the actual selection of linguistic contents, the Italian pedagogical grammars in question claim to open up their description of the language to the new theoretical insights underlying the communicative approach. Unique in the corpus is the approach taken by De Devitiis et al. (1984, 1989). These books call themselves 'grammars of English communication' and the authors state explicitly that they are organized according to 'broad notional/functional categories' (De Devitiis et al. 1984: v). Selection of contents is said to have been made through an analysis of 'the most widely used elementary and intermediate level English language textbooks' (De Devitiis et al. 1984: v). The obvious inspiration for the books by Devitiis et al. is Leech and Svartvik (1975), a reference grammar book published in the UK and aimed at university students which claims to employ 'a communicative rather than a structural approach' (Leech and Svartvik 1975: 11). After two introductory sections devoted to 'Varieties of English' and 'Intonation', the core of

Leech and Svartvik is the exploration of 'Grammar in use', organized on the basis of four types of 'meaning or meaning organization' (Leech and Svartvik 1975: 12). The final part of Leech and Svartvik is a 'Grammatical Compendium', where more traditional structural categories are arranged alphabetically and concisely presented. The contents and the organization of the first edition of Devitiis et al. (1984) are largely based on the notional categories illustrated in the third part of Leech and Svartvik (1975). This is thought to be enough to cater to students' 'grammar' needs. The second (1989) edition, however, which was prepared under the supervision of a grammarian from Longman, the publisher of Quirk et al. (1985) as well as Leech and Svartvik (1975),[4] saw the addition of a preliminary section called 'Language Structures', which contains a heterogeneous list of topics ('The sentence'; 'Replacing and omitting'; 'Personal, reflexive and reciprocal pronouns', etc.).[5]

Rather than going the way of selecting and organizing the contents according to notional/functional categories, as is done by De Devitiis et al. (1984), all the other grammars in the corpus appear to feature 'functional' sections. Pallini (1996), for example, in Chapter 3 includes morphosyntactic topics ('the imperative'; 'personal pronouns (object form)'; 'Present simple'; etc.) as well as, in a section called 'Notes', functional exponents ('Asking and giving directions'; 'Asking about likes and dislikes'; 'Asking and giving personal information'; etc.). A further section named 'Peculiarities' contains lexical sets (e.g. days of the week, seasons and months) and short comments on other lexical issues (e.g. translating *Signore/signora/signorina*). This is particularly representative of the corpus, where the strands of 'grammar' and 'pragmatics' seem to run parallel without displacing the way grammar is traditionally conceived of and described. Even in De Devitiis et al. (1989) many of the grammatical categories employed are those found in traditional and structural grammar, for example, in Chapter 6: 'Auxiliary and ordinary verbs: Auxiliary verbs and modal auxiliary verbs'; 'Ordinary verbs'; 'Verbs followed by the infinitive and/ or by the -ing form').

The inclusion of functional and lexical sections in Italian pedagogical grammars for EFL students as 'add-ons' to the main morphosyntactic core is particularly evident in those books (Bonomi et al. 1988, 1994; Camesasca et al. 1993, 1998; Pallini 1996; Pallini and Jeffries 1999) claiming to have sequenced the syllabus according to the principle of complexity: from 'simple to more complex', much in the way that this is very often done in coursebooks. We are thus faced with 'grammar books' that follow the sequencing of coursebooks and include morphosyntax, functions, lexis and exercises. As both the 'lexicogrammatical' *and* the 'communicative' sides of language teaching appeared to be somehow taken care of in these pedagogical grammar books for EFL learners, it is hardly surprising that what often happened in Italian classrooms in the 1980s and 1990s, after the novelty of communicative textbooks wore off, is that these supposedly ancillary grammar books ended up being used by English-language teachers as the main teaching textbooks, displacing, at least in the last three years of upper secondary school, communicative coursebooks.

Another aspect that made home-grown pedagogical grammars books for EFL students particularly appealing to Italian teachers vis-à-vis not only communicative textbooks but also UK-produced pedagogical grammars is the emphasis that they appeared to place on the learners' L1. As Prat Zagrebelsky's book from 1985 shows, the role of the L1 and of a comparative L1/L2 approach in grammar teaching was not ignored by the Italian applied linguists who attempted to make sense of grammar within a communicative approach. Her own suggestion of highlighting similarities, and not only differences, between native language and target language, including general laws of discourse organization, fits in with an approach that values learners' previous knowledge and contributions to the learning process. In the pedagogical-grammar-book corpus, claims can be traced in the introductory sections of several books that the presentation of the grammatical features of English capitalizes on learners' knowledge of Italian grammar. While Andreolli et al. (1986: iii) refer to L1 knowledge as (in a positive sense) 'linguistic and cultural baggage' which has been shown by cognitive psychologists to play a role in the acquisition of the L2, Bonomi et al. (1988: 6) mention the advantage of being able to use terminology which students are already familiar with (that of Latin-based traditional grammar). Pallini (1996) and Jeffries and Pallini (1999), two very popular books, call themselves 'constrastive English grammars for Italians'. The introductory section in Jeffries and Pallini (1999: 5) mentions that grammar is presented from the perspective of Italian students, 'highlighting contrasts and similarities between the two languages'.

Let us now provide a few examples of how the grammar in communicative language teaching issue is dealt with in the actual explanatory and illustrative sections of the grammar books in the corpus. If we were to pinpoint clues that the descriptions and examples of a grammar book have been influenced by the communicative turn, we might identify two pertinent aspects:

* the traditional concept of linguistic norm, based on formal, written, prescriptive conventions, being superseded by a more flexible concept accounting for different usages (formal v. informal, written v. spoken, etc.);

* the pedagogical presentation, in the form of examples, providing, as highlighted by Howatt with Widdowson (2004: 330), samples of language as a unified event — 'wholes' such as utterances, texts, conversations, or discourses.

Over the whole corpus there are in fact attempts to deal with the issue of linguistic variability but they usually boil down to the presentation of possible alternative examples labelled 'formal/informal', such as this pair from Bonomi et al. (1988: 247):

> This morning I found a sparrow, whose wing was broken, lying on the balcony (formal)
>
> This morning I found a sparrow with a broken wing lying on the balcony (informal).

Incidentally, Bonomi et al. (1988) is the only book that explicitly refers to the concept of 'norm' ('absolute necessity that the student be aware of the linguistic norm to abide by and refer to' (Bonomi et al. 1988: 5)). De Devitiis et al. (1984, 1989) and Andreolli (1998) make indirect mention of the issue of *where* the 'rules' presented in the explanations originate ('most common usage of the language' (De Devitiis et al. 1984: v)), with Andreolli (1998) going as far as providing a caveat showing the author's awareness of the growing phenomenon of English as a *lingua franca*: 'like any grammar book, this text cannot account for different usages originating from geographical variation and the evolution of the language. This phenomenon is particularly widespread in English, which is increasingly expanding as a lingua franca' (Andreolli et al. 1998: iii).

The examples above from Bonomi et al. (1988) are representative of the approach often taken by grammar-book authors in tackling register differences. To highlight how the degree of formality can be conveyed through different grammatical structures, the same sentence is presented in two labelled versions which only differ with respect to one grammatical feature (here the alternative between supplementary relative clause and post-modification through a prepositional phrase). It is apparent that the presence of a formal grammatical feature is not enough to make the first version a likely formal utterance, as it would be very hard to conjure up a natural formal context in which the communicative topic was 'a sparrow lying outside a balcony'. This example shows up another weakness of many grammar books in the corpus in relation to the 'communicative' concept of connectedness. Most of the examples provided are de-contextualized sentences, and they appear to have been concocted to fit the long lists of descriptive subsections rather than the other way round.

Conclusion

The genre of pedagogical grammar books for EFL students became increasingly popular in Italy between the mid-1980s and the late 1990s. After the first attempts at the implementation of communicative language teaching in Italian schools in the early 1980s, applied linguists, teachers and teacher educators had advocated a return to grammar, which was interpreted differently by those who thought of the communicative approach as an opportunity to revamp traditional views on grammar and grammar teaching (the 'innovators') vis-à-vis those who longed for a reinstatement of deductive grammar teaching alongside 'functional' practice (the 'traditionalists').

The analysis of a corpus of Italian pedagogical grammar books for EFL students has provided some evidence that in trying to make sense of developments in language teaching, authors of Italian grammar books mainly looked to the past. Indeed, the inclusion of functional inventories and lexical development sections in many Italian pedagogical grammars as well as a simple-to-complex organization of the subject matter led to their being used not *alongside* but *in place of* the main (communicative) textbooks in Italian English-language-teaching classrooms. Rather than 'revolutionizing' language teaching, the communicative approach, although much alluded to in the paratexts of these books, became the excuse for a return to grammar-teaching practices that had little to do with the development of the use of English in real-life situations. This was due to the influence of the local tradition of foreign-language teaching, often modelled on the teaching of classical languages, which valued grammar as an area of knowledge and deductive grammar learning as a highly intellectual activity. Apart from a few exceptions, in Italian pedagogical grammars for EFL learners little impact can be detected of the home-grown *educazione linguistica* movement and its 'progressive' view of grammar as a communicative resource.

In its attempt to contribute to the history of English grammaticography, the present chapter has deliberately adopted a narrow focus on one *local* incarnation of a grammaticographical genre. This narrowness of focus has enabled me to tap my 'insider' knowledge as an English-language learner and teacher for the past thirty years in the context analysed and thus complement grammaticological analysis with data about a specific context of practice (Smith 2016). As a contribution to the wider field of the history of language learning and teaching, it could be argued that, although the findings of the study cannot be easily generalized to other contexts, they do seem to point to a more general trend in language teaching history: that language teaching 'innovations' hardly stand a chance of success unless they take account of local educational traditions.

Bibliography

Abbs, Brian, and Ingrid Freebairn. 1977. *Starting Strategies* (Harlow: Longman)

——, and Ingrid Freebairn. 1979. *Building Strategies* (Harlow: Longman)

——, and Ingrid Freebairn. 1986. *Discoveries* (Harlow: Longman)

——, et al. 1980. *Communicating Strategies* (Bologna: Zanichelli; Harlow: Longman)

Ambel, Mario. (ed.). 1982. *Insegnare la lingua: quale grammatica?* (Milan: Mondadori)

Balboni, Paolo. 2009. *Storia dell'educazione linguistica in Italia: dalla legge Casati alla riforma Gelmini* (Turin: UTET Università)

Chalker, Sylvia. 1994. 'Pedagogical Grammar: Principles and Problems', in *Grammar and the Language Teacher*, ed. by Martin Bygate, Alan Tonkyn and Eddie Williams (London: Longman), pp. 31-44

Ciavatta, Paola, Giuliana Centazza, and Marisa Currò (eds). 1987. *Grammatica e insegnamento comunicativo* (Milan: Mondadori)

Cook, Vivian. 1989. 'The Relevance of Grammar in the Applied Linguistics of Language Teaching', *Trinity College Dublin Occasional Papers*, 22

Corder, S. P. 1972. *An Introduction to Applied Linguistics* (London: Penguin)

——. 1974. 'Pedagogical Grammars or the Pedagogy of Grammar?', in *Linguistic Insights in Applied Linguistics*, ed. by S.P. Corder and Eddy Roulet (Paris: Didier), pp. 167-73

De Mauro, Tullio. 1972. *Storia linguistica dell'Italia unita* (Rome: Laterza)

Ellis, Rod. 2002. 'Methodological Options in Grammar Teaching Materials', in *New Perspectives on Grammar Teaching in Second Language Classrooms*, ed. by Eli Hinkel and Sandra Fotos (Mahwah, NJ: Erlbaum), pp. 155-80

Elviri, Fiorella, Maria Cecilia Rizzardi, and Daniela Bertocchi. 1982. *Got the Message?* (Milan: Principato)

Gensini, Stefano. 1985. 'Le grammatiche dell'italiano: appunti per la discussione', *Lingua e Nuova Didattica*, 3: 3-13

Giacalone Ramat, Anna (ed.). 1983. *La lingua straniera nella scuola secondaria: un'indagine in provincia di Pavia* (= Supplemento a *Educazione Oggi*, March 1983)

Giscel. 1975. *L'educazione linguistica* (Padua: CLEUP)

Giunchi, Paola. 1986. 'Grammatica e insegnamento comunicativo', *Lingua e Nuova Didattica*, 1: 3-13

—— (ed.). 1990. *Grammatica esplicita e grammatica implicita* (Bologna: Zanichelli)

Grasso, Vincenzo, and Ugo Bottalla. 1958. *Nuova grammatica ragionata della lingua inglese* (Turin: Casanova)

Graustein, Gottfried, and Gerhard Leitner (eds). 1989. *Reference Grammars and Modern Linguistic Theory* (Tübingen: Niemeyer)

Howatt, A. P. R., with H. G. Widdowson. 2004 [1984]. *A History of English Language Teaching*, 2nd edn (Oxford: Oxford University Press)

Leech, Geoffrey, and Jan Svartvik. 1975. *A Communicative Grammar of English* (London: Longman)

Leitner, Gerhard. 1984. 'English Grammaticology', *International Review of Applied Linguistics*, 23: 199-215

—— (ed.). 1986. *The English Reference Grammar: Language and Linguistics, Writers and Readers* (Tübingen: Niemeyer)

—— (ed.). 1991. *English Traditional Grammars: An International Perspective* (Amsterdam: Benjamins)

Linn, Andrew. 2006. 'English Grammar Writing', in *The Handbook of English Linguistics*, ed. by Bas Aarts and April McMahon (Blackwell: Oxford), pp. 72-92

Lugarini, Edoardo, and Maria Cecilia Rizzardi. 1988. 'La riflessione sulla lingua', *Lingua e Nuova Didattica*, 2: 94-95

Mindt, Dieter. 1981. 'Linguistische Grammatik, didaktische Grammatik und pädagogische Grammatik', *Neusprachliche Mitteilungen*, 34: 28-35

Murphy, Raymond. 1985. *English Grammar in Use* (Cambridge: Cambridge University Press)

Nava, Andrea. 2008. *Grammar by the Book: The Passive in Pedagogical Grammar Books for EFL/ESL teachers* (Milan: LED)

——. 2014. 'Back to the Future. La grammatica pedagogica inglese di riferimento in Italia', in *Perfiles para la historia y crítica de la gramática del español en Italia: siglos XIX y XX. Confluencia y cruces de tradicionas gramaticográficas*, ed. by Felix San Vicente, Ana Lourdes De Hériz and Maria Enriqueta Pérez Vazques (Bologna: Bononia University Press), pp. 331-46

Noblitt, John. 1972. 'Pedagogical Grammar: Towards a Theory of Foreign Language Materials Preparation', *International Review of Applied Linguistics*, 10: 313-31

Palmer, Harold. 1924. *A Grammar of Spoken English, on a Strictly Phonetic Basis* (Cambridge: Heffer)

Prat Zagrebelsky, Maria Teresa. 1985. *Grammatica e lingua straniera* (Florence: La Nuova Italia)

Quirk, Randolph, et al. 1985. *A Comprehensive Grammar of the English Language* (London: Longman)

Simone, Raffaele (ed.). 1979. *L'educazione linguistica* (Florence: La Nuova Italia)

Smith, Richard. 2016. 'Building "Applied Linguistic Historiography": Rationale, Scope, and Methods', *Applied Linguistics*, 37: 71-87

Widdowson, H. G. 1978. *Teaching Language as Communication* (Oxford: Oxford University Press)

Notes to Chapter 17

1. In a seminal article, Leitner (1984) refers to the study of grammar writing and the principles on which grammars are based as 'grammaticology'.
2. The association *Lingua e Nuova Didattica* (*LEND*), which was founded in Rome in 1971, is aimed at the propagation of the principles of *educazione linguistica* and the development of innovative language-teaching practices.

3. I have translated the original Italian into English for this and other quotations from the paratexts in the corpus of pedagogical grammars.

4. Luciano Mariani, personal communication.

5. Changes in the second edition of Devitiis et al. (1989) were dictated by feedback from teachers, who felt that many familiar topics were missing from the first edition or at least were difficult to locate in the chapters organized according to notional/functional categories (Luciano Mariani, personal communication).

CHAPTER 18

❖

A Diachronic–Comparative Analysis of Three Foreign Language Teaching Manuals from the Perspective of Skill Acquisition Theory

Raquel Criado

The purpose of this chapter is to highlight the need to add a cognitive perspective to pedagogical and historical angles when assessing language teaching methods so as to obtain a deeper understanding of their potential contribution to language learning. This new perspective is based on Skill Acquisition Theory (SAT) from Cognitive Psychology. It distinguishes between declarative knowledge (knowledge about the linguistic system), procedural knowledge (instrumental knowledge) and automatized knowledge (the refinement of procedural knowledge or fluent and automatic deployment of communicative competence). The activities of the three middle lessons from three elementary textbooks were cognitively analysed. The three methods to which they adhered were the Grammar-Translation Method (G-T), Audio-Lingual Method (ALM) and the weak version of Communicative Language Teaching (CLT). The materials were dated 1973 (the first edition having been published in 1925), 1966 and 1984 respectively. All of them allegedly shared the same overarching goal: catering for students' communicative needs. The pedagogical tools of G-T and ALM were found to not be adequate to foster solid proceduralization, since meaningful and mechanical drills do not enable meaning–form relationships in the students' long-term memory. The early CLT materials were potentially more effective as proceduralization seems to be activated with communicative drills. The application of a cognitive perspective to the analysis of authentic textbooks contributes to enriching our knowledge of the History of Language Learning and Teaching and supports the call for interdisciplinary studies in this field.[1]

Introduction

In the history of language learning and teaching there have been a very wide range of different pedagogical attempts to provide the best possible way to learn a foreign language (FL). However, such a rich repertoire should not be taken as implying that most attempts have enabled students to master foreign languages successfully. Indeed, new methods are usually set up on the basis that previous methods have failed in some way or other.

In this chapter, I advocate and explain the rationale for an interdisciplinary approach to materials analysis to enable a more grounded understanding of the potential of such materials to contribute to language learning. More specifically, I argue for supplementing existing (evidently important) pedagogically based analyses in the field of History of Language Learning and Teaching (HoLLT) with cognitive analyses specifically based on Skill Acquisition Theory (SAT). If (foreign) language mastery is a type of brain-generated knowledge, it seems reasonable to apply insights from Cognitive Psychology to the evaluation of both new and old language teaching methods in order to enrich our understanding about why and how their materials seem to be more or less successful in leading students to language mastery.

SAT involves regarding the development of communicative language proficiency as a type of skill learning (DeKeyser 1998, 2009, 2015, etc.; Johnson 1996). It focuses on how language knowledge evolves from theoretical information about forms until language mastery is attained. Applications of insights from Cognitive Psychology in general, and SAT in particular, have so far been absent from the history of language teaching methods (e.g. Larsen-Freeman and Anderson 2011; Musumeci 2009; Richards and Rodgers 2014).

I focus on three methods which have had a large impact on Foreign Language Teaching (FLT) in both Europe and the United States: a form of the Grammar-Translation Method (G-T), Audio-Lingual Method (ALM), and the 'weak' version (cf. Howatt 1984: 279) of Communicative Language Teaching (CLT). Assuming a consensus that G-T and ALM have been largely discredited these days, I attempt to answer these two intertwined questions:

(1). Why did G-T and ALM not enable students to become communicatively competent?

(2). Is the weak version of CLT potentially more efficient than G-T and ALM at enabling students to become communicatively competent?

The remainder of this chapter is structured into four sections: 'The cognitive framework' includes an overview of key concepts from SAT, which are then applied to the analysis of the coursebook units in the following section. The findings of this analysis are discussed in the final section, which is followed by some concluding remarks.

The Cognitive Framework

The field of Second Language Acquisition (SLA) research has been enriched by a plethora of theories and approaches which attempt to account for how learners achieve mastery of a second or foreign language (L2): socio-cultural theory, emphasizing social, collaborative and interactive processes (e.g. Lantolf, Thorne and

Poehner 2015); 'emergentism' and a 'complex and dynamic systems' approach (e.g. Larsen-Freeman and Cameron 2008), which accentuate the complex and adaptive nature of language learning as emerging bottom-up from experiences with the L2 rather than top-down from grammatical principles; these, in turn, are related to 'usage-based approaches' (e.g. Ellis and Wulff 2015; Verspoor, de Bot and Lowie 2011), which link language learning to frequent input exposure, and so on.

The application of SAT to FLT settings makes sense because a) such contexts do not offer the same amount and quality of input as 'naturalistic' second-language acquisition environments (Criado 2016; DeKeyser 2015); and b) SAT 'highlights the influence of explicit instruction, meaningful practice and feedback [...], which are three main elements pertaining to traditional school teaching' (Criado 2016: 2).

According to SAT there are three kinds of knowledge: declarative, procedural and automatized. Procedural and automatized knowledge are frequently equated but there exist quantitative and qualitative differences between them (DeKeyser 2015; DeKeyser and Criado 2013). Declarative knowledge is factual knowledge or 'know-that': for instance, knowing that 'London is the capital of the United Kingdom'. As applied to language learning, declarative knowledge encompasses knowledge related to the grammar and phonological rules but also lexis and the socio-cultural, pragmatic and textual conventions of a language. In other words, it involves knowledge *about* the system, such as knowing the rule for the formation of the third person singular in the present perfect tense in English. Given that we can normally verbalize it (as in the case of this particular grammar rule), declarative knowledge is traditionally associated with explicit, conscious knowledge. Indeed, the use of declarative knowledge is low-risk in the sense that 'conscious attention is devoted to it before operations using it are undertaken' (Johnson 1996: 83). However, this also implies that it is slower to use than procedural knowledge: it places heavy demands on students' working memory as attention is required in its processing and retrieval (Johnson 1996: 84).

Procedural knowledge is 'know-how-to' or instrumental knowledge, which encompasses physical skills (e.g. driving, cooking, and so on) and cognitive skills (e.g. writing research papers). In language learning, procedural knowledge involves knowing *how to use* the linguistic system at both receptive and productive levels, although this does not mean that performance is fully fluent and error-free. This is because procedural knowledge needs to become automatized, as is the case, for example, with learners whose performance shows hesitation — since they need consciously to recall information about forms — and still contains mistakes.

The result of fine-tuning procedural knowledge is automatized knowledge, which implies executing the above-mentioned skills autonomously without the intervention of explicit reflection. Fully automatized procedural knowledge is usually associated with implicit knowledge (though see DeKeyser (2009), who makes clear that declarative and explicit knowledge on the one hand and procedural and implicit knowledge on the other do not always overlap). Translated into familiar terms in the field of language learning, automatized knowledge entails fluent language use for communicative purposes which is, ideally, both pragmatically efficient and formally flawless.

How can the learner move from declarative to automatized knowledge? SAT answers this by distinguishing three successive stages leading to skill mastery: declarative, procedural and automatic (DeKeyser and Criado 2013). Firstly, successful skill mastery involves the attainment of a solid, initial, declarative base out of which procedural and automatized knowledge are generated. Accordingly, SAT favours the strong position on the 'interface issue' (see Han and Finneran (2014) for a review), which ascribes a causal role to declarative knowledge for obtaining automatized knowledge. Secondly, the transition from one stage to the next is achieved by means of feedback and different types of extensive practice adjusted to each phase: controlled and accuracy-focused practice (declarative stage); gradually less controlled practice with a more balanced emphasis on accuracy and fluency (procedural stage); and, finally, practice which is fully focused on communicative meaning and fluency (automatic stage). Once proceduralization is obtained, automatization is gradually achieved through engagement in extensive practice so as to 'decrease the time required to execute the task ("reaction time"), the percentage of errors ("error rate"), and the amount of attention required (and hence interference with/from other tasks, or more generally "robustness")' (DeKeyser 2015: 95). Moreover, in order to attain full fluency, practice should not only be extensive *and* meaningful but also incorporate 'real operating conditions' (ROCs: see Johnson 1996) or 'psychological authenticity' (Gatbonton and Segalowitz 1988). These are aimed at making learners' attention gradually deflect from forms through simulation of the psychological and social pressures exercised in real life (for instance, by adding background noise or intensifying cognitive complexity).

Analysis of Grammar-Translation, Audiolingual and Weak CLT Materials

This section presents a cognitive analysis of three textbooks taken as representative of G-T, ALM and CLT:

(1). Girau, Lewis Th. 1973. *The New British Method/Método de Inglés por Lewis Th. Girau. Libro primero*, 49th edn (Barcelona: Gráficas Casulleras) [Girau]
(2). Modern Language Association of America. 1966. *Modern Spanish. A Project of the Modern Language Association*, 2nd edn (New York: Harcourt, Brace & World) [*MS*]
(3). Swan, Michael, and Catherine Walter. 1984a. *The Cambridge English Course. Student's Book 1* (Cambridge: Cambridge University Press) [*CEC*]

The first and the third books are targeted at English as a Foreign Language (EFL) learners whilst the second one is addressed to L1 English speakers wanting to learn L2 Spanish. All the textbooks are aimed at an elementary level and a representative lesson/unit from the middle of each one of them was selected for analysis so that marked methodological aspects of beginning and final lessons could be avoided as much as possible: number twelve out of Girau's twenty-five lessons; number twelve out of the twenty-six units in *MS* and number 16B out of *CEC*'s thirty-two units.

The analyses were carried out through close examination of the activities of the selected lessons. Firstly, the general focus was distinguished — whether forms, skills, or so on; secondly, the objectives and the means to reach them were identified (for instance, practising a certain structure by directing learners to use it while responding to prompts requiring their personal opinions). Thirdly, this information was used to identify the overall type of activity and the type of knowledge potentially activated (for example, the activity type might be 'communicative drill' and the type of knowledge fostered 'procedural').

1. Girau's *Método de Inglés*

Background

Girau's first edition is dated 1925. It was so successful that many further editions and impressions were issued until the 1970s, although without fundamental alteration to the preliminary material, structure, contents, exercises or page numbering.

Girau (1973) stresses in his preface that English is essential for anyone engaged in different branches of modern society (such as business, science, art, sport, and so on). Thus, it can be inferred that his textbooks, intended for classroom study, attempted to cater for students' communicative needs. However, Girau's manuals can be considered to be based on a form of G–T: undoubtedly, the core element around which the contents and pedagogical activities revolve is grammar, which had to be memorized and practised (in this order).

Girau's motto — 'No theory without practice. No practice without theory' (1973: 5) — accurately summarizes his approach to learning and teaching. In his preface, Girau clearly states that natural methods do not work for adults in a FL context due to the differences between L1 acquisition and adult L2 learning. He favours providing students with ample grammar practice but dismisses engaging in such activities without previous solidly anchored grammatical knowledge. Nevertheless, the grammatical rules included are not cumbersome and, as in Ollendorff's *New Method* (1835, and many other editions), copious examples of everyday oral language use are included.

Summary of the Lesson

All the lessons in Girau's textbook reveal the same organization. Lesson 12 is centred on English impersonal verbs. These are verbs mostly reflecting natural phenomena (e.g. 'it is raining' / *está lloviendo*). The impersonal construction 'there is/are' is also included. The structure of the lesson is as follows:

(1) Grammar explanation
This is the longest part. Firstly, it includes a rule statement in plain Spanish about impersonal verbs followed by bilingual conjugation of the verb 'to rain'. Afterwards there is explanation about the impersonal construction 'there is/are' with bilingual examples, followed by its bilingual conjugation in indicative and imperative modes;

(2) Vocabulary
This section comprises a bilingual list of words and phrases. Words are listed in English and followed by their Spanish equivalents, with English

phonetic transcriptions — the latter clearly reflects the influence of the Reform Movement;

(3) Dialogue

What the dialogue really involves is not any kind of 'model conversation' but a bilingual list of independent pairs of questions and answers arranged in two parallel columns, the left one with the English version and the right one with its corresponding Spanish translation (for example, 'Was there thunder in the country yesterday?' / *¿Tronó ayer en el campo?*). The dialogue includes many examples relating back to the grammatical explanations and words and phrases from the vocabulary list;

(4) Exercises (direct and reverse translation)

Both the form of the dialogue and the reverse translation exercises (L1 Spanish → L2 English) are reminiscent of Ollendorff's exercises, while direct translation exercises (L2 English → L1 Spanish) were not included in Ollendorff's own textbooks but added by his imitators (Sánchez 2009). According to Girau (1973: 16), the dialogues and the translations should enable the students 'to learn a variety of idiomatic phrases and sentences, which would otherwise be difficult to acquire'. The direct translation seems to have been designed to reinforce the receptive learning of lexical phrases following the dialogues while, in principle, the reverse translation was meant to enable learners to actively manipulate or put into oral practice the previously studied grammar rules and lexical items. Both types of translation are arranged as coupled questions and answers, without any semantic relationship between the different couples;

(5) Conversation

Fully written in English, this section is divided into independent paragraphs, each of which starts with two or three affirmative sentences in bold depicting a situation (even if very briefly) and which are followed by related questions whose answers can be readily found in the preceding 'introductory' sentences. For example:

It is not bad weather to-day. It is fine weather. It is neither cold nor warm. How is the weather to-day? Is it cold? (Girau 1973: 129)

Both the introductory sentences and the questions are comprised of the structures and vocabulary previously studied in this lesson. Alongside the reverse translation exercises, this type of 'conversation' unmistakably evokes the interactions in Berlitz's Method and the exercises in Ollendorff's method, which 'were intended to provide materials for "conversations" between teacher and students' (Howatt with Widdowson 2004: 161). Due to the nature of the questions and answers involved, the reverse translation and the conversation constitute *meaningful drills* (Paulston 1970), which entail processing that cannot be considered genuinely communicative, as the actual answers are always known beforehand by both the speaker and the listener;

(6) Exercises

There are two final exercises whose completion requires utilizing the previously studied grammatical points and vocabulary. The first involves completing sentences by filling between one and four gaps. The second exercise is a transformation drill where the students rewrite seven affirmative sentences interrogatively.

Cognitive analysis

The grammatical explanations, the bilingual vocabulary lists and the dialogues are targeted at instilling declarative knowledge in the students' long-term memory (LTM) in an explicit, deductive way. Furthermore, the controlled practice involved in the direct translation exercise seems to be aimed at both checking and improving students' memorization of the rules and lexical items and improving their comprehension (DeKeyser 1998), or, in cognitive terms, at refining and restructuring declarative knowledge. Controlled practice is equally involved in the two final exercises, whose degree of reliance on meaning is much more limited than those from the preceding exercises, especially in the transformation drill.

At the same time, a certain rudimentary degree of proceduralization can also be inferred due to the presence of reverse translation and the conversation, where language is somehow contextualized. Very embryonic situations underlie each pair of questions and answers in the reverse translation and the introductory bolded sentences of each set in the conversation. Accordingly, forms are, to an extent, associated with meanings as framed within such proto-situations. This, together with the fact that the language use in these exercises involves the frequent repetition (rehearsal) of the targeted grammatical rules and the vocabulary — which complies with the extensive practice tenet of SAT — may allow for the starting of form-meaning correspondences in students' minds.

Nevertheless, it should also be acknowledged that this use of language mostly involves the *reproduction* of meanings from one language to the other with hardly any creativity or personalization on the students' part (see Gatbonton and Segalowitz (1988) on 'creative automatization'). The learning situation does not resemble a (quasi-)communicative one but merely serves a language-learning goal for the purposes of achieving formal accuracy. This aspect accounts for the lack of complete, solid proceduralization and automatization. Therefore, it is clear that formal accuracy (declarative knowledge) is being fostered at the expense of fluency (full automatization).

2. Audio-Lingual Method (ALM)

Background

Modern Spanish (*MS*) was the outcome of a project within the American Modern Language Association (MLA). William Riley Parker (former Director of the MLA Foreign Language Program from 1952 until 1956), writes that '[t]his is an exciting book, whose publication will mark a number of "firsts" in the history of foreign language study in the United States' (*MS* 1966: xii).

MS perfectly matches the ambitions of the ALM. The preface to the second edition states the principles underlying this material, which unmistakably evoke behaviourism and are based on 'the memorization or assimilation of a series of dialogs drawn from life situations and the development of an *unusually high degree of fluency* achieved through repeated practice and verbal manipulation in a variety of drills' (*MS* 1966: xi; my emphasis). The memorization of such dialogues should make them 'immediately useful for conversational practice', and they constitute 'sentences one might actually want to speak someday in the classroom' (ibid.: xiii). Thus, 'the learner's hearing and speaking of Spanish, whatever his objective' are prioritized (ibid.: xiii). The approach to grammar is mostly inductive. The grammar drills should provide 'enough practice in the basic patterns of Spanish to enable the student to learn to use and respond to these patterns *automatically*' (ibid.: xiii; emphasis in original).

Summary of the lesson

The title of Lesson 12 is *Una visita al médico* [A medical appointment]. It focuses on: descriptive adjectives (*los Juegos Olímpicos* / 'The Olympic Games'); position of limiting adjectives (*es pura imaginación* / 'It's just imagination'); and several types of reflexive structures (*¿te cortaste?* / 'Did you cut yourself?').

Lesson 12 follows the same structure as all the twenty-five lessons and includes, in this order, the following elements:

(1)   An initial bilingual dialogue
      This dialogue should be listened to without looking at the English translation. It comprises sentences containing the targeted grammatical patterns and structures; for instance, *tiene que irse a su casa y acostarse* [You must go home and go to bed]. The dialogues should be properly memorized so that drills can be done very easily later (*MS* 1966: 19);

(2)   A writing exercise
      This consists of a dictation of several lists of Spanish words to check the students' comprehension of the phonetic differences between 'c' and 'z' in the written representation of /s/ (e.g. trozo / 'piece' and trece / 'thirteen'), since '[i] n American Spanish the letter *z* represents the same sound as the letter *s*' (*MS* 1966: 190);

(3)   Several structure-focused sections (corresponding with the grammatical constructions mentioned above). Lesson 12 has six such sections. Given that all

six of them display the same layout and elements (as in other lessons), I have chosen the middle one, section 66 — which focuses on reflexive pronouns — for the purposes of illustration:

(a) Bilingual examples with the targeted items in bold. For example, *¿Te cortaste?* / 'Did you cut yourself?';

(b) Bilingual synoptic charts followed by very brief metalinguistic notes in the students' L1, English. In this case, there is a chart with the reflexive pronouns in English and their equivalents in Spanish;

(c) Drills
Students should be able to perform the drills easily, in oral recitation in class, with their books closed (*MS* 1996: 19). Section 66 (ibid.: 195) includes a person–number substitution drill; for example, *No quieren bañarse por la mañana (la muchacha, tú, ella, nosotros, usted)* / 'They do not want to take a bath in the morning (the girl, you, she, we, you)'. This and the other types of drill in the remaining sections (except for translation drills, which convey a certain degree of attention to meaning despite the restricted co-text provided by the isolated sentences to be translated and the very controlled nature of the triggered output) are 'mechanical drills' (Paulston 1970);

(4)   Discussion in L1 English
This is 'not a set of rules to learn and follow, but a clear statement of how the pattern operates' (*MS* 1966: xiii). It provides an explanation of the different intricacies of the targeted structural patterns;

(5)   Reading
A dialogue in Spanish on the same topic as the initial one. It recycles — in written, receptive form — vocabulary (e.g. symptoms of flu) and several of the new constructions (e.g. *Tenga la bondad de sentarse* / 'Have the goodness to seat yourself') contained in the initial dialogue.

Cognitive analysis

Since the initial dialogue is seeded with examples of the targeted structures, in principle it allows for an implicit triggering of declarative knowledge given that the students' attention is not overtly directed or attracted to the targeted forms. Students' attention is explicitly drawn to the underlying structural patterns of these constructions in the subsequent structure-focused sections with their examples and synoptic charts, which are aimed at activating conscious declarative knowledge, mostly in an inductive way. After the drill performance, the 'Discussion' further contributes to the consolidation of the declarative knowledge underlying the structural patterns, this time in a deductive way.

In terms of SAT, *MS* does not foster proceduralization due to the nature of the type of drills implemented: mechanical drills. These only allow for the establishment of forms–forms chains in LTM (DeKeyser 1998) instead of meaning–form relationships because they can be performed without paying any attention to meaning at all in the process (similarly to Girau's transformation drill). Besides, the sentences to be repeated are not semantically related to one other and the type of language involved does not resemble that used in real communication.

The lack of resemblance with real-life communication accounts for the commonly remarked upon lack of transfer between the 'artificial' ALM class and the outside world (cf. Johnson 1996; Larsen-Freeman 2013). In cognitive terms, *transfer-appropriate processing*, according to which we retrieve knowledge best in contexts that are similar to those in which we originally acquired it, is not fostered. As Larsen-Freeman (2013: 112) states, in ALM 'the gap between the learning condition and the retrieval condition was too wide for successful transfer to take place'. In addition, as can be seen in this lesson from *MS*, ALM — and G-T too — failed to implement ROCs (see 'The cognitive framework' above). ALM was just concerned about 'getting the structures right when there is nothing else to focus attention on' (Johnson 1996: 171). Arguably, however, a very basic degree of proceduralization can be observed: the targeted structures are certainly contextualized in the final reading text (in the same way as the initial dialogue to be memorized), which comes after the abundant, oral, mechanical repetition of the structures in isolated sentences.

Overall, due to its reliance on behaviourism and mechanical drills, what *MS* (and ALM in general, by extrapolation) really fostered was the automatization of structures: their accurate and rapid production, without undue hesitations and pauses, resulting from constant repetitive practice. In Gatbonton and Segalowitz's (1988) terms, ALM just catered for automaticity (of structures), which they regard as one of the components of fluency, but not for the other component — the skill of pragmatic selection of utterances (that is, knowing what to say, to whom and when). As in Girau's textbook, with the same proviso that the target level of *MS* is an elementary one, it is clear that ALM was not suitable to foster the development of students' communicative competence.

3. Weak Communicative Language Teaching (CLT)

Background

The clear dissatisfaction on teachers', students' and scholars' part with regard to structural, behaviourist-based teaching due to its inability to enable students to communicate in foreign languages, paved the way for the development of CLT in the early 1970s. Advances in language theory and pedagogy on both sides of the Atlantic Ocean crystallized in CLT, which was premised on a functional, pragmatic and social view of language surpassing a merely structural view.

The *Cambridge English Course* series is one of the landmarks in CLT textbook development, following on from, for example, the *Strategies* series (Abbs and Freebairn 1977–) and *Communicate 1* and *2* (Morrow and Johnson 1979 and 1980 respectively). The *Cambridge English Course* leans towards the weak version of CLT (Howatt 1984: 279; Howatt and Smith 2014: 91), which is based on learning the foreign language to use it, while the strong version is targeted at using the foreign language to learn it (as in Krashen and Terrell's Natural Approach or

Task–Based Language Teaching). The particular book analysed here (*CEC*) is aimed at beginners and false beginners and is claimed to achieve a level between Waystage (A2) and Threshold (B1). It was designed around a multi-syllabus: 'Several intertwined syllabuses (lexical, structural, phonological, thematic, functional, notional, situational, skills) are required if we are to capture the complete range of language items and language uses which our students will need to master' (Swan and Walter 1984b: vii).

Summary of the lesson

CEC is structured into thirty-two units, each divided into four lessons (A, B, C, D). Lesson 16B was randomly selected out of the four lessons for Unit 16. The title of Lesson 16B is 'You look shy'. Its learning contents are the following:

> Students will learn to say more about people's appearances, relating them to professional and personality types.
>
> Structures: What does X look like?; look like + noun phrase; look + adjective; What is X like?
>
> Words and expressions to learn: I don't agree; some names of professions and adjectives for personality types. (Swan and Walter 1984b: 67)

Lesson 16B consists of four activities. Prior to the performance of the activities, the teacher should explain to the students the key unknown words included in the instructions of the activities and/or the boxes and the sample sentences (Swan and Walter, 1984b: 67). The activities are as follows:

(1)   In the first activity, the students have to look at six pictures of six different people and discuss who does what: for instance, 'D looks like a scientist. No, C looks more like a scientist'. This activity is to be performed in groups, as is the next one. The groups have to come to an agreement as to the assignment of the professions to each person;

(2)   In the second activity, the students have to look at a different set of six pictures with six people and discuss their personalities: for instance, 'What is A like, do you think? [...] I think he looks very bad-tempered'. A box of useful related adjectives is included.

As can be seen, in both activities the language forms are situationally contextualized thanks to the pictures. Indeed, *CEC* follows the British tradition of EFL courses published in the 1960s, which attempted to provide meaningful contexts in the form of pictures and other forms of 'situation' (Howatt and Smith 2014: 87);

(3)   In the third activity, the students have to write and read some things about themselves and also ask about other people: for example, 'I look shy, but I'm not'; 'What's your sister like? She's really bad-tempered';

(4)   The focus of the fourth activity is personality adjectives. The students are provided with very brief descriptions for each sign of the zodiac, which consist of personality adjectives, both new and reviewed from activities 2 and 3.

They are instructed to read their sign with a dictionary and say whether the descriptions are true of themselves.

All the activities are instances of *communicative drills*, which 'require conveying actual content unknown to the hearer' (DeKeyser 1998: 50) by means of certain pre-selected forms. The difference to the mechanical drills of *MS* and Girau's meaningful drills is evident. The activities are based on repetition but do not involve practice of isolated and decontextualized sentences. Although the forms are pre-determined beforehand, there are no right or wrong answers in terms of the content (contrary to Girau's and the *MS* textbooks). Indeed, the activities constitute examples of opinion-gap activities (Prabhu 1987: 47). At the end of each Lesson D, the students are told to study the corresponding language summary of each unit.

Cognitive analysis

Lesson 16B promotes declarative knowledge of the targeted forms in two different ways. Firstly, it is triggered in an explicit deductive mode when the teacher explains the meaning of unknown words and functional structures in the first two activities. Secondly, in the same activities such declarative knowledge is overtly reinforced in an inductive mode through the sample sentences that incorporate the targeted functional structures and which appear below the instructions. In activity four, declarative knowledge of new lexical items is also inductively triggered in an explicit way by students' searches for unknown words. Finally, the language summary is aimed at consolidating the learning of all the targeted forms (structures and lexis).

What distinguishes *CEC* from the two previous textbooks are the opportunities provided for the activation of procedural knowledge. The four activities are examples of communicative drills, which are candidates for triggering optimal proceduralization and, hence, later automatization (DeKeyser 1998). For cognitive purposes, one very interesting pedagogical feature of communicative drills is precisely that the actual meaning or content is not controlled by the teacher or author of the materials. In order to start the process of proceduralization, the students must engage in practice targeted at the conveyance of communicative messages whilst keeping the necessary declarative (formal) knowledge in working memory — which for that purpose has mostly been retrieved from LTM. In other words, they must focus on the actual content of the receptive or productive messages (the 'what' of communication) whilst being conscious of the forms they have to process and use (the 'how').

It seems that — in principle, at least — this lesson fosters 'transfer-appropriate processing'. As Larsen-Freeman (2013: 120) states: 'To increase the fidelity between situations of learning and retrieval, students should have a genuine need to successfully receive and convey the information at the core of the communication'. The above-mentioned pedagogical traits of communicative drills, the opinion gap to fill, the overall contextualization of language and the personalization featuring in the third and fourth activities conceivably all allow for facilitating a parallelism

— however basic — of language teaching conditions with the retrieval conditions of real-life communication.

Discussion

Two evident conclusions can be reached from the above analyses of the three textbooks. The first is that, in principle, declarative knowledge is catered for in all three of them as a prior cognitive stage. Girau's textbook relies on the explicit deductive-learning mode alone to trigger declarative knowledge. *MS* fosters it implicitly and inductively with the memorization of the initial dialogue and explicitly and inductively with the sample sentences and the synoptic charts; it is reinforced explicitly and deductively with the metalinguistic 'Discussion' following the extensive drill practice. *CEC* activates declarative knowledge explicitly both deductively (with the teacher's explanations of words and functional structures) and inductively (with the sample sentences of the instructions and the students' searches for words).

Secondly, the crucial cognitive difference between the three analysed lessons concerns proceduralization. Two cautions should be considered at this point: acknowledgement of the artificial nature of the classroom and the fact that the level targeted by the three coursebooks is elementary. The latter implies a higher degree of focus on the lower-level skills of communication (Johnson 1996), or form focus, in the overall teaching process, together with considerably shorter stretches of learner output than at more advanced levels. It also entails less leeway for attention to the pragmatic and socio-linguistic features of authentic communication and for the full implementation of ROCs in the practice activities.

With these caveats, the analyses revealed that Girau's textbook and *MS* did not provide avenues to begin the proceduralization of knowledge appropriately but *CEC* did. However, the number of practice activities presumably targeted at developing fluency is noticeably large in Girau's textbook (with its reverse translation and conversation activities) and above all in *MS*, whose total number of different drills in Unit 12 amounts to seventeen. Therefore, both seem to comply with the extensive practice principle of SAT — even though, obviously, none of the three textbooks can attain full proceduralization of the targeted forms in one single lesson, since students need constant opportunities for 'recycling' (Tomlinson 2011) or 'iteration' (Larsen-Freeman 2013). The weakness of Girau's textbook and *MS* from a cognitive perspective does not lie in the quantity but in the *quality* of the practice activities.

Furthermore, neither Girau's textbook nor *MS* respects the principle of transfer-appropriate processing: the knowledge-learning situation is too different from the knowledge-retrieval situation for authentic communication to occur or be developed. This is especially true in the case of *MS* due to the nature of the most abundant type of activities (mechanical drills). There are no opinion- or information-gaps to fill and there is no purpose to language exercises other than linguistic learning alone. Conversely, transfer-appropriate processing seems to be satisfied (partially, at least) in *CEC*, with its communicative drills. Furthermore, both *MS* and ALM are erroneously premised on the idea that by drilling all the patterns in the language classroom the learner will be able to use that knowledge naturally and spontaneously outside the classroom. As we have seen, for ALM the role of automatization is simply 'getting the structures right when there is nothing else to focus attention on' (Johnson 1996: 171). This clashes with the view of automatization in contemporary methodology, which aims at the development of communicative competence, including getting the forms right when all the attention is focused on the message (ibid.: 171).

To summarize, on the basis of the textbook analysis reported here the answer to the first research question — 'Why did G-T and ALM not enable students to become communicatively competent?' — is that in both cases inadequate pedagogical tools were supplied to ensure proceduralization out of the previously developed declarative base. As to the second research question — 'Is the weak version of CLT more efficient than G-T and ALM at enabling students to become communicatively competent?' — the answer is yes: it seems that *CEC* potentially offers a much more solid alternative for the activation of correct proceduralization than Girau's textbook and, especially, *MS*.

Conclusion

The rationale for this chapter was to highlight the value of supplementing pedagogical and historical perspectives in the evaluation of language teaching methods / materials with a cognitive angle which has so far been missing in the HoLLT literature. The three methods (G-T, ALM and CLT) to which the analysed textbooks adhere can be seen to be aimed at a similar overarching goal: catering for learners' communicative needs, which they attempt to satisfy by means of different pedagogical tenets and tools. Overall, the application of SAT to the analysis of the three units has contributed to untangling some of the reasons why G-T and ALM were not entirely successful at making their students communicatively competent, whereas (in principle) the weak version of CLT has the potential to be more effective.

This 'interdisciplinary' chapter may provide an example of a fruitful avenue for collaboration among different disciplines: Cognitive Psychology, SLA, FLT and HoLLT. Indeed, I would suggest that the combination of a cognitive perspective in the study of language teaching methods together with analysis of lessons from coursebooks can contribute to assessing reasons for the relative degrees of success and failure of past methods with greater precision and accuracy.

Bibliography

Abbs, Brian, and Ingrid Freebairn. 1977–. *Starting Strategies* (Harlow: Longman)

Criado, Raquel. 2016. 'Insights from Skill Acquisition Theory for Grammar Activity Sequencing and Design in Foreign Language Teaching', *Innovation in Language Learning and Teaching*, 10: 121-32

DEKEYSER, ROBERT MICHEL. 1998. 'Beyond Focus on Form: Cognitive Perspectives on Learning and Practicing Second Language Grammar', in *Focus on Form in Classroom Second Language Acquisition*, ed. by Catherine Doughty and Jessica Williams (Cambridge: Cambridge University Press), pp. 42–63

——. 2009. 'Cognitive-psychological Processes in Second Language Learning', in *Handbook of Second Language Teaching*, ed. by Michael Long and Catherine Doughty (Oxford: Blackwell), pp. 119–38

——. 2015 [2007]. 'Skill Acquisition Theory', in *Theories in Second Language Acquisition: An Introduction*, ed. by Bill VanPatten and Jessica Williams, 2nd edn (New York and London: Routledge), pp. 94–112

——, and RAQUEL CRIADO. 2013. 'Automatization, Skill Acquisition, and Practice in Second Language Acquisition', in *The Encyclopedia of Applied Linguistics*, ed. by Carol A. Chapelle (Oxford: Wiley-Blackwell), pp. 1–8

ELLIS, NICK C., and STEPHANIE WULFF. 2015 [2007]. 'Usage-Based Approaches to SLA', in *Theories in Second Language Acquisition: An Introduction*, ed. by Bill VanPatten and Jessica Williams, 2nd edn (New York and London: Routledge), pp. 75–93

HAN, ZHAOHONG, and ROSETTE FINNERAN. 2014. 'Re-engaging the Interface Debate: Strong, Weak, None, or All?', *International Journal of Applied Linguistics*, 24: 370–89

HOWATT, A. P. R. 1984. *A History of English Language Teaching* (Oxford: Oxford University Press)

——, with H. G. WIDDOWSON. 2004 [1984]. *A History of English Language Teaching*, 2nd edn (Oxford: Oxford University Press)

——, and RICHARD SMITH. 2014. 'The History of Teaching English as a Foreign Language, from a British and European Perspective', *Language and History*, 57: 75–95

GATBONTON, ELIZABETH, and NORMAN SEGALOWITZ. 1988. 'Creative Automatization: Principles for Promoting Fluency within a Communicative Framework', *TESOL Quarterly*, 22: 473–92

GIRAU, LEWIS TH. 1973 [1925]. *The New British Method/Método de Inglés por Lewis Th. Girau. Libro primero*, 49th edn (Barcelona: Casulleras)

JOHNSON, KEITH. 1996. *Language Teaching and Skill Learning* (Oxford: Blackwell)

LANTOLF, JAMES P., STEPHEN L. THORNE, and MATTHEW E. POEHNER. 2015. 'Sociocultural Theory and Second Language Development', in *Theories in Second Language Acquisition: An Introduction*, ed. by Bill VanPatten and Jessica Williams, 2nd edn (New York and London: Routledge), pp. 207–26

LARSEN-FREEMAN, DIANE. 2013. 'Transfer of Learning Transformed', *Language Learning*, 63: 107–29

——, and LYNNE CAMERON. 2008. *Complex Systems and Applied Linguistics* (Oxford: Oxford University Press)

——, and MARTI ANDERSON. 2011. *Techniques and Principles in Language Teaching*, 3rd edn (Oxford: Oxford University Press)

MODERN LANGUAGE ASSOCIATION OF AMERICA. 1966. *Modern Spanish: A Project of the Modern Language Association*, 2nd edn (New York: Harcourt, Brace & World)

MORROW, KEITH, and KEITH JOHNSON. 1979. *Communicate 1* (Cambridge: Cambridge University Press)

——, and KEITH JOHNSON. 1980. *Communicate 2* (Cambridge: Cambridge University Press)

MUSUMECI, DIANE. 2009. 'History of Language Teaching', in *Handbook of Second Language Teaching*, ed. by Michael Long and Catherine Doughty (Oxford: Blackwell), pp. 43–62

OLLENDORFF, HEINRICH GOTTFRIED. 1835. *Nouvelle Méthode pour apprendre à lire, à écrire, et à parler une langue en six mois, appliquée à l'allemand* (Paris: the Author)

PAULSTON, CHRISTINA BRATT. 1970. 'Structural Pattern Drills: A Classification', *Foreign Language Annals*, 4: 187–93

Prabhu, N. S. 1987. *Second Language Pedagogy* (Oxford: Oxford University Press)

Richards, Jack C., and Theodore S. Rodgers. 2014 [2001]. *Approaches and Methods in Language Teaching*, 3rd edn (Cambridge: Cambridge University Press)

Sánchez, Aquilino. 2009. *La enseñanza de idiomas en los últimos cien años: métodos y enfoques* (Madrid: SGEL)

Swan, Michael, and Catherine Walter. 1984a. *The Cambridge English Course. Student's Book 1* (Cambridge: Cambridge University Press)

——, and Catherine Walter. 1984b. *The Cambridge English Course. Teacher's Book 1* (Cambridge: Cambridge University Press)

Tomlinson, Brian. 2011 [1998]. 'Introduction', in *Materials Development in Language Teaching*, ed. by Brian Tomlinson, 2nd edn (Cambridge: Cambridge University Press), pp. 1-31

Verspoor, Marjolijn, Kees de Bot, and Wander Lowie. 2011. *A Dynamic Approach to Second Language Acquisition. Methods and Techniques* (Amsterdam: Benjamins)

Notes to Chapter 18

1. This work was supported by the Spanish Ministry of Economy and Competitiveness under Research Project Ref. FFI2013-44979-R. I am very grateful to two anonymous reviewers and to Dr Richard Smith for their very valuable comments. Any errors that remain are my sole responsibility.

CHAPTER 19

❖

The Impact of Governance
on Modern Languages in
Scottish Schools, 1962–2014

James Scott

Educationalists, linguists and politicians have debated the decline of Modern
Languages (MLs) in schools, both in the UK and across the Anglophone world.
Internationally, research has addressed pedagogical, motivational or societal
causes of ML decline but has rarely examined the nature or effectiveness of the
politico-educational governance which is intended to improve ML teaching and
learning. This first study of the political and educational governance of Modern
Languages in Scotland considers its interactions with ML improvement or decline
during the period from the introduction in 1962 of (relatively) broad-spectrum
Ordinary Grade qualifications to the introduction of 'new' National Qualifications
courses in 2014, using this timescale to analyse the nature and effectiveness of ML
governance in Scotland across the ten post-war phases of attempted curricular and
qualifications improvements. Through this historical approach, five long-term
periods of ML growth or decline have been identified and connections between
governance actions and ML outcomes analysed. The findings identify successful
and unsuccessful politico-educational governance strategies — specifically in the
ML context but with wider applicability to educational governance and attempted
improvement, both within and beyond Scotland.

Introduction

As in other Anglophone countries, Scotland's government, educational agencies
and media have identified Modern Languages (MLs) as a declining area in schools,
although only sporadic action has been taken to address the issues involved. Little
Scottish research has addressed this decline apart from papers issued by the Scottish
Centre for Information on Language Teaching (SCILT) in the 1990s. The key
SCILT paper, *Foreign Languages in the Upper Secondary School: A Study of the Causes
of decline* (McPake et al. 1999) (henceforth, *FLUSS*), identified certain issues and
considered their causes. *FLUSS* paralleled the last major ML report (HMI 1998)

by the Scottish evaluation body, Her Majesty's Inspectorate of Education (HMI, later HMIe and now subsumed within Education Scotland). Jointly, these papers created short-term media pressure on Scottish politicians to improve the status of MLs, paralleling events surrounding HMI's previous major ML evaluation (HMI 1990). Unfortunately, later HMIe reports on MLs (HMIe 2005a, 2005b, 2007a) and SCILT papers (Doughty 2013a, 2013b, 2013c) failed to achieve a comparable impact, reflecting the continued decline in Scottish political/societal prioritization of MLs.

Doughty's studies used five- to thirteen-year periods to analyse ML uptake and examination results, while *FLUSS* analysed five years drawn from a twenty-year period, but neither examined the full fifty-year period for which statistics are available. The timescale of the study reported on here, however, is sufficient to demonstrate that the decline of MLs in Scotland is not short-term. Two 'rise-and-fall' cycles have culminated in sustained decline for almost twenty years (see Figures 19.1 and 19.2). This chapter examines how, and how effectively, governance systems and actors have interacted with these trends, providing new insights into why national, local authority and school ML policies and initiatives often fail to improve pupil motivation, ML course enrolment or results (attainment) in ML examinations.

Methodology

A Mixed Methods Research (MMR) approach was used, offering a means of dealing with the need to use both predetermined and emerging methods of data collection and analysis (Creswell 2003:17). The study triangulates:

(i)   documentary evidence, including national, local authority and school documents relating to MLs;

(ii) qualifications statistics: Scottish Examination Board (SEB)/Scottish Qualifications Authority (SQA) data on language-course availability, course enrolment and attainment in the period from 1965 to 2014;

(iii) governance actors' testimonies: eighty completed questionnaires from governance agents at national, local authority and school governance levels and forty follow-up interviews. Respondents retain anonymity (using a five-digit code, M00XX) but are classified by occupation.

Modern Languages — A Subject Area in Long-Term Decline

Universal secondary education began in Scotland after 1945 (Paterson 2003: 14). Before this, MLs were a minority subject area. During the 1950s and early 1960s, the growth of secondary education, the arrival of more widely accessible Ordinary Grade qualifications in 1962, population growth, parental aspirations for qualifications and the decline of Classics combined to increase demand for ML qualifications and for the 'advanced' ML Higher course. By the mid-1960s, government statistics (Paterson 2003: 133; SEB 1965, 1966, 1967) confirmed that

MLs had grown significantly in curricular status and in the percentage of overall examination entries attracted. By 1965, MLs appeared a settled part of the Scottish core curriculum — alongside English, Mathematics, Science and Social Subjects — at least for able pupils.

Figures 19.1 and 19.2 draw upon national enrolment and attainment statistics for Scotland (SEB 1965–99; SQA, 2000–14) to illustrate the subsequent decline of ML qualifications. To remove the obscuring effects of changing pupil populations (which rose rapidly post-war, peaked in the 1970s and then declined equally rapidly), the tables calculate ML enrolment/attainment as a percentage of enrolment or attainment across all subjects at the same Scottish Credit and Qualifications Framework (SCQF) levels. Effectively, the tables show the 'market share' of pupil enrolment and examination passes (attainment) compared with all other subjects taken by fifteen- and sixteen-year-olds at SCQF Levels 3-5 (successively O Grades, then S Grades, then 'old' and 'new' National Qualifications); also Level 6 Highers, taken at age sixteen or seventeen; and Level 7 (originally Certificate of Sixth Year Studies, then Advanced Higher) at age seventeen or eighteen.

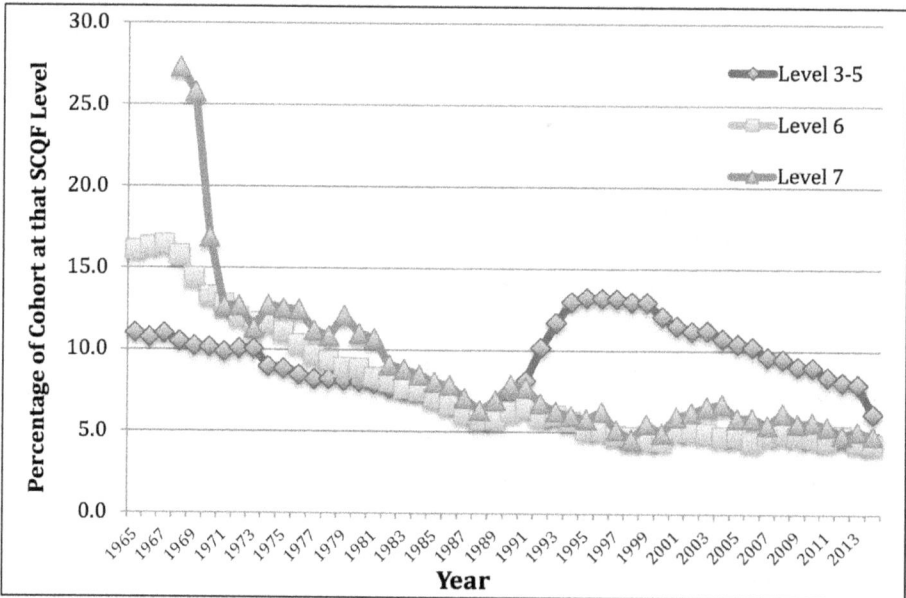

FIG. 19.1. ML Enrolments (1965–2014) at SCQF Levels 3–5, 6 and 7 as Percentages of Uptake in All Subjects at Those Levels

Figure 19.1 demonstrates five phases of ML course enrolment: (i) steady decline from the mid-1960s to the mid-1980s (due to comprehensivization; school-leaving age increase to sixteen; poor materials and pedagogy; and proliferation of alternative curricular courses, etc.); (ii) differing rates of growth at Levels 3–7 in the late 1980s to early 1990s (due to a political requirement for MLs to be compulsory to age sixteen); (iii) a stable period in the mid/late-1990s; (iv) decline from around 2000 (relaxation of the 'MLs to 16' policy; increased head-teacher curricular control);

and (v) an increased decline with the advent of the new Scottish *Curriculum for Excellence* curriculum in 2013 (continuing in 2015 and 2016, but beyond the scope of this chapter).

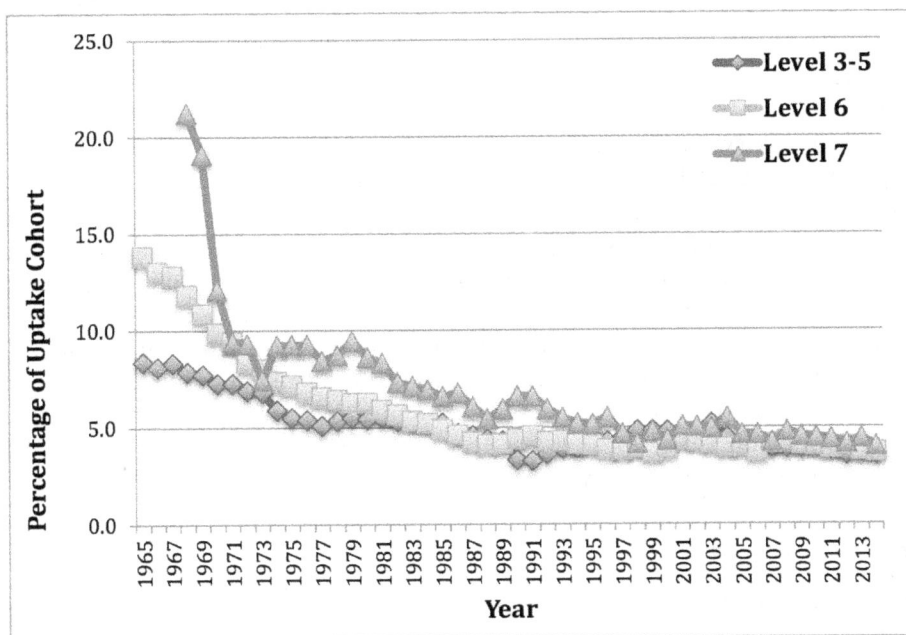

FIG. 19.2. ML Attainment (1965–2014) at SCQF Levels 5, 6 and 7 as Percentages of Attainment in All Subjects at SCQF Levels 3–5, 6 and 7

Figure 19.2 concentrates on pupils passing the Level 5 examination (the most able Fourth Year pupils: those most likely to proceed to Level 6), along with those passing Levels 6 and 7. The Level 5–7 attainment pattern is one of long-term decline with only a very limited recovery in the late 1980s and early 1990s.

The causes of these patterns are explored in subsequent sections of this chapter but it is necessary first to understand how MLs have been organized and controlled in Scotland and to note the key periods of change. These will then be examined against periods of ML growth or decline.

Governance of Modern Languages

Overview

The Scottish curriculum (including MLs) and qualifications are controlled by a three-layer hierarchical governance system comprising national, local authority and school layers. Each layer possesses considerable internal structure, including sub-hierarchies or, occasionally, networks (organic social systems, not the bureaucratic systems of hierarchy). For much of the period studied, the national layer has comprised a controlling 'First Triumvirate' of Scottish Ministers, civil servants and HMI, with a 'Second Triumvirate' of national agencies controlling curriculum, qualifications and teachers. The local authority layer contains local politicians, education officers and some central personnel. Head teachers interviewed saw themselves as a quasi-separate layer resident in both school and local authority levels, with the complexities inherent in such a situation. Other teachers lie wholly within the school layer, with the system completed by an outer 'cloud' of relatively disenfranchised 'governance actors': pupils, parents, unions, business and tertiary education.

This Scottish system contrasts sharply with England and Wales where, for example, Ball (e.g. Ball 2009; Ball and Junemann 2012) identifies multiple forms of school, multiple providers of qualifications, and the networked involvement of more 'actors' in the processes of governing education. Set against such complexity, Scottish education appears remarkably undifferentiated. Fewer than 5% of learners study in fee-paying schools (Paterson 2003: 14), with 95% in state-controlled comprehensive schools strategically directed by government but managed by local authorities. Evidence gathered for this study, both documentary and from respondents, suggests that issues generated by hierarchy, inter-layer contention and moderation of policy by lower layers have made major contributions to the ML patterns seen in Figures 19.1 and 19.2.

Governance and Structure

The Scottish governance system has experienced major change and shifting asymmetries of power since 1962. Five governance structures are identifiable across the period, from (i) the original hierarchical and highly centralist post-war structure to (iii) a more pluralistic system required by expansion in the 1950s to 1970s and the Thatcherite 'market economy' initiatives of the 1980s, and back to (v) an increasingly centralist post-devolution hierarchy, particularly since the advent of a majority Scottish National Party (SNP) government. Structures (ii) and (iv) are transitional models. Changes arose through expediency (driven by factors such as post-war expansion), political dogma (e.g. the Thatcher/Forsyth changes or SNP centralization) and tensions between Scottish and local governments (Bloomer 2013).

The first structure — in place in 1962 — was a relatively uncluttered hierarchical system of three nested governance layers: national, local authority and school. Some other structures existed, for example teacher unions (EIS and SSTA), headteacher associations and the local authority Education Directors' body. A few national proto-agencies also existed, notably the (repeatedly suspended) Advisory Council on Education in Scotland (ACES). At this time, ministers adopted a largely 'hands-off' approach to the curriculum (McPherson and Raab 1988), leaving civil servants (SED) and HMI, neither of whom evinced a vision for MLs during this period, to achieve a balance of vision, purpose and direction. The only other significant voice, ACES, was not a supporter of MLs (SED 1947).

The second (1970s) structure introduced a Second Triumvirate of national agencies, specifically to manage growth in areas previously directed by HMI. The First Triumvirate — unwilling to cede control but unable to absorb the increased qualifications, teacher and curricular workload (McPherson and Raab 1988: 288,

293, 323) — *had* to establish the Scottish Examination Board (SEB), the General Teaching Council (GTC and, later, GTC Scotland) and the Scottish Consultative Council on the Curriculum (SCCC and, later, Learning and Teaching Scotland (LTS) and then part of Education Scotland), possibly explaining the later difficulties experienced by all three. The agencies' constitutions permitted the First Triumvirate to control — sometimes directly — their workings and decisions, although an increasingly pressurized HMI (ibid.: 263–64) struggled to achieve this. Two of the three agencies remain, possibly reflecting a continuing workload beyond the capacity of the First Triumvirate in these areas. However, the third — the curricular agency — has experienced recurring difficulties, undergoing multiple reviews and eventual replacement of ACES, SCCC and LTS in turn. Documentary analysis indicates that none of these three agencies were, however, significant advocates of ML learning.

Alongside these national changes, local government was transformed in 1975 by the replacement of thirty-five County/City Councils by twelve Regional Councils. The largest, Strathclyde, became the largest education authority in Europe, and some of the larger regions developed significantly enhanced structures and expertise in governing education, including provision of specialist officers to lead/develop MLs. Their existence, however, represented an increasing political challenge to the UK government.

The third structure incorporated these changes and the subsequent changes introduced by the neo-liberal Thatcher administration and its Scottish Minister for Education, Michael Forsyth. Their attempted introduction of marketization of education into a hostile Scottish society fuelled a long-term Scottish Conservative collapse. However, the political outcomes — for Scotland and the UK — obscure both Forsyth's long-term effects on educational governance and his largely beneficial impact on MLs. This third structure introduced greater political control by Scottish Ministers, including a requirement for pupils to study an ML for at least four years, to age sixteen (whose impact may be seen from 1989 onwards in Figure 19.1, although less so in Figure 19.2), a moderation of the civil service / HMI balance in favour of civil servants, and an attempt to include previously isolated actors (particularly parents and business) in meaningful educational governance.

The fourth structure (1996 to 2007) introduced radical changes due to the Conservatives' second re-reorganization of local government (to remove the increasingly troublesome Regions) in 1996 and also the impact of devolved Scottish government from 1999. Although not well understood at the time, these two major changes, along with the Conservative demise in Scotland, transient Blairism, seven education ministers in as many years from 1995 and a rapid turnover of First Ministers in the early years of the new Scottish Executive generated significant politico-educational instability. The combined impact of national political turmoil and significant weakening of local authorities had profound effects for Scottish education, but particularly so for MLs, through the weakening of local authorities' ability to support specific subjects, coupled with the rapidly changing national agendas of the seven education ministers and the rapid replacement, abandonment and mutual interference of major educational initiatives. As discussed below, the unintended consequences of the many strategic decisions taken, changed and changed again in this period included allowing head teachers significant leeway to remove MLs from much of the secondary curriculum, failing to consolidate ML teaching in primary schools and the effective abandonment of the one major ML initiative intended to restore MLs to an appropriate place in the curriculum.

The fifth structure added what almost all respondents (except a few national and local authority respondents) describe as increasingly centralist control by the majority SNP government elected in 2011, although some nationally active respondents suggested this began around 2008. This is evident in increased ministerial/civil service control of education, the disappearance (again) of the curricular agency and the amalgamation of its remnants in a new body, Education Scotland, along with a smaller, apparently weakened (according to a majority of respondents) HMI.

Governance and Control

Despite these structural changes, the First Triumvirate has maintained control, albeit imperfectly. A large majority of respondents support this view, as typified by M0016 (local government leader), who describes 'a set of 3 linked hierarchies — national, local authority and school — which suffer from relatively poor linkages'. Some limited growth of networks, possibly leading to increased contention within the system, is evident but Scottish educational governance continues to happen 'in the shadow of hierarchy' (Scharpf 1993). Inter/intra-layer linkages were perceived by almost all respondents to be subject to contention and variably effective. M0050 (head teacher) provided a representative view: 'the structure is disconnected, with aspects of hierarchy and networks'.

The local authority level was initially strengthened, particularly in larger authorities, after 'regionalization' in 1975 but virtually all respondents agree that this strength was significantly compromised in most local authorities by the move to smaller 'unitary' councils in 1996. Councils' abilities to support/challenge their schools were further weakened by the financial crisis and the SNP–COSLA (Convention of Scottish Local Authorities) Concordat, causing staffing reductions and an associated loss of expertise and capacity (including almost all central ML officers). Head teachers, however, have gained increased freedom of financial and curricular operation as a result of the Forsyth initiatives, removal of national curricular guidelines in 2000 and the weakening of council capacity. This allows them much greater control of the existence (or otherwise) of ML courses in their schools than before 2000, as seen in Figures 19.1 and 19.2.

The overall result of these changes to educational governance is perceived by a large majority of respondents to have lessened Scotland's capacity effectively to govern, or improve, MLs (and the wider curriculum).

Governance and Agency

The stated view of successive Scottish government bodies is that the layers of Scottish governance operate in harmony, for example: 'public sector education in

Scotland is a partnership between central and local government' (Scottish Information Office 1977: 2). Challenges to this view come from Scottish academics, particularly Humes (1986), who suggested that the two Triumvirates operate an 'incestuous, self-regarding arrangement' (pp. 116–17). Other academics have seen the arrangement more positively, with McPherson and Raab describing a 'policy community' but rejecting the idea of partnership (1988: 3–4) and Arnott and Ozga (2009) having a more positive view. Most respondents see the system as elitist, for example: 'The national tier is by far the most important [and] works through the consensus of elites' (M0016).

The commonest view of respondents, that 'agency always trumps structure' (M0021, national agency officer) does not appear, on the basis of the available evidence, to hold true of 'elite' governance actors such as ministers, national agency leaders, local authority chief executives or political leaders of councils. A few, with only Michael Forsyth consistently identified by respondents or academic authorities (e.g. Humes 1995), have operated at moments when a combination of factors has allowed them significantly to change the direction of ML governance. Forsyth's impact on the enrolment patterns of Figure 19.1 is clear, but unique. No other high-level governance actor has individually generated notable improvement or halted decline.

Respondents' views *do* apply to middle/lower-ranking actors (especially head teachers and subject department leaders), who can (and have repeatedly been observed by respondents to) circumvent, subvert and/or re-interpret governance actions or policy emanating from higher hierarchical levels. This also applies to local authorities' increasing inability to support or challenge ML teaching, leaving curricular policy to head teachers. Most respondents confirmed that post-1996 local authority decline and weakening inter/intra-level linkages are leaving lower-layer actors to make their own decisions on a wider range of matters, despite national centralization of policy.

Effects of Governance on Modern Languages

Impact through Curricular Vision and Policy

Almost all respondents disputed the existence of a 'Scottish vision' for MLs, due to lack of consistency, negativity, intermittent commitment to MLs and/or a failure to communicate any vision to others. Representative responses included:

> There has not been a consistent vision for MLs. Originally, MLs were for an elite group. During the Forsyth period, there *was* a vision. Maybe it was a 'you've been told' approach, but it *did* produce results. (M0001, council senior officer)

Little longitudinal strategy is evident in the learning and teaching of Modern Languages. (M0040, head teacher)

Almost all respondents perceive that this partially accounts for the overall decline indicated in Figures 19.1 and 19.2.

This lack of vision can be traced even further back, however, to a 1907 Scottish

Office memorandum stating that: 'knowledge of a language other than the mother tongue is not a necessary part of the equipment of an educated mind' (SED 1947: 86). Although the attitudes of 1907 must have seemed distant in 1947, the memorandum was explicitly endorsed by the seminal 1947 ACES Report (ibid.: 19–21, 86). The 1947 Report rejected MLs for most learners of greater, average or lesser ability alike, suggesting that: 'the evidence is conclusive that very many children, perhaps even a majority, are incapable of progressing any distance [...] or of extracting any substantial benefit from their study [of MLs]' (ibid.: 20).

Although initially shelved by the Scottish Education Department (SED), the 1947 Report strongly influenced Scottish education from 1950 to the millennium (Paterson 2003) and so its rejection of any significant curricular place for MLs beyond the second year of secondary education (S2) was significant. The situation worsened in ACES's 1959 report (SED 1959), where MLs barely featured and were recommended to head teachers as optional throughout secondary education. Thus, throughout the 1950s to 1970s, MLs were officially merely an option for *some* 'elite' learners.

Nothing changed until the next major Scottish curriculum initiative, the Munn Report (SED 1977), in which MLs became compulsory in S1–S2 but remained optional thereafter. Only after Forsyth's Circular 1178 (SED 1989) did MLs become a core subject for all pupils in S1–S4 (and a compulsory experience for older primary school pupils). However, Forsyth's initiatives did not proceed smoothly. HMI's highly critical ML reports (HMI 1990, 1998) enumerate difficulties with the primary and S1–S2 phases. Union and media troubles also slowed implementation, causing the incoming Blair government to react by launching a 'ministerial action group' (MAG) on MLs.

The rapid political and structural changes in Scottish and local government at this time began to manifest themselves. MAG was a significant departure as previous national educational working parties were jointly organized by HMI and the agencies, not imposed by politicians. Although MAG's report, *Citizens of a Multilingual World* (CoaMW) (MAG 2000), was endorsed by the subsequent devolved coalition government, it was not implemented in secondary schools to any extent. Simultaneously, Circular 3/2001 (SED 2001) — left in place after the Curriculum Flexibility initiative (SED 2002) was abandoned for the overlapping Curriculum for Excellence (CfE) initiative (SED 2004) — gave head teachers unprecedented curricular freedom of action and a specific message about: 'not compelling' (SED 2001: 3) learners to study MLs.

The current policy initiatives, CfE and the '1+2' primary ML initiative, have already clashed in their impact on MLs. This mirrors the 'innovation overload' period of the 1990s–2000s, when up to six curricular initiatives were in the process of simultaneous development/implementation, with clashes of effect (and sometimes intent), abandonments and unforeseen interactions. The '1+2' initiative seeks to ensure that all primary pupils are actively learning a native language and two foreign languages by Primary 5 (in broad alignment with EU policy). This has, however, been counteracted by CfE's further curricular freedoms for secondary head teachers. The curricular distortion generated jointly by this freedom and by a perceived (by some head teachers and local authorities) reduction of time to study for the Level 3–5 examinations, has seen ML attainment in S4 examinations in 2014 fall by 40% (of the 2013 level) in French, German and Chinese and 20% in most other MLs (Scott 2015).

Impact through Qualifications Policy

The lack of a 'Scottish vision' for MLs is also evident in qualifications. Scottish qualifications policy lay with HMI until 1962, with SEB until 1999 and SQA since 2000, although policy is subject to consultation with politicians, civil servants and others. Qualifications in seven MLs were available in 1962: these, and subsequent changes, are shown in Table 1.

Phase	Language	From	Until	Peak S3–4 Uptake	Duration of availability (years)	Peak Enrolment Year(s)
Phase 1	French	Pre-1965	2015	42,626	50+	1981, 1996, 2003
	German	Pre-1965	2015	17,157	50+	1982, 1997
	Italian	Pre-1965	2015	1,108	50+	1983, 2001
	Portuguese	Pre-1965	1993	11	40+	1974
	Russian	Pre-1965	2014	384	50+	1970
	Spanish	Pre-1965	2015	6,573	50+	1982, 2011
	Gaelic (Learners)	Pre-1965	2015	540	50+	1985, 1996, 2008
Phase 2	Norwegian	1968	1993	41	26	1987
	Swedish	1968	1993	15	26	1968
	Danish	1976	1979	1	4	1976, 1979
Phase 3	Dutch	1974	1979	4	6	1979
	Hungarian	1974	1979	3	6	1975
	Persian	1976	1979	2	4	1978
	Polish	1976	1979	3	4	1976
	Afrikaans	1978	1979	2	2	1979
	Swahili	1978	1979	1	2	1978
Phase 4	Hebrew (Modern)	1981	1993	25	13	1991, 1992
Phase 5	Urdu	1998	2015	181	18+	2003
	ESOL	2007	2015	1075	9+	2014
	Chinese	1978	1979	4	2	1979
	Languages	2009	2015	245	7+	2013

TABLE 1. Provision of ML Qualifications (1965–2013)
N.B. Languages shaded have been withdrawn.

Twenty foreign languages have been offered to learners during the period considered. Of these, only eight remained in 2014. This provides a range of languages but should be considered against the peak uptake for each language — and in the knowledge that current enrolment levels are *well* below the peak in all languages except Spanish and English for Speakers of Other Languages (ESOL). Additionally, half of the eight MLs (Chinese, Gaelic (Learners), Italian and Urdu) are available on a limited basis and this is more pronounced in S5–S6 courses.

Questioning of respondents and documentary analysis were employed in attempting to ascertain the rationales and policy changes behind this fluctuating provision. 'Phase 1' in Table 1 represents the languages available in the immediate post-war period. Respondents with long experience of MLs (e.g. M0001, M0002, M0004, M0007 (all ML officers); M0022, M0029 (local authority leaders); and M0051 (head teacher)) all spoke of a subsequent period of language diversification in the 1960s and 1970s. This is evidenced by the nine MLs begun (and mostly terminated) during this time (Phases 2 and 3). No policy document or official circular could be located to substantiate a 'diversification policy' or explain the subsequent removal of most of the subjects concerned. Respondents suggested that low enrolment meant that most new languages were removed by SEB to minimize costs. When asked, SQA (the current examination body) indicated they retain no records of SEB's actions but confirmed that current qualifications must be financially self-sustaining, except specifically funded governmental priorities (currently, Chinese, Gaelic and Urdu).

Further deletions came in 1993 with Circular 1178 (SED 1989). The circular indicates Michael Forsyth was committed to MLs, primarily to support Britain's role in the forthcoming European Union, concentrating schools' efforts on EU languages — French, German, Italian and Spanish — along with the strategically important Russian and, 'where there is a demand for it' (SED 1989: 3), Gaelic, Classics and Asian languages.

It is difficult to reconcile subsequent changes: in recognition of growing ethnic diversity, Urdu and ESOL have been added, but Polish and Hebrew removed; also the economically significant Chinese was restarted but the economically important Portuguese and Russian were removed. Before Phase 5, respondents suggested various economic, political and ethnic rationales for addition/removal of languages but had no evidence for specific changes.

It is also difficult to identify a rationale for specific languages through analysing Scottish educational policy: no SEB/SQA document was available to illustrate or explain provision. The original ACES report (SED 1947) argues *against* French on educational grounds, but — to a limited extent — *for* Spanish and Italian. The Munn Report (SED 1977), almost uniquely among Scottish educational policy documents, addresses educational theory, attempting to base its recommendations upon this, but does not include MLs in its compulsory subjects for S3 and S4. Forsyth's Circular 1178 (SED 1989) is thus the clearest statement of a need for certain languages as a 'valid educational experience' (p. 1).

Impact through Curricular Initiatives

As seen in relation to vision, policy and curricular agencies, Scottish curricular governance has been generally weak. This trait may also be observed in the governance of major educational initiatives. Ten post-war 'waves' of attempted curricular and/or qualifications improvements were developed (and usually implemented) in attempts to improve either the whole curriculum, individual age-related stages of the curriculum or specifically MLs.

The initial (1950s–1960s) wave of initiatives to meet parental aspirations by improving the curriculum and introducing subject qualifications, at least for the more able, was generally effective. The second (1960s), however, was an ill-prepared attempt to introduce primary school MLs which, like its English equivalent (see Daniels in this volume), failed badly. Unfortunately, this was paralleled by the introduction of secondary 'drill and practice' materials just as this approach was becoming discredited across Europe.

The third (1960s–1970s) wave, a cross-party political move towards 'demo-cratization' of education, led to the raising of the school leaving age to sixteen and to comprehensive schools but was undermined by incoherent planning and development (Paterson 2003: 138) and a failure to provide accommodation, resources or training fit for radically changed school populations (Woodin, McCulloch and Cowan 2013) — with inevitable consequences for attendance, behaviour, motivation and attainment (Paterson 2003), not least in MLs (*FLUSS*). Scottish universities' simultaneous removal of ML Highers as entrance qualifications for many courses and the continuing diversification of Ordinary Grade courses further increased the drift from ML courses.

In the 1970s, a fourth wave attempted to replace 'drill and practice' with 'spoken, relevant language', resulting in improvements with average/less able learners but difficulties for the more able (*FLUSS*; HMI 1998). This approach persuaded the designers of Standard Grade ML qualifications to abandon key components, particularly Writing, causing a further decline in attainment. On reaching office, Michael Forsyth had immediately abandoned middle-school initiatives for a new curriculum for five- to fourteen-year-olds (and tests) for primary and S1–S2 learners and introduced the Munn curriculum and related Standard Grade qualifications for all S3–S4 learners, along with a revived Modern Languages in Primary Schools (MLPS) initiative. Issues abounded: the primary/lower secondary five-to-fourteen ML programme had no guidelines for primary ML courses; primary ML training experienced significant problems; and the lack of a compulsory Standard Grade Writing component impacted on Higher MLs. Union action against the unprecedented development workload seriously compounded these difficulties.

In a sixth wave, the Howie Report (SOED 1992) on S5–S6 courses and qualifications was also abandoned and immediately replaced by the Higher Still S5–S6 initiative and related National Qualifications (NQs), which were designed for S5–S6 *and* college learners but also found their way into S3–S4 course structures, resulting in two parallel qualifications systems (S Grade and 'old' NQs).

The unfavourable HMI ML reports (1990, 1998), the latter of which heavily criticized teachers, head teachers, directors of education and national leaders, generated the ML-specific seventh wave, Citizens of a Multilingual World (CoaMW), which joined the four Forsyth initiatives. When this was joined by an eighth wave — the secondary Curriculum Flexibility programme, with increased curricular control for head teachers — it is possibly unsurprising that MLs, undergoing curricular change from mid-primary to S6, lacking full guidelines, experiencing difficulties at the primary–secondary interface and neither consistently well taught nor resourced, were seen by many head teachers as a tempting target for reduction or deletion.

In a ninth development wave, the multiple major initiatives of waves five to eight were overtaken by a complete change of P1–S5 curriculum *and* the S4 qualifications through the appearance of the Curriculum for Excellence initiative and 'new' National Qualifications in 2010. This was again met with considerable concern by teaching unions (a concern substantiated by almost all respondents) but without the industrial action characteristic of the 1990s. The effects for MLs, however, have been more severe than in the 1990s. CfE formalized what had begun with Curricular Flexibility and so MLs became compulsory in S1–S3 only, although some schools have reduced this further. Respondents mostly see the subsequent '1+2' ML initiative as having potential if it can/will be implemented by councils and their schools at a time of financial and staffing shortage but see the continued indifference/aversion to MLs on the part of some council officers and many (particularly secondary) head teachers as a major challenge for MLs.

In summary, MLs have not been well supported, either through the implementation of major curricular initiatives or by the quality of governance applied to these. Of the twenty-one initiatives within the ten waves, commentators or respondents have identified only four as clearly benefitting MLs (and two of these date to before 1962). Seven initiatives have been seen to cause direct harm to ML enrolment and attainment and the remaining ten have variously caused benefit and harm or have simply been abandoned. In the light of this evidence, it appears self-evident that the operation of ML governance itself should be considered.

The Operation of Governance

The Extent of Cyclical Improvements

Local authority and school leaders in Scotland have been enjoined by governments and HMI (e.g. HMIe 2007b, 2007c) to improve teaching, learning and attainment through adopting a cyclical approach to governance, drawing heavily on the corporate PDCA (Plan-Do-Check-Act) Cycle developed by Dr W. Edwards Deming. Given the overlaps, abandonments and changes of direction embedded in the ten waves of ML/whole curricular initiatives considered above, compounded by significant political actions and changes in the 1970s, 1980s and again from the mid-1990s to date, it was important to establish whether any cyclical improvement approach had been considered or employed in ML developments, particularly for learning from prior successes or failures.

Early respondents suggested the PDCA cycle did not fully describe the complex processes of educational governance. Their views influenced the development of a more nuanced twelve-point cycle later used with all respondents in assessing the actions and impact of national, council and school governance actors and groups. The left-hand column of Table 2 shows the twelve stages. The remaining columns show respondents' evaluation of the quality of their own and others' governance of MLs.

Perceptions of Extent of Impact	National Actors' View of			Local Auth. Actors' View of			School Actors' View of		
	Nat	LA	Sch	Nat	LA	Sch	Nat	LA	Sch
Leadership	2.1	2.0	2.8	1.6	2.1	2.4	1.4	1.4	2.9
Research	1.1	0.6	0.8	0.7	0.9	0.8	1.0	0.8	1.4
Planning	1.9	1.7	2.0	1.5	2.1	2.3	1.5	1.0	2.7
Consultation	1.7	1.5	1.8	1.6	1.4	1.6	1.1	0.9	2.4
Policy	2.8	1.8	2.1	2.2	1.3	1.8	2.0	1.4	2.5
Development	2.1	1.8	2.4	1.6	1.6	2.1	1.4	1.5	2.8
Training	1.3	2.1	2.3	1.4	1.9	2.0	1.2	1.5	2.5
Resourcing	2.1	2.0	2.5	1.5	2.1	2.3	1.2	1.6	2.8
Management	1.9	1.9	2.7	0.8	1.7	2.1	1.0	1.2	2.8
Implementation	1.9	1.9	2.4	1.1	1.6	2.1	1.1	1.2	2.8
Evaluation	1.7	1.4	2.0	1.1	1.4	1.6	1.0	0.8	2.4
Amendment	1.3	1.1	1.6	0.9	1.4	1.5	1.0	0.8	2.4

TABLE 2. Effectiveness of ML Governance: Self and Mutual Perceptions

The eighty respondents were divided into three groups — national, local authority and school — of roughly similar size. National respondents see themselves as having weak to strong (in policy only) impact; local authority actors claim little impact. School respondents see themselves as having far greater impact on all aspects of ML governance except research. All groups perceive that school-based governance is stronger than the others. Schools and local councils see national actors as having little impact, while national and (particularly) school actors both perceive significant failures of impact by local authorities.

This common view that school-based governance — as implemented by head teachers and others — predominates inevitably raises questions about governments' and authorities' ability to implement ML initiatives that may not be supported by schools. This appears to be supported by the decline in ML course enrolment evident in Figure 19.1 after 2000 when head teachers gained far greater control of the curriculum.

Conclusion

The evidence considered in this chapter suggests improvements in MLs have been hampered by a lack of consistent (or shared) vision for, and appropriate action on, the role of ML learning and qualifications in Scottish society and the curriculum for over fifty years. Where a vision *has* existed, it has almost always portrayed MLs as undesirable, peripheral or optional for all or part of many/most learners' primary and secondary experiences.

Scottish politico-educational governance of ML at all levels has been characterized by inconsistency, has suffered repeated discontinuities and has not consistently embodied the 'partnership' stressed by successive Scottish Ministers. Repeated instances of abandonment of major developments, the unintentionally negative impacts of initiatives and the collateral damage caused by conflicting initiatives have come in the way of progress.

Despite possessing a well-respected evaluative arm, HMI(e), the governance system has at times failed to act on its findings. No documentary or respondent-based evidence was found of consistent use of the PDCA cycle, and the cyclical process of visualizing, planning, implementing, evaluating and amending initiatives does not appear to operate effectively at national or, in most cases, local authority levels.

The governance system's capacity to improve MLs has been limited by several issues. National political leadership of MLs faltered under multiple change pressures from the mid-1990s to the early 2000s. Significant governance discontinuities arose from nine Ministers in ten years (seven in seven), multiple simultaneous ML/whole-curriculum initiatives and three *very* different Scottish governments in three years. A majority of respondents dealing directly with government expressed concern about increased political centralization under the SNP since 2007, the enhanced control of civil servants and the perceived decline of HMI. Local government changes since 1996 have seriously impaired the vision, expertise and capacity of local authority teams. According to respondents, this has impacted negatively on primary and secondary MLs alike.

Governance issues have occurred across and within all governance layers as teachers, head teachers, councils, agencies and governments have attempted to improve MLs but, in so doing, have generated many of the issues inhibiting improvement. Expansion of head-teacher control, especially since 2000, has also impacted negatively, as many head-teacher respondents perceive MLs as 'difficult' (M0038), question the quality of their ML leaders and/or teachers and/or abandon MLs for subjects 'more likely to improve attainment' (M0035).

In what remains a layered hierarchical governance system, the long-term lack of focus on ensuring effective linkages between (and, at times, within) layers has also caused significant issues. Despite political insistence on 'partnership', the system is operated by the 'consensus of elites' (M0016) visible from documentary evidence and respondents' insights. Most individual respondents, however, admitted some responsibility for the ML decline. 'I blame myself, because [...]' was a common phrase: a majority of governance actors interviewed feel they should have seen the problem sooner / acted differently / persuaded others to 'do something'. However, the next commonest response (from a sizeable minority) was to blame someone else for the failures.

Commonality of purpose, consistency of vision, effectiveness of implementation or consistent use of evaluation and research have not consistently characterized Scottish attempts to improve MLs. This research may provide a new focus for improvements across these areas.

Bibliography

Arnott, M., and J. Ozga. 2009. *Education Policy and the SNP Government*, CES Briefing, 50 (Edinburgh: Centre for Educational Sociology)

Ball, S. J. 2009. 'Privatising Education, Privatising Education Policy, Privatising Educational Research: Network Governance and the "Competition State"', *Journal of Education Policy*, 24: 83-99

——, and C. Junemann. 2012. *Networks, New Governance and Education* (Bristol: Policy Press)

Bloomer, K. 2013. 'Tensions between Central and Local Government in the Administration of Scottish Education', in *Scottish Education, fourth edition: Referendum*, ed. by T. G. K. Bryce et al. (Edinburgh: Edinburgh University Press), pp. 1003-11

Creswell, J. W. 2003 [1994]. *Research Design: Qualitative, Quantitative and Mixed Methods approaches*, 2nd edn (London: Sage)

Doughty, H. 2013a. *Modern Language Entries at SCQF Levels 4 and 5: 2009–13* (Glasgow: SCILT)

——. 2013b. *French, German and Spanish at SQA Higher Grade. Uptake and Centres: 2000–13; Uptake and Attainment 2008–13* (Glasgow: SCILT)

——. 2013c. *Lesser Studies Modern Languages at SQA Higher Grade. Uptake and Centres: 2000–13; Uptake and Attainment 2008–13* (Glasgow: SCILT)

Her Majesty's Inspectorate of Education (HMI). 1990. *Effective Learning and Teaching in Scottish Secondary Schools: Modern Languages* (Edinburgh: SED)

——. 1998. *Standards and Quality, Primary and Secondary Schools, 1994–98: Modern Languages* (Edinburgh: SOEID)

Her Majesty's Inspectorate of Education (HMIe). 2005a. *Progress in Addressing the Recommendations of Citizens of a Multilingual World: A Report by HM Inspectorate of Education for the Scottish Executive Education Department* (Edinburgh: HMIe)

——. 2005b. *Progress in Addressing the Recommendations of Citizens of a Multilingual World: December update* (Edinburgh: HMIe)

——. 2007a. *Modern Languages: A Portrait of Current Practice in Scottish Schools* (Edinburgh: HMIe)

——HMIe. 2007b. *How Good is our School? The Journey to Excellence. Leadership for Learning: The Challenges of Leading in a Time of Change* (Edinburgh: HMIe)

——. 2007c. *How Good is our School? The Journey to Excellence. Part 4: Planning for Excellence* (Edinburgh: HMIe)

Humes, W. M. 1986. *The Leadership Class in Scottish Education* (Edinburgh: Donald)

——. 1995. 'The Significance of Michael Forsyth in Scottish Education', *Scottish Affairs*, 11: 112-30

McPake, J., et al. 1999. *Foreign Languages in the Upper Secondary School: A Study of the Causes of Decline*, Scottish Council for Research in Education Research (SCRE) Report No 91 (Edinburgh: SCRE)

McPherson, A., and C. D. Raab. 1988. *Governing Education: A Sociology of Policy since 1945* (Edinburgh: Edinburgh University Press)

Ministerial Action Group (MAG) on Languages. 2000. *Citizens of a Multilingual World* (Edinburgh: SED)

Paterson, L. 2003. *Scottish Education in the Twentieth Century* (Edinburgh: Edinburgh University Press)

Scharpf, F. W. 1993. 'Co-ordination in Hierarchies and Networks', in *Games in Hierarchies and Networks: Analytical and Empirical Approaches to the Study of Governance*, ed. by F. W. Scharpf (Frankfurt: Campus verlag), pp. 125-66

Scott, J. 2015. *The Governance of Curriculum for Excellence in Scottish Secondary Schools:*

Structural Divergence, Curricular Distortion and Reduced Attainment, OECD Evidence Paper < http://www.academia.edu/20171586/OECD_Evidence_Paper_2015>

Scottish Education Department (SED). 1947. *Secondary Education: A Report of the Advisory Council on Education in Scotland* (Edinburgh: HMSO)

——. 1959. *Report of the Working Party on the Curriculum of the Senior Secondary School: Introduction of the Ordinary Grade of the Scottish Leaving Certificate*, Circular 412 (Edinburgh: HMSO)

——. 1977. *The Structure of the 3rd and 4th Years of the Scottish Secondary School* [The Munn Report] (Edinburgh: HMSO)

——. 1989. *The Teaching of Languages Other than English in Scottish Schools*, Circular 1178 (Edinburgh: Scottish Education Department)

Scottish Examination Board (SEB). 1965-99. *Annual Enrolment and Attainment Statistics* (Dalkeith: SEB)

Scottish Information Office. 1977. *The Educational System of Scotland* (Edinburgh: HMSO)

Scottish Qualifications Authority (SQA). 2000–14. *Annual Enrolment and Attainment Statistics* (Dalkeith: SQA)

Woodin, T., G. McCulloch, and S. Cowan. 2013. *Secondary Education and the Raising of the School Leaving Age: Coming of Age?* (Basingstoke: Palgrave Macmillan)

CHAPTER 20

Pioneering, Consolidating and Monitoring

The Development of French Language Learning in England, 1960s–2000s, from the Perspective of a Middle-School Teacher

John Daniels

In this chapter I divide the recent history of school-based French learning in England into three periods: a 'pioneering phase' (1960s–70s) associated with the initial introduction of primary foreign-language learning via audio-visual methods and an extension of language learning to all secondary pupils; a 'consolidation phase' in the 1980s as foreign languages became embedded into the school curriculum; and a final 'monitoring phase' in the 1990s–2000s, associated with the introduction of the National Curriculum and emphasis on assessing pupil performance. Developments are shown to reflect the influences and pressures of the time as the wider political agenda impacted on school language-learning, in a climate where there was a 'perceived need for an increase in accountability of schools' (Pachler, Evans and Lawes 2007: 83). An examination of the teaching approaches marking these periods is followed in each case by an autobiographical account of how the developments were manifested within one English middle school and the particular responses they generated. This autobiographical aspect gives a distinctive character to the account, with the overall history of French teaching during this period being complemented by a teacher's perspective. In this respect the account is related to the notion of 'applied linguistic historiography', with its emphasis on the need to account for histories of practice and not just theory (Smith 2016).

Introduction

This account of the recent history of school-based French learning in England is based on consultation of the published literature of the time (for example, Stern 1967; Rapaport and Westgate 1974; Hawkins 1987, 1996), together with documents produced by Northumberland Education Authority and, later, the National

Curriculum. Textbooks have also been invaluable sources as a way to reconstruct changing influences and methodology as these are mediated into classroom learning. Finally, documents I produced myself as head of department in a middle school support my autobiographical commentaries on the nature of and ambitions for French learning from the 1960s to the 2000s.

Several underlying trends can be identified in this developing narrative. There is an increasing emphasis on communicative competence and the development of productive language skills (Savignon 1972; Littlewood 1981), with an increasing emphasis, also, on needs to monitor performance through graded testing (Page 2004) and, later, attainment targets. Changes in the relationship with the target culture are also evident, as the focus for school language learning became increasingly inward-looking in line with the need to respond to the demands of the National Curriculum.

Phase 1: 1960s–1970s

A 'pioneering phase' (audio-visual language learning)

> By about 1960 [...] it seemed as if a few highly promising and practical solutions to the language teaching problem were at long last in sight. The 'revolution' in language teaching caught the imagination of many teachers and the general public. (Stern, 1983:103)

This period saw a move away from more traditional language-learning systems in favour of new approaches, associated with audio-visual language learning. At the same time, there was 'the spread of opportunity for foreign language study to a new group of learners', with 'the tentative introduction of French into the primary curriculum' and an extension of language study, 'across the ability range' (Rapaport and Westgate 1974: 6).

The catalyst for primary foreign-language learning in England came with the Pilot Scheme proposal, launched by the government in March 1963. The 'enthusiastic response from schools and parents' led by 1970 to an 'estimated one third of all primary schools in the country including French in their curriculum' (Hawkins 1996: 159).

An explanation for this rapid expansion came from the perception that audio-visual language learning provided 'the practical solutions' (Stern 1983: 103) needed to enable younger pupils to acquire a foreign language. There was also the new importance given to languages with Britain's application to join the Common Market. Primary and middle-school head teachers wanted to engage with this new enthusiasm for language learning.

The Nuffield Introductory French course, *En Avant*, with its emphasis on speaking and listening and 'progression, in terms of controlled grammatical structures and graded lexical items' (Stern 1967: 122), provided the learning material required. What was also distinctive about *En Avant* was its use of narrative and dialogue, with each unit 'enlivened by dramatic situations' (ibid.). At the centre of the audio-visual learning process was the simultaneous presentation of images, in this case in the form of large posters, with sound in the form of 'magnetic tapes' — made possible by '[i]mprovements in the quality of sound-recording and the availability of reasonably priced tape-recorders' (Rapaport and Westgate 1974: 8).

There were, however, problems associated with the new primary French. According to the Plowden Report (Central Advisory Council for Education (England) 1967: 225), it was 'unfortunate that many schools and areas have chosen to add French to their curriculum without ensuring reasonable conditions for success'. The rather formal, teacher-centred methods adopted in audio-visual teaching were criticized, some language courses being 'completely out of harmony with good primary practice' (ibid.). For Rapaport and Westgate, the problem was that the 'educational needs of children in the junior school [...] have not been the starting point for the thought and planning of primary French' (1974: 1).

'Good primary practice' was at that time associated with an integrated learning approach, the emphasis being for children to discover and experience: 'Once the teacher brought autumn leaves into the classroom and talked about the seasons [...], now he will take the children out to see for themselves' (Central Advisory Council for Education (England) 1967: 199). It is evident from the comments of pupils and teachers at the time that primary French learning needed to take this into account. Indeed, Hoy reports that 'the most powerful incentive to learn French from the pupils' point of view was the opportunity to go to France', for '[i]f pupils were convinced they would never go to France they tended to condemn French as a waste of time' (Hoy 1977, quoted in Hawkins 1996: 163). One head teacher urged early contact with France and French people, 'otherwise the purpose isn't seen by the children. Enthusiasm can be lost. They need to see at once that French children exist' (Rapaport and Westgate 1974: 118).

Critical reports (Burstall 1970: 1974) led to the abandonment of language learning in most primary (but not middle) schools because the data suggested that an early start in language learning had not resulted in any substantial gain in proficiency (Hawkins 1996: 161). This led to what Johnstone has described as the 'collective trauma engendered by the negative evaluation of French in English primary schools' (2004: 190). It would be a further three decades before primary language-learning was reintroduced. However, languages were able to continue in middle schools, where the presence of a language teacher for pupils of 11+ made the provision of a language for primary-aged pupils easier to maintain.

Personal Experience in the 1970s: Drama as a Mechanism for Language Learning

As a student at Northumberland College of Education from 1968 to 1971, I trained to become a language teacher using the new *En Avant* materials. Sent out to local schools, we worked with small groups of pupils, introducing France and the French language into the classroom.

This was the introduction to a new world of flash cards and language games, French songs (preferably with actions) and a range of devices to promote spoken language. The first, oral stages of language learning involved pair work, as pupils learnt how to introduce themselves, saying who they were (given a French name to make things more authentic) and how old they were, and shaking hands enthusiastically.

Later, having been appointed as the first-ever language teacher at Coates Middle School — a school with five hundred pupils aged nine to thirteen situated near Newcastle-Upon-Tyne in south-west Northumberland — I made this report on middle-school language learning:

> Children coming to the school at nine begin French in their first year. The course, Nuffield's *En Avant* introduction to French, is followed [...] until they leave for the High School at thirteen. These four years are therefore a crucial introduction. They form the groundwork for future language learning and also, of equal importance, the pupil's attitude and motivation towards foreign languages. (Review of French teaching at Coates Middle School 1974, personal archive)

Operating the *En Avant* course meant, for the teacher, handling large posters while ensuring the tape-recorder was playing the correct section of dialogue — a juggling act, with the danger that the tape-spool would unwind out of control and end up on the classroom floor to the amusement of the class.

The narrative and dialogue elements of the course provided the opportunity for pupils to tell the story of each episode in their own words. There was the chance, also, to use the dialogue situations as the basis for drama and role-play work, engaging pupils with the language, through the creation of 'an imagined reality' (Verriour 1993: 49). So, in *En Avant 1* (used with pupils in Year 6, aged ten), the story of Georges, Xavier and Nicole going fishing one Wednesday morning could be acted out with pupils being given different roles, as a window-pole becomes the *canne à pêche* [fishing rod]; the chalk box, the *boîte de vers* [box of worms], and the individual pieces of chalk *les vers* [worms]. This was using drama as a mechanism for bringing the language to life — a way to develop productive language skills.

Creative language became possible in this situation, for, once a story had been acted out, it was possible to go beyond the script and use improvised drama to explore the language of what happens next. In *En Avant 2* (with pupils in Year 7, aged eleven), there is the missing *cric* [jack] incident as the *famille Léon* heads off for their summer camping holiday. Paul, responsible for having removed the *cric* from the car to make room for his fishing gear, is sent off to a nearby garage to find a *mécanicien*. He has to describe to him that there is *un problème* — *un pneu crevé* [flat tyre], and no jack. The roles of mechanic and members of the Léon family are given out and the action performed in front of the class, then practised out in groups. Placing pupils in more extended role-play situations outside the classroom will provide additional opportunities for more intensive language learning, as we shall see below.

A somewhat idealized representation of France — involving fishing trips and camping holidays — characterized the *En Avant* story lines. Later course books would provide a more realistic suburban view of France but usually without a narrative to follow or characters with which to identify.

Language learning in this period meant four thirty-five minutes lessons each week. Lessons were given entirely in French, with English strictly forbidden. This, together with the special nature of the teaching resources, made French stand out from other subjects. Rapaport and Westgate (1974: 122) reported that 'among all the groups of teachers there was a marked feeling that French was "different" and consequently functioning in isolation'.

The 'recognition of French as a special case' (Rapaport and Westgate 1974: 107) in the 1970s meant, in my experience, favoured treatment, with smaller groups of learners, language advisers providing additional funding and special features such as audio-loop connections (where pupils equipped with head-phones could listen to taped dialogue) made available in classrooms. The interest in and impact of audio-visual language learning was shown by an invitation to the Tyneside Branch of the Audio-Visual Language Association to give a demonstration lesson with a group of my pupils one Saturday morning in March 1973.

However, a concern to make French a 'less artificial subject in the middle school' and to bring 'children actually into contact with the language and culture they are studying' (French Scheme of Work 1973, personal archive), led to a walking expedition with pupils in the Jura region of Switzerland in 1974. This was to be the first of a long series of out-of-classroom learning experiences which I organized during my career.

Phase 2: 1980s

A 'Consolidation Phase' (Developing and Conforming to a School-Based Curriculum)

> The high hopes of the period were gradually eroded. The new methods did not produce spectacular results. The research was less conclusive than had been hoped. (Stern 1983: 103)

The 'pioneering' phase associated with audio-visual learning was followed by a period of consolidation as new systems were introduced and languages became embedded in the developing school curriculum. By the 1980s audio-visual learning had been replaced by a new approach associated with communicative competence, involving 'the expression, interpretation and negotiation of meaning' (Savignon 1972:124).

Communicative competence became a convenient way to describe the principal objective for school foreign-language learning: for example, 'to achieve a measure of practical, communicative competence in French' (Northumberland County Council 1983: 29). It was not always clear, however, exactly what this represented or how it could be achieved.

In his book *Communicative Language Teaching*, Littlewood suggested activities to 'help learners to go beyond the mastery of structures, to the point where they can use them to communicate in real situations' (1981: ix); and he stressed, also, the importance of learners being 'exposed to situations, where the emphasis is on using their available resources for communicating meanings as efficiently and economically as possible' (ibid.).

The Nuffield *Tricolore* course (which replaced *En Avant*) also placed 'the emphasis [...] on what pupils can do with what they have learnt: language for active use should gradually become the usable property of the learner' (*Tricolore 2*, Teacher's Book 1981: 4). This opened up an important consideration. Was school language learning to be focused on pupils being able to communicate in 'real' situations, as Littlewood suggests, or was assessment to be based on less ambitious targets associated with what could be achieved in the classroom, the language environment constituting, for the vast majority of pupils, the only place in which the language was encountered?

It was the GOML (Graded Objectives for Modern Languages) movement which provided, for many teachers, an answer to this question. The notion of communicative competence became focused through GOML on a particular aspect of pupil needs, associated with the kind of experience pupils might encounter in authentic situations — a school trip to France or school exchange, for example (Page 2004: 247). This initiative generated the same positive response among language teachers as the earlier introduction of audio-visual language learning had done in the 1960s: an 'enthusiasm sustained by an energy born of shared beliefs in the value of language learning and faith that languages for all would become a reality' (Holmes 2009: 18), for it was felt that graded objectives would 'shape the work of the classroom' (ibid.); indeed, for Page (2004: 247), GOML had 'changed completely the direction of MFL teaching in UK schools' and certainly did provide an outward-looking focus for language learning.

However, while new language learning initiatives were being introduced, what can also be seen to characterize this period was the increasing dominance of the centrally inspired school curriculum. Raggett and Clarkson, writing in 1974, had warned that 'historically, the teacher was concerned with the content of the curriculum in the classroom' and 'the more the area of relevant knowledge is circumscribed at a national level, the more the freedom of action of the teacher is reduced' (1974: 8). However, by November 1981, with the publication of *The School Curriculum* (DES 1981), a centralized approach began to be more evident. Local education authorities were responsible for implementing government policy in their own areas by setting out a policy document on curriculum following a period of consultation. The increased level of control being applied to schools by central government through local education authorities was apparent from the tone of language used: 'The policy statement should be studied carefully by the staff of each school, its implications considered, discussed and then applied to the school's curriculum. [...] Head teachers are asked to make appropriate arrangements for this action' (Northumberland County Council 1983: 51).

With this development of the school curriculum, the authority influencing language learning can be seen to have moved further away from purely language considerations to closer conformity with the educational environment in which school language learning operated. So, for example, the short, recommended, daily French lessons in the middle school, with the emphasis on speaking and listening, gave way often to just two isolated language sessions each week. Lessons tended to increase in length at this point, from thirty-five to forty-five minutes before finally stabilizing in the 1990s with lessons of one hour's duration, in spite of the fact that lesson times suitable for Maths and English might not be appropriate for early language learning.

The need to fill more extended, yet less frequent, periods of exposure to the target language led to the development of learning resources offering a range of different tasks and activities, capable of engaging pupils over a forty-five- or sixty-minute lesson.

Indeed language textbooks themselves became 'the guiding principle of language courses' (Sercu 2004: 626). There had been no textbooks for Year 7 pupils using *En Avant*, but now, set out in one attractive package full of illustrations and photographs, there came a series of listening comprehension exercises, reading, writing and speaking activities which were useful for school language learning. Activities were constructed in such a way as to reflect not just current language-teaching orthodoxies but also curriculum demands. So, to take a slightly later example, *Avantage* in 1992 'enable[d] effective assessing and monitoring' (pupil's book, back cover promotional statement).

Examining textbooks from this period is to appreciate the importance given to listening comprehension: 'As listening comprehension is such a vital skill and one in which all pupils can succeed, it is very much emphasised in these materials and used from the very first unit of stage 1' (Teacher's Book, *Tricolore 2* 1981:7). This was to remain the position into the following period too: 'Listening is assuming greater and greater importance in foreign language learning' (Nunan 1999: 200).

However, if listening comprehension is 'vital in the language classroom because it provides input for the learner' (ibid.), it may not be so well received by that learner, as Burstall had already discovered: 'There are certain aspects of learning French which children of all levels of achievement tend to reject, such as the enforced passivity, repetition and incomprehension of the tape-recorder' (Burstall 1970: 52).

Due to the increasing dominance of textbooks, early language learning can be seen to have become less distinctive, matching more closely the learning taking place in other classrooms. Kramsch, for one, complains about the 'prefabricated, artificial language of textbooks and instructional dialogues' (1998: 184) and the 'artificial and standardised environment of the classroom in which they had often become the central element' (ibid: 177) — comments which, while directed at language learning in the United States, can be seen to be equally relevant for English schools.

Personal Experience in the 1980s: Communicative Competence and an Intensive Language-Learning Response

> 'Mission Secrète' is a week's course of intensive French for pupils who have studied the language for three or more years. The purpose of the course is to stimulate language learning by creating a situation where French becomes natural to participants in a way that is not usually possible in the classroom. The course aims to give pupils the confidence to communicate effectively in a foreign language. ('Mission Secrète', Teachers' Notes 1989 — part of a package of materials designed to encourage other schools to engage in intensive language work)

To the language teachers at Coates Middle School, something seemed to be missing from the French programme available to learners. Years of textbook-based learning with the emphasis on listening-comprehension work were not, in our experience, sufficient to develop in learners an appropriate level of spoken language proficiency. Primary teachers interviewed by Rapaport and Westgate (1974: 117) had identified the same problem: '[T]he single most serious failing was that of not developing powers of productive usage among their children, [...] not enough were developing a command of the basic vocabulary and structures that could apply to new situations'. And for Hawkins (1987: x), 'much that has passed for language teaching [...] has been mere rehearsal not followed by performance'. Hawkins (1987) promoted intensive work in the context of developing what he describes as the acquisition stage of language learning — editing a class publication was one example he mentioned of intensive initiatives at school level.

Unaware at that stage of other intensive projects, I developed a series of annual intensive language programmes in the 1980s at Coates Middle School, working with fellow teacher Barbara Porter and with the support of the head teacher Peter Wolfenden. During each intensive session, there would be three French assistants to help maintain the French language input.

The intensive language work provided the missing 'performance' element, the chance for pupils to use the language in simulated situations outside the confining space of the classroom. And so, each year, a group of twenty-five twelve- and thirteen-year-old pupils arrived at an outdoor centre in the Lake District to begin an intensive French experience. The theme for the week, 'secret agent training', had 'the advantage of combining the facilities of an outdoor centre — with opportunities for hill-walking, map-work and caving — with a French situation: the participants are presumed to be training for clandestine operations in France' (Daniels and Porter 1991: 5).

The surveillance exercise provides an example of the kind of activities in which pupils engaged. The exercise unfolds like a military operation, with groups taken in Land Rovers to the drop-off points — two police and two secret-agent sections. They have walkie-talkies to ensure that, as the exercise proceeds, they can keep in contact with the other section across the open moorland, with special codes developed ensuring they are speaking to the correct group. The role of the police is to capture and interrogate the 'secret agents'. The secret agents have identity cards and have learnt the information they contain. They are given an alibi: in response to 'Qu'est-ce que tu fais?'[What are you doing?], they are to respond with 'Je regarde les oiseaux' [I'm bird watching]. There is a real sense of purpose and excitement as they head out on mission.

The activity is set up, explained and carried out entirely in French, involving a level of engagement and comprehension beyond anything pupils have experienced in the classroom. The drama 'provides contexts which are a substitute for real experience' (Fleming 2004: 187) and drives forward the intensive process, to make the unusual activities believable. Learners came into living contact with vocabulary they have previously known only from textbook illustrations. They walk cross-country, crossing streams, encountering sheep, climbing over stone-walls and suffering from Lake District weather. They have something real to talk about, a genuine need to communicate in French.

The hypothesis that some elements of classroom learning had not become fully acquired and needed the catalyst of the intensive experience to become available to pupils as active language elements was tested by comparing vocabulary knowledge of a number of key words before, during and after the intensive period: 'In addition to pupils learning new vocabulary, the research suggested that some elements of their vocabulary, only partially known through classroom learning, become activated by the intensive work, seen as a catalyst for such "dormant vocabulary"' (Daniels 2000: 13).

The comment by one pupil at the end of the intensive week points to how the experience might activate elements of vocabulary: 'Keep at it and you'll be impressed by what you can do. It's hard to speak in French at the start but you will soon get used to it. You remember words you will never use if you did not go' (Andrew, post-intensive week questionnaire 1990).

Phase 3: 1990s–2000s

A 'Monitoring Phase' (Introduction of the National Curriculum)

> In the 1990s, the government assumed more central control by introducing the National Curriculum that set out in some detail what was to be taught in each subject. (Page 2004: 247)

A way to address the problem of learning a language without any obvious performance element — central both in terms of motivating learners but also, for developing active language skills — is to provide early assessment opportunities. This is a way to show pupils what they can do with what they have learnt: 'Learners should not have to wait five years for official recognition of their success; the course should be divided into smaller steps, each of which would be rewarded' (Page 2004: 246). This had been the background to the development and introduction, starting in the 1970s, of Graded Objectives in Modern Languages (GOML), considered above.

Graded objectives became subsumed within attainment targets with the introduction of the National Curriculum in 1990, which set out 'clear, full and statutory entitlement to learning for all pupils. It determines the content of what will be taught and sets attainment targets for learning. It also determines how performance will be assessed and reported' (Department for Education and Science 1999: 3).

The nature of learning in each subject area is prescribed, and pupil progress measured. From a language perspective, attainment targets cover the four skill areas of listening, speaking, reading and writing, each linked to level descriptors. The data produced through this system enables the progress of an individual pupil to be measured, also the cohort of pupils and school progress as a whole, allowing comparison with other schools. Inspections by Ofsted (the national body set up by the government to monitor progress in schools) completed this process, ensuring the National Curriculum is being delivered effectively and there is continuous progress and improvement in standards.

The influence of GOML in the formulation of the attainment targets for modern languages is acknowledged (DES 1993: 16). Now, however, the assessment process is part of a whole, overarching system of government-organized learning procedures involving every aspect of education in schools: 'For each subject and for each key stage, programmes of study set out what pupils should be taught and attainment targets set out the expected standards of pupils' performance' (DFE 1995: v). There is, therefore, the same kind of requirement for languages to adapt to this format, to conform to the system, as occurred with the development of the school curricula in the 1980s (see above). Only, here, the necessary adjustments are more far-reaching.

Language publishers soon responded to the new structures: 'A rich variety of topics and tasks provide full and exciting coverage of the National Curriculum'; the 'course enables effective assessing, monitoring and recording of pupil progress to take place within the classroom routine' (*Avantage* 1992: back cover promotional statement). While the assessment of pupil levels was simplified for the teacher, there is the danger that monitoring and assessment 'all too often becomes the driver of teaching and learning' (Holmes 2009: 20).

Language teachers faced with delivering the National Curriculum and the rigorous examination of pupil progress through Ofsted inspections are likely to concentrate on using methods most likely to deliver the projected levels of attainment from their pupils — as their own performance, pay and promotion prospects are judged according to this criterion. This can lead to a further reliance on the textbook to provide the activities designed to achieve standards. For Holmes, '[o]ver-regulation has suppressed teacher and learner autonomy and arguably has impoverished the language learning experience many pupils receive' (2009: 20).

In this particular climate, it becomes possible for an official language document to produce the curious statement, '[i]t is also important that pupils see that languages exist beyond the classroom' (DfES, *Languages Review*, March 2007), suggesting how far a system of school-based language learning can become inward-looking and self-contained.

Personal Experience in the 1990s: Developing Language and Cultural Awareness through an Exchange Programme

> When the purpose of foreign language teaching changed [...] to preparation for communication with people living in a culture, the notion of travelling and having personal experience of another country became central to learning another language. (Byram 1997: 1)

> Attainment targets should 'enable pupils not only to communicate but also to develop their cultural awareness and contribute to their personal growth'. (Initial Advice, Modern Foreign Language Working Group, DES 1990a: 16)

It is a moment of culture shock, as pupils on an exchange visit are driven off in a French car on the 'wrong' side of the road to a strange house with people they do not know, tired after a long journey, and the food is not what they are used to — as their French Mum and Dad and a whole host of grandparents, brothers and sisters and neighbours look on at this small person who has just arrived from England.

This is not about listening to a cassette recording and linking the sound to illustrations of a French home: the image in the textbook has now materialized; this is the real France and a real French family. The twice-weekly hour-long language lesson, in the organized and predictable classroom environment, has been replaced by something altogether more challenging.

In common with many other schools, Coates Middle School operated an exchange programme, for ten years during the 1990s, with Collège Jean Macé in Saint Brieuc, Brittany, providing an authentic language and cultural experience. And, while an intensive experience (Phase 2, personal experience above) can simulate a French situation, it remained artificial. Here, the family pupils are staying with, the routines and business of someone else's house — because this takes place in another culture, in another language — all become much more dramatic; everything on that first, initial encounter appears totally different and only with time do the similarities appear.

Pupil diaries provide evidence of how pupils are able to 'develop their cultural awareness' (DES 1990a: 16) through an exchange programme. Christine's description of the house she is staying in, or Nichola's account of the food she is given, demonstrates a growing cultural awareness: 'It is very big and very strange. There are no carpets on the floor. There are blinds. The baths, shower and toilet are downstairs' (Christine, 12); 'For tea we had soup, then Claudine put a steaming pot on the table and inside it, it had rice with lobsters on the top! I didn't have any but I still had to watch everyone eat them' (Nichola, 11).

The short, five-day experience of living with a French family and going to a French *collège* can never provide a comprehensive experience of France but it does in many ways validate four years of language learning — French children do exist!

Conclusion: 'What went wrong?'[1]

Ofsted's (2008) examination of language learning in England from 2004 to 2007 'evaluates the strengths and weaknesses in modern languages from survey inspections of primary and secondary schools' (p. 1) This document enables us to assess the position of language learning just after the period considered here, and the impact of the National Curriculum introduced ten years before it ended.

While there was an increase in the number of schools taking up the new primary provision for language learning, the situation was far less satisfactory at secondary level, where those opting to learn a language at fourteen were seen to be 'rapidly declining', with 'major public concern about the decrease in the number of young people able to speak a language other than English' (Ofsted 2008: 4).

Holmes (2009: 19), writing at the same time, talked about the 'widespread disaffection with language learning', and a 'general malaise affecting head teachers, teachers and students alike with regard to the health of modern foreign languages by the start of the decade [i.e. the 2000s]'.

While Ofsted certainly found good practice — 'a third of schools surveyed from 2004/2007 showed considerable strengths in language teaching' (Ofsted 2008: 17) — 'the majority of teaching observed was satisfactory rather than good [...] a smaller proportion than in most other subjects' (ibid.). The report goes on to say: 'too close an adherence to the course book was often a feature of mundane and unexciting teaching' (p. 18).

Problems associated with productive language skills have been one of the recurrent themes of my account. This is reflected in the Ofsted report, for, while 'good progress' is reported in listening and understanding at Key Stage 3 (i.e. between ages eleven and fourteen), 'students' speaking skills were an area of particular weakness in both key stages' (Ofsted 2008:6). There was:

> insufficient emphasis [...] given to helping students 'to use the language spontaneously for real situations. [...] consequently too few students could speak creatively', or beyond the topic they were studying, by making up their own sentences in an unrehearsed situation. (Ofsted 2008: 12)

There is no mention of intensive work in this Ofsted report. One small paragraph covers what is termed 'extra-curricular provision', with a lack of precision about the number of schools engaged in visits and exchanges: 'although a decrease in visits has been suggested the evidence from the survey indicates they are reappearing' (p. 22).

It could be argued that a language curriculum set up as part of the National Curriculum and constructed with a focus on monitoring and assessment is likely to privilege those classroom language components most susceptible to measurement by testing procedures, with a focus on listening, reading and writing activities. This bias, according to the Ofsted report, does seem to exist in many language classrooms. The current system, then, has been failing to give adequate attention to the development of spoken language skills and to the communicative competence aspect of language learning.

From the funding and encouragement of audio-visual language learning in primary schools, through its insistence on curriculum development and the final introduction of the National Curriculum, the authority and influence of central government have been paramount. This has been an involvement which could be seen as inevitable as governments have sought to raise standards, but it seems to have produced an overall conformity of approach due to the need for each subject to adapt to the National Curriculum.

This recent history also suggests that, in order for teachers to focus on the pressing need to achieve targets set for improvement, less importance may be attached to France and French culture: a situation has arisen where a French exchange can be seen in some schools as an inconvenience, a distraction from the drive to achieve attainment targets and improved standards — particularly when there are concerns about the health and safety aspect of placing a student in an unknown household abroad. This is a climate in which it appears that assessment and monitoring, as they measure pupil progress, have become 'performance', providing in the absence of any more authentic experience a validation for the language learning that has taken place.

In this situation the potential and dimensions of school language learning may have become restricted, with there being, perhaps, too often an 'uncritical acceptance of the dominant educational culture' (Kramsch 1998: 183). The official discourse on foreign-language learning has come to construct it as a classroom-based, self-contained and self-sustaining system, measured with great rigour and intensity. Classroom language skills have often had the unpredictable carefully removed, even though this marks authentic communicative usage.

At the same time, in my parallel account of 'personal experience' I have ventured to provide examples from one school — one among many other possible school narratives from this period — to try and show how individual initiative can complement and compensate for official discourses, indicating that language-teaching history is also about the individual efforts on the part of teachers and learners, not just developments in overall policy (cf. Smith's call in 2016 for 'applied linguistic historiography' to place emphasis on practice as well as theory).

It is disappointing but perhaps not entirely surprising, therefore, to find language learning in decline in England, with the potential and ambition for school languages curtailed. The iceberg has been struck but those with authority for school language learning still appear to be dancing, carrying on as before, as though nothing much had happened.

Bibliography

BURSTALL, CLAIRE. 1970. *French in the Primary School: Attitudes and Achievement* (Slough: NFER)

——. 1974. *Primary French in the Balance* (Slough: NFER)

BYRAM, MICHAEL (ed.). 1997. *Face to Face: Learning 'Language and Culture' through Visits and Exchanges* (London: CILT)

CENTRAL ADVISORY COUNCIL FOR EDUCATION (England). 1967. *Children and their Primary Schools. The Plowden Report*, 2 vols (London: HMSO), II

DANIELS, JOHN. 2000. 'Intensive Language Work as a Catalyst for Classroom Learning and an Antidote for "Vocabulary Dormancy"', *Language Learning Journal*, 2: 13-18

——, and BARBARA PORTER. 1991. 'Mission Secrète: A French Immersion Programme', in *Le Nouveau Service Compris* (London: Mary Glasgow), pp. 5–8

DEPARTMENT OF EDUCATION and SCIENCE. 1981. *The School Curriculum* (London: HMSO)

——. 1990A. *National Curriculum, Modern Foreign Languages working group: Initial Advice* (London: DES)

——. 1990B. *Modern Foreign Languages for Ages 11 to 16: Proposals of the Secretary of State for Education and Science* (London: DES)

DEPARTMENT FOR EDUCATION. 1995. *Modern Foreign Languages in the National Curriculum* (London: DFE)

DEPARTMENT FOR EDUCATION and SCIENCE. 1999. *Modern Foreign Languages, Key Stages 3–4. The National Curriculum for England* (London: DFES)

DEPARTMENT FOR EDUCATION and SKILLS. 2007. *Languages Review* (London: DfES)

FLEMING, MICHAEL. 2004. 'Drama', in *Encyclopedia of Language Teaching and Learning*, ed. by Michael Byram (London: Routledge), pp. 185-87

HAWKINS, ERIC. 1987. *Modern Languages in the Curriculum* (Cambridge: Cambridge University Press)

—— (ed.). 1988. *Intensive Language Teaching and Learning: Initiatives at School Level* (London: CILT)

—— (ed.). 1996. *30 Years of Language Teaching* (London: CILT)

HOLMES, BERNADETTE. 2009. 'What is French for?', in *Looking Back — Moving Forward: The Legacy of Brian Page*, ed. by S. Fawkes and L. Parker (Leicester: Association for Language Learning), pp. 8–21

HONNOR, SYLVIA, and HEATHER MASCIE-TAYLOR. 1981. *Tricolore* (Leeds: Arnold-Wheaton)

HOY, PETER H. (ed.). 1977. *The Early Teaching of Modern Languages* (London: Nuffield Foundation)

JOHNSTONE, RICHARD. 2004. 'Early Language Learning in Formal Education', *Encyclopedia of Language Teaching and Learning*, ed. by Michael Byram (London: Routledge), pp. 188–93

KRAMSCH, CLAIRE, 1998. *Language and Culture* (Oxford: Oxford University Press)

LITTLEWOOD, WILLIAM. 1981. *Communicative Language Teaching: An Introduction* (Cambridge: Cambridge University Press)

MCNAB, ROSI, and FABIENNE BARRABÉ. 1992. *Avantage* (Oxford: Heinemann)

NORTHUMBERLAND COUNTY COUNCIL. 1983. *The School Curriculum in Northumberland: A Statement of Policy* (Morpeth: Northumberland County Council)

NUFFIELD FOUNDATION. 1968. *En Avant: Nuffield Introductory French Course*, 2nd edn (Leeds: Arnold)

NUNAN, DAVID. 1999. *Second Language Teaching and Learning* (Rowley, MA: Newbury House)

OFSTED. 2008. *The Changing Landscape of Language: An Evaluation of Language Learning 2004/2007* (London: Ofsted)

PACHLER, NORBERT, MICHAEL EVANS, and SHIRLEY LAWES. 2007. *Modern Foreign Languages: Teaching School Subjects 11–19* (London: Routledge)

PAGE, BRIAN. 2004. 'Graded Objectives', *Encyclopedia of Language Teaching and Learning*, ed. by Michael Byram (London: Routledge), pp. 245–48

RAGGETT, MICHAEL, and MALCOLM CLARKSON. 1974. *Planning and Organization: A School-Based Curriculum* (London: Ward Lock)

RAPAPORT, BARBARA, and DAVID WESTGATE. 1974. *Children Learning French* (London: Methuen)

SAVIGNON, SANDRA. 1972. *Communicative Competence: Theory and Classroom Practice* (New York: McGraw Hill)

SERCU, LIES. 2004. 'Textbooks', in *Encyclopedia of Language Teaching and Learning*, ed. by Michael Byram (London: Routledge), pp. 626–28

SMITH, RICHARD. 2016. 'Building "Applied Linguistic Historiography": Rationale, Scope and Methods', *Applied Linguistics*, 37: 71–87

STERN, H. H. 1967. *Foreign Languages in Primary Education* (Oxford: Oxford University Press)

——. 1983. *Fundamental Concepts of Language Teaching* (Oxford: Oxford University Press)

VERRIOUR, P. 1993. 'Drama in the Teaching and Learning of a First Language', in *Towards Drama as a Method in the Foreign Language Classroom*, ed. by M. Schewe and P. Shaw (Frankfurt am Main: Lang), pp. 43–57

Note to Chapter 20

1. Holmes 2007: 19.

INDEX

❖

This is a composite index to the three volumes of the History. References are to volume and page number: e.g., '3.116' refers to page 116 of volume 3. Where a locator refers to a chapter in French rather than English text, it is italicized.

www.ingramcontent.com/pod-product-compliance
Lightning Source LLC
Chambersburg PA
CBHW080540090426
42734CB00016B/3160